R
5/
S3 455
1 8 7

ANGELO STATE UNIVERSITY

3 0000 000 636 310

D1715860

SCHIZOPHRENIA AND AGING

THE GUILFORD PSYCHIATRY SERIES
Bertram J. Cohler and Henry Grunebaum, Editors

Schizophrenia and Aging: Schizophrenia, Paranoia, and
Schizophreniform Disorders in Later Life
Nancy E. Miller and Gene D. Cohen, Editors

The Invulnerable Child
E. James Anthony and Bertram J. Cohler, Editors

Self and Object Constancy: Clinical and Theoretical Perspectives
Ruth F. Lax, Sheldon Bach, and J. Alexis Burland, Editors

Parenthood: A Psychodynamic Perspective
Rebecca S. Cohen, Bertram J. Cohler, and Sidney H. Weissman, Editors

SCHIZOPHRENIA AND AGING

Schizophrenia, Paranoia, and Schizophreniform Disorders in Later Life

Edited by
NANCY E. MILLER / GENE D. COHEN
National Institute of Mental Health

THE GUILFORD PRESS
New York London

ANGELO STATE UNIVERSITY LIBRARY

The opinions expressed herein are the views of the individual authors and do not necessarily reflect the official position of the National Institute of Mental Health or any other part of the U.S. Department of Health and Human Services.

All material in this report is in the public domain and may be used or reproduced without permission from the Institute or the author. Citation of the source is appreciated.

Published 1987 by The Guilford Press
A Division of Guilford Publications, Inc.
72 Spring Street, New York, N.Y. 10012
Printed in the United States of America

Last digit is print number: 9 8 7 6 5 4 3 2 1

Library of Congress Cataloging-in-Publication Data
Schizophrenia and aging.

    (The Guilford psychiatry series)
    Bibliography: p.
    Includes index.
    1. Schizophrenia in the aged.   2. Aged—Mental
health.   3. Geriatric psychiatry.   I. Miller, Nancy E.
II. Cohen, Gene D.   III. Series.   [DNLM: 1. Aging—
psychology.   2. Schizophrenia—in old age.
WM 203 S3374]
RC514.S33455   1987   618.97′68982   87–14852
ISBN 0–89862–228–X

F O R

Manfred Bleuler
and
in memory of his father Eugen Bleuler

whose pioneering efforts, persistence, and compassionate interest in the unfolding lives of their patients yielded fresh insights into the role of developmental factors and the ameliorative influence of advancing age on the long–term course and ultimate outcome of the spectrum of schizo-phrenic illness.

Contents

Contributors

Hyo S. Ahn, M.D.
Johns Hopkins School of Medicine

Takamaru Ashikaga, Ph.D.
University of Vermont, College of
Engineering and Mathematics

Haroutun M. Babigian, M.D.
University of Rochester
School of Medicine

T. Peter Bridge, M.D.
Saint Elizabeths Hospital
Washington, DC

George W. Brooks
University of Vermont
College of Medicine

Monte S. Buchsbaum, M.D.
University of California
School of Medicine at Irvine

Luc Ciompi, M.D.
Social–Psychiatric University
Clinic, Berne, Switzerland

Carl I. Cohen, M.D.
Downstate Medical Center
State University of New York

Gene D. Cohen, M.D., Ph.D.
National Institute of
Mental Health

Bertram J. Cohler
University of Chicago

John M. Davis, M.D.
University of Illinois at Chicago

Lynn E. DeLisi, M.D.
National Institute of
Mental Health

Michael Drexler, B.A.
University of Colorado
Health Sciences Center

Maurice Dysken, M.D.
University of Minneapolis
GREEC V.A., Minneapolis

Carlton L. Ferrono, Ph.D.
University of Chicago

Caleb E. Finch, Ph.D.
The Andrus Gerontology Center and
Department of Biological Sciences
University of Southern California

David Garbacz, M.A.
Johns Hopkins School of Medicine

Ben Gierl, M.D.
Rush Medical College

Ann B. Goodman, M.A.
Nathan S. Kline Institute
Columbia University
School of Public Health

Barry J. Gurland, M.D.
Columbia University
Faculty of Medicine

Courtenay M. Harding, Ph.D.
Yale University
School of Medicine

Martin Harrow
Michael Reese Hospital
and Medical Center
University of Chicago

Robert K. Heaton, Ph.D.
University of Colorado
School of Medicine

Leonard L. Heston, M.D.
University of Minnesota

Dilip V. Jeste, M.D.
University of California at
San Diego, La Jolla, California

John S. Kafka, M.D.
George Washington University
Medical School

H. Richard Lamb, M.D.
University of Southern California
School of Medicine

Paul D. Landerl, M.S.W.
Howard Mental Health Services
Burlington, Vermont

Anthony F. Lehman, M.D., M.S.P.H.
University of Maryland
School of Medicine

Jary M. Lesser, M.D.
University of Texas
Medical School at Houston

Joanne Marengo, Ph.D.
Michael Reese Hospital
and Medical Center
University of Chicago

Thomas H. McGlashan, M.D.
Chestnut Lodge
Rockville, Maryland

Paul R. McHugh, M.D.
Johns Hopkins School of Medicine

Nancy E. Miller, Ph.D.
National Institute of
Mental Health

Allan F. Mirsky, Ph.D.
National Institute of
Mental Health

David Morgan, Ph.D.
The Andrus Gerontology Center and
Department of Biological Sciences
University of Southern California

George Niederehe, Ph.D.
University of Texas
Medical School at Houston

Susan Pauker, M.M.H.
Johns Hopkins School of Medicine

Thomas J. Pawelski, M.A.
Michael Reese Hospital and
Medical Center, Chicago, Illinois
Northwestern University

Godfrey D. Pearlson, M.D.
Johns Hopkins School of Medicine

Bruce Pfohl, M.D.
University of Iowa
College of Medicine

Michael Pogue–Geile, Ph.D.
University of Pittsburgh

Olive W. Quinn, Ph.D.
National Institute of
Mental Health

Peter Rabins, M.D.
Johns Hopkins School
of Medicine

Sir Martin Roth
University of Cambridge

Michele J. Rusin, Ph.D.
Emory University School of
Medicine, Department of
Rehabilitation Medicine
Atlanta, Georgia

Pamela Schwerdt
National Institute of
Mental Health

Carole E. Siegel, Ph.D.
Nathan S. Kline Institute
New York University
Medical Center

John S. Strauss, M.D.
Yale University
School of Medicine

Paul F. Teychenne, M.D.
Prince Henry Hospital
Matraille, Australia

Joseph Thomas, M.D.
Johns Hopkins School of Medicine

Rhett H. Tompkins, R.N.M.A.
Johns Hopkins School of Medicine

Ming Tsuang, M.D., Ph.D., D.Sc.
Harvard University
School of Medicine

Daniel R. Weinberger, M.D.
Saint Elizabeths Hospital
Washington, DC

Carol Wilder, Ph.D.
Teacher's College
Columbia University

J. K. Wing, M.D.
Institute of Psychiatry London

George Winokur, M.D.
University of Iowa
College of Medicine

Richard Jed Wyatt, M.D.
Saint Elizabeths Hospital
Washington, DC

Introduction:
Advancing Age and the Spectrum of Schizophrenic Illness

Nancy E. Miller

Gene D. Cohen

National Institute of Mental Health

This work stands as a tribute to the arduous life–long commitment of Eugen and Manfred Bleuler, who worked toward illuminating the tragic mysteries of chronic schizophrenic illness and uncovering clues to the origins and development of this disorder across time. The empirical studies, clinical papers, and review articles included here are each devoted to enhancing our understanding of the nature of schizophrenia as it is manifested in the latter half of life.

The volume represents an effort to review, consolidate, and comment critically upon the current status of theory, data, and clinical knowledge, with reference to the etiology, phenomenology, epidemiology, clinical course, treatment, and outcome of the full spectrum of schizophrenic disorder in older adulthood, while high-lighting implications for clinical care and pointing the way toward promising research horizons.

Since the turn of the century when Kraepelin first characterized dementia praecox as a disorder of young adulthood likely to culmi-nate in slow, progressive deterioration, prognosis for this illness has been viewed by clinicians and relatives alike with a mixture of pes-simism, resignation, and regret. While many parameters of schizo-phrenic illness have been intensively examined since Kraepelin's clinically astute observations, to a large extent such efforts have concentrated on individuals diagnosed with schizophrenia at the time of their initial hospitalization, typically in late adolescence, with some follow–up through the early years of the disease. Despite the writings of Eugen Bleuler, who as early as 1911 mentioned tendencies to improvement, noting the diminution of hallucinations and delusions and decreases in accompanying dysfunctional affects, American psychiatrists, with few notable exceptions, have uniformly viewed the outlook for chronic schizophrenia as bleak. Although this conviction was shaped by a host of scientific, political, and cultural factors, pessimism emerged, in part, as the legacy of an overly strong reliance on the results of cross–sectional studies, whose methodological limitations often served to obscure both individual differences and sequential causal events in explaining outcome in schizophrenia. Only in recent years, with the advent of a series of long–term studies primarily carried out in Europe—largely Switzerland, Germany, and England—where patients were followed past young adulthood into the farther reaches of middle age and beyond, has the prognosis for this illness begun to appear less hopeless. The course of illness was revealed to be far more complex and highly variable than previously suspected, and considerable clinical improvement was seen to occur, in some cases for the first time, in very old age. While these findings raised the hopes of at least some patients, many questions remained as to the predictability of such improvement and the phenomenological nature of such developments.

Despite the significantly shortened lifespan that accompanies schizophrenic illness, many affected persons live and suffer from its symptoms well into advanced old age. Yet, with the notable exception of the Bleulers and a few other important investigators, relatively scant attention has been paid to course and long–term outcome as individuals, diagnosed young with schizophrenia, subsequently age. Concomitant with this, and despite much clinical insistence to the contrary, a considerable body of empirical evidence suggests that severe schizophrenic symptoms can and do arise de novo in middle and later life, and that first onset of this disorder is not exclusively confined to those in young adulthood.

It is to the unraveling of these conundrums and to the fresh light that age as a variable can shed in enhancing our understanding of the precipitants, development, and fate of the spectrum of schizophrenic disorders that the scope of this book is devoted.

The study of schizophrenic illness has long been marked by a search for causal factors. New etiological clues to the origin and nature of the disorder that have emerged recently from basic structural and functional studies of the brain suggest intriguing parallels with clinical findings stemming from investigations of behavioral change and intellectual function. For example, a number of scientists have reported findings suggestive of cerebral atrophy, including enlarged ventricles and dilated cortical fissures and sulci in young schizophrenic patients.

Though many assumed that distinguishing the subtle pathology correlated with schizophrenic illness from the nonspecific atrophy which is a hallmark of normal advancing age would be nearly impossible, Weinberger and his colleagues herein describe how they found differences between the two. Although advancing age was indeed associated with large ventricles in both patients and controls, they discovered that in each age decade, schizophrenic patients had significantly larger mean ventricular size. Whereas ventricular enlargement was clinically mild in younger patients, when combined with the effects of aging it appeared to be quite marked, suggesting that elderly schizophrenic individuals may possess significantly less cerebral compensatory capacity than previously assumed.

In an interesting contrast, however, Pearlson and his colleagues in their computed tomography (CT) studies found no significant differences in ventricle–to–brain ratio between late–onset schizophrenics (paraphrenics) and age–matched controls. Since the relationship between schizophrenic and paraphrenic disorders remains incompletely understood, with the disorders clearly differing on such critical variables as degree of genetic loading, severity of personality deterioration, qualitative nature of manifest thought disorder and extent of intellectual impairment, the discrepancy between these findings leads to the intriguing suggestion that differential cerebral disease processes may be operative on the structural level in each of these two disorders.

In tandem with structural defects, neurochemical imbalances linked to advancing age may also significantly color the overt clinical picture in schizophrenia. In their chapter, Finch *et al.* note that throughout the brain, multiple mutually antagonistic systems must be properly balanced for adequate processing and output of information, such that both absolute levels of neurotransmitter systems, as well as differential levels of activity vis–a–vis opposing neural inputs, must be synchronized. Once reserve capacity is exhausted in the older brain and regulatory mechanisms are unable to bring the inputs into balance, the neural system no longer functions normally or optimally. Thus, imbalances among neurotransmitter systems can be affected by asynchronous aging–related reductions in different neural components. The authors speculate that that subgroup of schizophrenic individuals who manifest gradually remitting symptoms could be characterized by variously decreased dopaminergic, noradrenergic, and/or serotonergic levels with advancing age. For instance, symptoms may gradually diminish in some individuals with chronic schizophrenia because dopaminergic balance was restored during aging. On the other hand, symptoms of paraphrenia could arise from asynchronous aging, which could cause relatively greater cholinergic deficits than dopaminergic ones, leading to a relative dopaminergic excess. Despite some evidence in this direction from basic animal research, these hypotheses remain engaging but speculative.

Further research is clearly needed to define and clarify the complex brain functions underlying mood and information processing. A promising move in this direction is represented by the work of Bridge and Wyatt, whose findings strikingly reveal that those chronic schizophrenic patients most likely to experience symptomatic amelioration later in life are characterized by relatively greater platelet MAO activity. These results describing a significant relationship between catechol enzyme activity and cognitive status suggest the presence of important brain–behavior relationships in late–life schizophrenic illness which have largely gone unexamined in the past and which call out for further study.

Numerous investigators have attempted to better understand the disorders of schizophrenia as they are manifested in overt behavior and cognitive function. Inasmuch as schizophrenic illness typically develops in early adulthood, whatever patterns of cognitive change are seen to occur in affected individuals over the course of their later years could be attributed to either the aging process per se, to the progressive course of psychiatric disorder, or to an interaction between the two. The teasing apart of these dimensions are undertaken in a series of papers, beginning with a review of the neuropsychology literature, which comprises largely descriptive clinical studies, followed by an overview of the information–processing literature, wherein procedures are typically guided by more explicit experimental hypotheses derived from theoretical assumptions.

In the first instance, Heaton and Drexler carefully evaluate more than 100 clinical studies assessing neuropsychological function in schizophrenia. They accumulate impressive evidence to suggest that incontrovertible cognitive deficit is associated with the onset of schizophrenia, and that while this appears to be partially reversible in a subgroup of patients, others go on to manifest signs of progressive deterioration that is closely associated with unfavorable clinical course. Despite the many clinical reports indicating that the neuropsychological performance of some individuals improves considerably in old age, not a single empirical study of this phenomenon could be located. Heaton and Drexler caution that even the studies they cited that included older patients in their sample were often methodologically flawed by the investigator's failure to specify subject selection or the criteria used for psychiatric diagnoses. Furthermore, the presence, kind, and dosage of medication was typically not indicated, and level of premorbid intelligence was not controlled.

Harrow and his colleagues sought to determine whether the cognitive deficits commonly associated with schizophrenia appeared to vary as a function of advancing age. In effect, they attempted to delineate on the molar behavioral level what Finch and his associates hypothesized so boldly at the molecular neurochemical level, that is, increasing neural dysregulation with age. Harrow *et al.* also attempted to evaluate the impact of number of years of institutionalization on degree of concrete thinking and on qualitative intellectual ability in patients with chronic schizophrenia. They hypothesized that those individuals who had been continuously institutionalized would show greater impairment than those intermittently hospitalized. Surprisingly, the authors discovered that "revolving door" patients suffered as severe an intellectual deficit as that manifested by chronically institutionalized patients, with the loss of abstract ability coexisting with a general deficit in intellectual ability. Harrow *et al.* conclude that the defect states evident in chronic schizophrenia in old age probably reflect both the deteriorative course of the disease and its cognitive impact, together with the patients' low level of intellectual performance at baseline.

Neither Harrow *et al.*, Bridge and Wyatt, or Drexler and Heaton discovered any evidence to suggest that long–term hospitalization or iatrogenic effects of medication contributed in any significant way to the presence of cognitive deficits—although the cumulative impact of such factors on quality of life and long-term prognosis remain relatively unexplored.

The issue of the relative impact of environmental versus hereditary variables in the etiology of schizophrenia continues to be a question shrouded in conjecture and controversy, with convincing and dubious evidence falling on both sides of the equation. An interesting sidelight of this conundrum arises in the work of Mirsky and his colleagues, who by virtue of a rare and unique occurrence of nature, were able to carefully study and follow a set of monozygotic quadruplets, concordant for schizophrenia but discordant for severity of illness. Although these four sisters shared an identical hereditary background, differences in the way they were treated by significant others led to diverse expectations, self-images, and stress tolerances and hence to different phenotypic expressions of schizophrenic disease. Yet as Harrow *et al.* and other contributors to this volume discovered in the course of their studies, there was no definite indication after following these patients for over a quarter of a century that their schizophrenic illness had fully "burned out" with age. Although their functioning had improved significantly since their initial hospitalization, all four siblings continued to be considerably intellectually impaired.

In terms of cognitive function in schizophrenia, far less evidence is available regarding performance on information processing tasks than on neuropsychological tests, despite the fact that the former have been the predominant paradigm for cognitive experimentation in psychology for the past 25 years. In their review, Niederehe and Rusin could find few studies in any way pertinent to the cognitive aging of schizophrenic individuals, and even fewer data were available regarding information processing in late-onset schizophrenia. Accordingly, in an innovative move, the authors set out to examine the available literatures separately, first reviewing information processing in schizophrenia research, then assessing findings from the gerontological literature, searching for points of convergence and divergence. They found many similarities, the most prominent being slowed reaction time and distractibility in both elderly and schizophrenic persons. In sensory processing studies, both groups were deficient in accurately detecting items, and both tended to process fewer items from the display. In backward masking studies used to evaluate the time it takes to form sensory images, both groups required lengthier stimulus exposures and longer interstimulus intervals. Both manifested slowed processing of iconic information, though normal elderly were additionally hampered by slow decay or prolonged persistence of iconic information. Elderly and schizophrenic individuals also showed impaired pattern recognition, feature extraction, and preattentive processes. They seemed to acquire information more slowly in short-term memory and to form memory traces that were highly forgettable, though they demonstrated no difficulties in processes typically considered to be automatic (e.g., scanning) or to require minimal conscious effort (e.g., rote rehearsal).

The cumulative impact of such findings suggests that organizational schemas involved in information storage and response formation are critical determinants of the performance deficits shown by both elderly and schizophrenic subjects. In concert with the computerized tomography results reported by Weinberger *et al.*, these findings extrapolated from other literature would imply that age–linked differences for schizophrenic individuals parallel those for normal subjects and appear to be essentially additive to the performance deficits already associated with schizophrenia. The marked absence of reliable information about cognitive processes in individuals with chronic schizophrenia who have grown old highlights the need for prospective studies of cognitive change in schizophrenic patients with diverse outcomes, including those who progress to a severely demented state, those who manifest a persistent pattern of stable negative symptoms, as well as those who progress toward states of enhanced integration and health.

It should be noted that a number of important longitudinal studies have charted, if not the shifts in information processing strategies over time, then at least the changes in global intellectual and affective function that accompany normal advancing age—along with fluctuations in schizophrenic symptomatology that characterizes the course of the illness more generally.

A number of exceptionally informative longitudinal studies are alluded to and discussed in this volume, beginning with a presentation of data from the Iowa 500 on an unusually well–studied clinical cohort that has been conscientiously followed for almost 40 years. In reviewing their outcome data, Winokur, Pfohl, and Tsuang found that first–rank symptoms, bizarre behavior, depressed mood, and grandiose delusions significantly decreased with age, whereas avolition and cognitive deficits became increasingly more prevalent. Thus, those individuals diagnosed early with chronic schizophrenia and followed into old age manifested fewer difficulties over time in terms of active symptomatology but greater exacerbation of negative symptoms. Such findings suggest that different phases of illness carry with them profound implications for differential treatment and management interventions.

The impressive writings of Luc Ciompi and his colleagues deepen these understandings yet further. Based on his painstaking and committed efforts to detail processes of change over time, Ciompi underscores the recommendation, discussed eloquently by Strauss in the opening chapter of this volume, that outcome not be viewed within a single dimension but rather across a broad range of realms of function and adjustment. Strauss calls for the development of a more advanced, precise, and contextual model of schizophrenia, to supplement the natural history model of Kraepelin, the diathesis/ stress model of Rosenthal, the stimulus–window model, and many others. Ciompi and his European colleagues have seemingly heeded his plea, recognizing that to understand the unfolding of longitudinal processes and to decipher the causes and mechanisms of symptoms and their vicissitudes, descriptive life contexts and their meanings must be systematically examined. In his paper, Ciompi outlines a multicausal model of pathogenesis, focusing on diminished capacity for processing complex affective–cognitive information, which parallels in many ways the empirical evidence presented in the reviews of Niederehe and Rusin, and Heaton and Drexler. Such an approach is clinically relevant, suggesting, for example, the importance of clarity and simplification in the presentation of information. The model also yields suggestions aimed toward clarification of a mechanism of action in viable treatment approaches, such that regardless of whether the interventions are neurochemical or psychosocial in nature, and regardless of whether they operate at vastly different levels, the final common pathway would result in the dampening, filtering, and enhanced organizing of informational input.

Ciompi presents in detail data on long–term course and outcome in schizophrenia from three major European longitudinal studies undertaken by Bleuler, by Ciompi and Müller, and by Huber, Gross, and Schütter, respectively, that show a striking convergence: All report that schizophrenic individuals have significantly higher mortality rates than the general population. These findings have been confirmed internationally and are paralleled by epidemiologic data, presented in this volume by Babigian and his colleagues, based on evidence emerging from the Monroe County Psychiatric Case Registry in New York. The studies also agree that long–term course is extremely heterogeneous, but significantly more favorable than Kraepelin and others initially reported. Close to 25% of chronic patients appear to attain complete remission, and improvements are seen to occur in late life even after many years of severe and deteriorative illness. A more recent long–term follow–up of back ward patients with chronic schizophrenia in the United States, undertaken by Harding, Brooks, and Ashikaga, offers similar findings, emphasizing the marked variability of outcome with advancing age. As in the European studies, these investigators discovered a broad spectrum of adaptation in middle and old age, ranging from patients who were capable of sustaining considerable degrees of intimacy and living relatively independently, to those who lived in stark isolation and were unable to work to support themselves.

In an interesting development, the European investigators found that a family history of schizophrenia appeared to be completely unrelated to prognosis, whereas Kety *et al.* found a far more significant relationship between genetic factors and chronicity. Along with Strauss, and in consonance with Wing, Cohler, Lamb, Cohen, and Harding, Ciompi maintains that heredity has far less influence on long–term course than social and environmental factors. He argues that a vulnerability related to a defect of information–processing faculties decreases with advancing age, leading to marked symptomatic improvement, possibly because of the imbalances in neurochemical regulatory systems postulated by Finch. Ciompi also stresses the importance of premorbid personality on course of illness and reports that acute onset and positive symptoms are significantly associated with favorable long-term outcome. These factors have been cited as positive indicators by other investigators as well, but this has not been true across the board.

The careful work of McGlashan stands as a case in point. When this investigator attempted to identify positive markers of improvement early in the course of illness, he found that while late onset improvement occurred in a small subgroup of patients, the scope of improvement was highly variable and, more important, seemed nearly impossible to predict. Whether this failure to replicate the findings of others stemmed from the severity of illness of the clinical sample (patients referred to Chestnut Lodge as a last recourse following a long series of treatment failures), or from the retrospective nature of the study itself, or possibly was the result of other, unknown factors, remains to be more fully determined. There were indications that patients who eventually improved came from healthier families, displayed the presence and awareness of affect during illness to a greater degree, and remained in treatment at Chestnut Lodge for significantly longer periods, the latter suggesting some positive treatment effect worthy of further exploration. Despite difficulties in predicting precisely which individuals would improve with age, McGlashan expresses guarded optimism as he notes eloquently, echoing the words of Sigmund Freud, that these patients were not just better psychopathologically, but they also "recaptured something of the human striving for loving and for working."

At this juncture, not a great deal can be said with complete assurance about the definitive outcome and course of schizophrenic illness with onset in early life, particularly in the individual case. Yet if many uncertainties continue to surround our understanding of the pathogenesis and natural history of chronic schizophrenia, it should come as no surprise that even less is presently known about the relatively neglected schizophreniform spectrum of disorders with first onset in later life, known collectively as paraphrenia.

The syndrome was recognized early by Kraepelin, who distinguished it from dementia praecox on the basis of the preservation of motivation, the absence of negative symptoms, and the relatively intact, rather than degraded, personality function. In focusing on the historical development and permutations of psychiatric nomenclature in this arena, Roth subtly traces the broadening of the concept of schizophrenic illness through the writings of Eugen Bleuler and later of Kretschmer and the Scandinavian school. Ultimately, Roth favors a view intermediate between the original definition of Kraepelin, who set paraphrenia apart from dementia praecox, and that of his critics; i.e., somewhat equidistant between the "unifiers" and the "splitters."

Roth's own series of landmark studies have advanced knowledge of the phenomenology of late-onset schizophrenia considerably, and many of his findings have been subsequently replicated in clinical (Rabins, this volume) and epidemiologic (Siegel et al.; Heston) studies. His findings suggest that those individuals diagnosed as paraphrenic typically are female, unmarried, have no children, and have more disabling sensory deficits, particularly conductive deafness and blindness, than age–matched controls. In his chapter, Roth discusses what is known of the pathogenesis and course of this disorder in rich clinical detail, providing a host of vignettes and outlining its implications for differential diagnosis and treatment. He distinguishes among three forms of paraphrenia in late life: "late paranoia," which develops insidiously from a lifelong suspicious nature; "late paraphrenia with 'reactive' features," associated with a clearly defined onset, environmental precipitants, and florid symptomatology; and "'endogenous' late paraphrenia," with a symptom picture and degree of chronicity similar to paranoid schizophrenia of early onset, without deterioration of personality. Each of these variants of schizophreniform disorder, however, is also characterized by social isolation, deafness, and chronicity of course, thus yielding considerable overlap in the clinical picture. Further studies are warranted in order to investigate the utility of such proposed subgroups in predicting actual outcome and treatment response.

Roth advances a polygenic theory to explain the underlying hereditary basis of late paraphrenia, similar to the hypothesis proposed by Gottesmann and Shields (1982) that schizophrenia is determined by a combination of many genes, together with a host of contributory environmental factors. Thus, vulnerability to exogenous factors would be expected to vary as a function of the degree of genetic loading, a point of view not dissimilar from that advanced by Ciompi. The assumption, borne out by evidence of a lower risk of schizophrenia in first–degree relatives of late paraphrenics, is that those with schizophreniform illness first manifest in old age would be less predisposed genetically. The investigation of paraphrenia thus offers favorable opportunities for clarifying and enhancing understanding of the nosological and etiological basis of chronic schizophrenia.

While from a clinical descriptive point of view paraphrenia should be classified with schizophrenia, given its less prominent hereditary complement and differential outcome patterns, the disorder is not fully consistent with a schizophrenic picture. Those with paraphrenia may escape breakdown until they reach old age partially because of personality features that enable them to avoid emotionally taxing personal relationships. Further description and classification of paraphrenia will hopefully lead the way toward increased homogeneity of patient populations, which may in turn accelerate progress in the prediction of outcome, the discovery of further etiological factors, and the formulation of more effective treatments.

In contrast to the relatively hopeful scenario painted by Roth regarding course and outcome of late–onset schizophrenia, the picture presented by Heston, tracing the natural history of paranoid syndromes with onset in later life, is far less benign. Heston reports data from a 20–year study of autopsies of patients from the Minnesota State psychiatric hospital system. Patient charts were carefully evaluated and only those who retrospectively met full criteria for a DSM–III diagnosis of paranoia, with systematized, long–lived delusions, were included. As in many other studies presented in this volume—by Roth, Rabins, Siegel *et al.*, Gurland and Wilder, and others—these cases were admitted after the age of 45 and had significantly impaired hearing and/or vision. However, unlike those other studies, males predominated in this sample. Heston found that these patients were "utterly refractory" to treatment with phenothiazines and that no form of treatment appeared to have any appreciable effect, with the patients continuing to manifest persistent delusions, failing to develop insight, and being thoroughly unable to maintain themselves in the community. That these patients developed significantly more chronic illnesses than the general population and were seen to be at increased risk for death is intriguing.

Heston's autopsy findings also revealed an excess of various forms of brain pathology, suggesting the possibility of an etiological link between brain injury and the paranoid syndrome. Genetic factors predisposing to this vulnerability may be at play in that the later the age of onset, the less severe the course, less dramatic the manifestations of illness, and lower the recurrence risk to relatives. Together with Roth, Heston reasserts the need for further, more refined family studies of late–onset schizophreniform illness. Yet on the basis of their respective data, Roth and Heston see the long–term prognosis for this disorder quite differently.

As Roth was the first to discover, and others have since repeatedly replicated, paraphrenia is significantly associated with hearing loss. The impact of this symptom was investigated by Gurland and Wilder in their work on the US–UK Cross National Study of the Elderly. The investigators found that suspiciousness was significantly increased in persons complaining of hearing impairment. In addition, they found significant correlations between suspiciousness, having never been married, and "not feeling close to anyone," suggesting that these individuals may well have had lifelong difficulties in forging and sustaining intimate relationships, as Roth suggested. An important finding indicates that *duration* rather than quality of hearing impairment, appears to be the crucial stressor, associated as it is with decline in self–esteem, tendency to withdrawal, and proclivity to misinterpret interpersonal events. Since severe hearing loss was associated with *less* social isolation, it may be that it is the ambiguity of *mild* hearing loss that constitutes a potent stress. These data, however, are cross–sectional and depend largely on self–reports and interviewer ratings rather than actual patient evaluations. Further research of a longitudinal type is needed to trace the evolution of paraphrenia and the degree of its association with duration of chronic stress concomitant with hearing impairment. Understanding the phenomenological predisposition to late–onset schizophrenia and the timing of onset could yield invaluable knowledge about the vulnerability to schizophrenia at any age.

The entire question of timing, of that juncture in the span of an individual life when illness begins, stands in need of further sensitive evaluation. In examining the connections between stage in life course at onset of illness and placement of the individual in socio–historical time, Cohler reveals how shared cultural expectations about life events and the performance of characteristic roles at various points across adulthood lead to a sense of the individual being either "on time" or "off time." In this view, life satisfaction is ultimately determined by congruence between actual and expected accomplishment at a particular age. Thus, the chronic schizophrenic's psychotic episodes also disrupt his sense of personal continuity and his performance of expected life roles. In adolescence and young adulthood, for example, great pressures are exerted by society to forge meaningful intimate relationships, establish an identity, and select and succeed in a vocation. Lacking ego strength, resistance against stress, and the capacity to tolerate intimacy, the young schizophrenic person's efforts often culminate in painful failure or in feelings of desperation.

In his thoughtful chapter, Lamb reminds us that while some chronically ill individuals slowly, over a period of years, succeed in establishing a sense of identity and intimacy, many others abandon the struggle along the way, at best adjusting by maintaining a passive, constricted stance in life. Yet, with advancing age, many of the pressures that had led to psychotic decompensation in the past are removed or ameliorated, and later life is often characterized by a stabilization of illness.

With the advent of mid life, many individuals become newly aware of their own mortality and undergo a marked shift from a competitive outer world orientation to an increased preoccupation with their subjective, internal world. Thus, loneliness and lack of meaningful social contact may seem relatively less agonizing for the older person.

As Harding and her colleagues describe, on the basis of their extensive 25– to 50–year follow–up study, an inactive, even seclusive lifestyle in a pressureless setting may allow schizophrenic individuals to function at their highest levels for sustained periods without decompensation during their later years.

Lamb and Roth would agree that many individuals who decompensate for the first time in later life may have found and functioned in a long–term protected environment, such as living with parents or a supportive spouse, and only when these supports are lost does decompensation first occur. Whenever decompensation happens, most writers in this volume would agree that the key to helping individuals with schizophrenic illness to adapt is to provide supports appropriate to their needs, to reduce pressures, and at the same time to enable them to maximize their potential.

Unfortunately, the complexities and hazards of implementing this advice make it often easier said than done. The work of Wing, for example, clearly highlights the pitfalls, and sometimes iatrogenic effects, of efforts to provide support and assistance. On the one hand, impoverishment of interpersonal ties tends to be associated with increased slowness, underactivity, flatness of affect, poverty of speech, and social withdrawal, whereas an optimally stimulating social environment tends to decrease such symptoms. On the other hand, too much social stimulation can lead to feelings of being overwhelmed, with rapid relapse and the recrudescence of florid symptomatology. Somewhere between the Scylla of overenmeshment and the Charybdis of impoverished interpersonal relatedness lies an optimum social environment where the expectations of others are clear, predictable, and consonant with the individual's actual abilities and needs.

Lamb's chapter describes an interesting living arrangement organized to foster adaptation and optimal function in individuals with chronic schizophrenia. These room and care homes provide schizophrenic individuals with private rooms, three meals a day, and supervised medication, but minimal staff involvement, allowing them the optimal balance of support, structure, and personal freedom. While not perfect in all respects, such settings can come close to serving as "good enough" holding environments, enabling the individual to appropriate as much structure and distance as he needs.

Carl Cohen's landmark studies of older schizophrenic individuals residing in single room occupancy hotels (SROs) look at another type of living arrangement—one that has evolved less by design than by necessity, emerging as an unplanned response to the movement to deinstitutionalize chronically ill patients, and, in many instances, dispatch them to communities little prepared financially, emotionally, or professionally to receive and care for them. While SROs represent a less structured environment than the room and care service described by Lamb, such places frequently constitute a way-station or end-point in the life of a schizophrenic person.

Cohen describes a series of aged residents diagnosed with schizophrenia or paranoia who had been previously hospitalized for these conditions and contrasts them with a sample of "normal" elderly SRO residents. Not surprisingly, he found the psychopathologically impaired group to have significantly more women, with substantially lower rates of marriage, and higher degrees of social isolation. In agreement with the epidemiologic studies of Babigian *et al.*, Siegel *et al.*, Ciompi, Heston, Winokur *et al.*, and others, these residents underwent significantly more psychiatric *and* medical hospitalizations and spent more than twice as many days in general hospitals as did the normal elderly group. Although these results seem to be incontrovertible for those with early onset schizophrenia, their applicability to the late-onset schizophrenic disorders remains unclear. Heston, for example, reports significantly heightened risk of early death and physical, particularly cerebral, disorders in this group, while Roth reports rates not significantly different from that of the normal population.

In his study of the SROs, Cohen relates how, despite high rates of physical disorder, considerable psychopathology, near poverty-level income, minimal social support, little opportunity for neuroleptic use, and much hardship, a good number of these persons had, at least temporarily, found some modicum of relief and asylum from many of life's pressures. His work provides some moving clues to the everyday fabric of life in these run–down hotels and the manner in which quite markedly impaired human beings struggle to survive on their own in the community.

Gene Cohen reminds us that symptoms of schizophrenia in the elderly are often overlooked, or simply dismissed as inevitable precursors and concomitants of growing old. In a varied series of vignettes from his clinical practice, he describes the preventative and ameliorative impact of sensitively and respectfully educating physicians and family members about the episodic nature of the chronic course of illness, the meaning of negative symptoms, and the expectable exacerbations of disorder during periods of stress.

Together with Gierl *et al.*, Jeste and Wyatt, and others, Cohen underscores the critical importance of comprehensive medical, psychiatric, and psychosocial evaluation in these older patients. Particular attention should be paid to past drug history, recent stressors, and evaluating and correcting sensory and perceptual deficits, which often exacerbate suspiciousness and the attribution of hostile intent.

Often, when older individuals show signs of schizophreniform disorder, the consulting physician is tempted to resort to pharmacotherapy immediately. Many of the experts included here would hesitate considerably before administering neuroleptics in the face of nonspecific psychiatric symptoms such as agitation, social withdrawal, crying, confusion, etc., since such agents often needlessly complicate and obscure an accurate diagnosis. Moreover, toxic confusional states in older people are common side effects of drugs with central nervous system anticholinergic properties, including antipsychotics, anti–parkinsonian agents, and tricyclic antidepressants.

While neuroleptics are indisputably the most effective treatment for most varieties of schizophrenic illness, Jeste and Wyatt continuously urge restraint in their use because the risks of long–term administration can be considerable. For example, patients may develop tardive dyskinesia, a serious neurologic disorder that is potentially irreversible and that is more likely to occur, with less hope for remission, in the elderly than in any other age group. This finding is true whether schizophrenia is diagnosed early in life and treatment with neuroleptics has continued for many years, or whether paraphrenia, paranoia, or other schizophrenic illnesses have commenced later in life and treatment has just begun. Although the mechanism by which age increases the risk for onset and severity of tardive dyskinesia remains unknown, promising leads include pharmacokinetic factors—which may result from age–linked alterations in the absorption, metabolism, and excretion of drugs—and/or central factors—which could include age–linked changes in number and sensitivity of receptors, or alternately, reduced efficiency of homeo-static processes, as Finch has proposed.

Jeste and Wyatt outline a practical series of operational criteria for diagnosing tardive dyskinesia, including discussion of the phenom-enology, history, and course of illness; differential diagnosis; and treatment response. Since no fully satisfactory treatment has been found, neuroleptics for elderly persons should be prescribed most judiciously, in the smallest effective doses, over the shortest possible periods. In addition, their use should be discontinued or sharply cur-tailed at the first sign of tardive dyskinesia. Clearly, there is an urgent need for the creation and development of new antipsychotic agents free of neurologic side effects.

Taking these caveats into account, Gierl and his associates advocate the careful and judicious use of neuroleptics in the treat-ment of some subtypes of schizophrenic disorder. They indicate, in agreement with Roth, that while such treatment outcomes are often favorable in cases of paraphrenia, symptom remission is rarely accompanied by the development of insight. With patients suffering their first break in late life, the authors caution that delusional beliefs should not be directly confronted in psychotherapy, and the patient should be allowed to maintain a degree of interpersonal and physical distance. They also note that surprisingly few studies are available detailing treatment response in older patients with schizo-affective forms of illness, despite the fact that such individuals are at high risk for suicide. While there is some indication that these patients may respond to either neuroleptics or antidepressants, combined treatment with the two seems more efficacious. In all of this, a convincing case can be made for far greater use of psycho-social interventions for older patients with schizophrenic illness because of the increased risk of side effects, drug–drug interactions, and tardive dyskinesia with prolonged neuroleptic treatment.

Some thoughts on the technique and utility of psychotherapy are described in a humane and thoughtful clinical paper by Kafka, who describes his psychoanalytic relationship with a schizophrenic woman as it unfolds over more than three decades. In describing the oscillation of his patients' symptomatology, he underscores the importance of bridge building, of forging cognitive–affective links between periods of acute illness and remission. He would often clarify to his patient aspects of her delusional system during periods of remission, and when she was denying the severity of her illness, confront her with evidence of the extremes of her disturbance.

Kafka highlights how important it is for the therapist to tolerate ambiguity in attempting to understand, and empathize with, the logic and thought processes of the individual with schizophrenia. He suggests that the therapist who can communicate metaphorically on different levels of complexity simultaneously is more likely to be heard by the patient. The importance of timing is key here, enabling the formulation of interpretations to unfold during the presence of an optimal "therapeutic window" poised between psychotic and nonpsychotic states, wherein both psychotic mentation and the under-standing of fairly complex formulations can simultaneously coexist.

At all times cognizant of the intensity of his patient's projec-tions toward him, Kafka characterizes the nature of the transference in schizophrenia as a bond to numerous part–objects, that is, to separate and delineated qualities and characteristics of the therapist, rather than as a tie to the therapist as an integrated whole and a separate person. He presents a series of therapeutic strategies to assist the patient to more fully internalize features of the therapist's rational, respectful, and nonpunitive efforts to understand her symptoms.

Kafka reveals how, with advancing age, his patient's paranoia lessened, her use of denial diminished, and her capacity to protect herself from stressful situations increased. Though her vulnerability to psychotic episodes remained, her capacity to function with some modicum of pleasure in life continued to grow.

Systematic research is needed on the optimal use of psycho-therapeutic interventions in schizophrenic disorder, including studies of the therapist characteristics most effective with patients past mid–life; the kinds of approaches, interventions, and techniques linked with best outcome; and the subtypes of disorder for which these interventions are best indicated. All require thoughtful, serious, clinically informed empirical attention, both for those who have grown old with the disorder and for those with first onset in later life. In addition, process and outcome studies are urgently needed of psychotherapy *in conjunction* with pharmacotherapy, as well as research on treatment for the elderly in whom drug interventions are contraindicated.

Despite the fact that so much remains to be learned about the parameters, subtypes, course, etiology, and modalities of treatment best suited for alleviating the spectrum of schizophrenic disorder that occurs after young adulthood, it is clear that research interest has never been keener, and the light of hope provided by new knowledge has never burned brighter. It is our wish that the papers in this volume might bring us one small step closer to understanding and curing this mysterious and devastating psychiatric disorder.

SCHIZOPHRENIA AND AGING

PART

I

CLASSIFICATION AND EPIDEMIOLOGY OF SCHIZOPHRENIA

When does schizophrenia occur? How does it change with age? Do patients improve or get worse? Is schizophrenia related to mortality? The accumulation of information in computerized data bases enables us to answer some of these questions by examining the characteristics of large numbers of patients over substantial time periods.

Most studies confirm that the onset of schizophrenia is highest in young adulthood, with the peak incidence for females occurring later than for males. The prevalence of schizophrenia in treatment populations appears to decline sharply with old age, but it remains to be seen whether this is a function of diagnosis, treatment availability, higher mortality rates, or improvements.

The outcome for schizophrenic patients varies greatly, but these differences are not well defined nor are the causes as yet determined. Some attribute changes to psychosocial and motivational factors, others to environmental i' fluences, still others to biochemistry, while many see the problem as a combination of all of these. Differential mortality rates, especially the lower risk of neoplasms among schizophrenics, may add to our understanding of this illness. An updated model that integrates so many disparate variables is clearly called for.

1 Schizophrenia and Aging: Meeting Point of Diagnostic and Conceptual Questions

John S. Strauss

Yale University

The relationship of schizophrenia to the processes of aging is much like the riddle of the Sphinx: "What has one voice and yet becomes four–footed, two–footed, and three–footed? Man as he goes through the life cycle." We also have three age–related pieces of information about schizophrenia: A peak incidence in young adulthood (women about 6 or 7 years later than men), onset never occurring after age 45 (by definition), and the possibility of improvement, even at an advanced age.

Stating these facts is not just a device to suit the theme of this book. The relationship between aging and schizophrenia has been central from the time schizophrenia was first described. Its original title included "dementia" because a steady diminution of mental functioning had been noted similar to that often associated with the aging process. "Praecox" was used in the title because the disorder started at a relatively young age.

In the past 75 years, the name "dementia praecox" has been dropped, and more recent data have refined many of the earlier notions, sometimes radically. But the most crucial questions remain. The disorder does have a peak incidence in young adulthood, although with a rather broad, bell–shaped distribution. The peak incidence age and the differential for men and women are probably two of the most replicated facts about schizophrenia (Lewine, Strauss, & Gift, 1981). Surprisingly, they are virtually ignored in many conceptualizations, and possible explanations remain essentially unexplored.

The upper limit of incidence has been set at age 45 by DSM–III. It may be easy to ridicule the arbitrary cut–off point generated by descriptive psychiatry, but such thresholds do have the advantage of increasing reliability even if they do not always provide the best fit in the individual clinical case. The main question is why the onset of this disorder does not typically occur later, even much later, at age 55, 60, or beyond.

Only recently have we been forced to pay attention to the third fact about aging and schizophrenia. Kraepelin believed that the course of dementia praecox involved deterioration. He defined a variety of end states falling within a narrow range of severe dysfunction that he believed demonstrated one common disease process for the several syndromes of schizophrenia.

But since Kraepelin, the entire concept of outcome and prognosis has changed radically. Several investigators have shown that the course of schizophrenia is highly variable. Others have shown that there is not "an outcome," but several separable aspects of outcome. Our work suggests that, at follow-up, symptom severity, work functioning, social relations, and rehospitalization are relatively independent of each other (Strauss & Carpenter, 1974). To predict these outcomes, the symptom-based diagnosis of schizophrenia is only one of several important characteristics. Other predictors include premorbid social relations, past work functioning, and previous duration of hospitalization. Since each of these characteristics tends to be the best predictor of its corresponding outcome function, we have suggested that the process of outcome involves several open-linked systems of functioning.

These post-Kraepelinian findings about the complexity of prognosis and outcome are joined by important new data on the long-term course of schizophrenia. Bleuler (1978a), Ciompi (1980), and Huber, Gross, Schuttler, & Linz (1980), have shown how varied the course of schizophrenia is as a person becomes older and how, in some instances, major shifts toward improvement may occur even in late life. The diversity of outcome is so great, in fact, that anywhere from 8 to more than 80 "characteristic" patterns of the course of schizophrenic disorders have been described by investigators. The large number of patterns may imply no definable pattern at all. Rather, the variation in course may be determined by a range of cause and effect conditions occurring even in late life and after many years of illness.

What are these intersections of aging and schizophrenia trying to tell us about the nature of schizophrenic disorders? I have no definite answer to this riddle, but would like to speculate, hoping that the penalty for error is a bit less severe than the fate handed those who failed to guess the riddle of the Sphinx.

My major hypothesis is that the facts about age provide evidence that the etiology and course of schizophrenia involve psychosocial aspects of development encompassing both the individual and the environment—for example, in such interactive processess as the evolution of social expectations and the acquisition of age-appropriate social skills.

The peak incidence ages and the differential in age incidence by sex might be explained by considering the psychosocial stresses surrounding the issues of autonomy and responsibility. In the past, especially, those ages coincided with a man's starting a career and a woman's having to take care of an increasing number of children.

Strangely, no one, to my knowledge, has carried out the epidemio-logic studies that could explore such a hypothesis, for example, by comparing different cultures or by studying our culture and separa-ting out men who started careers late, women who have careers, or women who had children early. We have suggested elsewhere (Strauss & Carpenter, 1981) that both biological and psychosocial factors may determine age incidence peaks. Hormonal changes, maturation of the nervous system, and delayed genetic effects might contribute to onset. But certainly the psychosocial development hypothesis must also be taken seriously as a possible explanation for the age/sex differences.

The fact that schizophrenia is considered as never beginning after age 45 is more perplexing, but this, too, could be viewed as support for the developmental hypothesis. Anyone who gets to middle age without breakdown may have acquired "ego" strengths that preclude vulnerability to the degree of mental disorganization found in schizophrenia. Although this hypothesis is plausible, it would be more impressive if someone could explain in detail why such cognitive capacities should crystallize specifically by the mid-40s.

And what about the infinite varieties in the course of schizo-phrenia at even the most advanced ages? Several years ago, we described some longitudinal findings suggesting that the course of schizophrenia may be considered best in the context of development (Strauss, Kokes, Carpenter, & Ritzler, 1978). More recent and more long-term follow-up research has suggested that improvement may occur in late life because there are fewer social pressures at that time. This explanation focusing on one aspect of psychosocial development appears to be a good beginning, but it needs to specify the kinds of pressure that might be reduced in advanced age. My understanding of the aging literature and the reports and experiences of relatives and friends is that late life is a time with many stresses and, in fact, that older people often experience extreme demands, some entirely different from any they have faced before.

One exciting feature about this third piece of the riddle, the variability of the course of disorder even in late life, is that data are rapidly becoming available to help provide more definitive answers. For example, Harding and Brooks' long-term follow-up of a large number of schizophrenic patients will allow us to see what happens to them and their environments and how that may be associated with recovery, chronicity, or the many states in between. Our own intensive follow-up studies of work and other environmental factors in the course of psychiatric disorder suggest that rather specific cause-effect processes may exist that vary considerably from individual to individual and with the characteristics of his or her environment.

The rationale for exploring such individual-environment inter-actions has been strongly supported by recent large-sample studies of families, life events, and social networks in schizophrenia. These studies used controlled approaches to demonstrate the effect of suggest that the natural history model of schizophrenia, focusing on the individual alone, may be a bit like trying to explain the tides without noticing the moon. To untangle the riddle of aging and schizophrenia, I think we need to utilize a developmental research approach that goes beyond both the natural history paradigm and the study of particular environmental impacts on the individual.

To explain the course of disorder more adequately, we need to look at individuals in detail to see how they and their disorders evolve. Multi–cross–sectional studies, by their very nature, tend to wash out individual differences and sequential chains of events, thus providing few explanations for the variety of outcomes.

Consider the question of whether some people with schizophrenia improve late in life because of diminished stress. That hypothesis is certainly a valuable one, but a more complete explanation may be possible. Although we do not have elderly persons in our intensive follow–up studies, focusing on somebody in middle age may provide important clues about such processes.

One woman in our project has been schizophrenic (by any criteria) for more than 12 years, but she is a good worker. Sometimes, the severe exacerbations of her hallucinations and delusions occur just after she has been promoted. With each such exacerbation, she has had to leave her work as a machine operator in a factory and then, after her symptoms diminished, begin all over. Her work has been particularly important to her because other rewards in her life have been minimal. Her social relationships, for example, have been quite limited, and she very much regrets not having friends like other people do.

Recently, after becoming more floridly psychotic once again, this woman left her factory job and went to work as a cashier in a store. At last, she reported in our fourth follow–up interview, she could talk with people at work without being drowned out by machine noises. She also started group therapy and for the first time in her life began to feel somewhat comfortable with people. After telling a person about one experience that had bothered her for several years, she said she was amazed that her voices stopped for the first time in a very long while, and she felt depressed. If this woman continues to acquire new social skills and supports, will she become less vulnerable to psychotic relapse, as research would suggest? Will her development in this sense change the course of her disorder?

The experience of this patient points up the important role of skills as well as vulnerabilities, and of new environments as well. The way our subject described her promotions also suggests the importance of biological concepts of stimulus level and psychodynamic issues around the fear of success. Will our subject use her newly developing social skills and network to help buffer the stress of future promotions? We shall have to wait and see.

Although such histories do not prove causality, they do suggest that both people with schizophrenia and their environmental settings may change over time, change in ways that may be totally missed by issues around the fear of success. Will our subject use her newly developing social skills and network to help buffer the stress of future promotions? We shall have to wait and see.

Although such histories do not prove causality, they do suggest that people with schizophrenia and their environmental settings may change over time, change in ways that may be totally missed by many research methods. One explanation for a person with schizophrenia improving after many years may be diminution of stress. Another—not mutually exclusive—may be the acquisition of skills. A third possibility may be the development and/or loss of support systems. Research suggests that, most likely, changes in a person's work, family, friendship, and material environment, and in the person, interact in certain patterns to influence the course of disorder. Such changes might occur as the result of treatment, the action of others in the environment, chance, or the efforts of the individual. Certainly changes in levels of expectation, ability, and support that may occur with advancing age may be part of this more general phenomenon.

It is important to emphasize that the individual's own efforts may play a major role in such changes. Failures in coping in the past do not mean that the person is immutable, or that there have been no successes. Elsewhere (Breier & Strauss, 1983) we have reported that practically all the psychotic patients seen in our study describe the very active efforts they have made in attempting to manage their symptoms and that, frequently, they seem to succeed for extended periods of time. Such active involvement by the afflicted individual, perhaps learning new coping techniques in the process, may be an important part of the larger picture.

To understand the interaction between aging and schizophrenia, a model will be needed. The natural history model of Kraepelin provided a beginning. The diathesis/stress model of Rosenthal (1970) and others permitted a basis for considering environmental factors. The stimulus window model—specifying a narrow limit of stimulus levels within which someone with schizophrenia could successfully function—provided still greater specificity (Wing, 1975a). But if the ways in which age and schizophrenia interact are as complex as they seem, involving perhaps environmental demands, individual coping abilities, environmental supports, and biological processes, it will be essential to use our clinical and research experience to develop a more specific model, a model that describes several alternative pathways, by which these factors interact over time.

It appears to me that the psychosocial part of any such model must include three domains: (1) symptoms and their shifts, (2) the individual's vulnerabilities and strengths, and (3) environmental characteristics. Such a model will need to include consideration of individual environment interactions in the various life con-texts—work, friends, family, material setting. It will need to include descriptive factors such as the degree of structure needed by the individual and that provided by a work setting. It should also consider the meaning of situations, even at a relatively superficial level, describing such issues as autonomy, intimacy, and responsibility. Thus, to understand these longitudinal processes from a psychosocial point of view, we need to look systematically at symptoms, descriptive life contexts, and certain meanings of those contexts. Biological attributes related to stimulus management and integration need to be included as well.

Does the developmental hypothesis best answer the riddle of aging and schizophrenia posed by the available information? Major psychosocial factors have been demonstrated to be involved in the evolution of schizophrenic disorders. The probable interplay of these factors over time seems likely to require a longitudinal, probably developmental, perspective. More specific analyses of epidemiologic data, especially focusing on the age-sex differences in incidence for subgroups of persons, may be one way to provide relevant information. Increasingly detailed and focused attention on the life patterns of individuals with schizophrenic disorders is another crucial approach. In any such attempts, an explicit model for integrating the fragmented information now available will be essential.

Acknowledgment

This report was supported in part by NIMH Grants #MH-00340, MH-35777, and MH-34365.

2 Functional Psychoses in Later Life: Epidemiological Patterns from the Monroe County Psychiatric Register

Haroutun M. Babigian
Anthony F. Lehman
University of Rochester

As more people survive into the later years of life, the number of persons over age 45 with psychotic illnesses, including schizophrenia, also increases. For a large number, chronic illness began in early adulthood; a smaller number suffered the onset of psychosis after the age of 45.

A succinct summary of the epidemiologic literature is difficult because studies vary in their definitions of disorders and the manner in which data are grouped by age. However, some generalizations are possible. In a review of 10 studies, Neugebauer (1980) estimated the annual prevalence of functional psychoses among persons age 60 and over in the United States and Europe to be 35.1 per thousand; reported rates in individual studies ranged from 13.5 per thousand to 68.1 per thousand. In seven of these studies, the annual prevalence rates for schizophrenia ranged from 0 to 22.2 per thousand with a median of 3.2 per thousand, and for affective psychoses, from 0 to 13.6 per thousand with a median of 11.1.

Less information is available on the incidence of functional psychoses in later life, although case registers in England and Iceland showed annual incidence rates for schizophrenia among persons age 45 to 55 ranging from approximately 0.3 to 0.5 per thousand (Kay & Bergmann, 1980). Annual incidence rates for schizophrenia among persons 60 and over were 0.2 to 0.3 per thousand. These registers reported annual incidence rates of affective psychoses between the ages of 45 and 70 in the range of 0.8 to 3.0 cases per thousand.

The marked variability in the rates of functional psychoses across studies may be attributable to variations in both diagnostic precision and the thoroughness of case identification. For example, some studies failed to clearly differentiate between functional and organic psychoses and between psychotic and nonpsychotic major depressive disorders. Also, some studies included patients in nursing homes, while others did not.

The literature on utilization of services shows an overall trend for increased use of nursing home facilities and decreased use of standard inpatient psychiatric settings by older persons with psychoses over the past several years. Data specific to persons with psychotic disorders are sparse. Kay and Bergmann (1980) found that the percentage of inpatients aged 65 and over in state and county mental hospitals decreased by 36.6% between 1969 and 1973, paralleling declines seen in private and VA hospitals. During the same time, the number of persons over age 65 treated in nursing homes increased 101%.

During the 1971–75 period in the United States, persons 65 and over increased their overall utilization of mental health services by 38.9%. However, the various types of services differed dramatically. The number of persons over age 65 admitted to state and county mental hospitals decreased by 41%, whereas the admission rate increased by 30% for private psychiatric hospitals, by 5% for general hospital inpatient psychiatric units, and by 15% for outpatient psychiatric services.

In 1975 in the United States, 10% of persons aged 65 and older admitted to state and county mental hospitals were diagnosed with schizophrenia; lower rates of schizophrenia were diagnosed among the elderly admitted to private psychiatric hospitals (4.6%), general hospital psychiatric inpatient units (3.3%), and outpatient psychiatric services (6.2%).

Post (1980) presents some data on the elderly with functional psychotic illnesses, including schizophrenia, psychotic affective disorders, and paranoia. In the age groups over 35, schizophrenia tends to predominate in females. The marriage rate among persons with late onset functional psychoses is higher than among younger schizophrenics, but it is still considerably lower than among elderly depressive patients and the general population. People with late onset psychoses show no evidence of the downward drift in social class so prevalent among persons with early onset schizophrenia.

The final issue is that of risk of death among older persons with functional psychoses compared to the general population (relative mortality risk). Relative mortality risk for all persons in the Monroe County (New York) Psychiatric Case Register has been reported for the years 1960 to 1966 (Babigian & Odoroff, 1969). Age–specific relative risks for persons over age 45 ranged from 1.9 to 3.2 for men and 2.2 to 3.6 for women, with an overall trend for the relative mortality risk among psychiatric populations to increase with age for both sexes.

Mortality data from the National Psychiatric Case Register of the Netherlands (Giel, Dijk, & van Weeden–Dijkstra, 1978) indicated that mortality rates among schizophrenics age 40–64 were approximately twice those expected based on general population rates. However, for schizophrenics over age 65, the observed mortality rates were quite close to those in the general population. Other studies (Innes & Miller, 1970; Singer, Garfinkel, Cohen, & Srole, 1976) reported higher mortality rates among general psychiatric populations but did not provide specific information on older psychotic patients.

PURPOSE

This paper presents data from the Monroe County Case Register on the epidemiology and patterns of utilization of psychiatric services for functional psychoses among persons over age 45 between the years 1965 and 1975. The following questions are addressed:

1. What are the incidence and prevalence rates of treated functional psychoses among persons aged 45 and older in Monroe County?
2. How did these prevalence and incidence rates change from 1965 to 1975?
3. What was the pattern of service utilization among older persons with functional psychoses during this 10–year period?
4. Who are these people, that is, what are their demographic characteristics?
5. What is the relative risk of mortality among these persons compared to the same age groups in the general population of Monroe County?

METHOD

Data were taken from the Monroe County Psychiatric Case Register. Monroe County, New York, is a relatively small urban county, including the city of Rochester and surrounding area, with a 1970 population of 711,917. The Case Register, initiated in 1960, records utilization of psychiatric services by county residents. More detailed descriptions of the Case Register and its uses are presented elsewhere (Babigian, 1977; Gardner, Miles, Iker, & Romano, 1963; Liptzin & Babigian, 1972). Virtually all providers of psychiatric services in Monroe County submitted data for the Register from 1960 through 1975, with most private psychiatrists also supplying information until approximately 1973. To ensure optimal comprehensiveness, relevance, and accuracy of data, the period from 1965 through 1975 was selected for this study.

Annual Treated Incidence and Prevalence

For the years 1965, 1970, and 1975, counts of new Register cases reporting no previous psychiatric care (annual treated incidence cases) were generated and aggregated by category of most frequent diagnosis received that year. Because of the limited reliability of diagnoses across the spectrum of psychiatric providers, all individuals with diagnoses of schizophrenia, affective disorders, and paranoid or other psychotic disorders were classified under "functional psychoses" for most analyses. Age/sex adjusted incidence rates per 1,000 county population were computed, using the formula:

$$\frac{\text{Number of new cases in age/sex group}}{\text{County census in age/sex group}} \times 1,000$$

Procedures for determining annual treated prevalence were based on 1965, 1970, and 1975 Register counts of all individuals who received any psychiatric treatment in the respective year, categorized by most frequent diagnosis received during that year. Diagnostic groupings were defined and treated prevalence rates computed in a fashion analogous to that described above for treated incidence.

Utilization of Services

Utilization rates of psychiatric services by diagnostic and age groups were based on the population receiving psychiatric services during the respective years. Categories of service utilization included: inpatient treatment at the state psychiatric facility (Rochester Psychiatric Center or RPC), treatment at other psychiatric inpatient centers, emergency department care, and treatment in other outpatient settings, including day care and partial hospitalization. Unduplicated raw counts of utilization and age/sex adjusted rates per 1,000 county population were computed, using the procedure described earlier. Utilization counts consisted of unduplicated counts of individuals treated at some time during the year in each service. Duplications were allowed across services, but not within any service.

Mortality

The relative risk of mortality among persons with functional psychoses compared to the entire county population was assessed. All individuals making contact with the Register during the years 1960 through 1975 and having a diagnosis of schizophrenia, paranoia, affective disorders, or other functional psychotic disorder were included. Mortality risk was computed as the ratio of deaths to person-years at risk in each age/sex group. This ratio for the psychotic group was then divided by the respective ratio for the county population to produce the relative mortality risk. Relative risks were computed for major psychotic disorders and major causes of death.

RESULTS

Incidence

The incidence of all reported psychiatric disorders combined rose from 7.6 per 1,000 in 1965 to 9.0 per 1,000 in 1975 (see Figure 2–1). This reflected primarily the increase in nonpsychotic, nonorganic disorders among the young. The treated incidence of all psychiatric disorders among persons aged 45 to 64 remained essentially unchanged.

The sharp decline in incidence among the elderly, from 6.0 per 1,000 in 1965 to 4.0 per 1,000 in 1975, was attributed to the decline in treatment for organic brain syndromes among the elderly by the mental health system. Neither the incidence of treated psychosis nor of other psychiatric disorders changed significantly for those over 65.

The incidence rates of schizophrenia and paranoia by age and sex reflect a pattern of earlier presentation of males than females for these disorders, with the highest rates for males in the 15– to 24–year age group and for females in the 25– to 44–year age group (see Table 2–1). Overall rates for males were higher than for females.

Incidence rates for schizophrenia and paranoid disorders decreased with age, whereas the rates for affective disorders and other psychoses increased. The overall downward trend in the incidence of these disorders between 1965 and 1975 is difficult to explain, but may be related to changes in diagnostic practices and changes in the locus of care from inpatient settings to outpatient settings and nursing homes.

Prevalence

In general, prevalence reflected the same patterns as incidence (see Figure 2–2). The treatment rates for psychoses declined modestly, but significantly, over the 10–year period for all age groups. The dramatic increase in the young and middle age group of "other disorders" was due in part to increases in treatment for alcohol disorders and neurotic depression.

The treated prevalence rates for schizophrenia and paranoia were roughly comparable for males and females over the 10–year period, with the highest rates in the 35– to 54–year age groups (Table 2–2). Although the incidence of schizophrenia and paranoia decreased with age, their prevalence remained relatively constant across all age groups because of the chronic nature of these disorders.

Demographic Analysis

Examination of marital status, sex, and race of psychotic patients treated in 1975 revealed that the youngest group (15 to 44 years) was predominantly male and single, while the older groups were dispro-

Figure 2–1
Annual Treated Incidence Rates of All
Psychiatric Disorders in Monroe County

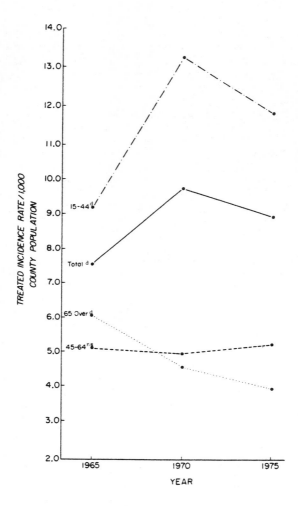

ns = not significant
a = $p < .05$
b = $p < .01$
c = $p < .001$
d = $p < .0001$

Table 2-1

Incidence of Schizophrenia, Paranoia, Affective Disorders, and Other Psychoses, Reported in Monroe County, 1965, 1970, and 1975

Age	1965 Schizophrenia/Paranoia Male n	rate	Female n	rate	Total n	rate	Other[a] Total n	rate	1970 Schizophrenia/Paranoia Male n	rate	Female n	rate	Total n	rate	Other[a] Total n	rate	1975 Schizophrenia/Paranoia Male n	rate	Female n	rate	Total n	rate	Other[a] Total n	rate
15–24	52	1.16	34	.68					94	1.63	35	.55					69	1.10	30	.46				
25–34	40	.99	44	1.04	251	.97	27	.10	41	.91	38	.81	247	.84	44	.15	47	.92	23	.43	205	.65	50	.16
35–44	38	.96	43	1.03					14	.36	25	.61					16	.41	20	.49				
45–54	21	.58	27	.69	61	.45	92	.68	15	.38	15	.35	46	.32	87	.60	15	.41	16	.40	35	.25	60	.42
55–64	4	.14	9	.29					7	.24	9	.27					0	.00	4	.12				
65–74	5	.28	4	.17	12	.18	43	.65	0	.00	4	.17	8	.12	36	.52	6	.34	7	.28	20	.27	30	.41
>74	1	.11	2	.13					2	.19	2	.11					0	.00	7	.35				
Overall	161	.74	163	.67	324	.71	162	.35	173	.73	128	.48	301	.59	167	.33	153	.62	107	.38	260	.49	140	.27

[a]Affective disorders and other psychoses.

Table 2-2
Rates Per 1,000 Annual Treated Prevalence of Schizophrenia and Paranoia
in Monroe County, New York

Age	1965 Schizophrenia/Paranoia Male n	rate	Female n	rate	Total n	rate	Other[a] Total n	rate	1970 Schizophrenia/Paranoia Male n	rate	Female n	rate	Total n	rate	Other[a] Total n	rate	1975 Schizophrenia/Paranoia Male n	rate	Female n	rate	Total n	rate	Other[a] Total n	rate
15–24	242	5.40	142	2.84					323	5.61	203	3.19					293	4.66	123	1.88				
25–34	289	7.15	297	6.99	1,839	7.10	157	.61	357	7.92	324	6.91	1,929	6.58	195	.67	456	8.89	320	5.95	1,796	5.73	282	.90
35–44	398	10.10	471	11.25					314	8.01	408	10.03					269	6.89	335	8.18				
45–54	345	9.48	365	9.29					342	8.70	443	10.31					301	8.19	372	9.37				
55–64	178	6.39	219	7.08	1,107	8.23	511	3.80	202	6.89	260	7.94	1,247	8.64	476	3.30	217	7.11	282	8.15	1,172	8.29	413	2.92
65–74	134	7.51	172	7.39					101	5.90	146	6.17					106	5.98	156	6.30				
>74	58	6.11	119	7.74	483	7.32	300	4.55	63	6.10	120	6.76	430	6.24	313	4.54	69	6.51	126	6.31	457	6.26	267	3.66
Overall	1,649	7.60	1,785	7.34	3,429	7.46	968	2.11	1,702	7.15	1,904	7.09	3,606	7.12	984	1.94	1,711	6.88	1,714	6.14	3,425	6.48	962	1.82

[a]Affective disorders and other psychoses.

portionately Caucasian females, either married or widowed (Table 2–3). The proportion of people still single after age 45 was considerably larger among psychotics than the 12%–15% reported among persons with other types of psychiatric disorders.

The decrease in proportions of white males and the increase in white females with age was seen only in the psychotic diagnostic group. Among other types of disorders treated in 1975, the proportion of white males in each age group remained between 40% and 50%, with a clear majority of white females (53.8%) only in the oldest group.

Figure 2–2
Annual Treated Prevalence Rates of All
Psychiatric Disorders in Monroe County, NY

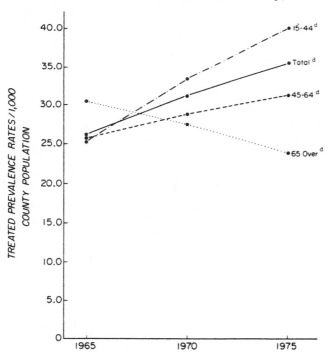

ns = not significant
a = $p < .05$
b = $p < .01$
c = $p < .001$
d = $p < .0001$

Table 2–3
Marital Status, Race, and Sex of Psychotics Treated in 1975, by Age

	15 to 44		45 to 64		65 & over		Total	
	n	%	*n*	%	*n*	%	*n*	%
Marital status								
Single	1,146	55.1	473	29.8	246	34.0	1,865	42.5
Married	559	26.9	736	46.4	248	34.3	1,543	35.2
Separated/								
divorced	349	16.8	256	16.2	66	9.1	671	15.3
Widowed	24	1.2	120	7.6	164	22.7	308	7.0
Race/sex group								
White[a] male	943	45.4	599	37.8	231	31.9	1,773	40.4
White[a] female	789	38.0	864	54.5	473	65.3	2,126	48.5
Black male	190	9.1	60	3.8	10	1.4	260	5.9
Black female	156	7.5	62	3.9	10	1.4	228	5.2
Total	2,078	47.4	1,585	36.1	724	16.5	4,387	100.0

[a]Includes other ethnic groups.

Utilization of Services

An analysis of first contact in the psychiatric service system of all individuals having a most frequent diagnosis of psychosis in 1975 revealed that nearly 60% of the elderly psychotics had their first contact with the system prior to 1961. Fewer than 10% of the psychotic individuals over 45 years old had their first contact with the psychiatric service system in 1975.

The rates of utilization of services by psychotic individuals aged 15 to 44 changed very little from 1965 to 1975, other than a modest decrease in rates of treatment in the state facility inpatient programs. In contrast, hospitalization rates at the state facility decreased sharply for persons over age 45 with psychotic disorders. This probably reflects the vigorous growth in nursing home services during that decade. Both older age groups also showed increased rates of utilization of outpatient services over the 10–year period. In the oldest group, outpatient service was the only type of care that did not show a utilization decrease between 1965 and 1975.

Mortality

Psychotic populations from the Register demonstrated modest rates of excess mortality relative to the overall county population. Table 2–4 shows the age–specific relative mortality risks obtained for individuals having at least one diagnosis of schizophrenia or affective disorder. In both groups, excess mortality peaked in the 15- to 34–

Table 2–4
Relative Mortality Risk for Psychotic Population by Age

Age group	Schizophrenia		Affective disorder		All psychotic	
	No. of deaths	Relative risk	No. of deaths	Relative risk	No. of deaths	Relative risk
15 to 24	65	2.64***	5	2.59*	70	2.64***
25 to 34	133	2.42***	14	2.77***	147	2.45***
35 to 44	230	2.05***	30	1.98**	260	2.04***
45 to 54	441	1.70***	119	1.67***	560	1.69***
55 to 64	503	1.30***	321	1.49***	824	1.37***
65 to 74	485	1.11*	588	1.32***	1,073	1.21***
75 & over	589	1.06	976	1.20***	1,565	1.15***
Total (age adjusted)	2,449	1.24	2,054	1.38	4,503	1.31

Note. Significance test for relative mortality risk not equal to 1.00 (z statistic): * $p<.05$; ** $p<.001$; *** $p<.0001$

year–old group, with mortality for the young psychotic populations ranging from 2 to 3 times that of the overall population in the same age groups. Elderly persons with schizophrenia or affective disorder exhibited mortality risk only slightly, but still significantly, higher than those of the general population.

Both older psychotic groups were at considerably greater risk of death by suicide than the general population, with suicide occurring more frequently among individuals with affective disorders in the middle age group (see Table 2–5). Slight to moderate excess mortality was also observed for all other causes of death, with the exception of neoplasms. The psychotic population died from respiratory and digestive disorders at approximately twice the rate of the general population.

DISCUSSION

The treated incidence and prevalence rates for functional psychoses among all age groups remained quite stable over the 10–year period compared to rates for other types of psychiatric disorders. The treated incidence and prevalence rates for functional psychoses among the elderly found in the Monroe County Register were consistent with rates reported in previous studies (Kay & Bergmann, 1980; Neugebauer, 1980).

In general, utilization of psychiatric treatment by the elderly decreased dramatically over the 10–year period compared to the nonelderly groups. Much of this decrease may be attributed to the

Table 2–5
Relative Mortality Risk for Psychotic Population by Age Group and
Cause of Death

Cause of death	Schizophrenia		Affective disorder		Overall	
	45–64	>64	45–64	>64	45–64	>64
Neoplasm	.92	.62***	1.04	.68***	.95	.66***
Nervous/sensory	1.06	.45***	1.48	1.23*	1.17	.87
Circulatory	1.13*	1.00	1.58***	1.32***	1.26***	1.17***
Respiratory	2.25***	1.66***	2.32***	1.52***	2.27***	1.59***
Digestive	2.32***	1.41	1.55	1.00	2.11***	1.19
Accidents	1.90***	.91	1.48	1.49*	1.78***	1.22
Suicide	6.36***	2.51**	10.08***	7.83***	7.39***	5.36***
Other causes	2.26***	1.23	2.45***	1.17	2.31***	1.20*

Note. Significance test for relative mortality risk not equal to 1.00 (z statistic): * $p<.05$; ** $p<.001$; *** $p<.0001$

shift in the locus of care for persons with organic brain disorders from inpatient psychiatric settings to nursing home facilities. However, treatment rates among the elderly for other types of psychiatric disorder, including functional psychoses, failed to keep pace with the striking increases in treatment rates for younger patients, which were directly related to the establishment of three new Community Mental Health Centers in the Rochester area during 1967–68. The needs of the elderly were among the last to be addressed by these new centers (Babigian, 1977).

Assuming that the true prevalence and incidence rates for psychiatric disorders among the elderly remained constant, these changing patterns in care suggest that the elderly may be underserved by the mental health system. The shift in the locus of care for many of the elderly from inpatient settings to skilled nursing facilities and the observed lag in their use of outpatient mental health services raise questions about the accessibility and quality of mental health care received by the elderly.

The mortality rates among persons over age 55 with schizophrenic disorders were similar to those in the general population and were lower than the mortality rates among elderly persons with affective disorders. As has been reported elsewhere (Tsuang, Woolson, & Fleming, 1980), the relative mortality risk of neoplasms was less among schizophrenics than in the general population, but deaths from other causes were slightly higher among persons with functional psychoses compared to the general population.

The relative risk of suicide was substantially higher in persons with either schizophrenia or affective disorders than in the general population, and the relative risk among persons with affective disorders was substantially higher than among schizophrenics throughout late life. It was noteworthy that the suicide risk among schizophrenics dropped from 6.4 among persons age 45 to 64 to 2.5 among persons 65 and over. The entire issue of excess mortality among patients with functional psychoses compared to the general population deserves further attention.

RECOMMENDATIONS FOR FUTURE RESEARCH

1. The changing pattern of mental health service utilization among the elderly requires more careful scrutiny. In particular, the quality and quantity of care they are currently receiving and their quality of life in alternative facilities outside of psychiatric inpatient settings should be assessed.

2. Now that DSM-III is in place and better defined diagnostic criteria are available, further population-based epidemiologic studies are needed to clarify the patterns and types of psychiatric disorders among the elderly.

3. The excess mortality among psychotics needs to be investigated, focusing more attention on specific kinds of disorders and the possible relationships between psychiatric disorders and medical illnesses.

3

Mental Illness Among the Elderly in a Large State Psychiatric Facility: A Comparison with Other Age Groups

Carole E. Siegel

Nathan S. Kline Institute

New York University Medical Center

Ann B. Goodman

Nathan S. Kline Institute

Columbia University School of Public Health

Although organic brain syndrome (OBS) disorders account for most of late onset psychiatric illness, reviews of European literature (Bridge & Wyatt, 1980a) suggest that substantial numbers of patients exhibit severe paranoid symptoms for the first time in late life. They further report that 10% of all first admission elderly psychiatric patients suffer from paraphrenia, a distinct part of the schizophrenia spectrum characterized by paranoia and onset in the middle or older years.

Few American studies report on such paranoid type illnesses among the elderly. Thus, a descriptive study of a large inpatient cohort of elderly patients in a New York State psychiatric center was conducted to explore the following questions:

1. Does the distribution of diagnoses in the elderly population differ from that of younger age groups?

2. Among the elderly, what are the patterns of age of onset for the various diagnoses, and specifically, what is the incidence of late onset paraphrenia?

3. What is the prior inpatient experience of the elderly mentally ill?

SETTING

Rockland Psychiatric Center is one of 23 adult mental hospitals operated by the State of New York. Completed in the early 1930s, its peak inpatient population of close to 9,000 was reached in the mid–1950s. By 1970 the patient census had almost halved to about 5,000; its present census is approximately 1,400.

Since 1972, the hospital has served as an admission facility only for residents of Rockland County and the western portion of Westchester County, both middle–class suburban catchment areas. Active short–term inpatient psychiatric facilities serve both of these counties, so that acute patients requiring less than 30 days hospitalization may have received inpatient care elsewhere. However, patients from the two counties requiring longer hospitalizations eventually would have been admitted to Rockland Psychiatric Center. Concomitantly, discharges have been largely to the two catchment areas, facilitated by the presence of an unusually large number of skilled nursing homes and health–related facilities.

Since the mid–1970s the hospital has participated in a state–sponsored unified services plan in both catchment areas, which has facilitated the development of close cooperative agreements among public and voluntary mental health service providers. Both catchment areas possess a wide range of geriatric treatment services, organized to prevent institutionalization of the elderly. Therefore, the network of mental health services available within the catchment area is believed to be as extensive as any currently available. Since 1975, there has been an active policy of admission diversion away from the state center to other service settings within the two counties.

DATA

An automated mental health information system, the Multi–State Information System (MSIS), operating in the hospital since the mid–1960s, was the source of information about admission, psychiatric diagnosis, and discharge status (Laska and Bank, 1975). Descriptive data were gathered for all mental hospital inpatients (based on unduplicated counts) who received care at Rockland Psychiatric Center between January 1, 1972 and December 31, 1976. Patients were characterized by age (either at the beginning of the period or at initial admission in the period); sex; the latest DSM–II diagnosis recorded during the period; age at first recorded hospitalization; and amount of prior inpatient hospitalization, whether accumulated continuously or in several episodes. The latter two variables were used to differentiate those with longstanding psychiatric illness (chronic) from those with more recently developed illness. Those who had accumulated less than 1 year of prior hospitalization were labeled as brief–prior; this included new cases. Those with 1 to 10 years prior experience were labeled intermediate chronics, and those with more than 10 years as long–term chronics.

The diagnostic groupings considered in this study were schizo-phrenia (DSM–II codes 295, except 295.3); paranoid conditions (DSM–II codes 295.3, 297); organic brain syndrome (DSM–II codes 290–294, 309.0, 309.2–9), and other (all other DSM–II codes). These groupings were formed in order to specifically investigate the relative magnitude of schizophrenia, excluding paranoid type (295.3), in relation to paranoid states (297) and paranoid schizophrenia (295.3) grouped together as paranoid conditions. Among the elderly, paranoid conditions would most closely approximate the nosologic group termed paraphrenic in European studies.

DSM–II, the classification scheme mandated by the state during the cohort period, was used in the study, and somewhat limited the interpretation of the data. In particular, the reliability and validity of diagnoses were open to question because of the absence of specified criteria. A small validation study carried out by Craig, Goodman, and Haugland (1982) on a subsample from the cohort of patients of all ages in the hospital during 1975–76 revealed good overall reliability (Kappa=0.73) between the DSM–II study diagnosis and a more structured DSM–III criterion checklist.

Moderately good reliability (Kappa=0.67) was demonstrated be-tween the DSM–II and DSM–III diagnoses of schizophrenia, including paranoid schizophrenia and paranoid states, although the DSM–III criteria include age at onset before 45 years; schizophrenia with late onset is classified as atypical psychosis by DSM–III. However, as a major focus of the study was the difference among elderly patients with a DSM–II diagnosis of schizophrenia or paranoid conditions, ac-cording to age at onset (including after age 45), it was perhaps for-tuitous that the data preserved a degree of specificity that would be lost if the diagnosis of atypical psychosis were arbitrarily imposed.

RESULTS

Cross–Sectional Comparison of the Elderly with Other Age Groups

During the 5 years between January 1, 1972 and December 31, 1976, 6,825 persons were hospitalized in Rockland Psychiatric Center; 1,518 (22%) were age 65 and over. Of the total, 41.7% were age 15–44, 36.1% were age 45–64, 13.1% were age 65–74, and 9.1% were age 75 or older. Schizophrenia accounted for 32.3%, paranoid condi-tions for 19.1%, OBS for 16.0%, and other diagnoses, predominantly alcoholism, for 32.6% of the total cohort.

Figure 3–1 displays the distribution of diagnosis and sex ratio by age group. In contrast to the under 65 age groups where schizophrenia and "other" were the major diagnoses, among those 65 to 74, OBS, paranoid conditions, and schizophrenia accounted for roughly equal

Figure 3–1
Percent Distribution of Diagnosis and Sex Ratios (SR)
for Age Groups: All Patients in Rockland
Psychiatric Center, 1972–76

NOTE: SR=number of males per 100 females.

proportions, whereas "other" diagnoses constituted only 19%. After age 75, however, OBS constituted 55% of the diagnoses, far outnumbering the other categories.

The proportion of patients with paranoid conditions among the elderly was significantly greater ($p<.001$) than among those less than 65. The proportion of schizophrenics dropped from 39% of those 45 to 64 years to only 6% of those 75 or older.

For the total cohort, most of the paranoid condition group were paranoid schizophrenics (DSM–II code 295.3), and only 84 (1.2%) were diagnosed paranoid states (DSM–II code 297). In the 65–74 age group, only 26 (2.9%) were diagnosed paranoid states; in the over 75 age group, 43 (6.9%) had this diagnosis. In total, paranoid states constituted 4.5% of the elderly group, whereas paranoid schizophrenics constituted 22%.

Among the young, "other" was the most prevalent diagnostic grouping, and almost half that group were alcoholics (44%). Among the elderly, 17% were diagnosed "other," and 50% of this group had affective disorders.

Females predominated among the elderly, with the ratio of males to females decreasing in linear fashion from 180/100 for the youngest age group to 41/100 for the oldest group. For all but those over 75, the sex ratio for OBS favored males, whereas females predominated among the schizophrenic and paranoid groups except among the youngest.

Figure 3–2 shows the age and sex distribution by diagnosis of the total cohort. The number of those diagnosed as schizophrenic dropped sharply after age 65, but approximately equal numbers were diagnosed schizophrenic in the younger age groups. More males were admitted prior to age 45, and more females between 45–64. Paranoids, although relatively fewer than the schizophrenics, declined much more gradually in number after age 65, with equal numbers in the under–45 and 45–64 age groups. The male/female ratio shift for these age groupings was similar to that seen for schizophrenics. The OBS group increased in number with increasing age, except for age 65–74. For all age groups under 75, males predominated.

The age distribution of schizophrenia and paranoid conditions differed significantly from each other ($p<.001$) for the total cohort, males, and females, with the direction of the differences the same for males and females (see Table 3–1). The bulk of schizophrenics and paranoids were in the younger age groups, but whereas 11.5% of schizophrenics were over 65, 31% of paranoids were elderly. For the age groups under 65, schizophrenics outnumbered paranoids approximately two to one, whereas for patients 75 and older there were approximately four paranoids to every one schizophrenic (ratio 0.24).

Age of Onset Among the Elderly

Figure 3–3 displays the diagnostic–specific patterns of age of onset (as defined as age at first recorded admission in the MSIS data base)

Figure 3-2
Age and Sex Distributions for Diagnostic Groups: All Patients in Rockland Psychiatric Center, 1972–76

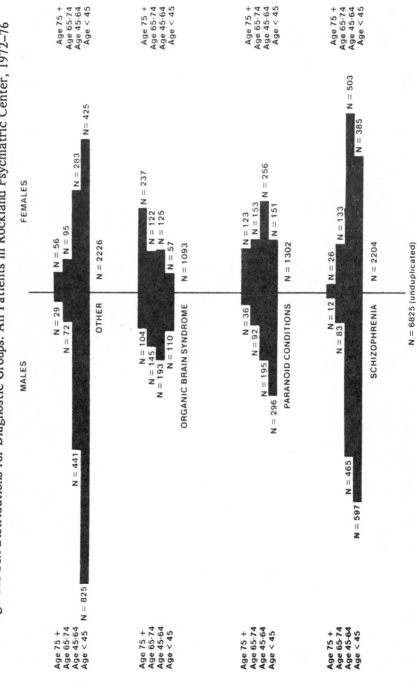

Table 3-1
Percent Distribution of Schizophrenia and Paranoid Condition by Sex
and Age: All patients in Rockland Psychiatric Center, 1972–76

Sex/age	Schizophrenia	Paranoid	Ratio schizophrenia/paranoid
Total			
15–44	44.5	34.3	2.19
45–64	43.9	34.6	2.14
65–74	9.8	18.8	0.88
75+	1.7	12.2	0.24
Total	n=2,204	n=1,302	1.69

X^2=249.2 df=3 p<.001

Males			
15–44	51.6	47.8	2.02
45–64	40.2	31.5	2.38
65–74	7.2	14.9	0.90
75+	1.0	5.8	0.33
Total	n=1,157	n=619	1.87

X^2=267.6 df=3 p<.001

Females			
15–44	36.7	22.1	2.54
45–64	48.0	37.5	1.96
65–74	12.7	22.4	0.87
75+	2.5	18.1	0.21
Total	n=1,047	n=683	1.53

X^2=178.4 df=3 p<.001

among the elderly. Forty–five percent had a first recorded admission at age 65 or over, and 28% were admitted before the age of 45. Among the elderly, 56% of schizophrenics and 61% of paranoid schizophrenics were first admitted before age 45. The modal age of onset for the 69 elderly patients diagnosed as paranoid states was in the mid–years (45–54). Onset for schizophrenics was predominantly early and declined sharply with age, while age of onset for paranoid conditions declined more gradually.

More than half of the OBS and "other" (mostly affective disorders) diagnoses had late onset with first recorded admission at age 65 or older. The bimodal distribution of age of onset among the total elderly cohort was thus explained by the predominantly early onset for schizophrenia and paranoid conditions and the late onset of OBS and "other" conditions (see Table 3–2). Nevertheless, it is notable

Figure 3-3
Age on Admission by Diagnosis Among the Elderly: All Patients in Rockland Psychiatric Center, 1972–76

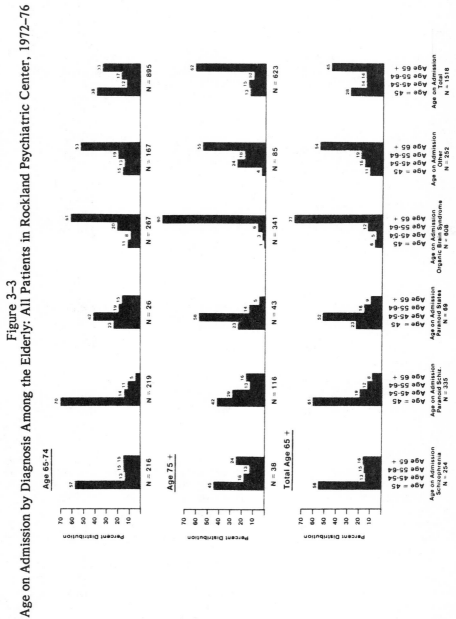

that 44% of elderly schizophrenics and 39% of elderly paranoid schizophrenics had a first recorded hospital admission after age 45.

Prior Inpatient Hospitalization

Of those patients over age 65 at the time of the study, 736 (48%) had brief or intermediate prior hospitalization, with slightly under half of this group (43%) having less than 1 year's experience (see Table 3–3). Three–fourths of the long–term chronics had accumulated more than 20 years of hospitalization. A significantly ($p<.001$) greater proportion of paranoids over 65 had more than than 10 years of prior inpatient hospitalization (86%) than of schizophrenics (76%).

Among the 316 elderly patients classified as brief–prior, 31 were diagnosed schizophrenic and 17 were paranoid. The ratio of schizophrenia to paranoid was 1.8 among the brief–priors and 0.8 among intermediates. Schizophrenics and paranoid conditions represented 8% each of patients with less than 10 years prior hospitalization. For long–term chronics, 25% were schizophrenic and 44% were paranoid, giving a schizophrenia to paranoid ratio of 0.6.

For the 45–64 age group, proportionately more paranoids had less than 10 years of prior hospitalization (38%) than schizophrenics (30%). This was also the case for those under 45, where the proportion of paranoids with less than 10 years of prior hospitalization was 93% and for schizophrenics, 74%.

DISCUSSION

Schizophrenia and "other" diagnoses each accounted for 32% of the total cohort, paranoid conditions 19%, and OBS 16%. However, the proportionate breakdown was strikingly different for the different

Table 3–2

Distribution of Diagnosis Among the Elderly by Age of Onset

| | Age of onset | | | | | | | | Total | |
| | <45 | | 45–54 | | 55–64 | | 65+ | | | |
	n	%	n	%	n	%	n	%	n	%
Schizophrenia	141	33	34	17	38	18	41	6	254	16
Paranoid conditions	219	52	100	49	51	24	34	5	404	27
Organic brain syndrome	34	08	30	15	73	35	471	69	608	40
Other	28	06	41	20	47	22	136	20	252	17
Total	422	100	205	100	209	100	682	100	1,518	100

Table 3–3
Prior Cumulative Hospitalization by Age and Diagnosis:
Rockland Inpatient Cohort, 1972–76

Age/diagnosis	Prior hospitalization							
	Brief <1 year		Intermediate 1–10 years		Long >10 years		Total	
	n	%	n	%	n	%	n	%
>64 years								
Schizophrenia	31	12.2	31	12.2	192	75.6	254	100
Paranoid conditions	17	4.2	39	9.7	348	86.1	404	100
OBS	162	26.6	307	50.5	139	22.9	608	100
Other	106	42.1	43	17.1	103	40.9	252	100
Total	316	20.8	420	27.7	782	51.5	1518	100

Total table X^2=346.3 df=6 p<.001

Schizophrenic vs. paranoids X^2=16.7 df=2 p<.001

45 to 64 years								
Schizophrenia	199	20.6	89	9.2	680	70.3	968	100
Paranoid conditions	124	27.5	46	10.2	281	62.3	451	100
OBS	130	40.9	108	34.0	80	25.2	318	100
Other	586	80.9	58	8.0	80	11.1	724	100
Total	1,039	42.2	301	12.2	1,121	45.6	2,461	100

Total table X^2=905.8 df=6 p<.001

Schizophrenic vs. paranoids X^2=9.7 df=2 p<.01

<45 years								
Schizophrenia	584	59.5	146	14.9	252	25.7	982	100
Paranoid conditions	373	83.5	43	9.6	31	6.9	447	100
OBS	124	74.2	27	16.2	16	9.6	·167	100
Other	1,105	88.4	91	7.3	54	4.3	1,250	100
Total	2,186	76.8	307	10.8	353	12.4	2,846	100

Total table X^2=314.3 df=6 p<.001

Schizophrenic vs. paranoids X^2=87.2 df=2 p<.001

age groups. The increased prevalence of OBS was the predominant factor in the change in diagnostic mix with age. Paranoid conditions emerged as the second most prevalent diagnostic category among the elderly, while the number of schizophrenics declined sharply. The two age groups under 65 had diagnostic distributions similar to that of the total cohort, but the proportion of schizophrenics decreased to 17% for those over 65, and to 6% for those over 75, while the proportion with paranoid conditions increased to 26%.

It is startling that in Rockland Psychiatric Center during the 1972–76 period, there were 982 schizophrenics under 45, 968 aged 45–64, and only 254 schizophrenics over 65. Whereas almost four times as many schizophrenics were in the 45–64 year age group as in the over–65 age group, the number of paranoids in both age groups was about equal (approximately 400–450). To the extent that we can make longitudinal assumptions from cross–sectional data, we may well ask, what happened to the elderly schizophrenics?

The period of this particular cohort fell squarely within the period of active deinstitutionalization in New York State. The shifting ratio of schizophrenics to paranoids as age increased and the sharp decline in the absolute number of schizophrenics over 75 may be strongly related to the impact of deinstitutionalization on this cohort. Schizophrenics and paranoids may have been differentially placed in the community. Several researchers (Bleuler, 1978a; Ciompi, this volume), in connection with long–term follow–up studies, have suggested a reduction in symptomatology among schizophrenics, with complete remission evidenced for some. Our data suggest that community placement was viable for a large subgroup of chronic schizophrenics, whereas this was not the case for paranoids (including, in our analysis, paranoid schizophrenics). These paranoids may well exhibit and retain more florid or "positive" symptoms requiring active drug management, making their placement in community residences more difficult.

We noted that the elderly patients were fairly well split between those with brief or intermediate prior hospitalization and long–term chronics. Among brief and intermediate priors, schizophrenics and paranoids each accounted for 8%, the bulk of these groups being diagnosed OBS. However, among the long–term chronics, schizophrenics accounted for 25% while paranoids accounted for 44%. When did the buildup of paranoids begin? Our data allow us to suggest that this buildup begins well before age 65. The elderly paranoid conditions ("paraphrenic") and the elderly schizophrenic groups both predominantly comprised those with early onset (<45). However, more of the elderly had been first admitted between 45 and 54 with a diagnosis of paranoid conditions than with schizophrenia (25% versus 13%). In fact, for paranoid states this figure was 52%. The incidence rate of late–onset paranoid or "paraphrenic" conditions was 5%, less than the 10% rate reported by others (Bridge & Wyatt, 1980a; Kay & Roth, 1961; Roth, 1955); however, when combined with late–onset schizophrenia (6%), the percentage was close.

Furthermore, an examination of the data on the culmulative prior hospitalization experience of the total cohort leads us to speculate that the excess buildup of paranoids over schizophrenics begins after the close of young adulthood between 35 and 63. Only 7% of young paranoids were chronic in contrast to 26% of schizophrenics, but for the 45–64 year group, 62% of paranoids and 70% of schizophrenics were chronic.

Among other hypotheses that might explain the relative increase in paranoid conditions among the elderly, we are presently investigating (Goodman & Siegel, 1986):

1. Changes in diagnoses over time
2. Lower mortality rates among paranoids

Some other aspects of our data require comment. In Rockland, only 8% of the elderly suffer affective disorders. Roth (1955), in Britain, finds affective disorders in almost 50% of patients over 60. This surprising difference in diagnostic mix may be the result of deinstitutionalization and an active admission diversion policy of this state psychiatric hospital which admits only the most seriously ill and directs many less disabled elderly to community facilities or nursing homes.

We also found that 44% of elderly schizophrenics and 39% of elderly paranoid schizophrenics had their first recorded hospital admission after age 45. These patients may have been ill before age 45, but since these proportions are substantial, we must consider whether these illnesses do begin after age 45. If so, the DSM–III criterion for schizophrenia requiring age of onset prior to 45 is questionable.

Further study is needed to distinguish clinical patterns relating to the course of illness from patterns relating to administrative decisions such as deinstitutionalization or admission diversion, and to better characterize the nature of the late–onset schizophrenic and paranoid patient, exploring alternative hypotheses to account for the shifting ratio of paranoids to schizophrenics.

PART

II

LONGITUDINAL STUDIES: COURSE OF ILLNESS AND PROGNOSTIC INDICATORS

Longitudinal studies don't provide definitive answers, either, to the course of schizophrenic illness. Many factors are clearly involved. European researchers have found substantial evidence for improvement with age, and several American investigators have uncovered similar data. Long–term findings tended to be more positive than those recorded for short–term follow–up of released chronic patients. But no reliable predictors have been identified, and outcomes vary widely.

Several hypotheses about the cause and course of schizophrenia have been put forward. Most postulate some combination of heredity and environment. The Genain quadruplets are a dramatic example of identical heredity with different degrees of severity of schizophrenia. Ciompi suggests a defect in information processing that responds to less stressful environments in vulnerable people. Other studies point to a possible immunological defect in nonparanoid schizophrenics and to significantly shortened lifespans in all schizophrenic patients.

4 Review of Follow-up Studies on Long-Term Evolution and Aging in Schizophrenia

Luc Ciompi

Social–Psychiatric University Clinic

Berne, Switzerland

In the first systematic follow–up investigation focused on senescence in schizophrenics that exists to my knowledge, Christian Müller (1959) stated that elderly schizophrenics provide an excellent test for the different etiologic theories on this puzzling illness. In spite of this, the latter half of the course of this disorder has received far less research and clinical attention than the first half. Since Kraep- elin, schizophrenia has been viewed pessimistically as a process of slow progressive deterioration resulting from chronic illness com- bined with old–age impairment. Yet, as early as 1911, Eugen Bleuler mentioned tendencies for improvement:

> Many patients really improve by diminution of hallu- cinations and delusions . . . The affects related to the pathological phenomena diminish in various ways, partly in the same way as in healthy people who accommodate to disagreements, and partly by simple splitting.

These tendencies have largely been confirmed, first by Müller's study and, during the last decade, by several major European follow– up investigations, one of them our own. To some extent, they are changing our whole outlook on schizophrenia. Three major questions have received some interesting new answers. They concern:

1. The evolution of schizophrenia during the second half of life

2. The factors related to this long–term evolution

3. The relationship between schizophrenia and aging, including senile or arteriosclerotic deterioration.

THE LONG–TERM EVOLUTION OF SCHIZOPHRENIA

The current state of knowledge on the long–term evolution of schizophrenia has been reported in several excellent reviews (Bleuler, 1972, 1978; Langfeldt, 1937; Stephens, 1970; Strauss & Carpenter, 1972; Vaillant, 1964). In his comprehensive study on prognosis, Stephens (1970) listed 32 follow–up studies covering more than 5 years; however, only four of them exceeded 20 years (Beck, 1968; Bleuler, 1968; Noreik, Astrup, Dalgrad, & Holmboer, 1967; Rennie, 1939). We added 12 studies in our 1976 monograph (Bender & Hirschmann, 1966; Bleuler, 1972; Bruck, Heiss, & Trappl, 1968; Ehrentheil, Davis, Casey, & Alsenberg, 1962; Favorina, 1965; Gross & Huber, 1973; Henisz, 1967; Hinterhuber, 1973; Huber, Gross, & Schüttler, 1979; Lindelius, 1970; Romel, 1970; Sutter & Chabert, 1967).

One of Stephen's main conclusions was that outcome depends primarily on the concept of schizophrenia adopted by the investigator. When bad outcome itself is used as a diagnostic criterion for "true schizophrenia", the overall prognosis cannot be other but overwhelmingly bad. Such a confusing tautology has to be discarded for another reason as well—long–term studies have shown that late remissions can occur even after many years of severe illness. Thus, a valid diagnosis could logically only be determined in old age, leading to a *post hoc*, clinically impractical situation for an illness that frequently begins in young adulthood. On the other hand, the long–term prognosis becomes favorable, according to Stephens, in a majority of cases when a broad concept of schizophrenia is adopted.

Another crucial methodological problem was emphasized by Strauss and Carpenter (1972), who claimed that outcome cannot be viewed in one single dimension, but rather must be considered on numerous levels (e.g., psychopathology, work, social relations, hospitalizations)." This is even more evident when we look at very long evolution including senescence.

The three recent European studies that provide the most significant new information on the long–term course of the illness (Bleuler, 1972; Ciompi & Müller, 1976; Huber, Gross, & Schüttler, 1979) have not completely solved these problems, but present at least some important advantages. They are all based on the same Bleulerian and partly Schneiderian diagnostic criteria, which are independent of outcome and occupy an intermediate position between the very narrow concepts of, say, the Scandinavians and the very broad ones that were widely used in the United States until the recent introduction of DSM–III. Sampling procedures and methodology are also quite comparable. In spite of inevitable methodological limitations related to sample mortality, representativeness, validity of retrospective information, assessment techniques, etc., the results are strongly cross–validated by a striking convergence of many findings. The sample size in all three studies was considerable and together included about 1,000 cases over at least 2 decades (Table 4–1). As our own investigations provided the longest catamneses and

Table 4–1
Comparison of Some General Data on Three Recent
Long–Term Follow–up Investigations

	Bleuler 1972	Ciompi and Müller 1976	Huber, Gross and Schüttler 1979
Schizophrenia concept	E. and M. Bleuler	E. and M. Bleuler	E. and M. Bleuler K. Schneider
Sample			
Number of cases	208	289	502
Average duration of follow–up (years)	22	36.9	21.4
Location	Psychiatric University Hospital Zurich	Psychiatric University Hospital Lausanne	Psychiatric University Hospital Bonn
Delineation of catchment area	Unclear	Clear	Unclear
Criterion of inclusion	First and/or succeeding admissions	First admissions	First and/or succeeding admissions
Factors of selection	Not investigated	Investigated	Partly investigated
Representativeness	(+)	(++)	(+)
Method of investigation	Continuous personal knowledge	Personal follow–up examination by semi-structured interview at home; study of hospital records and other documents	Personal follow–up examination

are the only ones that were systematically extended into old age, they are of particular interest here.

Our follow-up study on schizophrenia was part of the so-called "Lausanne Investigations," an extended research program initiated by Christian Müller in 1963 to systematically explore the long-term evolution of the main psychiatric illnesses into old age (Müller, 1981). The initial sample consisted of 5,661 psychiatric patients of all diagnostic groups who had been hospitalized during the first decades of the century in a Swiss catchment area of about 500,000 inhabitants. Age groups were chosen to obtain catamneses systematically extending into old age, covering an average 30-40 years. All patients included in the study were born between 1873 and 1897 and had a first psychiatric hospitalization before the age of 65; if alive, they were reexamined between 1963 and 1969, at an age of 65-97 years.

Thanks to extremely favorable conditions in Switzerland, information was obtained for over 97% of the initial cases. A detailed study of the causes of death as compared to the general population provided information on selection factors for the reexamined minority of survivors. In this framework, of 1,642 cases diagnosed as schizophrenic at first admission, 289 survivors (92 male and 197 female) remained after careful diagnostic reassessment by operational criteria, following exclusion of doubtful cases. These survivors were personally reexamined in their homes an average 36.9 years after their first admission, at an average age of 75.2 years for men and 75.8 years for women.

Follow-up examination included a semi-structured interview with the patient and all available additional information from relatives, nurses, family, doctors, authorities, and hospital files. Detailed statistical comparisons between the initial and the reexamined patients shed light on favorable as well as unfavorable biases introduced by sample attrition, thus permitting a more realistic evaluation of the results. Outcome and course of disorder were individually assessed across five dimensions: evolution of psychotic symptomatology, the development of additional disorders and of psycho-organic deterioration, the nature of social adjustment over time (housing, work, social autonomy, interpersonal relations), and global overall evolution. All five dimensions were systematically correlated with general, premorbid, psychopathological, and situational variables.

Results of particular pertinence for this discussion include the following (for further details, see Ciompi, 1980a):

1. Overall mortality was higher for schizophrenics than for the general population. If the expected value for the latter is considered as 100%, mortality amounted to 173% for the initial sample (161% for men and 185% for women, with significant differences for different diagnostic subgroups and for late as compared to early onset schizophrenics).

2. The long-term evolution of schizophrenia was clearly better than generally believed. According to the criteria established by

Bleuler (1972), complete and lasting social remission occurred in 26.6% of the cases and mild end–states in 22.1% (Table 4–2). Even using our own more stringent severe criteria, 20.1% had been completely free of any residual for at least 5 years, and 42.6% were markedly improved. Thus, the evolution was relatively favorable in about half to two–thirds of the cases. As already mentioned, remissions occasionally occurred even after many years of severe illness.

3. A "typical" evolution of schizophrenic disorder does not exist. On the contrary, schizophrenic disorder manifests an enormous variety of evolutionary forms. Only by extreme schematization could the more than 30 forms of evolution—resulting from various combinations of different types of onset, course, and end–states—ultimately be reduced to the 8 main evolutionary types represented in Figure 4–1. These correspond to the 8 categories distinguished by Bleuler in 1972. (Huber *et al.* (1979), initially differentiated more than 70 forms that were eventually condensed to the 12 main categories presented in Table 4–3.) The most frequent types in our series were those of an undulating (25%) or continuous course (24%); 10% of the cases remitted after a single episode. We also observed phase-wise–increasing (12%) and continuous–decreasing (10%) patterns. The other evolutionary forms represent various less frequent combinations, with the severest possible form (acute beginning and continuous evolution to severest end–state), resembling Bleuler's "catastrophic schizophrenia," being observed in 6% of the cases.

4. In cases with persistent disorder, patients typically began with a great variety of acute productive initial symptoms but later developed strikingly uniform residual states, mainly characterized by amotivational and other negative–unproductive symptoms. Such residual states clearly predominated in 55.7%; only in 18.3% could

Table 4–2
Long–Term Outcome (Stable End–States Over ≥ 5 Years)

	Bleuler 1972		Ciompi and Müller 1976[a]		Huber, Gross and Schüttler 1979[b]	
Complete remission	20%	53%	27%	49%	26%	57%
Mild end–states	33%		22%		31%	
Intermediate end–states	24%		24%		29%	
Severe end–states	24%		18%		14%	

[a] 9% unstable or uncertain.

[b] As a consequence of another categorization, the comparison with figures of Huber *et al.* (1979) presents some difficulties. It is made on the basis of their data reported on page 141 (Table 32).

Figure 4-1
Long–Term Evolution of Schizophrenia

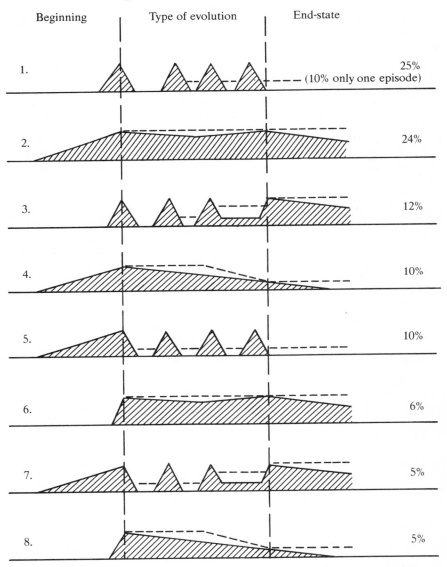

Note. Average follow–up 36.9 years, n=228. Dotted line = alternative forms of evolution within the same type.

the initial paranoid, catatonic, or hebephrenic pictures still be distinguished (the remaining 26.6% were classified as remissions). This marked difference between acute and chronic schizophrenia could be related to certain differences in etiology.

While Bleuler and Huber *et al.* did not systematically investigate mortality and/or causes of death, on the other three points, Bleuler's and Huber's findings were very similar to ours—even if Huber *et al.* (1979) conceptualized the long–term courses, according to their own concepts, in a more complex way. The proportion of favorable outcomes (remissions and mild "end–states" in Bleuler's sense) across three studies was, as Table 4–2 shows, 53%, 49% and 57%, respectively.

Additional support for these findings comes from two eastern studies known to us only through some quite extensive German summaries. Sternberg (1979, 1981) reported repeatedly on extended epidemiological investigations on 1,035 schizophrenics over 60, treated and followed–up through several decades in the Moscow psychiatric dispensaries. He claimed that the available information

Table 4–3
Types of Evolution According to Huber *et al.*, 1979

I.	Monophasic course to complete remission	10.0%	Favorable
II.	Polyphasic course to complete remission	12.1%	22.1%
III.	Pure chronic psychosis	4.2%	
IV.	With only one phase to pure residual states	6.2%	Relatively
V.	Primary phasewise, then escalating course to pure residual states	10.0%	favorable 26.1%
VI.	Escalating, with second positive turn, to pure residual states	5.8%	
VII.	Phasewise–escalating, primary escalating, or simple course to structural deformation	6.2%	Relatively
VIII.	Continuous course to pure residual states	5.4%	unfavorable
IX.	With several phases to pure residual states	12.9%	24.5%
X.	Escalating–simple course to mixed residual states	9.6%	
XI.	Escalating–simple or primary simple course to mixed residual states	7.2%	Unfavorable 27.3%
XII.	Escalating, escalating–simple or primary simple course to typical schizophrenic defect psychoses	10.5%	

Phasewise course = acute episodes with return to initial state.
Escalating course = acute episodes without return to initial state.

on psychopathology, hospitalizations, situational variables, families, genetics, etc., was exceptionally complete, as his sample had the great advantage of also including the ambulatory treated schizophrenics of a given catchment area, instead of being based on hospitalized patients only. Follow-up data covered 40 to 50 years in about 60% of the cases, and 20 to 39 years in the remainder.

Sternberg generally confirms the above findings, observing a general tendency to improvement after a more or less extended period of "maximal psychotic activity." Three main types of evolution were distinguished, each including several subgroups: remitting, escalating, and continuous, the second being a kind of combination of the first and the third. In the remitting type, the peak of the acute productive "intensity of illness activity" occurred in the fifties and sixties, which is astonishingly late (60% of the acute attacks occurred after the age of 50), whereas it occurred before 40 in the great majority of the escalating and continuous cases. It should be noted that this conceptualization is quite close to the one introduced by Huber *et al.* (1979). Unfortunately, the fragmentary information available hinders an appropriate evaluation of the validity of these findings.

The same is true for Marinow (1974, 1981), who reexamined a sample of 405 hospitalized, Bulgarian male chronic schizophrenics after 15, 20, 25, and 30 years. At the last follow-up, only 56 cases were left. His tables of comparison with Bleuler's, Huber's, and our own findings yield many similar results, particularly those concerning the overall long-term outcome, which was favorable in 49% of the cases (remissions 16%, mild end-states 33%, intermediate end-states 27%, and severe end-states 25%). Symptomatology, work capacity, and social adjustment were separately evaluated. The proportion of favorable cases tended to decrease from the first follow-up to the fourth, but this was probably the result of sample attrition.

FACTORS RELATED TO LONG-TERM EVOLUTION

It is not possible to present here the full details of the extended literature on predictors and other factors related to outcome. Again, only some overall results from our own long-term studies will be compared to those of others.

In our series, harmonious versus disturbed premorbid personality, good versus poor premorbid adjustment, acute versus insidious onset, productive versus unproductive initial symptomatology, and undulating versus continuous course were significantly related to good versus poor long-term outcome. On the other hand, among the variables statistically unrelated to evolution were gender, constitution, intelligence, and surprisingly, heredity as measured by presence of schizophrenia or other mental disorders among close family members.

Corresponding correlations, including those on heredity, were found by Bleuler (1972, 1978) and especially by Huber *et al.* (1979), the latter finding, paradoxically, an even better long–term course in cases with heavier hereditary charge. Contradictory results are reported in the literature in respect to this important point. Bleuler (1972, 1978) for instance mentions a great number of studies with similarly negative findings concerning the influence of heredity on long–term course. Kety *et al.* (1976) and others found on the contrary, although usually not in long–term observations, indices for a close relationship between genetic factors and chronicity. Sternberg (1979) observed that remitting and escalating courses had a higher genetic loading than chronic–continous ones.

Some genetic correlations were found associated with the age of onset. In addition, unfavorable long–term course was significantly more frequent in men than in women. A possible interpretation of these observations is that genetic factors are mainly implicated in creating a particular vulnerability or disposition for acute psychotic reactions, whereas long–term course is more dependent on environmental influences.

As to the other predictors mentioned, our results correspond quite closely to those usually reported in the literature, with the exception perhaps of the often ambiguous findings concerning premorbid personality, which are probably related to methodological problems. It must, however, be emphasized that the nature of all these correlations is statistical. In the province of the single case, the long–term course remains almost unpredictable.

Other factors related to outcome, among them organic, biologic, environmental, and situational variables, are known from short–term investigations. Among the former, the still–contradictory findings on correlations between ventricular enlargement and chronic unproductive schizophrenia deserves special mention (Andreason, Smith, Jacoby, Dennert, & Olson, 1982; Huber *et al.*, 1979). Among the latter, the syndrome of "institutionalism" that is related, according to the studies by Wing and Brown (1970), to the socially understimulating environment typical of understaffed old–style hospital wards, homes, etc., is of particular importance.

On the other hand, overstimulation contributes to, and exacerbates, acute psychotic relapses. The interesting statistical correlations between psychotic relapse and stressful "life events" must certainly be put in the same context (Birley & Brown, 1970; Dohrenwend & Egri, 1981; Jacobs & Myers, 1976). Similar findings are suggested by modern crisis research (Caplan, 1964; Jacobson, 1974) and additional evidence for the influence of environmental factors comes from the well–known studies by Brown *et al.*, (1972) and Vaughn and Leff (1976*a,b*) concerning a higher tendency to relapse for patients with close contacts to families with "high expressed emotions." Finally, the markedly better evolutionary tendencies in developing as compared to industrialized countries found by the International Schizophrenic Study (Sartorius, Jablensky, & Shapiro, 1978; WHO, 1979) could also be related to environmental influences.

In short, the provisional conclusion can be made that the course of schizophrenia is statistically related to (1) the premorbid phase, certain personality characteristics that are in part genetically determined and in part acquired, and (2) in the succeeding phases, to a great range of environmental and possibly biological factors. Several of the most consistently reported predictors such as type of onset and nature of initial symptomatology, as well as the evolutionary type itself could all be based, as we hypothesized in our monograph (Ciompi & Müller, 1976), on personality–specific coping and reaction patterns.

SCHIZOPHRENIA AND AGING

As pointed out earlier, prior to Müller's 1959 study, only scattered observations were available regarding the influence of aging on schizophrenia. Some studies found aggravating effects and some found ameliorating effects of senescence (e.g., Barucci, 1955; Bychowsky, 1952; Fleck, 1950; Jaser, 1928). Some of these investigators postulated an antagonistic and some a cumulative interaction between schizophrenia and senile or arteriosclerotic dementia. Müller (1959), in his systematic exploration of 101 schizophrenic patients over 65 (hospitalized an average 25 years), found in a majority of cases an easing and calming influence of the aging process, more marked in terms of social adaptation than on psycho– pathology *per se*. An aggravation of schizophrenic symptoms was observed in only a small minority of cases. Although psycho–organic intellectual deterioration seemed to occur with approximately the same frequency in schizophrenic patients as in a comparable sample of the general population (about 10%), a certain "petrification" was observed in a minority of the 36 cases who could still be reexamined 10 years later (Müller, 1971).

These questions were explored again with care in our 1976 study (Ciompi & Müller, 1976). It confirmed and differentiated most of Müller's initial findings, especially those concerning the predominant ameliorating influence of aging. The calming down of affects and drives, often leading to better interpersonal relations, was, however, frequently combined with increased indifference and social dependency. Senile or arteriosclerotic deterioration, with 8.0% severe and 16.9% intermediate cases, was probably slightly more frequent than in a comparable general population (3–6% severe and 6–15% intermediate cases according to different field studies—see Ciompi, 1980a); a direct control group was not available.

More severe intellectual impairment was significantly related to an unfavorable course of schizophrenia. Except for this correlation, however, analysis of the interaction between the two disorders in 23 specially selected cases revealed that schizophrenia and senile or arteriosclerotic dementia are two clearly distinguishable, independent diseases that can be fortuitously combined in the individual patient. The disorders appeared completely independent from each other in time of onset and/or nature of symptomatology. Often we observed a simple mixture of both without any noticeable interference. Sometimes, a superimposed senile or arteriosclerotic dementia could lend a certain organic "coloration" to the symptom picture, or lead to a transient aggravation of schizophrenic symptoms (e.g., of delusions or hallucinations). But most frequently, typically schizophrenic features tended to progressively disappear behind the classical picture of organic dementia.

In summary, the relationship between old age and schizophrenic symptoms appeared complex, with an initially ameliorating, but in advanced stages sometimes also transitorily aggravating, and (through a superimposed senile dementia) finally destructive influence of the aging process. Clearly, manifestation of schizophrenia appears even in old age as very different from a typically psychoorganic disease. As in the general population, only a minority of cases develops a specifically organic deterioration.

CONCLUSIONS

The main results of the reported long–term follow–up studies can be summarized as follows. Apart from reconfirming the presence of increased mortality, the long–term course of schizophrenia appears to be clearly better than hitherto believed. Outcome is far from uniform, but on the contrary, is characterized by enormous variability, with possible improvement and even remission after many years of severe illness. These findings are incompatible with the old idea of a progressive organic deteriorative process. More plausible is the notion of a highly variable period of greatest "illness activity" within an open life process, leading—sometimes within a few months and sometimes only after decades—in a majority of cases to marked improvement, and in about 25% of cases to complete remission.

Long–term evolution seems to be influenced by a wide range of variables. Among them, premorbid personality and adjustment and coping patterns appear to play an outstanding role. The more integrated and harmonious they are, the better the long–term evolution. Hence, the main impact of heredity, but also of certain familial and other psychosocial influences, could be located in the premorbid period. The long–term course seems to depend more on environmental than on biologic factors. In my view, the following three central questions have not been sufficiently understood and therefore need further exploration:

1. What is the nature and the genesis of the premorbid vulnerability?
2. What is the relationship between genetic factors and long–term evolution?

3. How much is the variability in long–term course determined by environmental, genetic, and/or other biological factors, and how do these different factors interact?

Some creative ideas are also needed for integrating the scattered pieces of knowledge on schizophrenia instead of focusing on only one particular variable. To stimulate further thinking and research in such a direction, as a final point let me briefly present a somewhat provocative but nevertheless plausible multicausal schizophrenia model with three phases; this idea has been fully developed in a book on logic and affectivity (Ciompi, 1982). Based on combined psychodynamics, systems theory, and Piagetian views, it attempts to integrate genetic and biological as well as psychosocial and environmental influences into the following comprehensive concept.

As shown in Figure 4–2, in the *first, premorbid phase*, variable clusters of genetic and other biological factors on the one hand and of psycho– and socio–dynamic factors on the other lead to a vulnerable premorbid personality with deficient coping patterns. Many indices, coming particularly from the current research on cognition, communication, family dynamics, and psychophysiology, and possibly also on disturbances typical of minimal brain damage, suggest that this vulnerability could consist mainly of a diminished capacity for processing complex affective–cognitive information (see also Ciompi, 1981a,b).

In the *second phase*, this vulnerable information processing system is overtaxed by too many or too complex demands, particularly when they occur during periods requiring major cognitive–affective adjustments, such as puberty or young adulthood. This critical overstimulation leads eventually, with complex and stressfully escalating vicious circles between biologic and psychosocial factors, to increasing difficulties with behavior and communication, finally culminating in acute productive psychotic symptoms.

In the *third phase*, long–term evolution is mainly determined by the interaction of preexisting deficient coping patterns with a great variety of favorable and unfavorable environmental and situational influences, including the consequences of the acute illness itself. Different pathways through this complex network of interwoven influences could determine different subgroups of schizophrenia, and thus explain the almost unpredictable variety of long–term evolutions that can be observed. On this basis, many chronic residual states, characterized mainly by "negative symptoms" (such as flatness of affect, indifference, withdrawal, negative self–concept, lack of plans and hope for the future, etc.), could represent a kind of "social artifact" (Ciompi, 1980b).

Such a concept of schizophrenia has interesting theoretical and practical implications. If a central feature of schizophrenia–prone people is a partly inborn and partly acquired vulnerability leading to a diminished capacity for processing complex information, then one essential treatment of schizophrenics should consist of utmost

Figure 4–2
Three–Phase Model of Schizophrenia

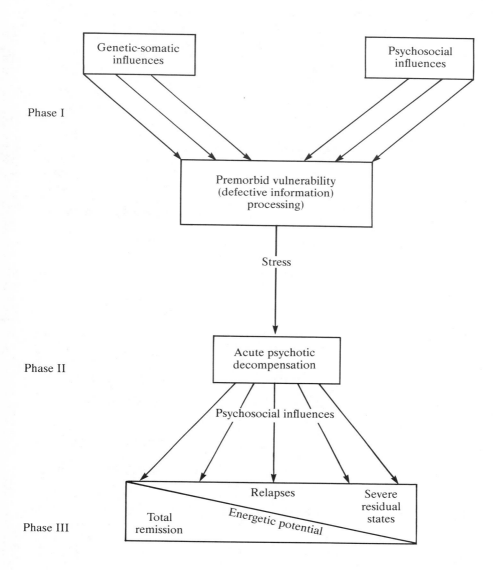

clarification and simplification of all information input in the widest sense (cognitive–affective messages of all kinds, psychosocial-situational demands, environmental stimuli, etc.). Even the curative and preventive action of neuroleptics, damping and filtering the informational input, could be understood on this basis. The same is true for the negative influence of "high expressed emotions."

The sufficient protection against overstimulating stress, the explicit formulation of clear and concrete therapeutic goals, the shaping of small and natural therapeutic settings with a relaxing ambiance, the systematic modification and education of the sur-rounding "social field" (family, therapeutic team, etc.) aiming first at minimizing contradictions and ambiguities in communication, as well as unifying the interpersonal feedbacks that constantly validate or invalidate the behavior of the patient are other important aspects of the needed simplification of informational input. In fact, most of the current biologic as well as combined psychosocial, behavioral, educational, and family dynamics approaches with proven therapeutic or preventive effects on the course of schizophrenia could be viewed in this way (Ciompi, 1981b, 1982; Mosher & Keith, 1980). Thus, the synthesis between the results of the reported longitudinal studies on the aging process and other current research on schizophrenia seem not only to lead, as Müller prophesied in 1959, to new insights into the nature of this still so enigmatic illness, but also to new and useful therapeutic approaches.

RECOMMENDATIONS

Further research on the relationship between schizophrenia and aging is recommended in the following areas:

1. Carefully investigate the long–term course of schizophrenia into old age in a cohort of former schizophrenics who are now living in the community, in order to replicate the findings of the major European follow–up studies that show a general tendency for improvement during the second half of life.

2. Include in the sample not only schizophrenics according to the DSM–III criteria, but also schizophreniform psychotic states accord-ing to Schneiderian or PSE–criteria of shorter duration, as well as similar late–onset states to determine whether these conditions have the same or different long–term course.

3. Investigate the influence of genetic, biologic, and social factors on long–term course to replicate the European finding that heredity has little influence on long–term course compared to social and environmental factors. The aim of this research should be to determine that part of the variance of long–term course attributable to genetic, biologic, and psychosocial factors.

4. Investigate more closely the validity of the vulnerability model, especially as related to a defect of information processing faculties.

5. Examine the hypothesis that vulnerability decreases in old age. Vulnerability may consist of a special affective sensibility, measurable through biophysiological parameters, that decreases in relaxing environments and increases in stimulating environments, but that declines globally with advancing age, contributing to the observed tendency to improvement.

5 A 40-Year Follow-up of Hebephrenic-Catatonic Schizophrenia

George Winokur

Bruce Pfohl

Ming Tsuang

University of Iowa College of Medicine

There are two reasons to be interested in what happens to hebephrenic schizophrenics. The first is to determine the effect of aging on the clinical picture of the patient. This would indicate whether longevity changes the nature of treatment. Perhaps more importantly, it would also confirm whether the disease starts with an active process and ultimately becomes inactive, leaving simply a defect state. If, in fact, there is an active process that stops at a particular point, it would be best to test for etiological factors prior to the time that the process becomes quiescent.

The use of a 40-year follow-up also enabled us to look at the question of differential mortality and cause of death. Since the diagnosis of hebephrenic-catatonic schizophrenia (nonparanoid schizophrenia) can be made according to fairly rigorous criteria (Tsuang & Winokur, 1974), we can compare these patients to other kinds of rigorously defined schizophrenics on rates of mortality and on particular cause of death.

METHOD

Two separate but overlapping patient groups were examined. The first group was studied to determine the progression or regression of specific symptoms in patients who have been systematically diagnosed as having hebephrenic-catatonic schizophrenia. The data came from a large project called "The Iowa 500" (Morrison, Clancy, Crowe, & Winokur, 1972; Tsuang & Winokur, 1975). Two hundred schizophrenics were admitted to the study. All had been inpatients at the Iowa Psychopathic Hospital between 1935 and 1945. Of these, 116 were diagnosed by clinicians in the hospital as hebephrenic, 14 as catatonic, 8 as uncertain, and 62 as paranoid at the time of index admission. The nonparanoid group was also referred to as the hebephrenic–catatonic group (*n*=138). A set of systematic criteria (see Table 5–1) were formulated from the material to separate hebephrenic–catatonic patients from paranoid patients (Tsuang & Winokur, 1974).

Follow–up interviews and hospital charts of the patients with an original clinical diagnosis of hebephrenic–catatonic schizophrenia were evaluated. Fifty–two patients fulfilled the systematic criteria for hebephrenic–catatonic schizophrenia and also had been followed for 12 or more years; 17 had reached the age of 60 or more in the follow–up. The symptoms seen at index hospitalization in the entire group of 52 were compared with those of the older subgroup. The symptoms at last follow–up were also evaluated for those over 60 years of age. The symptoms and criteria for rating them are pre-sented in Table 5–2. The methodology and patients in this study are more completely described in another publication (Pfohl & Winokur, 1982).

As many of the hebephrenic–catatonic schizophrenics had died, we were interested at looking at differential mortality in the hebephrenic–catatonic schizophrenics versus the paranoid schizo-phrenics. The diagnoses used were based on the initial clinician's workup. Thus this part of the study compared 158 nonparanoid (hebephrenic–catatonics) and 62 paranoid patients on mortality and the different causes of death.

Table 5–1
Diagnostic Criteria for Hebephrenic–Catatonic Schizophrenia

A thru D must be present

A. Age of onset and sociofamilial data (one of the following)
   1. Onset before age 25
   2. Unmarried or unemployed
   3. Family history of schizophrenia

B. Disorganized thought

C. Affect changes (either 1 or 2)
   1. Inappropriate
   2. Flat affect

D. Behavioral symptoms (either 1 or 2)
   1. Bizarre behavior
   2. Motor symptoms

Table 5-2
Symptom Definitions for Use in Evaluation of Charts and
Personal Follow-up Interviews

_____

Social performance
    Moderately impaired self-care
        Tends to dress in a sloppy manner, uncombed hair, etc.
    Severely impaired self-care
        Does not adequately feed self or eliminate bodily excretions in
        bathroom without help; must be present at least 1 month to
        score as present.
    Moderately impaired social interaction
        Initiates interaction with others less than twice a week.
    Severely impaired social interaction
        Ignores or walks away from attempts by others to interact most
        of the time.
    Productivity less than 50%
        Productivity is less than one-half what it was at highest level.
    No ability to do any work
        Unable to do even simple housekeeping-type chores.
    Avolition
        Loss of interest, withdrawal, aversive, seclusive, lack of
        motivation, inert.
Motor symptoms
    Hypoactive or catatonic
        If left to self, spends at least half of waking hours in one
        location.
    Waxy flexibility
        Does not resist changes in body position on manipulation by
        examiners but maintains whatever position left in for at least 1
        minute.
    Bizarre behavior
        e.g., arranges all objects in a room in shape of triangles; walks
        in a circle around anyone he/she passes.
    Mannerisms
        Spends more than one-half hour per day with some simple
        repetitive movement, e.g., tapping knee with hand.
    Tics and grimaces
        Sudden muscle contractions followed by immediate relaxation.
    Aggressive/assaultive behavior
        Patient strikes someone else or throws an ashtray across the
        room. In most cases, such behavior would occur only once or
        twice a year even though it was scored as continuously present
        for the stated time period.

Table 5–2 (continued)

Affect and Mood
  Elevated mood
    Elated: smiling, laughing, displaying enthusiasm without evidence of depressive symptoms for at least 4 weeks in a row.
  Depressed mood
    Depressed: crying, frowning, expressing dissatisfactions for at least 4 weeks in a row without evidence of symptoms of elation.
  Flat affect
    Reference in chart to decreased range of emotion or flat facies.
  Inappropriate affect
    Expressing a definite emotional reaction that is contrary to what situation should logically elicit.
Speech form
  Decreased speech
    Less than 10 words per day or mute.
  Blocking
    Sudden pause without finishing the thought after which patient never does finish the thought he/she was leading toward.
  Loose association
    Ideas slip off one track on to another that may or may not be related.
  Incoherence
    Unable to understand what idea patient is trying to express at least 1/4 of time.
Speech content
  First–rank symptoms
    Thought broadcasting, withdrawal, or thoughts heard as if spoken aloud; made feelings, impulses, thoughts, or actions; voices keep a running commentary on actions.
  Persecutory delusion
  Grandiose delusion
    Grandiose or religious delusions
  Other delusions
  Auditory hallucinations
Sensorium
  Orientation problems
    Present if more than 5 days off on date or more than one day on day of week.
  Memory deficits
    Remembers less than two of three objects at 5 minutes or does not know name of own hometown.
  Cognitive deficits
    Cannot calculate change from a dollar, misses more than 25% of serial sevens, or cannot say how an orange is like an apple.

Table 5–3
Progress and Regression of Symptoms

	Index Admission				Follow–up	
	n=35	(%)	n=17	(%)	n=17	(%)
Mean age	22		29		64	
Social performance						
Moderately impaired self–care	29	(83)	8	(47)	8	(47)
Severely impaired self–care	7	(20)	1	(6)	4	(24)
Moderately impaired social						
interaction	23	(66)	10	(59)	14	(82)
Severely impaired social						
interaction	6	(17)	5	(29)	8	(47)
Productivity less than 50%	31	(89)	17	(100)	16	(94)
No ability to do any work	8	(23)	6	(35)	8	(47)
Avolition	22	(63)	11	(65)	15	(88)
Sensorium						
Orientation problems	6	(17)	1	(6)	13	(77)
Memory deficits	5	(14)	1	(6)	9	(53)
Cognitive Deficits	6	(17)	0	(0)	4	(24)
Affect and mood						
Elevated mood	2	(6)	0	(0)	0	(0)
Depressed mood	6	(17)	4	(24)	0	(0)
Flat affect	19	(54)	8	(47)	15	(88)
Inappropriate affect	24	(69)	14	(82)	9	(53)
Motor symptoms						
Hypoactive or catatonic	14	(40)	8	(47)	10	(59)
Waxy flexibility	2	(6)	1	(6)	0	(0)
Bizarre behavior	14	(40)	8	(47)	4	(24)
Mannerisms	9	(26)	5	(29)	4	(24)
Tics and grimaces	0	(0)	3	(18)	2	(6)
Aggressive/assaultive behavior	17	(49)	8	(47)	4	(24)
Speech form						
Decreased speech	9	(26)	6	(35)	13	(77)
Blocking	8	(23)	5	(29)	7	(41)
Loose association	20	(57)	15	(88)	15	(88)
Incoherence	16	(46)	7	(41)	12	(71)
Speech content						
First rank symptoms	8	(23)	7	(41)	1	(6)
Persecutory delusion	22	(63)	12	(71)	2	(6)
Grandiose delusions	9	(26)	3	(18)	0	(0)
Other delusions	15	(43)	9	(53)	4	(24)
Auditory hallucinations	19	(54)	9	(53)	3	(18)

RESULTS

Table 5–3 shows the presence of specific symptoms and character-istics in two groups, the 35 patients of the 52 who were diagnosed hebephrenic–catatonic schizophrenic but were not followed up to the age of 60 and the subgroup of 17 who were.

In comparing the index symptoms of the subgroups, the 7–year difference in age at index admission was particularly notable. The group that was not followed up to age 60 was not only younger at index admission (22 vs. 29) but also was significantly more likely to suffer from moderately impaired self–care. More of the younger group showed severely impaired self–care and had orientation prob-lems, memory deficits, and cognitive deficits. Though none of these differences reached significance, they were all in the same direction, implying that early hospitalization is associated with more severe impairment. However, there are other possibilities. Three factors increase the likelihood of the patient being followed past age 60: (1) having late–onset schizophrenia, (2) requiring more than 12 years of institutionalization at a mental health facility, and (3) being admitted early in the 1935–45 period.

Because the early onset and the late onset group did not differ significantly (except in frequency of moderately impaired self–care), they were combined and their symptoms at time of onset were com-pared with the follow–up symptoms after age 60 of the subgroup. There was a marked change in symptomatology. The elderly schizo-phrenics were significantly more likely to have problems with orientation and memory and to show flat affect and a decrease in amount of speech. They were significantly less likely to have perse-cutory delusions and auditory hallucinations.

Thus, negative symptoms, i.e., flattened affect and decreased speech, became more prominent, while such positive symptoms as paranoid delusions and auditory hallucinations became relatively less frequent. Other trends went in similar directions. Aggressivity de-creased, blocking increased, loose associations remained stable, and incoherence became more frequent with age. First–rank symptoms dissipated with age, as did grandiose delusions and other delusions. Avolition, which was present to a high degree at onset, became more prevalent with age. Cognitive defects became more frequent. De-pressed mood disappeared with age. Inappropriate affect diminished slightly, and bizarre behavior decreased with age.

One can conclude from the data that delusional and hallucinatory behavior and aggressiveness become less of a problem with advancing age. Negative symptoms such as avolition and monotony and flatness become more of a problem, though they are obviously present from the very beginning.

These patients had been diagnosed as having hebephrenic–cata-tonic schizophrenia on the basis of nonparanoid symptoms. What is very striking is the fact that most of the patients had delusional and hallucinatory symptoms at the beginning of their illness. These later became considerably less important.

Based on systematic evaluation of the data (the original clinical diagnosis versus the final diagnosis in follow–up), the transition from hebephrenic–catatonic schizophrenia to paranoid schizophrenia was almost nonexistent, but the transfer of diagnosis from paranoid to hebephrenic was not uncommon. At admission, 69% of the 200 schizophrenics were nonparanoid; some 35 years later, 85.5% were classified nonparanoid.

Finally, mortality and cause of death were examined in the 138 originally diagnosed hebephrenic–catatonic patients versus the 62 paranoid patients (Table 5–4). The paranoid patients were significantly older at time of index admission, 34 years $\pm$ 9 versus 26 $\pm$ 6 for the nonparanoid (t=6.16, p<.001). Thus, more deaths would be expected in the older group. In fact, 47% of the paranoids at time of follow–up had died versus 36% of the nonparanoid patients. Even without age adjustment, however, the difference was not significant. Most interesting was the difference in cause of death. None of the paranoid patients died of infectious diseases, whereas 11 of the 49 nonparanoid deaths were due to infectious diseases (X^2=5.84 with Yates correction, p<.025).

DISCUSSION

The data in this paper suggest that the appropriate diagnosis of nonparanoid or hebephrenic schizophrenia is based on the presence of such negative symptoms as avolition and flatness. These symptoms start early and are accompanied by such positive symptoms as

Table 5–4
Mortality In Paranoid Versus Nonparanoid
(Hebephrenic–Catatonic) Schizophrenics

	Paranoid	Nonparanoid
Length index admission	40 days	50 days
Age at admission	33.9$\pm$9.11	26.14$\pm$6.17 (p<.001)
Deceased at follow–up	29 (49%)	49 (36%) (ns)
Cause of death		
Infectious diseases	0/29	11/49 (p<.025)
Circulatory diseases	11/29	12/49 (ns)
Suicides and accidents	5/29	9/49 (ns)

delusions, hallucinations, and assaultiveness. As time wears on, the positive symptoms become less prevalent, but the negative symptoms either do not change or become more prevalent. In contrast, in paranoid schizophrenia the individual has delusions or hallucinations but none of the negative symptoms. Both diagnoses are associated with a chronic course, but the end point is different. In late life, the hebephrenic–catatonic schizophrenic is mostly beset by negative symptoms, although he almost invariably had positive symptoms early in the illness.

This way of diagnosing or separating hebephrenic from paranoid schizophrenia differs from the usual diagnosis of paranoid schizo-phrenia. Generally, paranoid schizophrenia is diagnosed in the pres-ence of a massive set of paranoid delusions or hallucinations. In fact, all schizophrenics, paranoid and nonparanoid, suffer from these symptoms. No doubt such illnesses as have been called paranoia, late paraphrenia, or paranoid state could be included under the rubric of schizophrenia of a paranoid type. These illnesses typically do not culminate in flat affect and avolition. The follow–up material into old age supports the idea that paranoid schizophrenia may develop into nonparanoid schizophrenia, but the reverse is unusual.

The question of mortality poses an interesting problem. Those patients in this study who were followed to 60 years of age tended to have an earlier onset and a more severe clinical picture. No doubt one of the reasons for no follow–up was death, raising the question of whether or not early onset hebephrenic–catatonic schizophrenics have a higher death rate than later onset patients with the same diagnosis. If this were so, it would indicate that schizophrenia is not trivial as a cause of mortality. The data in this paper do not settle this issue by any means. However, it would be possible to evaluate this problem by taking all the patients who ended up with a diagnosis of hebephrenic–catatonic schizophrenia ($n=171$), separating them for mean age of onset, and looking at the difference in death rate in those above versus those below the mean age of onset. Should the ones below the mean age of onset also be younger at time of index admission, presumably they should have had a lower mortality as they were further from the years of a high prevalence of mortality. If, on the other hand, the early onset group had a higher mortality, it would support the idea that schizophrenia is a lethal disease and that those with a milder form of the disease live to an older age.

Finally, the question of cause of death is a matter of some significance. In the past, schizophrenics had a high rate of death by infectious disease, particularly tuberculosis. As the years passed, such deaths became less likely, and it was assumed that the pheno-menon was simply due to poor nutrition or crowding in hospitals. However, paranoid schizophrenics did not have a high death rate from tuberculosis. We do not, however, have the data at this point to show whether they suffered from equal amounts of institutionalization. It is possible that the hebephrenic–catatonic patients had a decreased resistance to infection; but with the development of antibiotics and the decreased incidence of exposure to such agents as the tubercle bacillus, it may be difficult to detect increased mortality in con-temporary mortality studies. If this finding is valid, there may be some kind of immunological defect in schizophrenics that is now hidden. The defect may manifest itself in other ways that should be investigated.

These are some of the leads that the present study suggests. The findings, however, are clear enough. Schizophrenics in old age become less of a problem in terms of active symptomatology and more of a problem in terms of passive or negative symptoms. They thus require a different kind of management than they did when they were younger, and this is useful to keep in mind.

6 Late Onset Improvement in Chronic Schizophrenia: Characteristics and Prediction

Thomas H. McGlashan

Chestnut Lodge

Rockville, Maryland

Chronic schizophrenia has been classically regarded as a deteriorating condition. Morrison, Winokur, Crowe, and Clancy (1973), for example, found little or no evidence of functional improvement after 2 to 3 years of continuous illness. In contrast, a variety of studies emerging from Europe have contested this pessimistic outlook. In an investigation covering three British mental hospitals, Wing and Brown (1970) noted clinical improvement in about 20% of patients hospitalized at least 4 years. The improvement consisted of decrements in social withdrawal, flatness of affect, and other negative or defect symptoms. In Norway, Flekkoy, Lund, and Astrup (1975) found a tendency for improvement in 42 of 148 chronic schizophrenics on 10–year follow–up. Huber, Gross, Schuettler, and Linz (1980) from Germany noted a development toward more stable remissions in patients after age 50.

From Switzerland, where the strongest statement to this effect has come, Bleuler (1969, 1974) asserted that the average schizophrenic patient shows no further deterioration after 5 years of illness. In fact, he found many patients improving with age, the alterations over time being in the direction of improvement versus impairment by a ratio of 6:1 (1974). He wrote:

> The improvements are manifold: some of the patients who had hardly ever uttered coherent sentences, start to speak normally on certain occasions: others behave suddenly in a normal way on leave, during hospital entertainments, or while they are suffering from a physical disease. Other patients suddenly take up social activities when they have been apathetic for many years. . . . In old age, schizophrenics may not only become less excited, less aggressive, and less active regards their delusions, but many of them

start to develop an active inner life, true interests, and a
sounder activity than before (pp. 246–247).

Ciompi (1980) and Mueller and Ciompi (1976), also working in Switzerland, essentially replicated Bleuler's observations and found
between 10% and 15% of patients with a chronic course progressing
toward calming and improvement with advancing age. They specifically noted five cases of striking improvement after "decades of the
most severe illness" in their sample of 289 long–term follow–ups.

In America, corroborating data has emerged from only one
center. Harding *et al.* (Daum, Brooks, & Albie, 1977) in Vermont
reported surprisingly good outcome at 20–year follow–up on a
stratified subsample of patients originally selected for chronicity.
They especially noted a strong tendency toward independent living
8–12 years post–index discharge, with psychopathology and social
disability diminishing more rapidly as the patients reached age 50.

Such complementary findings have more or less put to rest
doubts about the reality of eventual amelioration in chronic schizophrenia for at least some patients. Less unanimity exists, however,
about the specific phenomenology of these long–term developments
or whether they can be anticipated or predicted early in the course of
the disease. Mueller and Ciompi (1976) found that improvement over
the long term was associated with many of the factors classically
demonstrated to predict short–term outcome in schizophrenia such as
good premorbid social and work adaptation, few premorbid personality disorders, marriage, completion of education, acute onset,
undulating course, initial symptoms of depersonalization, dereali-
zation, depression, and the absence of indifference and withdrawal.

American investigators, on the other hand, have been more
impressed with the attenuated power of these predictors as follow–up
periods lengthen. Stephens and Astrup (1963), for example, found that
one–half of their process schizophrenic cohort were deteriorated on
13–year follow–up, yet they failed to identify any predictors of these
developments. Twenty of Vaillant's 51 remitting schizophrenic patients from his original Massachusetts Mental Health Center study
(1980) proved to develop a chronic course at 10–year follow–up.
These 20, however, did not differ from the 31 patients with sustained
remissions on any of Vaillant's now classic criteria of reactivity
(acute onset, affective symptoms, nonschizoid premorbid personality,
precipitating factors, marriage, confusion on admission, family history of affective psychosis).

To summarize, late onset improvement appears to occur in some
chronic schizophrenic patients but with a debatable predictability.
Further work is needed to track this phenomenon more closely and
refine its nature and degree of randomness. This study, utilizing
specified schizophrenic subgroups from the Chestnut Lodge follow–up
study, attempts to make further inroads in these directions. Several
questions are addressed. Does psychopathology in schizophrenia
diminish with age? Can late improving schizophrenic patients be

identified, and what are they like? Finally, can such a development be predicted at the time patients enter the hospital?

METHODS

Chestnut Lodge is a small, private psychiatric hospital that specializes in the long-term residential treatment of severely ill (and usually chronic) schizophrenic and borderline patients. Included in this follow-up study were all patients without organic brain syndrome or primary alcoholism discharged between 1950 and 1975 who were between 16 and 55 upon admission and who were treated at Chestnut Lodge for a minimum of 90 days. This minimum maximizes the probability of thorough diagnostic records being available. Following admission virtually all patients are withdrawn from medication, observed, and evaluated at a staff conference in three months. Three kinds of data were collected in the study: outcome, diagnostic, and predictor.

Outcome data were collected, following informed consent, an average of 15 years after discharge (range 2–32 years) via interviews with the subjects and/or significant others. The majority of interviews were by phone and averaged 2 hours in length. Interviews were conducted and rated by the author or by research-trained social workers. Interviews contained structured and unstructured segments and assessed multiple dimensions of outcome over the entire period since discharge from Chestnut Lodge. Twenty-eight outcome variables were rated for this study and covered dimensions of demography, treatment, psychopathology, employment, social activity, and global functioning. Some ratings pertained to the entire follow-up period, others to the last year of follow-up, and the rest to current status and situation (see Table 6–1). The average interrater reliability for these assessments was .75 (kappa).

Diagnostic evaluation was conducted independent of knowledge about outcome. Because clinical chart diagnoses are notoriously unreliable and subject to changing criteria, all study subjects were rediagnosed according to current systematic criteria using detailed historical sign and symptom information abstracted from the clinical chart. Because medical records are often very incomplete, we conducted a pilot audit of key demographic, predictor, and diagnostic variables from a random sample of chart abstracts. This revealed an average of 12% missing data, which was considered sufficiently low to render the medical record a valid source of diagnostic information.

Using these data, each study subject was rated on the following eight diagnostic systems: the New Haven (Astrachan *et al.*, 1972), Feighner (Feighner, Robins, Guze, Woodruff, Winokur, & Munoz, 1972), Research Diagnostic Criteria (Spitzer, Endicott, & Robins, 1977), and DSM–III (APA, 1980) systems for schizophrenia; the Gunderson (Gunderson & Kolb, 1978), DSM–III schizotypal, and DSM–III borderline personality disorder systems for borderline syndrome; and

Table 6–1

Outcome Dimensions

Variable	Total follow-up period	Last year of follow-up	Current
Demographic			
Living situation			+*
Marital status	+		+
Socioeconomic status			+
Treatment			
Percent of time hospitalized	+*	+*	
Number of hospitalizations	+		
Percent of time on medication	+*		
Percent of time in psychosocial therapy	+		
Psychopathology			
Percent of time symptomatic	+*	+*	
Severity of symptoms	+*		
Problems with: Alcohol	+		
Drugs	+		
Law	+		
Suicide attempts	+		
Clinical diagnosis	+		
Employment			
Percent of time working	+*	+*	
Further education	+*		
Social function			
Frequency contact with friends		+*	+*
Frequency contact with family		+	
Closeness of relationships		+*	
Number of social organizations			+*
Global function			
Global functioning	+*	+*	+*

* = significant difference between late improving and chronic poor outcome cohorts, $p.<01$.

the DSM–III system for affective disorders. The average interrater reliability for assignment of diagnosis using these systems was .66 (kappa).

Predictor and demographic data were collected, like the diagnostic data, from the abstracted clinical records. Many of the variables rated were chosen from the classic literature on prediction, prognosis, premorbid adjustment, and follow–up in schizophrenia (Astrachan, Brauer, Harrow, & Schwartz, 1974; Bland, Parker, & Orn, 1976, 1978; Bromet, Harrow, & Karl, 1974; Carpenter & Stevens, 1979; Garmezy, 1970; Goldberg, Schooler, Hogarty, & Roper, 1977; Harrow, Bromet, & Quinlan, 1974; Hawk, Carpenter, & Strauss, 1975; Herron, 1962a; Hogarty & Goldberg, 1973; Hogarty, Goldberg, & Schooler, 1974a, 1974b; Keith & Buchsbaum, 1978; Kokes, Strauss, & Klorman, 1977; Mueller & Ciompi, 1976; Pollack, Levenstein, & Klein, 1968; Rosen, Klein, & Gittleman–Klein, 1971; Sartorious, Jablensky, & Shapiro, 1977, 1978; Stephens, 1970; Stephens & Astrup, 1963; Stephens, Astrup, & Mangrum, 1966; Strauss & Carpenter, 1974, 1977; Strauss, Kokes, Klorman, & Sacksteder, 1977, Strauss, Klorman, & Kokes, 1977; Vaillant, 1962, 1964, 1978; Zigler & Phillips, 1961). Other variables were chosen as promising new additions to be tested.

In all, 111 variables were collected, rated, and tested as predictors. Covered were dimensions of patient demography, premorbid functioning, family history, and growth and development. Also included were indices of psychopathology evident both prior to and during admission to Chestnut Lodge as well as diagnostic assignments made using the diagnostic systems outlined above. See Table 6–2 for a categorical list. The average interrater reliability for all except the diagnostic variables was .64 (kappa and intraclass correlations).

ANALYSIS

For this study, patients were included if they satisfied specified criteria for schizophrenia or schizoaffective disorder. The criteria for schizophrenia were from DSM–III. A schizoaffective diagnosis was assigned if the patient met all of the DSM–III criteria for schizophrenia *and* for affective disorder (bipolar or unipolar) minus their respective exclusion criteria. Schizoaffective patients were included because a preliminary analysis comparing this sample ($n=39$) with the entire DSM–III schizophrenic sample ($n=110$) failed to demonstrate any differences on several key demographic (sex, marital status), predictor (age first symptoms, length of previous hospitalizations), and outcome measures (hospitalization, employment, social activity, symptoms, and global functioning). Given this, the schizophrenic and schizoaffective samples were pooled, and special subgroups for further study were selected from this collective sample.

A first brief analysis involved calculating Pearson product moment correlations between age at follow–up and global psychopathology to test for any relatedness.

Table 6–2
Predictors

Variable	Time frame covered	
	Before admission Chestnut Lodge	At admission Chestnut Lodge
Demographic		
Age admission Chestnut Lodge		+
Sex	+	+
Marital status	+	+
Highest educational level (2 variables)	+	+
Highest occupational level (2 variables)	+	+
Socioeconomic status (2 variables)	+	+
IQ		+
Premorbid		
Childhood asociality	+	
Phillips Scale	+	
Quantity useful work	+	
Quality useful work	+	
Quantity social relations	+	
Quality social relations	+	
Heterosexual functioning	+	
Pre–Chestnut Lodge admission morbid		
Age first symptoms mental illness	+	
Age first hospitalization	+	
Stressors to first episode	+	
Number previous hospitalizations	+	
Total length previous hospitalizations	+	
Family		
History of mental illness (4 variables)	+	+
Parental psychopathology (4 variables)	+	+
Family dynamic functioning (8 variables)	+	+
Growth and development		
Obstetrical difficulty (3 variables)	+	
Constitutional/environmental trauma (5 variables)	+	
Psychopathology		
Global psychopathology		+
Length continuous symptoms		+
Signs and symptoms (41 variables)	+	+
Elgin 10 Scale (11 variables)	+	+
Diagnosis		
Chart diagnosis		+
Study diagnosis		+
Diagnosis by diagnostic systems (9 variables)		+

The central analyses proceeded as follows. From the collective sample, 18 patients were identified as late onset improvers. They were defined as patients who had accumulated at least 10 years in hospitals, including Chestnut Lodge, but who, upon long–term follow–up, obtained a global functioning score of moderate or better over the previous year of follow–up. At first they were statistically compared (using t test and chi–square) with 49 patients who had a chronic poor outcome using the same global measure. This analysis revealed that the 18 late–improving patients had remained in Chestnut Lodge for a significantly longer period of time than the other cohort (mean length of stay 97 months versus 52 months, $p<.01$, 2–tailed t test). The comparison group of 49 was narrowed to 18 patients with the longest stays at Chestnut Lodge in order to match the cohorts on this variable.

The samples then consisted of 18 schizophrenic patients who improved after many years of illness and 18 who did not despite comparable exposure to treatment at Chestnut Lodge. These samples were characterized and compared on the outcome dimensions mentioned above using t and chi–square statistical tests. Similar tests were applied to the diagnostic and predictor variables outlined to identify those with particular discriminating power between the two groups. Variables discriminating with $p<.2$ were then entered into a stepwise linear discriminant function analysis (Anderson, 1959) with a jackknife classification (Mosteller & Tukey, 1977).[1] This identifies those variables that together maximally discriminate, characterize, or predict membership in the two cohorts. The jackknife classification is a technical modification designed to minimize error arising from deriving and testing the linear discriminant equation upon the same subjects.

RESULTS

Psychopathology and Age. Product moment correlations were calculated between age at follow–up and global functioning at follow–up as rated on the 100–point Health–Sickness Rating Scale (Luborsky, 1962). As shown in Table 6–3, the correlation was small and nonsignificant for the population as a whole ($n=149$). Breaking this down between the schizophrenic and schizoaffective cohorts, however, revealed a modest though significant correlation for the latter but not for the former diagnostic subgroup. That is, global score increased—indicating greater health—with advancing age for the schizoaffective population.

Cohort Comparison: Total Sample Characteristics. The late improving (LI) and chronic poor (CP) cohorts were, collectively, followed up

---

[1] This linear discriminant function analysis was conducted using the BMDP computer program with an F to enter of 3 and an F to delete of 2.99.

Table 6–3
Psychopathology and Age

Cohort	n	Correlation	p value
Total sample	149	.06	ns
Schizophrenic sample	110	–.07	ns
Schizoaffective sample	39	.38	.01

a median of 16 years after discharge from Chestnut Lodge. They averaged 49 years of age and had spent a median of 6 years in Chestnut Lodge. There were 22 males and 14 females. On the average, they experienced their first symptoms at age 19, their first hospitalization at age 21, and came to Chestnut Lodge at age 27 after four previous hospitalizations totaling about 3 years in length. Unquestionably, their picture at admission was a profile of established chronicity. As such, they are typical of the schizophrenic patients treated at Chestnut Lodge over the years.

Cohort Comparison: Outcome. At follow–up, all of the LI schizophrenics were alive, and 16 gave us interviews. In contrast, two of the CP group were dead, one by suicide. Only four of this cohort were intact enough to be interviewed, and our information came for the most part from significant others.

Since the LI cohort were selected on the basis of better global functioning, it is to be expected that they would compare favorably to the CP group on many other outcome dimensions. Indeed, taking $p<.01$ as the cut–off level of significance, the LI group scored better than the CP group on 17 of the 28 outcome variables measured (see asterisks in Table 6–1). The majority of LIs were living on their own or with their own families. In contrast, virtually all of the CPs were institutionalized or dependent upon their families of origin. The LIs experienced symptoms of moderate intensity about 50% of the time, whereas the CPs had been continuously symptomatic and unable to function. The LIs spent less than 25% of the follow–up period in hospitals and less than 50% of the same period on medicine. The CPs, in contrast, were on medicine more or less continuously by virtue of their lengthy hospitalizations. The LIs had been employed more than half the time, and 9 of the 18 had engaged in some further education. They visited friends at least every other week and described these relationships as moderately close. The CPs, in contrast, were basically unemployable and friendless. The differences between the groups, in short, were striking and highlight the multidimensional nature of improvement in the LI group. These patients were not just better psychopathologically; they had also recaptured something of the human striving for loving and working.

Table 6–4
Significant Predictors

Variable	n	Test	p value
Family closeness	36	t test	.01
Elgin 10: Atypical symptoms	34	t test	.04
Dysphoria	34	chi–square	.05
Feighner criteria for schizophrenia	36	chi–square	.05
DSM–III criteria for schizotypal personality	36	chi–square	.02

better psychopathologically; they had also recaptured something of the human striving for loving and working.

Cohort Comparison: Prediction. Can late clinical improvement in chronic schizophrenia—which we can identify and demonstrate as valid—be anticipated by the patient's early history of illness and functioning? The answer to this—based upon a conservative assessment of the results to be outlined—is negative.

Statistical testing of well over 100 predictor variables (as outlined) yielded only five with $p<.05$. These are listed in Table 6–4. Family closeness refers to the degree of boundary differentiation and cohesiveness in the patient's family of origin as reconstructed from descriptions in the medical record. LI patients score higher or healthier on this dimension. Atypical symptoms from the Elgin Scale refer to manic or depressive features mixed with those of schizophrenia. LI patients demonstrated these to a greater degree. Dysphoria refers to complaints of feeling dysphoric, empty, lonely, or anhedonic—either at admission or before. Such complaints were more frequent in the late improvers. The final two predictors identify the degree to which patients satisfy other diagnostic criteria in addition to DSM–III schizoaffective psychosis or schizophrenia (the latter diagnostic categories, incidentally, did *not* discriminate the groups). The CP cohort satisfied the Feighner criteria for schizo– phrenia *more* frequently but satisfied the DSM–III criteria for schizotypal personality *less* frequently than the LIs.

From a clinical perspective the first four predictors could be said to "make sense." That is, it might be anticipated that patients who eventually improve come from healthier families, fail to satisfy the currently most stringent criteria for schizophrenia, and display the presence and awareness of affect during illness to a greater degree. The latter especially is in line with other studies. The higher frequency of schizotypal personalities among the LIs, however, was

Sixteen predictor variables that discriminated the two groups at $p<.02$ were entered into a linear discriminant function analysis with jackknife classification. The resultant function that best discriminated membership in the two groups consisted of four variables: (1) family closeness (as described above), (2) the presence of manic or depressive symptoms in the present illness, (3) the degree of social anxiety or sensitivity to criticism, and (4) the presence of suggestive evidence for minimal brain dysfunction in the first decade of life. LIs scored higher than CPs on the first three variables and lower on the fourth. Again, these dimensions make clinical sense when taken individually. However, they fail to provide a compelling profile as an aggregate. Furthermore, this capacity to discriminate statistically was modest at best; and the function correctly classified cases into the two groups only 83% of the time (two LIs and four CPs classified incorrectly). Given the number of potential variables tested and the power of this method of analysis, one is again struck with the paucity of significant relationships.

Of equal if not greater note was the lack of distinction between the two outcome cohorts on many dimensions that have frequently been demonstrated to correlate with outcome, such as marital status; premorbid occupational, social, and sexual functioning; childhood asociality; Phillips Scale scores; age of symptom onset; precipitating stress; and family history of mental illness. Length of illness prior to admission also failed to discriminate, but one would not expect this dimension to have much predictive power in a study comparing two groups with established chronicity.

In all, the failure of most variables to predict outcome was more impressive than the success of those that did, especially when one realizes that with over 100 variables tested, five could be found significantly different (at $p<.05$) by chance alone. As such, the variables discriminating between the two cohorts in this study should be regarded as tentative rather than definitive.

Late Improving Schizophrenia: Case Vignettes. Although the LI patients were clearly better as a group, there the similarity ended. As individuals they were very different from one another at follow-up. It is impossible to convey the heterogeneity we found without expanding this communication into a monograph. As such, a brief elaboration of two contrasting cases will have to suffice.

Gregory S. came to Chestnut Lodge at age 28 with a diagnosis of paranoid schizophrenia after two previous hospitalizations. He remained at Chestnut Lodge for 11 years and was followed up approximately 17 years after discharge. At follow-up and for the entire follow-up period he lived alone in an apartment and worked as a computer software specialist. He had not required any further hospitalization and sought no further treatment, somatic or otherwise. Although functional and self-sufficient, he remained symptomatic enough to warrant a follow-up diagnosis of schizoid personality with paranoid features. The social worker who interviewed him on the phone captured something of the quality of his life, as can be gathered from her follow-up summary:

> Mr. S. finds satisfaction in his ability to do competent work and to "hang in" despite paranoid concerns that his co-workers are trying to make him quit or throw him off track due to their own failures. . . . He has some perspective that these people aren't necessarily making errors in order to hurt him. His reality testing in other areas seems largely intact. . . . He is an isolated, lonely man who finds some gratification in remaining physically fit and through his annual holidays in the wilderness where he finds an isolated area in which to hike and explore. . . . He dreams of retirement as a recluse away from the terrors of city life. . . . He expressed gratitude with the chance to talk although the intimacy of the contact was probably uncomfortable for him since he felt pressure to complete the interview in one sitting. He has not really internalized (an individuated sense of himself) but feels obligated to do what his parents would want him to do. He idealizes his mother as the person giving his life purpose and protection from a cruel world, despite the fact that his mother is dead and his contact with her during the period before this was minimal. Her capacity to remain a viable introject with whom he plays out a dependent relationship is striking.

Benjamin T. came to Chestnut Lodge at age 31 with a diagnosis of paranoid schizophrenia after approximately 10 years of intermittent illness requiring at least five hospitalizations. He remained at Chestnut Lodge for 8 years and was followed up 10 years after discharge. He had been working successfully for years selling insurance and had recently married. He required no further hospitalizations but had remained on a maintenance dose of antipsychotic medication for the whole follow-up period. He saw his Chestnut Lodge therapist in intensive psychotherapy for about 5 years after discharge until moving away from the Washington area, after which he saw someone in his locale, mainly for support and medication. Although active socially, he did not consider any of the relationships very close. He continued to experience symptoms of anxiety and a tendency to grandiose thinking apparent in political and philosophical ruminations.

He proved to be quite articulate in his phone interview. He recognized his continuing propensity for illness and elaborated upon his daily efforts to accept uncertainty as a fact of life and differentiate "honest mistakes" from the distortions of "illness." He acknowledged having "hard times" but added that he also had many years of experience in coping with them. As such, his "bad periods" were milder in frequency and scope. As he said, "It's a matter of degree. Compared to 15 years ago, I can recover from troubled periods in a couple of hours"—often through the application of "persistence and hard work." He found himself far more capable of relatedness and comfortable with "caring for others and being cared for." He attributed a great deal of this to his work with his former therapist, who he acknowledged still "operates inside of me . . . I haven't completely let go of him." As such, he too drew support from continuing relatedness with an idealized introject but not, like Gregory S., at the expense of investments in the real world.

DISCUSSION

To recapitulate, late onset improvement can occur in a small subgroup of patients with chronic schizophrenia. These changes range widely in scope and quality. For some (largely described in the literature) it consists of an amelioration of disruptive behaviors leading to better institutional adjustment. For others (e.g., those selected for this study) the change can be more far reaching and extensive, amounting to a significant return of normal functioning although seldom (if ever) without lingering disability. Those who improve are difficult to profile, and their differences seem more compelling than their similarities.

Late improvement seems particularly difficult to predict. Although our results are at variance with the findings of some, it appears that the classical predictors of short–term outcome in schizophrenia have questionable value for predicting outcome after years of illness. It may be, of course, that we looked at the wrong predictors. Indeed, those we tested were all referrable to the patient's deep past, i.e., admission to Chestnut Lodge and/or earlier. As such, this ignored the whole arena of process and treatment. The patients who improved did spend a longer time at Chestnut Lodge than those who did not. This implies some kind of treatment effect worthy of exploration. With luck, we hope to get a systematic handle on these patients' hospital courses as well, but that is another study for another time. Nevertheless, it appears to be an important area to investigate.

The relationship of late improvement with aging is also unclear. Although such changes usually occur when the patient is older—almost by definition—it is not a phenomenon unique to *old* age. Two of our patients at follow–up were in their early thirties. Furthermore, we were unable to find any overall systematic change in the level of schizophrenic psychopathology with aging in our larger sample. The schizoaffectives were a modest exception suggesting some linkage of affective processes with age. Nevertheless, before speculating upon the nature of any such linkages, it would be important to replicate this finding.

In summary, the disease process we call schizophrenia presents us with many mysteries, not the least of which is its retreat after years of hegemony in a few fortunate individuals. The nature of this process is highly variable and questionably predictable. Nevertheless, it is very real and worthy of note and further exploration.

Acknowledgments

The author wishes to acknowledge the help of many people who have contributed to the project in general and to this paper in particular: Polly Curry for project coordination and manuscript preparation; Allison Benesch for chart abstraction and diagnostic evaluation; John Bartko and Robert Welp for statistical consultation; Lawrence Abrams, John Cook, William Flexsenhar, Kathleen Free, Wendy Greenspun, Lee Goldman, Anita Gonzalez, Brian Healy, Tom Martin, Jim Miller, Jack O'Brien, Terry Polonus, Steven Richfield, Rochelle Spiker, Holly Taylor, Barry Townsend, Susan Viosinet, Denise Unterman, Robert Welp, and Donald Wright for chart abstraction; and Dexter Bullard, Jr., John Cameron, David Feinsilver, and Wells Goodrich for institutional support and guidance.

This study was supported in part by NIMH grant MH 35174–02 and by the Fund for Psychoanalytic Research of the American Psychoanalytic Association.

7

Aging and Social Functioning in Once-Chronic Schizophrenic Patients 22-62 Years After First Admission: The Vermont Story

Courtenay M. Harding

Yale University

George W. Brooks

Takamaru Ashikaga

University of Vermont

John S. Strauss

Yale University

Paul D. Landerl

Howard Mental Health Services, Burlington, Vermont

Disturbance in social functioning and the disorders of schizophrenia have always been intertwined. This relationship is reflected in premorbid descriptors, diagnostic criteria, and prognostic indicators. Poor premorbid social adjustment has been noted in schizophrenia by many investigators (Garmezy, 1974; Gittleman–Klein & Klein, 1969; Phillips, 1953), as has deterioration of social relations during the course of disorder (APA, 1980; Kraepelin, 1902). The patients themselves have described feelings of isolation and estrangement (Kaplan, 1964; Laing, 1971; Sechehaye, 1951; Strauss and Carpenter, 1981). Objective measures have recorded disordered emotional responsivity (Abrams and Taylor, 1978; And reason, 1979; Reid, Moore, & Zimmer, 1982). Bizarre behavior and speech or withdrawal quite often alienates relatives and would–be friends. Hospitalization removes patients from their natural settings and breaks many family and community ties. Finally, the negative signs and symptoms, such as apathy and blunted affect from chronic schizophrenia, occurring after long or multiple hospitalizations, continue the problem of social isolation and alienation noted after discharge by investigators in short–term follow–up studies (Brown *et al.*, 1966; Davis, Dinitz, & Pasamanick, 1974; Lamb & Goertzel, 1977; Sanders, Smith & Weinman, 1967).

Are all these patterns incurable and irreversible? A survey of long-term (more than 10 years) studies reveals a heterogeneity of diagnostic criteria, sample selection, unspecified constructs, and a wide variety of methodological problems, which make analysis of findings difficult (Bachrach, 1976; Erickson, 1975; Harding & Brooks, 1984; Shapiro & Shader, 1979; Stephens, 1978; Strauss & Carpenter, 1974). The question remains. Do these once profoundly socially disabled patients continue to lead isolated lives, barren of social contacts, across long periods of time? A second question naturally follows. Does the impact of age, *per se*, augment this deterioration in functioning?

This chapter focuses on findings from the Vermont Longitudinal Research Project, a long-term follow-up of patients whose first admission, primarily for schizophrenia, occurred 22 to 62 years ago. A brief description of the project's history, sample, design, and findings regarding outcome is provided. In addition, assessments of current social function and the relationship between age and domains of function are made.

HISTORICAL OVERVIEW OF THE PROJECT

The Vermont Longitudinal Research Project began in 1955 when George Brooks, M.D., now Superintendent of Vermont State Hospital, secured funds (OVR-SP180) to institute a pioneering rehabilitation program for his backward chronic patients. When selected for the rehabilitation program, these subjects were middle-aged, poorly educated, mostly single, lower class individuals. They had an average of 10 years total disability and 6 years continuous hospitalization. Seventy-nine percent were considered schizophrenic according to DSM-I (1952), and nearly all were committed at state expense.

The rehabilitation program met Bachrach's eight criteria for model demonstration programs (1980), and most participants were discharged either to early versions of halfway houses and job placements or to their families. A book about the program, entitled *The Vermont Story* by Chittick, Brooks, Irons, and Deane, was published in 1961.

Five to ten years after entry into the project, 269 patients from the program who were considered to be the most chronic of the rehabilitated group were followed up (Deane & Brooks, 1967). Two-thirds of the subjects were out of the hospital, a proportion considered remarkable at the time. The subjects were maintained by constant attention from counselors and the allocation of diverse other resources as well. The expectations of the counselors for this group of patients were either stabilization at that minimal level of functioning or deterioration. These expectations were not unlike those held today by clinicians dealing with similar chronic patients.

In the mid-1970s, a pilot long-term follow-up study was conducted with a stratified subset (Daum *et al.*, 1977). At that time, nine out of ten subjects from the original cohort were located with one simple letter of inquiry to their last known address.

From a research standpoint, Vermont is similar to Scandinavia and Switzerland (Ciompi, 1980). Its small population of a half million people is geographically stable—nearly all subjects, their children, other family members, the original project team, caseworkers, and family physicians still live within state borders. George Brooks has maintained contact with many members of the cohort or their families for more than 30 years (much as Manfred Bleuler [1972] has with his patients). Vermont also has central recordkeeping because it has only one state hospital. In addition, this state hospital has a research orientation, which is aided by collaboration with nearby schools of medicine and psychology.

Because of this research atmosphere, excellent patient records are maintained. These records facilitate retrospective ratings that increase the value of long–term cross–sectional assessment and provide valuable data for serial longitudinal documentation of patterns, shifts, and trends demonstrated by this group of chronic patients struggling to reintegrate into the community.

THE LONG–TERM FOLLOW–UP STUDY

Design and Procedure

The study focused on four major questions:

- Do such subjects improve symptomatically and/or functionally?
- In what ways do they improve?
- For those who do, when do they improve?
- Are there any predictors of who improves?

In order to address these issues, the long–term follow–up study comprised four substudies:

The Life History Study.—In this part of the project, the data were arranged to provide descriptive biographies with particular emphasis on critical events, environmental buffers, and personal strengths.

The Long–Term Course and Outcome Study.—A cross–sectional assessment of subjects was made to determine current state and status at time of discharge from the rehabilitation program. Data were gathered from hospital and vocational rehabilitation records as well as extensive interviews with the subjects, relatives, and service personnel. Structured and standardized assessments were used to measure a variety of psychopathologic and social functioning domains (see Table 7–1). Field interviewers were blind to all record information, and all instrument batteries were subjected to interrater and test–retest reliability assessment.

From these measures, diagnostic and social functioning assessments at several points in time were generated, with the focus on

Table 7-1
Domains Measured in the Course and Outcome Study

Diagnosis	Physical health
Symptomatology	Interpersonal relationships
Quality of life	Occupational functioning
Self-care skills	Psychosexual adjustment
Life events	Recreational activities
Psychiatric treatment	Degree of independence
Readmissions, episodes, and	Community support systems
intervals	Global assessment of adjustment

changes between index release and the present. In addition, the longitudinal portion documented a year-by-year follow-up across multiple domains during the intervening 20 years.

Prediction of Long-Term Outcome Study.—The ratings from hospital records were used to predict current status. Data from case records were abstracted and rated by record reviewers who had no knowledge of postdischarge status.

Control Substudies.—A variety of small substudies, such as assessment of the parametric characteristics of the hospital population in 1954, determined original sample selection and degrees of bias. A detailed discussion of the general design and the sample may be found in the literature (Harding & Brooks, 1980, 1984; Harding, Brooks, Ashikaga, Strauss, & Breier, under review-A, B; Harding & Strauss, 1985).

FINDINGS

Brief Overview of Outcome

Ninety-seven percent of the original cohort were located and/or accounted for. The 190 still alive were contacted, and families of the 72 deceased were interviewed. Only 7 subjects were not found.

Although all subjects were rediagnosed by DMS-III (1980) criteria using hospital records stripped of all diagnostic references and post-index discharge material, the preliminary analyses used the diagnosis of schizophrenia made by Dr. George Brooks employing DSM-I standards at the 5-year follow-up mark. At that point, he had known patients for as long as 10 years and was familiar with each one's history and presenting symptomatology. Based on Brooks' diagnoses, data from all currently living schizophrenic subjects ($n=149$) were analyzed for this report.

A picture of current status more than 20 years after deinstitutionalization began to emerge from the set of demographic descriptors of the living schizophrenic subjects. Sixty percent of the subjects were over 60. Half the subjects had less than a high school education; however, that was the average for Vermonters in that era. Fifty-six percent of the subjects were still single; 14% were married, and an additional 7% were widowed.

Only 3% of the subjects were still residing in the state hospital, 43% had had one or two readmissions, and 21% had no further hospitalization over the 20 years. Of the 61 subjects (40%) residing in boarding homes, about 17% showed superior functioning and were actively involved. This group did not actually need much supervision. Half of those subjects under retirement age were engaged in some kind of productive enterprise.

Social Functioning of Older Schizophrenics

The domain of interpersonal relationships is a complex and challenging one to assess. A good deal of attention was paid to this domain because of the vast literature on the inability of schizophrenic patients to interact with others and the relative absence of a support system (e.g., Hammer, MaKiesky-Barrow, & Gutwirth, 1978; Pattison, deFrancisco, Wood, Frazier, & Crowder, 1975).

We constructed an instrument called the Star Chart to update some of the principles originally developed in the sociogram (Moreno, 1960). With the set of structured probes and codes derived from the Community Care Schedule [CCS] (Schwartz, Muller, Spitzer, Goldstein, & Serrano, 1977), the Social Adjustment Scale for Schizophrenia [SAS II] (Schooler, Hogarty, & Weissman, 1978), and the Vermont Community Questionnaire items, questions were asked in a mutual participation model while the subjects helped draw the chart. These questions evoked data about the nature and degree of support systems and also the interdependence and affective quality of the relationships with significant people in the subjects' lives.

From the Star Chart, the Life Chart probes, and a variety of structured questions derived from the SAS II, the Personal Resources Inventory [PRI] by Clayton and Hirschfeld (1978), and the Structured and Scaled Interview to Assess Maladjustment [SSIAM] (Gurland *et al.*, 1972), both cross-sectional and longitudinal pictures of interpersonal relationships emerged, which allowed investigation of a wide variety of questions. The primary question, of course, was: Were these subjects, once diagnosed as schizophrenic, isolated with little or no social contacts or supports?

As a first look at this question, a pair of findings from the Strauss-Carpenter Levels of Function Scale (Hawk *et al.*, 1975) on frequency and quality of social contacts was selected to highlight the field observations and showed the following:

Frequency of Current Social Contacts
Meets with friends at least once a week	56%
Meets with friends once every 2 weeks	9%
Meets with friends once a month	9%

Only "over the back fence" or work	18%
Never	5%
NI	3%
Quality of Social Contacts	
One or more close relationships	19%
One or more rather close relationships	24%
One or more moderately close relationships	33%
Only superficial relationships	15%
Only saying hello to neighbors	6%
NI	3%

Thus, 65% met with friends at least once every week or two. The quality of relationships reflected considerable richness and variation—43% had one or more close or rather close friends, and an additional 33% had one or more moderately close friends. In similar items, such as quality of companionship or adequacy of social supports, the findings were similar.

Particular styles of interpersonal relationships were revealed by field observations. Three styles were noteworthy: the Niche Group, the Loners, and the Self-Regulators.

The Niche Group.—The Niche Group was a cluster of people who were placed in situations that, over time, enabled them to fit in and flourish. One woman went as a boarder with a family and 15 years later had become "the grandmother." She was integrated into and valued by the family with whom she lived. Another woman went to work at a guest lodge and had become assistant manager. More remarkable was the fact that she was once shy and stand-offish, but had become a gregarious manager, well-liked by the guests, many of whom return year after year. In some situations, people may not flourish but function at a higher level of productivity, intimacy, and independence than might have been expected given their history. Several of the marriages in the cohort demonstrated this situation.

The Loners.—The Loners were a small group of middle-aged single men and a few women who lived over commercial buildings in the middle of town. They appeared to have made a distinct choice to live by themselves because they felt they could not get along with others well enough and needed the buffer of living alone. They seemed to have no friends and worked only sporadically.

The Self-Regulators.—The Self-Regulators were a group who had found ways to socialize to a degree that was comfortable. They "regulated" their interactions. At first glance, "the hermit" appeared to represent the extreme of social isolation. He lived in an old fishing shack by the river. However, everyone in town knew him. He had forged a place as "the town character." He was well-liked, amiable, and had "drinking buddies," but no close friends and no family connections. The trombonist was a lively woman in her 70s who performed in a jazz quintet that played concerts for the community to brighten the lives of senior citizens in centers and nursing homes. Her zest for life was remarkable, but she also had no close friends.

The Self-Regulators, as a group, socialized only at arm's length, when and where they chose to do so. They differed from the Niche Group because they were more active in the selection and creation of their styles. This group seemed to function not much differently from many ordinary people, except that they gauged their tolerance level due to the disorder and adjusted for it very finely.

Clearly, many chronic schizophrenic patients were *not* isolated with little or no social contact. The long-term findings were more positive than those heretofore recorded for short-term follow-up of released chronic patients.

Age and Outcome

Age at follow-up, age at admission, and time since first admission have often been key measures in prognostic studies. The age in the Vermont cohort for the subgroup of DSM-I schizophrenia ranged from 41 to 85 years. Age, *per se*, was tested for correlation with social functioning and other measures of outcome. We were particularly interested in whether current age correlated with outcome status. Ages were grouped in the following manner: less than 50 (n=24 or 16%), 50–64 years (n=59, 40%), and greater than 64 years (n=66, 44%).

Grouped age was cross-tabulated with the following variables, which represent a variety of domains:

> Gender
> Percentage of social relations
> Quality of social relations
> Quality of companionship
> Adequacy of social supports
> Residence
> Ability to meet basic needs
> Strauss/Carpenter total outcome score
> GAS score
> Overall community adjustment
> Symptoms
> Fullness of life

Findings revealed that age appeared to have no significant relationship with any of the measures. It was possible that our broad age groupings were less sensitive than finer discriminations which might have been assessed with traditional or even nonparametric correlational methods, when appropriate. Effects of current age were obviously vitiated by heterogeneity in two other temporal variables also of potential importance in considering outcome, i.e., length of course and age at first admission. To demonstrate this interaction, all 61-year-olds in the schizophrenic sample were tabulated. Age at first admission was found to differ radically, ranging from 18 to 40 years, with matching variability in length of course.

Another way of looking at the same problem, length of course or catamnesis (time since first admission or onset), a standard measure in follow-up studies, was examined. Every subject with a 42-year course was chosen, and the same heterogeneity appeared. Age ranged from 57 to 84. Age at first admission broke down into three or four separate groups (15, 21-24, 26-27, 42), at once distinguished as prognostically different indicators (e.g., admission at age 15 is considered by most investigators to be very different from admission at 42).

The problem of heterogeneity across key measures points to the need for partial correlation analysis in which the association of age with outcome is assessed, partialling out the effects of age at first admission and length of course. As an example of this, we explored the relationship between the Global Assessment Scale score (Spitzer, Gibbon, & Endicott, 1975) and length of course for each of the three individual age groupings. A significant rank correlation existed between age and course (tau=-.33; $p<.01$), with smaller correlations for the two younger age groups (middle age [tau=-.12; $p< .17$]; youngest age [tau=-.19; $p<.07$]). Being over 64 with a short course and thus later onset was associated with a good GAS score rating. It should be emphasized that a "short course" in the present study constituted a 20- to 29-year period.

CONCLUSIONS AND COMMENTS

Findings from these analyses suggest that:

1. These once-chronic patients have improved (more functional, less symptomatic) far more than would have been predicted an average of 32 years post discharge out of the program.
2. Although these patients with schizophrenia began with severe impairments in interpersonal relationships, this disability was considerably ameliorated for some.
3. Analysis by age or length of catamnesis has been too gross to detect many of the complex interactions that may account for more variance in outcome functioning.

These findings underscore the complexities in understanding the course and outcome of patients with chronic schizophrenic disorders. They support a growing body of results from other studies of the same kinds of patients (e.g., Bleuler, 1972; Ciompi, 1980) that show a significant number of subjects improving considerably over time. Some even recover completely.

Findings of a wide range of potential outcomes suggest that the secure but gloomy pessimism of the past must be exchanged for less certainty and at least guarded optimism. This change in attitude emphasizes the importance of a renewed effort in research to understand the complexities of clinical course and their treatment implications. Clearly, treatment must be more flexible and creative to maximize the possibility of recovery.

Acknowledgments

This research was supported by NIMH Grant No. 29575 and the Biomedical Research Grant from the College of Medicine, University of Vermont. The authors also wish to acknowledge the contributions of Carmine M. Consalvo, Ph.D., Counseling Services of Addison County, Vermont, and former field interviewer in the Vermont Project.

8
The Genain Quadruplets: A 25-Year Follow-up of Four Monozygous Women Discordant for the Severity of Schizophrenic Illness

Allan F. Mirsky

Olive W. Quinn

Lynn E. DeLisi

Pamela Schwerdt

National Institute of Mental Health

Monte S. Buchsbaum

University of California at Irvine

A rare set of monozygotic quadruplets, concordant for schizophrenia but discordant for the severity of the illness, was hospitalized at the National Institute of Mental Health in the mid–1950s. The women were studied intensively by a group of mental health scientists. The information was summarized and integrated in *The Genain Quadruplets* (Rosenthal, 1963). The women (who were named by Rosenthal for this publication Nora, Iris, Myra, and Hester, i.e., NIMH, in order of birth) were examined with virtually all of the methods extant at the time for studying schizophrenia and psychological deficit.

In Rosenthal's summary of the life history and test data obtained in the Genains, he suggested the diathesis–stress theory as a reasonable way of accounting for the variations in the severity of their psychiatric illness. Although they shared an identical heredity (diathesis), differences in the way they were treated by their parents and significant others in their environment led to different expectations and self–images and consequently to different phenotypic expressions of the schizophrenic disease.

Early physical and developmental differences provided a rationale for dividing the set of four into two sets of "identical twins." The more competent pair, Nora and Myra, were more favored and fussed over. Iris, second–born and physically closer to Nora and Myra, was most often bracketed with Hester, the smallest and physically the least prepossessing. Hester and Iris, treated as the less competent and capable pair, more or less fulfilled that expectation. This is a greatly simplified but reasonably accurate summary of the earlier view of the Genains.

In the spring of 1981, we invited the Genains to come back to NIMH for additional study. Rosenthal and his colleague Quinn had maintained close contact with the quadruplets over the years and had urged the Genains to return for further studies employing techniques that had been developed subsequent to their first 3–year stay. They returned accompanied by their 82–year–old mother and, for part of the stay, by Myra's husband and two sons.

Arrangements were made for the entire family to be evaluated as NIMH outpatients. The sisters were then hospitalized on a research ward of the Adult Psychiatry Branch, NIMH, Saint Elizabeths Hospital, Washington, D.C. for a medication–free evaluation. On this occasion, which lasted for approximately 3Ü months, we tested the Genains with the full battery of neurobiological test procedures that have evolved over the last 25 years.

The full report of the tests has been described in a series of detailed papers (Buchsbaum *et al.*, 1984; DeLisi *et al.*, 1984; and Mirsky *et al.* 1984). We report here the results that pertain to the purposes of this volume. First, let us recapitulate some of the significant life history of each of the quadruplets.

THE QUADRUPLETS

Nora

Nora became overtly ill in 1951 at age 21, resigned from a 2–year position as a stenographic clerk, and was first hospitalized for psychiatric illness 14 months later, at age 22. From 1952 until her admission to NIMH in early 1955, Nora was hospitalized four times for periods of 2–4 months and received a total of 19 trials of ECT. During the 3–year NIMH hospitalization, she was described as withdrawn, hallucinatory, delusional, and slow of speech, with a diagnosis of "schizophrenic reaction, catatonic type." After being discharged from NIMH, she was transferred to a state hospital where she remained for 18 months. She then lived with her mother and had a series of clerical jobs in each of which initial success rapidly deteriorated. She remained out of the hospital until 1967, when she spent another year at NIMH. She has been an outpatient since 1967, except for 4 months in 1979. She had been living in a family care home and most recently in her mother's home.

Iris

Within 7 months of Nora's hospitalization, Iris, too, was first hospitalized at the age of 22. Her symptoms included numerous somatic complaints, insomnia, the belief that she was being watched, auditory hallucinations, and posturing. (Her resignation from her job had followed Nora's by 6 months.) During the 3-year NIMH admission, her diagnosis was "schizophrenic reaction, catatonic type." After her stay at NIMH, she was transferred to a state hospital where she remained for more than 12 years. In her last 2 years as a hospitalized patient, an unsuccessful attempt was made to train her as a beautician, and she was placed in a half-way house in a city near the hospital. She required two subsequent, short-term hospitalizations in 1977 and 1979, and since then has been living in a foster care home and attending a day care center.

Myra

Myra was first diagnosed as schizophrenic (catatonic type) in 1955 during the first NIMH evaluation of the quadruplets. Her symptoms included marked psychomotor retardation, hysteroid symptomatology, multiple somatic complaints, and periods of depression and anxiety. She held a few clerical jobs in the Washington, D.C. area subsequent to the NIMH hospitalization while living in a half-way house. She married in 1966 and is the mother of two sons, aged 11 and 17.

She received no medication and appeared to be functioning without psychiatric problems until 1976, when she became paranoid and delusional regarding her new employer and job. She was admitted to a state hospital for 2 months, was treated with trifluoperazine, and reports that her symptoms lasted no more than 4 months. She returned to secretarial work in 1978. In April 1979, she again developed an acute paranoid psychosis following family stress, attempted suicide by an overdose of medication, and was placed under outpatient psychiatric care. During this period she was on minimal doses of trifluoperazine. She had a brief 3-week hospitalization in April 1980 for difficulties related to Parkinsonian side effects of the medication and in October 1980 reportedly attempted suicide by an overdose of medication.

Hester

Although the first NIMH hospitalization was her first hospitalization, Hester apparently had emotional and functional problems for a number of years, resulting in her withdrawal from high school after the 11th grade. She was described as "fearful, withdrawn, irritable, confused, and later hallucinatory." By the time she was 24 she was clearly psychotic and was diagnosed as having a "schizophrenic reaction, catatonic type" during her 3 NIMH years. She was transferred from NIMH to a state hospital where she remained until October 1970. Although her course has remained chronic and unremitting, she has been maintained on medication as an outpatient for the past 10 years. She lives with her mother and helps with household chores. Table 8-1 summarizes the quadruplets' hospitalization (prior to our follow-up study) and the current level of social functioning.

Table 8–1
Summary of Adult Social History of the Genain Quadruplets

	Nora	Iris	Myra	Hester
Hospitalization				
Age at first hospitalization	22 years 2 months	22 years 9 months	24 years 8 months	24 years 8 months
Number of hospitalizations	8	6	4	3
Total time in hospital	6 years, 2 months	15 years, 10 mos	4 years, 4 months	15 years, 9 months
Last hospitalization	1979	1979	1980	1971
Social Functioning				
Educational Level	High school graduate	High school graduate	2 years business college	3 years of high school
Ever worked	Yes	Yes	Yes	No
Usual occupation	Secretary/clerk	Secretary/clerk	Secretary	None
Currently employed (1981)	No	No	No	No
Total time worked	Approximately 7 years; 4 jobs for pay; 2 lasted about 3 years	Approximately 28 months; 6 jobs for pay; 1 lasted 15 months	Unknown; 6 jobs before onset of illness, at least 6 years, all for pay	None

Most recent job	CETA trainee 12/79–4/80	Prior to illness onset	On and off throughout illness	Never worked
Heterosexual adjustment	Never married, occasional dates (2 times month) with expatients from halfway house	Never married, occasional dates in hospital; intense rivalry with Hester for male patients	Married, frequent tense conflicts with mate	Never married, eloped with fellow patient, lived together 1 week; intense rivalry with Iris for male patients
Parental status	No children	No children	Two sons	No children
Current social role	Attends program at social rehab. center for expatients 5 times/week; looking for volunteer work	Attends program at social rehab. center 5 times/week; often leaves after a short time	Housewife (unable to do household chores—unwilling?)	Stays home with mother, helps around house
Financial support	Supplementary Security Insurance	Supplementary Security Insurance	Husband's income	Social Security Disability
Living arrangements	With mother, Hester	Board and care home	With husband in own home	With mother, Nora
Friendships (nonfamily)	Expatients	Expatients	No friends, except those of husband	No friends

Adapted from Table 1, DeLisi *et al.* 1984.

THE 1981 FOLLOW-UP STUDY

Method

The procedures employed in the behavioral studies of the Genains were designed to measure performance in four different domains: attention, memory, neuropsychologic function, and personality. Two of the tests were essentially identical to measures employed in the late '50s—the continuous performance test of visual attention (CPT) and the reaction time (RT) paradigm. Further, for most of the behavioral tasks we were able to examine the Genains both on and off medication—the latter after a period of at least 2 weeks free from the phenothiazine drugs they were taking on admission to NIMH.

Seven techniques were used to assess attention or arousal. Five of these techniques are described here.

For the RT set index, the subject had warning or preparatory intervals (PI) of 2, 4, and 8 seconds before the imperative or "respond now" stimulus was presented. The RT data were combined into a single weighted average or "set index" (Zahn, Carpenter, & McGlashan, 1981) to consolidate the information. This testing procedure was virtually the same as that used by Rosenthal (1963) on the first NIMH admission of the Genains.

In the RT crossover method, a series of four trials, all isotemporal (with the same PI or preparatory interval) was presented in the context of a larger random series of trials in which PIs varied from 0.5 to 11 seconds. The extent to which the subject can benefit from the regularity in this small regular series and begin to respond more rapidly is the operational measure of set (Steffy, 1974, personal communication). Three isotemporal series with PIs of 3, 7, and 11 seconds were used. All stimuli were auditory. A so-called crossover measure was calculated, defined as the difference between the first trial RT and those at the three succeeding regular trials of the same PI within the isotemporal four-trial series.

CPT was administered to all subjects in three forms: the X-task, in which the subject is asked to press a response key whenever the letter X appears on a video display but to avoid pressing for other letters; the AX-task, in which the critical stimulus is the letter X immediately preceded by the letter A; and the "dynamic" version of the X-task, in which the stimulus duration and interstimulus interval vary as a function of the performance of the subject. The parameters of the standard X and AX-task are: stimulus duration = 0.20 sec, interstimulus interval = 0.8 sec, allowable response time = 0.7 sec, total stimuli = approximately 600, total critical stimuli = 150 (X-task) and 120 (AX-task).

The Stroop Test (Jensen, 1965; Stroop, 1935) involves the presentation of three stimulus displays via slide projector. In the first slide, color patches are the stimulus material, and the subject is required to name the colors. The second slide presents color names printed in inks that match the lexical content, whereas in the third slide, the color names and the inks do not match. The difference in time required to read the color names on slides two and three is thought to reflect susceptibility to interference and distraction.

Autonomic indices of arousal, measures of heart rate, and various measures of skin conductance level were obtained. These measures were recorded under baseline (resting conditions) and in response to the stimulus of a reaction time task. The data analysis was performed according to standard techniques (Zahn et al., 1981).

Several memory tests were administered that have been used to define changes in information processing in the encoding and organizing of information after administration of psychoactive drugs and in groups of persons suffering from various types of psycho– and neuropathologic conditions. These included a selective reminding task (Weingartner, Caine, & Ebert, 1979); a learning task requiring the recall of 32 related words in two clusters (Weingartner et al., 1981); a task requiring subjects to predict their recall performance (Groninger, 1979), and the free and cued recall of acoustically and semantically processed words (Craik & Tulving, 1975; Weingartner et al, 1980).

The Luria–Nebraska scale (Golden, Hammeke, & Purisch, 1978, 1980) was administered to all the subjects while on neuroleptic medication. This test also yielded an estimate of full scale IQ that could be compared with the premorbid IQs published by Rosenthal (1963).

The Rorschach test was administered to all the quadruplets when they were free of medication. The protocols were scored blind by standard determinants and the values compared with those obtained in the 1950s as reported by Rosenthal (1963).

The neurological procedures included an extensive series of genetic identity tests; biochemical determinations from blood, urine, and cerebrospinal fluid of various catecholamine compounds with particular emphasis on dopamine and norepinephrine; procedures related to the identification of possible preexisting viral infection of the central nervous system; neuroradiological and neurophysiologic tests [CT scan, PET scan, evoked potential and EEG brain maps, and brain stem evoked potentials (BSEP)]. No gross signs of neurological disease were found in any of the women. Myra showed evidence of tardive dyskinesia. "Soft" neurological signs were found in all the quadruplets; the total number of signs were: Nora, 6.0; Iris, 2.5; Myra, 2.0; and Hester, 5.5.

Results

Three of the 1958 tests were repeated in 1981: the CPT, RT, and the Rorschach Test. Results for the two time periods are presented in Table 8–2.

In 1958, none of the quadruplets was on medication, and CPT test scores reflected the hierarchy based on severity of illness. Myra, last ill and least impaired, performed the task, albeit within the "poor

Table 8–2
Tests Performed in 1958 and 1981 on Genain Quadruplets

CPT†

Test	1958 Examination		1981 Examination			
			X task		AX task	
	X task	AX task	On meds	Off meds	On meds	Off meds
Myra	89.4	72.5	82.0	78.7	30.8	35.8
Nora	28.7	27.5	98.7*	25.3	80.8*	21.7
Iris	1.3	3.3	98.0*	64.7	80.0*	56.7
Hester	—	—	80.7	27.3	42.0	13.3

Reaction Time

	Global Assessments‡	Set Index	
		On meds	Off meds
Myra	normal	312*	771
Nora	impaired	323*	–
Iris	—	273*	2113
Hester	—	526	–

Rorschach Test

	Mean Rank	Mean Rank	Rank Change
Myra	1	1	0
Nora	3	3	0
Iris	4	2	+2
Hester	2	4	–2

Adapted from Table 1, Mirsky *et al.* 1984.
† % correct responses; — untestable; * scores within the normal range; ‡ for details see Rosenthal (1963)

CPT" range. Nora, Iris, and Hester, in that order, showed decreasing ability to function in the test situation. In 1981, when tested on/off medication, Nora, Iris, and Hester showed remarkably better performance; and when tested on medication, Nora and Iris had scores within normal limits. Both Nora and Hester showed marked impairment when tested off medication. Only Myra, still considered the most nearly intact of the quadruplets, had poorer CPT scores in 1981 than in 1958.

Scores on RT, like CPT, paralleled severity of illness in 1958; similarly, in 1981 the RT (on medication) was improved, and again Nora and Hester exhibited greater impairment when off medication than did Myra and Iris.

Global rankings on the 1958 and 1981 Rorschach tests did not parallel the rank order of severity of schizophrenic illness, and only Iris and Hester showed any change. Part of the problem in assessing these test results stems from the complexity of the 1958 Rorschach information.[1] At both times, however, none of the quadruplets had normal records; all the records were compatible with some degree of psychotic or organic pathology.

On all tests of attention (CPT, RT, Steffy technique, Stroop), the quadruplets functioned better on medication. When taken off medication, Nora and Hester showed greatly impaired performance; decrements in performance were considerably less for Myra and Iris . Figure 8-1 shows the dramatic differences in response to medication between Nora and Hester, on the one hand, and Myra and Iris on the other.

In view of aging concerns, it is important to note that even without medication the quadruplets as a group performed better in 1981 than in 1958.

Neuropsychologic assessment provided a basis for comparison of intellectual functioning in the two periods. The Luria–Nebraska examination of the quadruplets, administered in 1981, yielded an estimate of full scale (WAIS) IQ. The estimates are presented in Table 8-3, where they are compared with scores on the Henmon–Nelson administered in 1947, when the quadruplets were 16 years old, years before any of them had had a psychiatric diagnosis. The 1981 estimates were markedly similar to those obtained 35 years earlier. Only Iris's score differed by more than three points from the 1947 values.

Evoked potential brain maps were obtained off medication in the context of an attention test. There were no comparative data from the earlier period.

BSEP showed that, as a group, the Genains showed significant slowing of conduction time compared with age–matched controls. The significance of the finding of abnormality is unclear except as further evidence for brainstem dysfunction in schizophrenia.

---

[1]One rating provided by Singer (Rosenthal, 1963) predicts the following order of severity of illness: Myra (least ill), Nora, Iris, Hester.

Figure 8–1
Representative Tests of Attention and Memory
Genain Quadruplets On and Off Medication

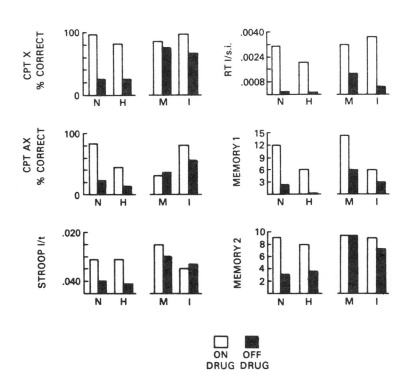

Adapted from Mirsky *et al.* 1984.

Table 8–3
IQ Scores, Genain Quadruplets, 1946 and 1981

	Herman Nelson IQ age 16	Luria Nebraska (WAIS estimate) age 51
Myra	87	89
Nora	99	97
Iris	89	82
Hester	77	80

Adapted from Table 4, Mirsky *et al.* 1984.

Generally, CT scans did not distinguish the quadruplets from one another. All were normal; there was no ventricular enlargement and little atrophy.

The PET scan data suggest that Nora and Hester have lower glucose uptake values in the frontal lobe's activity than have Myra and Iris. It will be recalled that Nora and Hester showed a greater drop in performance and more personality deterioration when taken off psychotropic medication.

SUMMARY AND DISCUSSION

The Genain quadruplets at age 51 are functioning about as well as they ever have in their adult lives. Their identical genetic endowment is reflected in identical CT scans and similar biological and bio-chemical abnormalities (BSAEP abnormality; low DBH; high PEA; Buchsbaum *et al.*, 1984; DeLisi *et al.*, 1984).

For most of their lives they have been viewed as two pairs: Nora and Myra, and Iris and Hester. The data obtained in their maturity and the striking effects seen when they were taken off medication suggest that the true pairing, if any, is Myra and Iris, Nora and Hester, with the latter pair showing greater evidence of functional brain disturbance. In this connection, it may be significant that Nora was the first born and Hester the last. From an obstetrical point of view, a case could be made for the first and last born sustaining more brain injury than the other two.[2] These observations, however, did not become salient until the Genains were studied at maturity.

---

[2]The facts pertaining to Hester's birth are in dispute (Rosenthal, 1963, pp. 39–40), but her birth weight (1361 gm) is clearly indicative of greater prematurity than her sisters (Nora, 2041 gm; Myra, 1928 gm; Iris, 1503 gm). Rosenthal speculated that "Hester may have suffered handicaps from which she was never to recover" (Rosenthal, 1963, p. 544).

In considering the possible effects of aging upon the expression of schizophrenic illness in these women, a number of other factors must be considered. Medication has reduced the severity of symptoms in Nora, Hester, and, to a lesser degree, Iris. Myra's marriage has taken her out of the Genain home for varying periods of time, and at those times there has been less turmoil in interquadruplet interactions. Nora has finally abandoned all thought of becoming fully employed and self-sustaining, and while she may feel a sense of failure in this respect, the concomitant reduction in pressure probably relieves some stress. Hester, though still at the bottom in status within the group, has gained some importance from a recent serious physical illness and faces fewer demands for service to other family members.

Mrs. Genain appears to grow more tolerant of her daughters' disabilities as she grows older. Whether through a diminution of energy, sheer discouragement, or an increase in wisdom, she no longer believes that she can change her daughters or make things right for them. These are but a few examples of the kinds of changes which have occurred with the passage of time, but not necessarily as a result of the aging process.[3]

It is by no means clear in the case of the quadruplets that their schizophrenic illness has "burned out" with age. Unquestionably they have improved greatly since they were first admitted to NIH in 1955, and there is time yet for further improvement.

A group of only four cases will not allow us to confirm or contradict any hypothesis; however, the special nature of these four women (odds of occurrence about one in a billion) gives us the right to speculate that the schizophrenic phenotype and the course of its expression will ultimately be understood as a combination of biochemical abnormality, functional (if not structural) brain damage, and life stress. The specific combinations of factors leading to the varied expression of the illness is unknown, but may be revealed to us with further study.

---

[3]Since this manuscript was prepared, Mrs. Genain has died and the quadruplets (now age 56) function more-or-less independently. Myra and Nora share the primary responsibility for keeping the Genain enterprise afloat, and they have financial help and other support provided by various state and community agencies.

BIOLOGICAL PARAMETERS

Several investigators are examining the biological factors that may relate to schizophrenia. One hypothesis relates asynchronous aging changes in opposed neural systems to improvement in early onset schizophrenia as well as to the development of late onset paraphrenias. Other researchers are finding cerebral atrophy in schizophrenic patients, which when combined with normal age-linked changes may have definite implications for exacerbating the course of disorder.

Another study found that schizophrenics most likely to experience symptomatic amelioration across the lifespan were those with relatively greater platelet MAO activity after controlling for age, race, gender, and medication. Activities of platelet MAO and plasma DBH were directly related to cognitive impairment.

9

Aging and Schizophrenia: A Hypothesis Relating Asynchrony in Neural Aging Processes to the Manifestations of Schizophrenia and Other Neurologic Diseases with Age

Caleb E. Finch

David Morgan

University of Southern California

A substantial fraction of diagnosed schizophrenics seems to gradually improve over several decades of adult life. In contrast, other neurologic disorders resembling schizophrenias in some respects, the so–called paraphrenias, worsen with age. It is proposed that the incidence and time course of these disorders may be a function of organic age changes in monoaminergic and other neurotransmitter systems. Our major hypothesis is that asynchronies in the aging changes of opposed neural systems can, in principle, modify early, adult onset psychiatric disorders such as schizophrenia, and in other individuals such asynchronies could increase the risk of brain disorders altering motor control, emotion, and cognition.

OVERVIEW OF AGING PROCESSES IN THE BRAIN

Neuronal Loss

Aging does not uniformly impair all brain systems: in humans and in a wide variety of short– and long–lived mammals, age changes appear to be selective. Consider the issue of neuronal loss. Contrary to popular assumptions, many human brain systems do not normally lose neurons even at advanced ages, e.g., the inferior olive (Monagle & Brody, 1974) and other brain stem nuclei. Initially, considerable neuron loss was believed to occur in the cerebral cortex (Brody, 1976; Henderson *et al.,* 1980). However, recent detailed accounts have revised these estimates downwards to a 10–30% reduction in cortical neurons over the lifespan (Haug *et al.*, 1983). Neuronal loss also occurs with age in the noradrenergic locus ceruleus (Vijayashankar & Brody, 1979; Wree, Braak, Schleicher, & Zilles, 1980), in the dopa-

Mann *et al.*, 1984), in the dopaminergic substantia nigra (McGeer, McGeer, & Suzuki, 1977), and in the putamen (Bugiani, Salvarini, Perdelli, Mancardi, & Leonardi, 1978).

Less well documented, but of potentially greater relevance, is the loss of dendritic arborization, spines, and synaptic terminals (Buell & Coleman, 1979; Geinisman & Bondareff, 1976). According to the synaptic doctrine, the pertinent measure of information processing capacity in the aging central nervous system is the number of viable synaptic contacts, rather than the number of neurons themselves. One means by which the brain might store information is the selective elimination of synapses irrelevant to or competing with the desired circuit, thereby enhancing the remaining connections (Eccles, 1973). Such a theory would explain the loss of synapses with age and place a finite limit on the lifetime memory capacity of an individual.

Appel (1981) recently suggested that mature neurons require end organ trophic support for survival, much like developing neurons. A reduction in the number of synaptic contacts would decrease the retrograde transport of such a factor, leading to cell death when trophic support became insufficient. In such a manner, terminal loss may be the primary lesion in the aging nervous system, and neuron loss a secondary event. In reciprocally innervated systems such as substantia nigra and striatum, cell loss in one region may produce a secondary neuron degeneration in the other, generating a positive feedback spiral with devastating consequences. Such transneuronal degeneration events are well known to occur in tightly coupled neuronal systems following acute lesions (Cowan, 1970).

Genomic Functions

Efforts to find age–correlated alterations in genomic functional aging have not detected global changes. The bulk RNA content is decreased in some neural types, e.g., the nucleolar volume decreases after 60 years in neurones of the human substantia nigra, but does not decrease in locus ceruleus neurons until after 80 years (Mann & Yates, 1979). Cell body RNA content also decreases differentially, with the least loss in hippocampal pyramidal cells and the greatest loss in the inferior olive (Mann, Yates, & Stamp, 1978). The nucleolar volume and cell body RNA content represent largely ribosomal (noninformational) RNA.

Evaluation of complex (informational) nuclear RNA obtained from the cortex of pigtail macaques showed no change of yield or sequence complexity between 4 and 20 years (Farquhar, Kosky, & Omenn, 1979). Similar results were obtained for nuclear and poly-somal poly(A)RNA of the laboratory rat brain (Coleman, Kaplan, Osterburg, & Finch, 1980). In rodents, as in long–lived primates, RNA loss with age is not general, but is limited to some brain regions and cell types (see Chaconas & Finch, 1973). Differential rates of age changes between brain regions and cell types arise in most parameters, including accumulations of age pigments and changes in the levels of enzymes (reviewed in Finch, 1977), and neurotransmitter receptors (Severson & Finch, 1980).

Neurotransmitter Functions

In the last decade, many reports have described changes in neuro-transmitter metabolism and membrane receptors for synaptically active drugs in human and mammalian models. Most changes are small (10%–35%) during the average life span (Finch, 1977; Rogers & Bloom, 1985). In nearly all cases, age changes in neurotransmitter-related functions indicate reduced function: levels decrease, turnover slows, receptors decline, etc. The absence of change in many param-eters with age, however, is of major importance. Just as for neuronal loss and RNA metabolism, there is considerable cell and pathway specificity in vulnerability to age changes in neurotransmitter functions.

In relation to the schizophrenias and paraphrenias, the effects of age on the following neurotransmitters are of particular interest: the dopaminergic pathways of the mesocortical and mesolimbic systems, the noradrenergic pathways from the locus ceruleus to the cerebral cortex and hippocampus, the serotonergic projections from the raphe to the limbic system, and also opioid systems and cholinergic projec-tions. There is some evidence for age–related decreases in each of these neurotransmitter systems (see Table 9–1).

NEUROLOGICAL IMBALANCE, THRESHOLDS, AND ASYNCHRONOUS AGING

A useful, albeit simplistic, model of human basal gangliar dysfunction supposes an antagonism between dopaminergic and cholinergic inputs (Figure 9–1), which, when out of balance, results in movement and thought disorders (Barbeau, 1962). A relative dopaminergic deficit results in rigidity and akinesia. A selective reduction of cholinergic function would lead to choreiform movements. Throughout the brain, many mutually antagonistic systems are operating and must be properly balanced for the appropriate processing and output of information. An imbalance in the relative activities of these inputs may arise due to disease, age, or experimental intervention. Use of the latter has demonstrated that different systems have different thresholds for functional expression of an imbalanced condition.

One system having considerable redundancy is the nigrostriatal dopamine system. Experimental lesions in rodents indicate that loss of dopaminergic neurons and striatal dopamine of up to 70%–90% may not impair normal movement (Ranje & Ungerstedt, 1977). Intra-ventricular transplant studies of embryonic substantia nigra show that reinnervation of the dopamine depleted striatum to merely 3%

Table 9-1
Aging Changes in Human Brain Neurotransmitter Systems

Measure	Region	Change	Reference
Dopaminergic systems			
Dopamine levels	Caudate nucleus	Decrease	1, 6, 18
	Putamen nucleus	Decrease	5
		No change	1, 3
	Hypothalamus	No change	1
Tyrosine hydroxylase	Caudate nucleus	Decrease	7, 13
		No change	20
	Substantia nigra	Decrease	7
		No change	20
DOPA decarboxylase	Caudate nucleus	Decrease	7, 13
	Substantia nigra	Decrease	7
3H-spiperone binding	Caudate nucleus	Decrease	21
	Substantia nigra	Decrease	21
3H-ADTN binding	Caudate nucleus	Decrease	21
Noradrenergic systems			
Norepinephrine levels	Caudate nucleus	No change	6
	Hypothalamus	No change	6
	Cerebral cortex	No change	6
	Hippocampus	Decrease	6
	Substantia nigra	Decrease	23
	Midbrain	Decrease	15, 19
Tyrosine hydroxylase	Cerebral cortex	No change	20
	Hippocampus	No change	13, 20
	Hypothalamus	No change	13, 20
Monoamine oxidase	Cerebral cortex	Increase	20
	Hippocampus	Increase	20
	Hypothalamus	Increase	6, 20
	Midbrain	Increase	19, 20
3H-dihydroalprenolol binding	Cerebellum	Decrease	12
	Cerebral cortex	No change	12
Cholinergic systems			
Choline acetyl transferase	Caudate nucleus	Decrease	13
		No change	6
	Cerebral cortex	Decrease	13, 17
		No change	4, 6, 25
	Hippocampus	No change	6
Acetylcholine esterase	Substantia nigra	Decrease	13

Table 9–1 continued

Measure	Region	Change	Reference
Cholinergic systems (continued)			
3H–QNB binding	Cerebral cortex	No change	16
	Caudate nucleus	No change	16, 25, 26
3H–atropine	Cerebral cortex	Decrease	25
Serotonergic systems			
Serotonin levels	Cerebral cortex	No change	6
	Hippocampus	No change	6
	Hypothalamus	No change	6
3H–5–HT binding	Cerebral cortex	Increase	22
Opioid systems			
Beta–endorphin levels	Hypothalamus	Decrease	2, 8, 9
Met–enkephalin levels	Hypothalamus	Increase	11, 24
3H–etorphine binding	Cerebral cortex	Decrease	10
	Caudate nucleus	Decrease	10
	Hippocampus	Decrease	10
3H–dihydromorphine binding	Cerebral cortex	Decrease	14
	Caudate nucleus	Decrease	14
	Hippocampus	Decrease	14

References

1. Adolfson *et al.*, 1979
2. Barden *et al.*, 1981
3. Bird & Iverson, 1974
4. Bowen *et al.*, 1976
5. Carlsson & Winblad, 1976
6. Carlsson *et al.*, 1980
7. Cote & Kremzner, 1974
8. Forman *et al.*, 1981
9. Gambert, 1981
10. Hess *et al.*, 1981
11. Kumar *et al.*, 1980
12. Maggi *et al.*, 1979
13. McGeer & McGeer, 1978
14. Messing *et al.*, 1981
15. Nies *et al.*, 1973
16. Perry, 1980
17. Perry *et al.*, 1981
18. Riederer & Wuketich, 1976
19. Robinson, 1975
20. Robinson *et al.*, 1977
21. Severson *et al.*, 1982
22. Shih & Young, 1978
23. Spokes, 1979
24. Steger *et al.*, 1980
25. White *et al.*, 1977
26. Yamamura, 1981

The preparation of this table in 1984 was greatly assisted by privileged access to the superb review of Joseph Rogers and Floyd Bloom (1985). For an updated review, see Morgan *et al.* (in press).

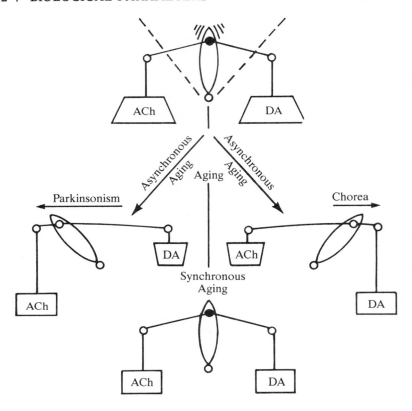

Figure 9–1. Cholinergic–dopaminergic antagonism in the basal ganglia. The relative influence of cholinergic and dopaminergic processes (represented here as weights) on the output of the basal ganglia (indicated by the quivering needle) are depicted to be in a dynamic balance (top center). If either process begins to dominate, the output is biased toward one or another abnormal manifestation, presented here as rigidity (cholinergic excess, Parkinsonism) or choreiform movements (dopaminergic excess, Huntington's disease). Aging may impact upon this system either synchronously (bottom), with approximately equal reductions in both activities, or asynchronously (sides) with a greater reduction in one of the two antagonistic inputs. The imbalanced condition produced by asynchronous aging will manifest itself behaviorally if the imbalance exceeds a threshold level (indicated here by dashed lines).

of the original dopamine content is sufficient to overcome amphet-amine–induced rotational asymetries (Schmidt, Ingvar, Lindvall, Steneri, & Bjorkland, 1982). Clinical observations support the concept of a high threshold for the nigrostriatal system before imbalanced transmitter functions are expressed as abnormal behaviors (Bern-heimer, Birkmayer, Hornykiewicz, Jellinger, & Seitelberger, 1973).

In contrast, small lesions of the catecholaminergic nucleus A2 in the brainstem cause permanent increases of blood pressure liability in rats (Talman, Snyder, & Reis, 1980). Similarly, graded lesions of the tuberoinfundibular dopamine system produce graded increases in prolactin output from the pituitary (K.E. Moore, personal com-munication).

The basis for different thresholds in response to partial neuronal lesions is unclear, but rests in part on the capacity of negative feed-back systems, both local (autoreceptors, uptake, metabolic enzyme activity, clearance rates) and transneuronal (direct feedback loops, postsynaptic receptor supersensitivity, modulation of release by other transmitters, i.e., opiates and dopamine) to adjust the new steady state condition to one of balance between antagonistic inputs. In support of this notion, acute haloperidol injections cause a compens-atory increase in striatal dopamine turnover, presumably mediated via autoreceptor blockade; however, in the tuberoinfundibular dopa-mine system, no increased turnover is detected at short intervals following haloperidol administration (Gudelsky, Annunziato, & Moore, 1978).

In addition to appropriate feedback regulation, the compromised system must have sufficient reserve capacity to restore a balanced condition. In this respect, the *absolute* level of the transmitter system is important, as well as the *differential* level of activity with respect to opposing neural inputs. Each input has some reserve capacity or safety factor. Once this reserve capacity is exhausted, and regulatory mechanisms are unable to bring the inputs into balance, the neuronal system will no longer function normally.

Thresholds for neuronal dysfunctions can, therefore, be con-ceptualized as the limits of compensatory mechanisms to maintain a balanced condition between antagonistic transmitter systems. Once these limits are exceeded, the compromised input will no longer be able to influence the output of the neuronal network. Under such conditions, the information conveyed by the impaired transmitter system will be lost. The now unopposed inputs will have no resistance to their influence on the neuronal system. The loss of information combined with the unbridled activity of the remaining inputs could then result in behavioral disturbance.

The therapeutic value of drugs that act directly at postsynaptic sites may rest on their capacity to restore the balance between opposing neuronal inputs. These drugs tonically stimulate or inhibit in a general, nonspecific manner that precludes the direct transmission of information. However, by restoring the balance amongst opposing inputs, they restrain the previously unopposed inputs and reinstate the conditions whereby the compromised input can have some influence on the output of the neuronal system.

The balance among transmitter systems can be affected by asynchronous, aging–related reductions of different neuronal components. These asynchronies may exacerbate or attenuate a given disease state depending upon the nature of the asynchrony and the disease. Examples of how asynchronous aging might interact with two age-linked disturbances are presented below.

Huntingtonism

Huntingtonism has interesting parallels with schizophrenia in several regards: (a) most cases (90%) occur before midlife (30–40 years), but after puberty (Bruyn, 1968; Brackenridge, 1973); (b) positive dopaminergic imbalances are implied by the efficacy of treatment by dopamine antagonists and the exacerbation of symptoms in most patients by L–DOPA (a dopaminergic and noradrenergic indirect agonist) (Klawans, 1970); (c) the late–onset forms of Huntingtonism are rela-

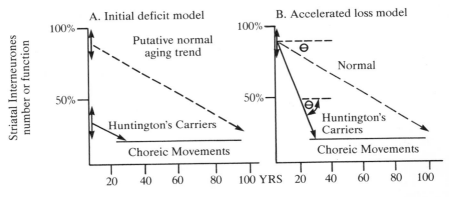

Figure 9–2. Two mechanisms for the age–related incidence of Huntington's chorea. The onset of choreic movements is assumed to result when deficits of striatal neurons (either number or function) reach some critical threshold (solid horizontal lines). The onset is hypothesized to occur when the Huntingtonism lesion summates with normal age–related trends for progressive striatal cell loss or functional impairment. In the initial deficit model (A), the rate of striatal impairment is the same as in normal aging. The threshold for chorea is reached when the congenital deficits, which were initially insufficient to cause neurological abnormalities, are summated to threshold with the normal aging trend. In the accelerated loss model (B), the rate of impairment is greatly accelerated above the normal aging trend. No information is available about the time course of striatal neuron loss in Huntington's chorea (Finch, 1980).

tively mild (Bruyn, 1968); and (d) genetic factors are involved—dominant alleles for Huntingtonism but complex genetic factors for schizophrenia (Kety, Rosenthal, Wender, Schlusinger, & Jacobsen, 1975). This view of Huntingtonism can serve as a model for conceptualizing age changes in the expression of schizophrenia.

A key to the analysis of Huntingtonism is the implied threshold for the expression of symptoms. The adult onset implies that the inherited allele is initially not expressed. In a study by Klawans, Paulson, Ringel, and Barbeau (1972), L–DOPA transiently evoked chorea–like movements in 33% of prospective but asymptomatic carriers, whereas controls were unaffected. Further evidence for cryptic damage is the reduced striatal glucose metabolism in presymptomatic carriers (Kuhl et al., 1982). We suggest two possible models (Figure 9–2). In the *initial deficit mechanism*, carriers could have congenital deficits in striatal neurone number or function that were insufficient to cause chorea until the deficit summated with the normal age–trend for loss or impairment of striatal neurons to reach a *critical threshold for chorea*. Alternatively, in the *accelerated loss* mechanism, the loss or impairment of striatal neurons could be accelerated during aging in Huntingtonian carriers. The age when striatal deficits approach the critical threshold could also be functions of congenital variations in the number or functions of striatal neurons; genotype–controlled variations in neuronal numbers are known in inbred mice.

The mildness of late onset (after 50 years) in Huntingtonism has been commented on by some clinicians (Bruyn, 1968). A possible mechanism for this is the age–correlated trend for reduction of nigro–striatal dopaminergic functions, which could reduce the positive dopaminergic imbalance caused by striatal neuron pathology (Finch, 1980). Similarly, the trend for dopaminergic impairments during aging would tend to partially correct the effects of striatal neuronal loss with age, thereby reducing the risk of senile chorea (Martin, 1968) which might otherwise be higher. In both these cases, the threshold *per se* for chorea need not be modified by age; instead, age–changes in the opposing dopaminergic functions would attenuate the *extent* of the imbalance. Such thresholds should be conceptualized in terms of the differentials between opposing neural systems as well as in terms of their absolute levels.

Parkinsonism

The clinical manifestation of schizophrenia in mid and late life can also be considered in the context of what is known about the age–linked onset of Parkinsonism. The increase of Parkinsonism after midlife may result from different etiologies, including delayed effects from viral encephalitis (Schwab et al., 1956) and genetic predispositions (Martin, 1973; Mjones, 1949). The greater susceptibility of Parkinsonism relations to neuroleptic–induced Parkinsonism

(Myrianthopoulos *et al.*, 1962, 1969) is consistent with genetic poly-morphisms, resulting in congenital subthreshold dopaminergic defi-cits. (In contradiction to this view, however, a recent study failed to detect any concordance between identical twins for Parkinsonism (Duvoisin *et al.*, 1981).) The greater susceptibility of the elderly to Parkinsonian side effects of neuroleptics (Ayd, 1961) is consistent with subthreshold dopaminergic deficits, which reached the threshold for expression when further compromised by dopaminergic blockade. The onset of Parkinsonism 20 years or more after encephalitis-associated damage to the basal ganglia (Schwab *et al.*, 1956) might also be viewed as the summation of an initially subthreshold lesion with the normal age–correlated changes. Given the 1% per year loss of striatal dopamine (Riederer & Wuketich, 1976; Carlsson & Winblad, 1976), a greater incidence of Parkinsonism might be predicted by the 8th or 9th decade. Bugiani and colleagues (1978) ingeniously sug-gested that the loss of striatal neurons might protect the elderly against Parkinsonian–like consequences of dopaminergic deficits alone.

Another phenomenon possibly involving interactions of age changes in the basal ganglia with pathologic lesions is the age–dis-tribution of "on–off symptomology in Parkinsonism;" during L–DOPA therapy, younger patients are more likely to have "uneven" symp-toms, including dyskinesis, than are older patients (Granerus *et al.*, 1979). Because dementia was prevalent in the older Parkinsonisms, these authors suggested that the older group involved "multineuronal" damage. We further propose that *asynchronies in the loss or dysfunction of the opposing (counterbalancing) systems during aging* (e.g., dopaminergic versus cholinergic and gaba–ergic) *will lead to individual variations in the risk for different types of motor disturbances with age, including senile tremor, bradykinesia, and chorea.* Asynchronies could result from differential rates of decline, as well as variations of initial levels. Thus, dopaminergic deficits could be produced by a relative decline of dopaminergic systems compared to cholinergic or gaba–ergic losses. On the other hand, a synchronous decline of opposing systems might *protect* against some types of motor disturbances.

Schizophrenia

The onset of schizophrenia is uncommon after 30 years (Loranger, 1984). A gradual diminution of schizophrenic symptoms is observed clinically during midlife in 20%–40% of subjects (Bleuler, 1974; Bridges, Cannon, & Wyatt, 1978; Ciompi, 1980). Given the symptomo-logic heterogeneity in schizophrenia, it is clearly possible that the "spontaneous remitters" are a unique category of disorder that should be separately classified from the majority. Regardless, it is probable that the subgroup of schizophrenics with gradually remitting symp-toms results from variously decreased dopaminergic, noradrenergic, serotonergic, or opioid activity with age.

In view of the increased dopaminergic receptors observed in the caudate and putamen of schizophrenics (Lee & Seeman, 1980; Snyder, 1981), it is interesting that a trend for decreased dopaminergic receptors may occur with normal aging in the caudate and nucleus accumbens. Thus, some schizophrenics may gradually diminish in symptomatology because dopaminergic balance was restored during aging (Figure 9–3). This model predicts that schizophrenic symptoms would transiently reappear with doses of amphetamine or other dopaminemimetics that are subthreshold for symptoms in the normal elderly. Decreases with age of other neurotransmitters or neuromodulators could also be involved, e.g., some evidence suggests associations of schizophrenic symptoms with excess endorphins (Pickar *et al.*, 1982; van Ree & DeWied, 1981) or norepinephrine (Hornykiewicz, 1982; Sternberg, Van Kamen, Lerner, & Bunney, 1982). Those schizophrenics who did not progressively improve with aging would be predicted to maintain their neurochemical characteristics because of synchronous aging.

Paraphrenias

The late–life onset of the schizophrenia–like paraphrenias involves hallucinations and paranoia, but without personality disintegration (Kay & Roth, 1961; Post, 1980). The paraphrenias could be viewed as

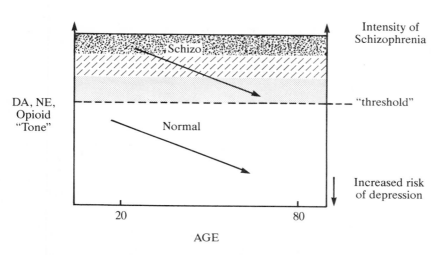

Figure 9–3. Interaction of aging–related decreases in brain transmitter function and the intensity of schizophrenic symptoms. In this model, schizophrenia is viewed as a relative hyperactivity of one or more neurotransmitter systems, with dopamine being the primary candidate.

the result of asynchronous aging, which causes relatively greater cholinergic deficits than dopaminergic ones and leads to a relative dopaminergic excess. The rarity of typical schizophrenic anxiety in the elderly paraphrenics could result from changes in monoamine systems tending toward depression, which might protect against global personality disorders. Trends for hippocampal deterioration as inferred from Golgi-stained neuronal profiles (Scheibel, 1978) might also protect against a full schizophrenic syndrome, if dopaminergic excess arises. On the other hand, because hippocampal tumors in younger adults may be associated with schizophrenic symptoms, including hallucinations of smell and sound such as observed in the paraphrenias (Malamud, 1967), primary hippocampal age changes could be involved in the paraphrenias.

CONCLUSIONS

This discussion of aging, neurotransmitter balance, and neurological disease is very speculative. Whether or not these hypotheses relating the schizophrenias and paraphrenias to aging processes are borne out, it is clear that further research attention should be focused on neurotransmitter interrelationships during aging. Far too often in the past, studies have dealt with just one neurotransmitter system at a time in the examination of age-correlated changes. Most neuroscientists would agree that complex brain functions involving mood or information processing are built in the interplay of several types of neurotransmitters and circuit regulation. In the future, a better theory of macroscopic circuit functions should result from pursuing these directions.

10

Cerebral Atrophy in Elderly Schizophrenic Patients: Effects of Aging and of Long-Term Institutionalization and Neuroleptic Therapy

Daniel R. Weinberger

Dilip V. Jeste

Richard Jed Wyatt

National Institute of Mental Health

Saint Elizabeths Hospital

Washington, D.C.

Paul F. Teychenne

Prince Henry Hospital

Matraville, Australia

Over the past 5 years, research studies of schizophrenic patients evaluated by computed tomography (CT) have proliferated. This landmark radiological technique has revealed findings suggestive of cerebral atrophy in some schizophrenic patients. The findings include enlarged cerebral ventricles, dilated cortical fissures and sulci, and, possibly, reduced radiodensity of the cerebral parenchyma. Although negative studies have appeared, the majority of the controlled investigations have confirmed these findings (for review, see Weinberger, Wagner, & Wyatt, 1983).

For a variety of reasons, most investigators have concentrated on schizophrenic patients in the third and fourth decades of life. In fact, only one study has included patients over 60 years of age (Johnstone, Crow, Frith, Husband, & Kreel, 1979). In elderly populations where CT findings consistent with cerebral atrophy are common, it would be more difficult to differentiate subtle pathology, possibly related to the schizophrenic illness, from the nonspecific concomitants of normal aging.

Now that an association between schizophrenia and CT findings suggestive of cerebral atrophy has been demonstrated, a study of elderly schizophrenic patients offers some potentially novel insights and may help answer the lingering concern about the role of psychiatric treatment in the etiology of cerebral atrophy. Our effort at such a study addressed three specific questions: (1) Are the CT findings described in young schizophrenic patients observable in elderly patients who have been ill for many years? (2) What impact does the aging process have on cerebral atrophy? (3) Is cerebral atrophy caused by many years of psychiatric treatment, especially institutional and somatic?

METHOD

Seventeen chronic schizophrenic women were selected from a single ward of Saint Elizabeths Hospital, Washington, D.C. These patients had spend the majority of their adult lives as inpatients in mental hospitals. They fulfilled both Research Diagnostic and DSM–III criteria for the diagnosis of chronic schizophrenia. These patients, furthermore, had no history of neurological disease or disorder, had not abused alcohol, and had no other known cause of cerebral atrophy. Control subjects were chosen from a sample of healthy volunteers who had undergone CT scanning for other purposes. These individuals were carefully screened to exclude cases with neurological problems.

Table 10–1 shows the demographic features of the two groups. The schizophrenic patients were slightly, but not significantly ($p=.15$, two–tailed t test), older. They had spent a mean of 34 years as hospital inpatients and had been on neuroleptic medication for a mean duration of 18 years. While race is not known to be associated with cerebral atrophy, the groups were racially comparable. The inclusion of a few males in the control group, if anything, biased against finding larger ventricles in patients, as normal males tend to have larger ventricles than do normal females (Gyldensted, 1977).

Patients and controls underwent CT scanning at the Clinical Center, National Institutes of Health, Bethesda, Maryland. The same machine was used for all subjects, with window width and level set by technicians who were unaware of the research proposals and whose intent was to achieve optimum soft tissue resolution. Each scan

Table 10–1
Characteristics of Samples

	Controls	Schizophrenics
Sample size	16	17
Age (±SD)	66 ± 9	72 ± 12
Sex	10 F, 6 M	17 F
Race	11 W, 5 B	7 W, 10 B

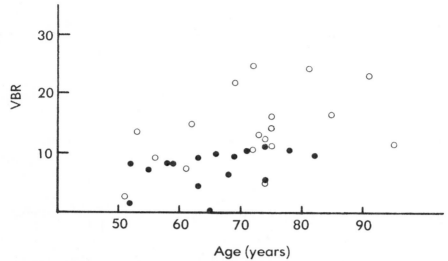

Figure 10-1. Ventricular size as a function of age. For patients: Spearman rho=.52, p=.04. For controls: rho=.44, p=.07.

consisted of from 8 to 12 near horizontal cross sections ("slices") of 10–mm thickness. The slices appeared on self–developing prints reduced from actual size by a minification factor of 3.3.

Ventricular size was quantified using a planimetric measurement that has been described in detail elsewhere (Weinberger, Torrey, Neophytides, & Wyatt, 1979a). This method yields a ventricular-to-brain ratio (VBR) that reliably approximates ventricular volume. The VBR of each patient and control was determined in identical manner. A caliper was used to quantify cortical structures involved in cortical atrophy. In each case, the width of the sylvian fissures, the interhemispheric fissure, and the mean width of the three broadest cortical sulci were measured. This method also is described in detail elsewhere (Weinberger, Torrey, Neophytides, & Wyatt, 1979b).

RESULTS

Comparison of "Atrophy" Measures

The first question addressed by this study was whether the CT findings observed in young schizophrenic patients are seen in older patients as well. Figure 10-1 shows the VBR values for the patients and control subjects. The group means were significantly different (7.7±3.2 for controls, 14.2±6.4 for patients; ANCOVA: $F=9.5$, $p<.005$), a finding consistent with other studies. There was, however, consid–

Table 10–2
Comparison of Mean VBRs by Decade

Age	Schizophrenics	Controls
50–60	8.5	7.3
61–70	14.7	6.3
71–80	13.7	9.4
81–90	10.5	9.7 (*n*=1)
<90	17.5	––

erable overlap between the groups. In each age decade, the schizo-phrenic patients had larger mean ventricular size (Table 10–2), and advancing age was associated with larger ventricles in both patients and controls.

For the cortical atrophy measures, the difference between patients and controls was less obvious. Figure 10–2 shows the distribution of widths for the sylvian and interhemispheric fissures and cortical sulci. Although there was a trend for dilated cortical sulci in the schizophrenic patients, this did not reach statistical significance.

Effects of Aging

The cerebrospinal fluid–filled spaces of the brain increase in size with age as shown in many CT studies of normal aging (Barron, Jacobs, & Kinkel, 1976; Earnest, Heaton, Wilkinson, & Manke, 1979; Gyldensted, 1977; Meese, Kluge, Grumme, & Hopfenmuller, 1980; Zatz, Jernigan, & Ahumada, 1982). The present study was consistent with these reports. For the controls as well as the patients, increasing age was associated with larger VBR. Furthermore, the variability of normal ventricular size became greater in later years. As Figure 10–1 illustrates, the degree of increase in VBR with age was similar in both the schizophrenic patients and the control subjects, though the variance appeared to increase more in the former group. The data did not suggest a meaningfully different effect of age on VBR for the two groups, and the samples were too small to make more conclusive comparisons.

To further explore differential effects of age, the values from this study were compared to those from a similar study (Weinberger *et al.*, 1979*a*) that found a mean VBR of 3.5 for a sample of normal volunteers between the ages of 20 and 50 (mean age 30). This was half the mean VBR of the controls (mean age 66) in the present study. In the earlier study, the mean VBR for schizophrenic patients was 8.7, almost 40% less than that of the patients reported here. Clearly, both groups showed an aging effect, which does not obscure the finding of larger ventricles in the elderly chronic schizophrenic

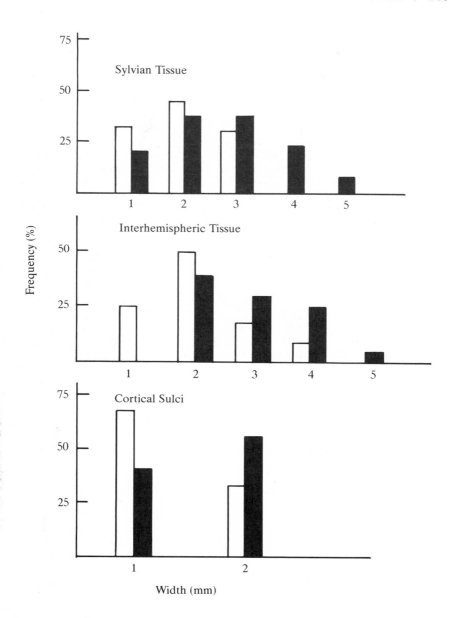

Figure 10–2. Distribution of widths: open bars are controls, closed bars are patients. Sylvian tissue, interhemispheric tissue, cortical sulci.

patients. The normal subjects, if anything, appeared to show a slightly greater percentage increase in ventricular size with aging. This is most probably a "law of initial values" phenomenon, in that the ventricles of the normal patients have considerably more room for expansion. We should, however, add a note of caution—ours was not a prospective longitudinal study of patients and controls as they age, but a cross–sectional study comparing subjects from different age groups.

The effect of age on cortical structures was not directly addressed by the data. The sample per decade was too small for statistical analysis. However, in a similar study of younger patients (Weinberger *et al.*, 1979*b*), no controls had sylvian or interhemispheric fissure width in excess of 3 mm or cortical sulci width greater than 2 mm. These limits were exceeded by more than 25%, 50%, and 35%, respectively, of the controls in the older age group. The distribution of widths was similarly shifted to the right for the older schizophrenic patients compared to their younger counterparts. Thus, both groups showed aging effects. It is interesting that the group difference in cortical structures observed between younger patients and controls was not found in the older samples. This has also been reported elsewhere (Johnstone, Crow, Frith, Stevens, Kreel, & Husband, 1978). In contrast to its effects on VBR, aging appears to obscure the difference in cortical parameters between schizophrenic patients and controls. This may be a result of the limitations inherent in making precise cortical measurements on CT scans. True differences in the effect of age on the cerebral cortex may possibly exist between the two groups.

Effects of Institutionalization and Drug Treatment

In light of their extreme duration of institutionalization and drug treatment, the elderly patients in this study were an ideal group for observing the cerebral toxicity of drug and institutional treatments. Do these forms of therapy cause cerebral atrophy in the form of enlarged ventricles and dilated fissures and sulci? To demonstrate this, the effect of age must be isolated. The simplest way is to add the normal aging effect (i.e., the mean VBR of elderly controls minus the mean VBR of the young controls) to the mean VBR of the young schizophrenics. The result should approximate the inherent schizophrenic VBR plus the effect of aging 36 years, assuming the effect is directly additive. If the sum is considerably less than the VBR of the elderly schizophrenic patients in the present study, then secondary causes of enlarged VBR must be considered (e.g., drug and institutional therapy).

We found the computed VBR to be 12.9, only 11% less than the actual VBR. This is probably within the expected error of the method. It appears, therefore, that the effects of prolonged institutionalization and drug treatment on ventricular size are minimal. The finding that elderly schizophrenic patients have much larger ventricles than do their younger counterparts is consistent simply with the effects of normal aging. In fact, relative to their control populations, the older patients had less deviant VBRs than did the younger patients.

The effect of treatment on cortical structures is more difficult to assess. Since the difference between patients and controls disappears in the elderly, it seems unlikely that psychiatric treatment is a cause of cortical atrophy.

DISCUSSION

This investigation was an attempt to resolve three issues germane to the study of schizophrenia and aging. Although the results must be viewed as preliminary, they are consistent with other reports and tentative conclusions seem justified.

Cerebral Atrophy

The first conclusion is that cerebral atrophy, seen on a CT scan as enlarged ventricles and less frequently as dilated cortical fissures and sulci, exists in elderly chronic schizophrenic patients in a more extreme form than can be explained solely on the basis of advanced age. In other words, the findings described in young schizophrenic patients were confirmed. One potential problem with this conclusion involves the control group. If it did not truly represent elderly individuals, then the results might be spurious. A review of other studies of ventricular size in healthy elderly subjects shows considerable variability of normal ventricular size (Barron et al., 1976; Earnest et al., 1979; Zatz et al., 1982). In Table 10–3, the present study is compared with two other reports that used similar methodology. Our controls were very much like those of Barron et al. and

Table 10–3
Normal Means ± SD Ventricular Size (VBR):
Summary of Three Studies

Age	Barron et al.	Earnest et al.	Present study
50–59	5.2 ± 0.6	—	6.9 ± 3.1 (n=5)
60–70	6.4 ± 0.8 (n=15)	10.5 ± 2.9 (n=13)	6.3 ± 3.7 (n=6)
70–79	11.5 ± 1.2 (n=15)	10.9 ± 4.4 (n=17)	9.4 ± 2.7 (n=4)

somewhat different from those of Earnest *et al.* These discrepancies probably reflect idiosyncracies involved in performing planimetry (for a discussion of methodological issues see Weinberger *et al.*, 1983). Nevertheless, all of the controls cited in Table 10–2 have smaller mean ventricles than do the patients in this study. Some of the patients in this study had quite dramatic ventricular enlargement. Figure 10–3 shows examples of such CT scans. Although the findings are nonspecific and not diagnostic, their appearance is striking. Most neuroradiologists would consider these scans as showing marked cerebral atrophy.

Cortical atrophy also may be found in elderly schizophrenic patients to a greater degree than in similarly aged healthy individuals. This finding, however, is not clear. In fact, the only other CT study of elderly schizophrenic patients (Johnstone *et al.*, 1978) did not show this. We believe two primary reasons account for the inconsistency. First, the effects of aging obscure differences between patients and controls. Second, cortical atrophy is difficult to quantify. The method is less precise and less reliable than the VBR technique. If large samples were employed, the statistical differences might have been more persuasive.

Aging Effect

The second conclusion is that, at least for ventricular enlargement, the age factor is additive to the schizophrenia factor. Aging does not appear to influence ventricular size in a qualitatively distinct manner for either schizophrenic patients or normal controls. The additive nature of the aging factor may have clinical implications. Whereas ventricular enlargement is clinically mild in younger patients, when combined with the effect of aging it may become quite marked. Patients with this degree of atrophy may have less cerebral compensatory capacity. Further study is necessary to clarify the implications of this finding.

Treatment Effect

Since the first report of enlarged ventricles in schizophrenia, the finding has been questioned as a possible effect of drugs and institutionalization. This now appears unlikely. Most studies in young patients have failed to show a correlation between ventricular size and either duration of hospitalization or drug treatment. Two recent reports have described large ventricles in first episode schizophreniform patients prior to any psychiatric treatment (Nyback, Wiesel, Berggren, & Hindmarsh, 1982; Weinberger, DeLisi, Perman, Targum, & Wyatt, 1982).

The present study supports these other investigations. When our results are compared to those of a previous study of younger patients, the larger ventricles in the older patients are consistent solely with the additive effects of aging. No evidence for neuroleptic therapy or

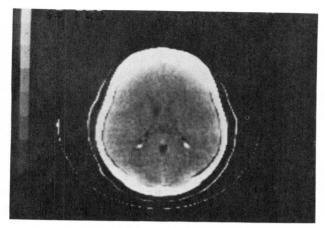

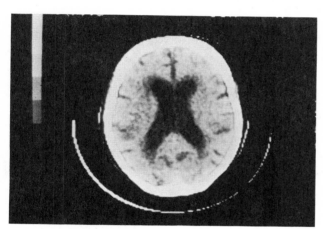

Figure 10–3. CT scans of three chronic schizo-phrenic patients showing enlarged ventricles. Two and three also show cortical atrophy.

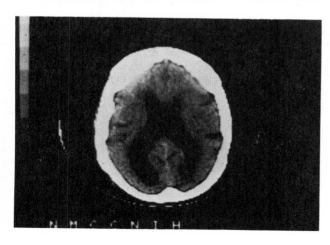

chronic institutionalization as a cause of cerebral atrophy was found. From this observation, it may be inferred that subtle environmental factors have little impact on ventricular size.

A recent study by Reveley, Reveley, Clifford, and Murray (1982) is relevant here. Comparing ventricular size of adult twins from 11 monozygotic twin pairs, they found that ventricular size among twins correlated at the 0.98 level. This landmark finding suggests that, in spite of the vagaries and stresses of day to day existence, in the absence of neurological disorder the primary determinant of ventricular size is congenital. One interesting case was a 72-year-old chronic schizophrenic patient who, despite 30 years of hospitalization and 20 years of continuous neuroleptic treatment, showed no evidence of either enlarged ventricles or cortical atrophy.

Implications for Future Research

The most obvious need in this area is to confirm these preliminary findings. It cannot be overemphasized that the findings reported here would be confirmed most conclusively in a longitudinal study. Our cohort comparison has limitations for investigating long-term effects. Questions about the etiology and pathogenic relevance of ventricular enlargement are probably best considered in younger patients where aging is less of a complication.

This study raises certain issues that are particularly germane to schizophrenia in later life. Foremost among them is the question of how schizophrenic dementia relates to cerebral atrophy. It has long been known that many elderly schizophrenic patients achieve a "burned out" state that in many ways is clinically indistinguishable from senile dementia. One could hypothesize that large ventricles in early life predispose a schizophrenic patient to such burn out. Perhaps the effects of aging, which have only minor implications for cognitive function in most individuals, are especially problematic in cases with preexisting atrophy. This could be tested by evaluating cognitive performance in elderly chronic schizophrenic patients grouped according to ventricular size. Grouping patients by ventricular size has been productive in research with younger patients and it may help reduce the problems of heterogeneity common to samples of schizophrenic patients. This strategy should prove useful in research with elderly populations as well.

11

Schizophrenia in the Senium: Symptom State, Platelet Monoamine Oxidase Activity, and Cognitive Function

T. Peter Bridge

Richard Jed Wyatt

Saint Elizabeths Hospital

Washington, D.C.

Schizophrenic patients have been classically described (Kraepelin, 1971; Bleuler, 1950) as deteriorating progressively across the life span to a regressed, demented state. Nevertheless, the literature does not uniformly support this invariable deteriorating course (Bridge, Cannon–Spoor, & Wyatt, 1978). Only ten studies could be identified that followed the course of schizophrenic illness into the senium. The majority of these studies, either by Russian or European investigators, found a variable but substantial proportion of patients who had decreased schizophrenic symptomatology during the post-involutional years. The Russian investigators in particular noted the greatest symptomatic improvement in the involutional years (ages 55–64) (Molchanova 1975; Zukhovski, 1976). They also reported, and their views were amplified by Manfred Bleuler (1976), that the late life decrease in schizophrenic symptomatology was accompanied by positive changes such as improved sociability, work capacity, and interpersonal relatedness.

If, in fact, schizophrenic symptoms do change ("burn out") in later life, what causes the change? Although a number of psychopharmacologists have also observed this symptomatic change, none has suggested a late onset of drug responsiveness (Davis, 1974; Imlah, 1976). Reduced hepatic function, distribution changes, or end organ sensitivity changes often necessitate reduction of phenothiazine dosages in the elderly, but Davis (1974) states that these "burnt out" patients often do as well with no medication at all. Among the numerous biological variables correlated with schizophrenic symptomatology, one that also appears to vary with age is the change in activity of the enzyme monoamine oxidase (MAO).

Reporting on elderly psychiatric patients and controls, early studies by Robinson, Nies, and colleagues (Robinson, *et al.*, 1972; Nies, Robinson, Lamborn, and Lampert, 1973) demonstrated increases in platelet MAO activity with advancing age. Examination of this phenomenon in our laboratories using a recently developed, complete platelet population collection technique (Wise, Potkin, Bridge, Phelps, Cannon–Spoor, & Wyatt, 1980) produced similar findings. In our study of a population of psychiatrically normal adults, platelet MAO activity increased with age after 50 (Bridge, Wise, Potkin, Phelps, & Wyatt, 1981). As with Robinson's and Nies' (1972, 1973) earlier work, these are cross–sectional data and are limited as such. Interestingly, however, Breakefield and colleagues have observed increases in fibroplast MAO activity in cell cultures from older individuals as well as in cell cultures that become senescent (Breakefield, Giller, Nurn- berger, Castiglione, Buchsbaum, & Gershon, 1980). Such evidence suggests that the increase in platelet MAO activity observed in the postinvolutional years may be a developmental phenomenon, rather than solely a cohort effect.

During the last decade, reduced activity of platelet MAO has been widely observed in chronic schizophrenic patients (Wyatt, Potkin, Bridge, Phelps, & Wise, 1980). The majority of studies show this reduction, although at least part of the decrease is probably due to neuroleptic drugs (Jackman & Meltzer, 1980; DeLisi *et al.*, 1981).

In studying elderly populations, both early and contemporary investigators concur on the importance of identifying neuroanatomic and neurochemical correlates in dementia generally and in schizo- phrenia specifically. Although considerable evidence exists for a cholinergic deficit in senile dementia of the Alzheimer type (SDAT), noradrenergic changes have been reported in both SDAT and schizo- phrenic patients, (Mann, Lincoln, & Yates, 1980; Mann & Yates, 1981; Adolffson, Gottfries, Roos, & Winblad, 1979*b*; Vijayashankar & Brody, 1979; Bondareff, Mountjoy, & Roth, 1981; Kleinman, Bridge, & Karoum, 1980; Farley, Price, & McCullough, 1978). We, therefore, decided to examine two of the enzymes important in catechol- aminegic metabolism with respect to cognitive function in a group of elderly schizophrenic patients and controls.

METHOD

To assess the relationship of advancing age and platelet MAO activity upon schizophrenic symptomatology, psychiatric patients over age 50 whose first hospital records were available were examined. They were included in the study if their initial records indicated a Research Diagnostic Criteria (RDC) diagnosis of schizophrenia (Spitzer *et al.*, 1977) as determined by two board certified psychi- atrists. Interviews by the same two psychiatrists and the patients' hospital records for the year prior to the interviews provided a present–state diagnosis by RDC criteria. A total of 34 patients, 29 female and 5 male, with a mean length of hospitalization of 19.4 years, satisfied these criteria.

Subjects were further classified as RDC negative, i.e., they did not currently qualify for an RDC diagnosis of schizophrenia, or RDC positive, i.e., they were still diagnosed as schizophrenic and had not manifested major symptomatic change. Then a consensus RDC subtype diagnosis, based on individual examination of the patient's entire history and simultaneous interview of the patient, was rendered by the same two psychiatrists. Subjects were categorized as paranoid (PARA+) or nonparanoid (PARA−) and as auditory hallucinations/delusions present (AH/D+) or absent (AH/D−).

All patients had platelet MAO activity (expressed as nM product/mg protein/hr) determined by methods (Wise et al., 1980) with high reliability, as shown by an intraclass correlation of 0.93 for subjects sampled at two separate times. Plasma DBH activity was also measured by methods described elsewhere (Nagatsu & Udenfriend, 1972). Peripheral measures were chosen because they are minimally invasive. Simultaneous assessments of peripheral and central MAO activity have not been performed in humans; therefore, the ability of a peripheral measure to reflect central noradrenergic activity remains speculative.

Those patients receiving neuroleptics ($n=14$) also had serum neuroleptic concentrations determined by a radioreceptor assay (Rosenblatt, Pert, Coleson, van Kammen, Scott, & Bunney, 1979). For statistical analysis, all neuroleptic dosages were converted to chlorpromazine equivalents (Wyatt & Torgow, 1976). The diagnosing psychiatrists were blind to all biochemical determinations at the time of the interviews.

Since phenothiazines have been reported to reduce platelet MAO activity in chronic dosage (Jackman & Meltzer, 1980; DeLisi et al., 1981), a subsample of patients ($n=20$) who had received no neuroleptics during the previous 6 months was identified. Medication was generally discontinued for side effects or "drug holidays." Patients were matched by age, race, and gender to 23 controls who had no symptoms nor histories of major or functional psychiatric illness. The patient group (16 females, 4 males) had 12 institutionalized subjects, while the control group (19 females, 4 males) had 11 institutionalized subjects. The institutionalized controls all had primary degenerative dementia characterized by dementia; absence of clouded consciousness; impaired abstract thinking, judgment, or other higher cortical disturbances; personality changes; insidious onset; and absence of all other specific causes of dementia. No controls were receiving phenothiazines, and no subjects in either group were taking tricyclic antidepressants or MAO inhibitors.

Control subjects also had platelet MAO activity and DBH activity determined. Controls and nonmedicated patients were further evaluated on the Folstein Mini–Mental State Exam (MMSE), a rapid assessment instrument with scores ranging from 0 to 32; less than 20 indicates dementia (Folstein, Folstein, & McHugh, 1975).

RESULTS

Most importantly, of the 34 patients who qualified for a Research Diagnostic Criteria diagnosis of schizophrenia at the time of admission, only 12 continued to demonstrate symptomatology sufficient to warrant an RDC diagnosis of schizophrenia (see Table 11-1). Since only the first and last years of hospitalization were considered, when this symptomatic change took place is unknown. Nonetheless, this does support the European/Russian view that many schizophrenics demonstrate reduced symptomatology as they age.

Statistical analyses of demographic data, biochemical determinations, and diagnostic data from the elderly schizophrenics were performed by two-tailed t tests for independent groups and multiple linear regression analysis. White and black patients did not differ significantly with respect to MAO activity, DBH activity, or Mini-Mental State scores. Females tended to have greater MAO activity than males ($p<0.1$), consistent with previous studies of younger schizophrenics and older normals, but the small number ($n=4$) of males did not allow for any conclusive statement. None of the symptom classifications showed significant differences between groups with respect to DBH activity, but all three classifications significantly separated the patient group by high and low MAO activity in bivariate comparisons.

Several studies have indicated an inhibitory effect of chronic neuroleptic dosage upon platelet MAO. Although a rigorous on-off study was not possible for these older patients, Table 11-2 shows no mean differences between those patients on or off neuroleptics with respect to platelet MAO activity. Among medicated patients, the difference in MAO activity by RDC classification was significant, as in the full sample. The AH/D and PARA pairs did not, however, demonstrate significant differences in platelet MAO activity.

Table 11-1
Platelet Monoamine Oxidase (MAO) Activity by Symptom
Classification Groups for Elderly Schizophrenics

	MAO (mean)	Age (mean)	n
RDC positive	22.3**	73.9	12
RDC negative	33.5	79.8	22
Paranoia present	23.4	69.7	14
Paranoia absent	28.9	76.5	20
Auditory hallucinations/delusions present	21.6*	73.8	8
Auditory hallucinations/delusions absent	30.0	75.1	26

Note. $n=34$; *Significant at $p<.01$; **Significant at $p<.001$

Table 11-2
Neuroleptic Usage and Platelet Monoamine Oxidase (MAO) Activity

Group	All patients on neuroleptics	All patients off neuroleptics	RDC+ patients on neuroleptics	RDC− patients on neuroleptics
n	14	20	7	7
MAO (nM/mg/hr)	26.4	25.2	22.8	33.6*
CPZ† + equivalents, dosage mg			132.5	341.8
Duration of treatment, years			21.8	21.0
Serum neuroleptic level (ng/ml/CPZ)		826.0	506.8	

*Significant at $p<.01$; †CPZ = chlorpromazine

Within the medicated subsample, neuroleptic dosage, calculated in chlorpromazine equivalents, correlated negatively with age ($r=-.58$, $p=.08$). In contrast, platelet MAO activity tended to correlate directly with neuroleptic dosage ($r=.48$, $p=.08$), and reached significance when the effects of age were partialed out ($r=.64$, $p=.02$). When the effects of neuroleptic dosage and age were partialed out, the correlation with RDC classification remained significant ($r=.64$, $p=.02$). The other two classification groups did not demonstrate significant correlation with platelet MAO activity, and no significant correlations were found for serum neuroleptic levels with any of the other independent variables.

The multiple linear regression analysis showed that, in both the medicated and nonmedicated samples, only the RDC +/– classification significantly increased the explanatory power of the main effects model after controlling for the effects of the demographic variables and drug dosage/serum neuroleptic levels (Table 11–3). The AH/D/ +/– classification, however, tended toward significance in the nonmedicated group.

It is interesting to note that of the 14 medicated patients, 6 had their neuroleptic treatment discontinued after participation in this study. After 12 months neuroleptic-free, the drug-free platelet MAO activities showed an intraclass correlation with the medicated value of 0.79 for these patients.

The matched patient and control groups were not significantly different with respect to age, race, or gender, and there were no across group differences for either plasma DBH activity or MMSE scores. Within and across groups comparisons by institutional status,

Table 11–3

Select Results of the Regression of Platelet Monoamine Oxidase Activity (nM/mg/hr) on Demographic Variables, Neuroleptic Dosage, and Diagnostic Status

Independent variables	Medicated ($n=14$)	Nonmedicated ($n=20$)
Age	.12	.33*
Gender	–2.17*	–2.62*
Neuroleptic dosage[a]	.01	——
Serum neuroleptic level (pg/ml)	.06	——
Research diagnostic criteria symptoms, presence/absence	7.34	12.68*
Auditory hallucinations/delusions presence/absence	2.71	2.28
Paranoia, presence/absence	3.6	6.88

[a]Calculated as chlorpromazine equivalents; *Significant at $p<.05$

as seen in Table 11–4, showed that the institutionalized control subjects were significantly older than those living in the community. The institutionalized control subjects also had increased platelet MAO activity, but this was most likely reflective of the age difference. Furthermore, the institutionalized subjects were more likely to have evidence of cognitive impairment, which was at least partially attributable to the older age of these subjects.

Examining the data by demented/nondemented status (MMSE below/above 20), no differences within or across groups emerged for age, but the demented controls demonstrated greater platelet MAO activity than either the demented schizophrenic or the nondemented controls. Furthermore, the schizophrenic patients and the controls revealed divergent patterns of plasma DBH activity across demented/nondemented status. Low DBH activity was associated with dementia in the control group while the reverse was seen in the schizophrenic sample. This relationship reached significance, however, only in the control group.

These patterns from the bivariate data were generally confirmed in the correlational analysis. Age and MAO activity were significantly correlated for controls ($r=0.49$, $p=.02$), for patients ($r=0.47$, $p=.01$), and for the entire group ($r=0.54$, $p=.001$). Age was significantly correlated inversely to MMSE scores, and plasma DBH activity tended to have an inverse relationship with age.

Since age has important and evidently divergent relationships with the other variables (MAO, DBH, MMSE scores) in this sample, age was used as the independent variable in the simple or bivariate model of the multiple regression analysis predicting the dependent variable, MMSE scores.

In the simple model, age explains 37% of the variance in MMSE scores in this group of older schizophrenics and elderly controls (Table 11–5). In the main effects model, age continued to be a significant variable, and the entire set of variables explained 63% of the variance in the MMSE scores. It should be noted that dummy variables for race, gender, institutional status, and schizophrenic status were included in the analysis. Although age as a predictor of MMSE scores became much less significant in the main effects model, gender and race did not significantly predict MMSE scores in this sample. Having initially controlled for age, first in the simple model and then in the main effects model, both platelet MAO and plasma DBH activities were significant predictors of the MMSE scores in the main effects model.

Since institutional status was also a highly significant variable in the main effects model, the relationship of the two enzymes' activities to MMSE scores were examined across the four groups: hospitalized schizophrenics, community dwelling schizophrenics, nursing home residents, and community dwelling controls. The community based sample demonstrated a significant negative relationship of platelet MAO activity with cognitive performance on the MMSE. The institutionalized sample did not, however, show any

Table 11-4
Mean Patient/Control Group Variable (± Standard Error of the Mean)
by Institutional Status and Demented/Nondemented Status

	Schizophrenics	Control	T test
Age			
Institution	75.5±3.3	82.5±2.0	ns
Community	69.3±3.6	70.1±2.2	ns
T test	ns	T=5.9, p<.0001	
Demented	75.1±3.4	80.5±2.3	ns
Nondemented	68.0±5.9	74.1±3.9	ns
T test	ns		
Platelet monoamine oxidase activity[a]			
Institution	27.5±2.0	42.5±3.5	T=3.86, p<.0009
Community	24.3±3.4	30.7±4.1	ns
T test	ns	T=5.9, p<.0001	
Demented	28.7±2.2	34.1±3.9	T=3.4, p<.003
Nondemented	23.5±2.7	30.7±4.1	ns
T test	ns	T=2.2, p.=3	
Serum dopamine beta hydroxylase activity[b]			
Institution	37.9±6.2	30.0±5.3	ns
Community	53.8±10.5	45.4±6.8	ns
T test	ns	ns	
Demented	50.2±8.2	29.9±5.3	T=2.07, p<0.05
Nondemented	34.6±6.5	45.4±6.8	ns
T test	ns	T=1.99, p<.05	
Mini-Mental State Exam scores			
Institution	15.4±1.7	8.5±1.5	T=2.26, p<. 01
Community	19.6±2.6	28.0±1.5	T=2.98, p<. 009
T test	ns	T=9.3, p<0.0001	

[a] MM/ng/hr
[b] mM/L/min

Table 11–5
Multiple Linear Regression Analysis on Mini–Mental State Exam
Scores (MMSE) for Entire Sample and for Institutional Subgroups

All subjects (n=43)			
Main effects model	SSE 1327	F Ratio	12.86
	DFE 37	Prob	.006
	MSE 35.9	r^2	.63
Dependent variable:	MMSE		

Independent variables	Parameter estimate	T ratio	Prob
All subjects (n=43)			
Intercept	32.8	5.21	.0001
Age	−.26	−2.47	.02
INST[a]	9.45	4.28	.001
MAO[b]	−.19	−1.98	.05
DBH[c]	−.08	−1.98	.05
SCZ[d]	−1.94	−.94	.35
Nursing home (n=11)	F ratio=.45	Prob=.72	r^2=.13
Intercept	−7.50	.07	.94
Age	.07	.16	.88
MAO[b]	−.05	−.34	.75
DBH[c]	.09	.92	.38
Hospitalized schizophrenics (n=12)	F ratio=2.42	Prob=.14	r^2=.48
Intercept	30.33	3.90	.0005
Age	−.32	−2.39	.04
MAO[b]	.07	.26	.80
DBH[c]	−.08	1.06	.31
Control (n=12)	F ratio=12.96	Prob=.005	r^2=.87
Intercept	49.98	6.86	.0005
Age	.25	−1.82	.12
MAO[b]	−.29	−3.52	.01
DBH[c]	.13	−3.44	.01
Nonhospitalized schizophrenics (n=8)	F ratio=5.04	Prob=.07	r^2=.56
Intercept	13.45	2.03	.11
Age	.22	−1.20	.29
MAO[b]	−.35	−1.96	.11
DBH[c]	.20	−3.25	.03

[a] INST = Institutional status
[b] MAO = Platelet monoamine oxidase activity, mM/mg/hr
[c] DBH = Plasma dopamine beta hydroxylase activity, mM/L/min
[d] SCZ = Schizophrenic diagnosis

significant relationship between platelet MAO activity and cognitive performance.

For all groups except the nursing home residents, plasma DBH activity had an indirect relationship with cognitive performance on the MMSE, reaching statistical significance again in the community based sample. Among nursing home residents, lower plasma DBH activity was associated with poorer performance on the MMSE. The fact that this relationship did not reach statistical significance within this group may be attributed partially to sample size and partially to the minimal range of variation in performance on the MMSE (i.e., all within the demented range).

DISCUSSION

Among a group of older chronic psychiatric patients, all with symptomatic evidence of schizophrenia consistent with RDC at the time of their admission, approximately two-thirds (22 of 34) no longer qualified for an RDC diagnosis of schizophrenia at the time of this study. The symptomatic and nonsymptomatic groups did not differ on age, race, gender or neuroleptic dosage (calculated in chlorpromazine equivalents) for those receiving medication. Although no clear evidence of any neuroleptic effect upon platelet MAO activity appeared in this cross-sectional analysis, the data were analyzed separately for those patients who were and those who were not presently receiving neuroleptics.

Among both groups, patients with greater MAO activity were more likely to be asymptomatic. The previously reported direct relationship between age and platelet MAO activity was evident only in the nonmedicated group. The more specific subgroups of schizophrenic patients (i.e., with auditory hallucinations and delusions or with paranoia) had lower platelet MAO activity, but the differences were not statistically significant in this sample. The failure to replicate the observed association of subtype diagnoses in younger schizophrenic patients with decrements in platelet MAO activity may reflect: (1) the ability of the symptomatic/asymptomatic paradigm to explain a greater proportion of the variance in enzyme activity than the other two models; (2) the age of the subjects; or (3) the examination of the subtyping data after having controlled for the variance due to demographic and neuroleptic medication variables.

The interrelationship among schizophrenia, platelet MAO activity, and age are, at the least, complex. Whatever enduring effects exposure to neuroleptics may have upon platelet MAO activity, the elderly schizophrenic patients from this sample most likely to demonstrate symptoms of schizophrenia appeared to be those with low platelet MAO activity, after controlling for the effects of demographic variables and medication. It would be interesting to observe longitudinally the fluctuations of clinical state, platelet MAO activity, and neuroleptic usage. More importantly, however, these data argue for a reexamination of psychiatry's classically held view that schizophrenia is a chronic disease whose generally unremitting course leads to a terminal, regressed demented state. Further large scale studies can speak more conclusively to this, but our data are consistent with those European studies that have followed schizophrenic patients' symptom state longitudinally.

Changes in the catecholamine system were also associated with dementia as reflected in peripheral enzyme measures present for some of the subjects in this study. Only the nursing home residents, the group most likely to manifest Alzheimer changes, showed a direct relationship between cognitive performance and plasma DBH activity. By history, the nursing home patients demonstrated a steady, rather than decremental, decline in cognitive function, consistent with Alzheimer changes rather than multi-infarct dementia. This group, among the four subsamples, showed a pattern of reduced DBH activity associated with dementia that agrees with Cross, Mann and Vijayashankar's studies of Alzheimers patients. From the data in this sample, the nursing home residents would be the group most likely to demonstrate a combined pattern of reduced DBH activity (therefore reduced formation of NE) as well as increased MAO activity (therefore increased metabolism of NE) associated with poor performance on the MMSE. The opposite pattern, however, reached significance for the community based sample.

Why the community based sample, in particular, demonstrated these indirect relationships of catechol enzyme activities and cognitive performance is hard to explain. Although none of the schizophrenic patients were taking neuroleptics at the time of the study, prior chronic neuroleptic usage might possibly have enduring metabolic effects upon these enzymes. Although difficult to conceptualize, other, now unspecified, effects of institutionalization may possibly alter the relationship of these catechol enzymes to cognitive performance. Certainly across all groups a significant relationship of catechol enzyme activity and cognitive performance appears, after controlling for age and institutional status. A larger, more comprehensive study that considers institutional status as well as diagnostic groups in both pre- and postmortem assessments is needed.

COGNITIVE AND PSYCHOLOGICAL VARIABLES

Cognitive deficit is associated with the onset of schizophrenia and appears to be partially reversible in some patients. Some studies show that such deficits are not dramatically affected by age, and that some patients even improve in old age. Hospitalization is not the determinant, and drugs and ECT do not explain the impairment either. The cognitive deficit of schizophrenics appears much like that shown by neurological patients with diffuse brain disorders. It also closely resembles the type of cognitive impairment seen with normal advancing age. The effect of such neuropsychological deficits on everyday function and long-term prognosis has yet to be investigated.

Performance on information processing tasks was compared for normal elderly and for schizophrenics, and both manifested similar types of impairment. However, several questions remain. Do the processes of aging in some way offset the processes of schizophrenia, leading to remission of cognitive symptoms? At what juncture in the information processing sequence does function break down? In the past it was assumed that the problem centered on attentional mechanisms alone, but the solution promises to be far more complex.

12

Schizophrenic Deficits in Intelligence and Abstract Thinking: Influence of Aging and Long-Term Institutionalization

Martin Harrow

Michael Reese Hospital and Medical Center

The University of Chicago

Joanne Marengo

Michael Reese Hospital and Medical Center

The University of Chicago

Michael Pogue–Geile

The University of Pittsburgh

Thomas J. Pawelski

Michael Reese Hospital and Medical Center

Northwestern University

The current research was designed to examine relationships among major defect state symptoms (i.e., intellectual ability and concrete thinking), institutionalization, and aging in chronic schizophrenic patients. Intellectual skills and abstract thinking are purported to deteriorate gradually over the course of schizophrenic disorders. However, the relative impact of duration of disorder versus length of hospitalization on cognitive deficit remains unknown.

Several investigators have attempted to distinguish between behaviors arising from the basic disease process and the effects of being removed from the community on a semipermanent or periodic basis. Wing and Brown's (1970) longitudinal study suggested that a number of schizophrenic behavioral deficits can be remedied by introducing environmental change. In contrast, Johnstone *et al.* (Johnstone, Cunningham, Gold, Crow, & Macmillan, 1981) employing a cross–sectional design, reported that the deficit states developed by chronic schizophrenics constituted aspects of the deteriorative process and were minimally due to environmental circumstances or long–term institutionalization.

Severe intellectual deficit and concrete thinking were viewed as major features of schizophrenia prior to the modern treatment era (Benjamin, 1944; Goldstein, 1944). Since the widespread use of phenothiazines and with the introduction of current psychotherapeutic and milieu therapy techniques, the clinical picture of schizophrenia has changed. Many believe that very severe decline and deterioration has either been reduced or eliminated. However, concrete thinking and intellectual dysfunction have not been studied extensively in multiyear, chronic schizophrenics whose disorder began before the phenothiazine era.

Investigations by our own research team suggest that concrete modes of thought are demonstrated only in certain types of schizophrenia (Harrow & Quinlan, in press), and are a prominent feature in chronic schizophrenia (Harrow, Buckley–Marengo, Growe, & Grinker, 1979). In addition, when severe deficits in abstract abilities appear, they are primarily associated with a more general intellectual deficit (Harrow & Adler, 1974; Harrow, Adler, & Hanf, 1974).

Recent research has also introduced some doubts as to whether a loss of abstract abilities is a prominent feature of acute schizophrenia (Wright, 1975; Oltmanns & Neale, 1975, 1978). Our studies suggest a deficit in abstract ability during acute psychopathological states (Buckley–Marengo & Harrow, 1979a). However, symptomatic remission appears to instigate a return of abstract capacities for many schizophrenic patients during the early course of the disorder (Buckley–Marengo & Harrow, 1979b).

We have also studied the effects of aging and chronic institutionalization on positive cognitive symptoms (Andreasen & Olsen, 1982). Our results showed no age–related differences within either continuously or intermittently hospitalized chronic schizophrenic groups on positive types of thought disorder, such as bizarre–idiosyncratic thinking (Harrow, Grossman, Silverstein, & Meltzer, 1982; Harrow, Silverstein, & Marengo, 1983; Marengo, Harrow, Lanin-Kettering, & Wilson, 1985).

The current research was designed to examine whether various areas of cognitive deficit and intellectual dysfunction in the chronic schizophrenic are primarily associated with long–term institutionalization and the effects of aging. The specific experimental questions were:

1. With the advances in pharmacological and psychotherapeutic techniques, are defect–state or negative symptoms, such as severe intellectual deficits and concrete thinking, still present in the chronically institutionalized multiyear schizophrenic?
2. Do continuously institutionalized schizophrenics show greater intellectual deficit and concrete thinking than a parallel sample of intermittently hospitalized schizophrenics?
3. Is the concrete thinking of the chronic schizophrenic a function of general intellectual deficit, or is it a separate independent factor?

4. Are intellectual deficit and concrete thinking a function of age in chronic schizophrenia, and how does age interact with differences in the length of institutionalization?

METHOD

Subjects

A group of 39 continuously hospitalized chronic schizophrenic patients and a group of 38 revolving–door (intermittently hospitalized) chronic schizophrenic patients were investigated. For comparison purposes, a group of acutely disturbed young schizophrenic patients was also studied.

The continuously hospitalized chronic schizophrenics were inpatients at a Chicago–area long–term care state psychiatric hospital and had been hospitalized for at least eight of the last 10 years. In contrast, the revolving–door chronic schizophrenics, although inpatients at the same state hospital, had a history of intermittent hospitalization and community tenure rather than continuous hospitalization. The revolving–door patients had their first hospitalization at least 5 years prior to assessment, with at least three separate readmissions since that time.

All the patients in these two groups met the criteria for a schizophrenic diagnosis according to the New Haven Schizophrenia Index (Astrachan *et al.*, 1972), and all had hospital admission diagnoses of schizophrenia. All had been floridly psychotic (i.e., delusional and/or hallucinating) at some point in the course of their disorder. At the time of assessment, however, four of the continuously hospitalized group and four of the revolving–door group showed no evidence of an active psychosis. All the continuously hospitalized patients and 85% of the revolving–door patients were receiving antipsychotic medication at the assessment period.

The continuously institutionalized group had spent significantly more time hospitalized (median=104 months) than had the revolving–door group (median=38 months). The revolving–door group had significantly more hospital admissions (median=6.1 admissions) than the continuously institutionalized schizophrenic group (median=1.6 admissions). These figures document the differences between the two groups in their previous hospital histories and also suggest the severity of disorder present in *both* of these chronic schizophrenic groups.

Despite their differing hospitalization histories, the two groups appeared similar on several premorbid variables. All patients in both groups were selected for and had completed at least 10 years of education. The two groups did not differ significantly in the amount of education completed (median=11.7 years), nor in their age at first hospitalization.

The two groups did differ in current age, with the continuously institutionalized sample being older (mean=43.7 years) than the revolving–door group (mean=31.9 years). To control for this age difference and to investigate possible age–related effects, both the continuously hospitalized and revolving–door patient samples were divided into three age groups: under 35 years (*n*=37), 35 to 44 years (*n*=21), and 45 years and older (*n*=19).

The acute schizophrenic subjects were inpatients from a private short–term treatment hospital in the Chicago area. They met the same diagnostic criteria as the long–term state hospital samples (i.e., evidence of psychotic episodes, a score of at least 4 on the New Haven Schizophrenia Index, and a hospital diagnosis of schizophrenia). These subjects were assessed early in the course of their disorder and were generally younger (mean=20.7 years), better educated (median=12.2 years), and had shorter hospitalization histories (median=5.5 months) than the chronic patients.

Assessment of Intellectual Deficit

Four tests assessing different aspects of cognitive functioning and potential intellectual deficit were administered to the three patient groups. The Information Test of the Wechsler Adult Intelligence Scale (WAIS) was employed to measure general verbal intelligence and long–term recall, and the Comprehension Test of the WAIS was used to assess social problem–solving and social comprehension (Wechsler, 1955).

Assessment of Abstract and Concrete Thinking

Two indexes of concrete thinking were used, the Object Sorting Test (Goldstein & Scheerer, 1941) and the Proverbs Test (Gorham, 1956).

The classical system of administering Part 1 of the Object Sorting Test (OST) was used. The patient was presented with a series of objects. The examiner selected one object (the "starting object"), and asked the patient to find all the other objects that belonged with it. Then the patient was asked to give his/her reason for the selection. This procedure was followed with seven different starting objects.

The OST is composed of two parts: (a) sorting objects into conceptual groups, and (b) verbally discussing the concept used. With sorting behavior the examiner has an opportunity to observe a number of intellectual processes that enter into conceptual thinking. These observations include how rigid or narrow and how fluid or loose the concept formation of the subject is as he/she compares objects to others within a realm, decides on a group, and determines which objects do not belong to the realm (Rapaport, Gill, & Schafer, 1968).

Concrete thinking, defined as the inability to formulate a concept designating a common quality among the chosen set of objects, was assessed through the subject's verbal statements. A response was considered concrete if the generalization or abstract response was not stated, even though it may have been implied. For example, the starting object was a pipe. A patient's concrete response was, "Ashtray for ashes, cigar is like a pipe, matches to light it." "Smoking objects" would be an appropriate abstract conceptualization. If the patient was unable to sort, refused to sort, or only sorted upon the examiner's insistence, the patient's response was also scored concrete. Each response was scored on a 3–point scale (Himmelhoch, Harrow, Tucker, & Hersch, 1973). A maximum of 21 points (7 objects x 3 points) reflects the highest score for concreteness. Satisfactory interrater reliability ($r=.87$) was achieved.

In the second measure of concreteness, the Gorham Proverbs Test, the patient was asked to explain the meaning of 12 proverbs. Concreteness was defined as the tendency to use the key words and ideas from the proverb in their literal form, such as responding to the proverb, "While the cat's away the mice will play," with a discussion of cats and mice.

Responses were systematically scored for concrete thinking by first dividing each proverb into two components (e.g., When the cat's away/the mice will play) and then judging the patient's interpretation of each element on the dimensions of abstract–concrete, abstraction (including inaccurate abstractions), and concreteness. The highest total score for each index summed across proverbs was 24 (12 proverbs x 2 components). Satisfactory interrater reliability ($r=.92$) was achieved for this scoring system. All tests were scored blind as to patient group membership. Further details and criteria for scoring these constructs are found in Marengo, Harrow, and Rogers (1980).

The Proverbs and Part 1 of the OST both assess performance on the dimension of abstract–concrete thinking. However, the nature of the response process differs in terms of the conceptual demands required by the structure of the tests.

The Proverbs Test requires abstract, symbolic thinking and typically does not assess concreteness as a function of perceptually bound thinking. The subject must manipulate symbols, make inferences about relationships, and function at a high level of cognitive activity, entirely on a verbal–intellectual plane. The more complex the proverb and less direct the solution, the greater the claim on language and higher cognitive skills. The Proverbs Test is also vulnerable to differential language skills and subcultural variation. The lack of perceptual cues to help structure the response and the difficult verbal–abstract challenge can lead to considerable deviance in thinking by the patient.

In contrast, the OST requires action accompanied by speech and cognitive work, reminiscent of earlier stages of cognitive development (sensorimotor and concrete operational levels of thinking). The subject begins and organizes the task with the support of tangible modes of thought, directly choosing and manipulating objects and using the auxiliary support of his/her senses. The objects are familiar and, in almost every case, can be sorted on the basis of stereotyped, customary concepts. Memory and passive registration of input may be as much a part of the OST as the active processes of selection and abstraction.

At times, the use of objects that lend themselves to conventional, everyday experience and conceptions (e.g., silverware) may serve to obscure a disorganization in the process of active, high–level concept formation (Rapaport *et al.*, 1968). The OST confronts the subject with numerous alternative objects that demand active concept building and delimiting. The concept must be either used or created amidst many associative possibilities, which can lead to deviant responses by some disturbed patients.

Because of these differences, the scores from the two instruments show low to moderate correlations with each other in some types of samples, and higher correlations with other groups. In this study, a correlation of *r*=.42 was obtained.

AGING AND COGNITIVE DEFICIT IN SCHIZOPHRENIA

Aging and Intellectual Deficit

The first major question investigated concerned the potential influence of aging on cognitive functioning and deficit symptoms in schizophrenia. Tables 12–1 and 12–2 present the means and standard deviations for intellectual performance and concrete thinking for the various age groups.

A series of 2x3 ANOVAs (institutional group x age group) were conducted on the WAIS data. The ANOVAs for the Information Test

Table 12–1
Mean Scores of Schizophrenic Groups on Measures of
Intellectual Ability

Type of schizophrenic sample	Age	WAIS Information		WAIS Comprehension	
		M	*SD*	*M*	*SD*
Continuously institutionalized chronic schizophrenics	below 35	5.6	2.6	4.0	3.1
	35–44	7.1	2.9	5.0	3.1
	>44	6.7	4.1	5.5	3.6
Intermittently hospitalized chronic schizophrenics	below 35	7.8	3.6	6.7	3.7
	35–44	7.4	3.4	6.0	4.9
	>44	6.8	1.9	6.2	2.8
Young nonchronic private hospital schizophrenics	below 35	11.3	3.1	9.7	4.1

Table 12–2
Mean Scores of Schizophrenic Groups on Measures of
Abstract and Concrete Thinking

Type of schizophrenic sample	Age	Object sorting concreteness[a]		Proverbs abstractness[b]	
		M	SD	M	SD
Continuously	below 35	4.8	3.6	7.1	7.6
institutionalized	35–44	4.6	5.0	6.6	6.1
chronic schizophrenics	>44	6.9	6.7	5.9	7.8
Intermittently	below 35	3.1	2.6	11.1	6.1
hospitalized	35–44	10.0	7.0	5.2	6.4
chronic schizophrenics	>44	7.8	8.2	3.0	5.1
Young nonchronic private hospital schizophrenics	below 35	2.9	3.7	14.5	6.6

[a] Higher scales denote more concrete thinking.
[b] Higher scores denote increased abstract abilities.

of verbal intelligence showed no significant main effect for age (F (2,73)=.09, $p<.30$) and no significant interaction (F (2,73)=.56, $p<.30$). Similarly, there was no significant main effect on Social Comprehension for age (F (2,73)=.10, $p<.30$) and no significant interaction (F (2,73)=.44, $p<.30$).

Separate analyses also indicated no significant differences in intellectual performance between younger versus older patients within the continuously institutionalized schizophrenic group; all age groups showed severe deficits on each measure of intellectual performance.

Similarly for the revolving–door schizophrenics, increasing age was not associated with intellectual deficit. Thus in chronic schizophrenics under 60 years old, increasing age was not found to be a potent predictor of increased intellectual deficit.

Aging and Abstract–Concrete Thinking in Schizophrenia

Our findings on the association between age and abstract–concrete thinking for both continuously institutionalized and revolving–door schizophrenic samples suggested some age–related difficulties in abstraction for the chronic schizophrenics. A 2x3 ANOVA showed a significant main effect for age on concrete thinking as measured by the OST (F (2,64)=3.95, $p<.05$). Patients over 45 years of age were consistently more concrete on the OST than the younger (under

35 years of age) schizophrenic group, with some variability shown by the intermediate (35–44 years old) group. A 2x3 ANOVA that tested for the effects of age across continuously hospitalized and revolving–door groups also indicated a greater deficit in abstract performance for older schizophrenics on the Proverbs Test (F (2,71)=3.02, $p<.05$). Thus, schizophrenics who were older than 45 years of age performed more poorly when compared to the younger (under age 35) schizophrenics on both the Object Sorting Test measure of concreteness and the Proverbs Test of abstract performance. It should be emphasized, however, that this sample did not include subjects who were over 60 years of age.

Several factors could account for the greater difficulties in abstract thinking among the older schizophrenics:

1. There may be some deterioration in cognitive functioning specific to schizophrenia over time. With increasing age, schizophrenics may show increasing deficits in complex cognitive areas that are sensitive to such deficits, such as the abstract–concrete dimension.

2. People of all types (i.e., normals, disturbed patients, and schizophrenics) may show increased difficulty with advancing age in complex cognitive areas such as the abstract–concrete dimension.

3. The poorer performance of older schizophrenics on the abstract–concrete dimension may be related, in part, to the secondary psychological effects of reduced striving, leading to reduced performance when complex cognitive functioning is demanded.

LONG–TERM INSTITUTIONALIZATION IN SCHIZOPHRENIA AND COGNITIVE DEFICIT

Institutionalization and Intellectual Performance
in Schizophrenia

The second major question investigated concerns the effect of long-term institutionalization on cognitive deficit in schizophrenia. In general, both the continuously hospitalized and revolving–door samples demonstrated below average intellectual functioning across the two WAIS tests. Mean levels of general verbal intelligence (Information Test) and social problem–solving (Comprehension Test) fell into the dull–normal ranges (IQ=89 or below). Absolute levels of performance were lower on the Comprehension than on the Information Tests, suggesting a relatively greater deficit in social judgment for these chronic schizophrenic groups.

Although not significant, the continuously institutionalized schizophrenic sample showed the poorest overall intellectual functioning of the groups, with only 26% above the dull normal range of intelligence. The relatively low level of intellectual functioning in the revolving–door schizophrenic patients constituted a somewhat unexpected finding. While we did not have direct measures of pre-morbid intellectual functioning, all these patients had at least 10 years of education, and more than half were high school graduates.

To approximate initial intellectual ability level, the sample was divided into three educational groupings: patients who (a) did not finish high school, (b) completed high school, and (c) had some college education. Comparisons of continuously institutionalized versus revolving–door schizophrenics within each educational group showed similar dysfunction when educational achievement was controlled. Further analysis indicated that patients with more education tended to perform better on the intellectual tasks and to show more abstract thinking than patients with less education. The magnitude of this trend was equal for both continuously hospitalized and revolving–door samples.

In contrast to the two chronic state hospital schizophrenic groups, the sample of young nonchronic schizophrenic patients from a private hospital setting showed significantly less intellectual deficit. They generally performed at average and bright–normal intellectual levels (Table 12–1). Although follow–up data indicate that some of these schizophrenics subsequently showed poorer adjustment in other areas of life, they did not show severe intellectual defect symptoms at hospitalization in the early course of disturbance or at subsequent posthospital follow–ups (Buckley–Marengo & Harrow, 1979*b*; Harrow, Grinker, & Silverstein, 1978).

In modern times, most young schizophrenics are not likely to spend many years on the back wards of state hospitals, and the severe continuously hospitalized schizophrenics are more likely to have had initially low intellectual levels and poor integrative ability. Thus, some of the deficit seen in very chronic schizophrenics may be a consequence of initially lower ability levels, rather than a function of lower educational achievement, lower social class, or of the basic disease process. If this formulation is accurate, then initially lower ability levels could explain some of the extremely poor cognitive performance found in the two chronic schizophrenic samples.

Intellectual Deficit in Schizophrenic Patients in the Postphenothiazine Era

One goal of the present research was to assess whether the chronic schizophrenic patients with severe cognitive deficits could still be found in the postphenothiazine era with its milieu therapy and other modern treatment techniques. Thus, the sample of continuously institutionalized schizophrenics was divided:

1. Schizophrenics whose first psychotic break occurred after 1959 (postphenothiazine era).
2. Schizophrenics whose first psychotic break occurred between 1954 and 1959, and the majority of whose hospitalizations occurred since 1959 (predominantly postphenothiazine era).

3. Schizophrenics whose first psychotic break occurred prior to 1954 and who were hospitalized at least 4 years prior to 1959 (predominantly prephenothiazine era).

Although sample sizes were small, the comparisons of pre- and postphenothiazine era schizophrenics showed no significant differences in intellectual function across the two measures of cognitive ability. Severe chronic schizophrenics whose first psychotic break occurred in our modern treatment era can still demonstrate severe intellectual dysfunction similar to those schizophrenics whose first psychotic break occurred during the prephenothiazine era.

Hospitalization and Abstract–Concrete Thinking in Schizophrenia

The data on concrete thinking and deficits in abstract thinking for the schizophrenic samples are presented in Table 12-2. The 2x3 ANOVA (institution group x age group) on the OST measure of concrete thinking and the 2x3 ANOVA on the Proverbs Test measure of abstract thinking showed no significant main effects for type of hospitalization in these chronic schizophrenics.

As a group, the chronic schizophrenics showed high levels of concrete thinking and significant deficits in abstract performance. This included difficulty in abstracting the qualities of immediate stimuli when dealing with routine and simple objects, such as those found in the OST.

For example, a 53–year–old male patient, who had been continuously hospitalized for 18 years, responded when asked to sort other objects that belonged with the pipe: "I don't see anything at the present time that would go with that. We'll leave be as it is now. I prefer to leave as is." This response was given despite the availability of an ash tray, cigar, and other items relevant to smoking.

About 70% of the continuously institutionalized schizophrenics were unable to give any abstract response (even an incorrect one) for over half the proverbs. For example a 55–year–old woman, continuously hospitalized since 1950, responded to "When the cat's away the mice will play," with "When the cat's there he'll bite the mice and kill them."

In contrast, the young nonchronic schizophrenic patients had only mild difficulties on the abstract–concrete dimension. Concreteness was considerably more prevalent ($p<.01$) within the two chronic state hospital samples than in the young nonchronic schizophrenic group. Furthermore, none of the nonchronic schizophrenics showed extreme concrete modes of behavior as many of the multiyear patients did. However, other results suggest that schizophrenics who have yet to demonstrate a chronic disturbance have some limited impairment on the abstract–concrete dimension when compared to parallel samples of disturbed nonschizophrenic patients (Buckley–Marengo & Harrow, 1979a).

Concrete Thinking and Intellectual Ability in Schizophrenia

The relationship between performance on the abstract–concrete dimension and the indexes of intellectual ability was analyzed separately. The significant correlations between intelligence scores and abstract thinking on the Proverbs Test ($r=.51$, $p<.001$) and concreteness on the Object Sorting Test ($r=-.49$, $p<.001$) indicated that abstract–concrete thinking was associated with overall intellectual functioning.

The scores of nine chronic schizophrenics who showed above-average intellectual functioning were analyzed, and six were able to abstract successfully. These data provide strong evidence that the loss of abstract ability coexists with a general deficit in intellectual ability.

Equally striking was the apparent vulnerability to concrete thinking found in some patients who were functioning at average levels of intelligence. Abstract ability seems to be influenced by several factors, with intellectual ability being one such factor, if not the most important. Other factors, particularly acute psychopathology, have also been found to influence abstract ability (Buckley–Marengo & Harrow, 1979a).

In many areas of human functioning, the most complex skills and abilities are the first to be disrupted or interfered with by pathological processes. The abstract–concrete dimension may be especially affected by psychopathology because it is a complex cognitive function involving symbolic manipulation.

CONCLUSION

In this paper we have focused on the potential effects of chronic institutionalization and aging on defect state–negative symptoms in schizophrenia. In addition, we also collected data on the potential effects of chronic institutionalization and aging on positive cognitive symptoms (Andreasen & Olsen, 1982). We employed a comprehensive measure of bizarre–idiosyncratic thinking and a number of individual measures of bizarre–idiosyncratic thinking (Harrow et al., 1982; Harrow & Quinlan, 1985; Harrow et al., 1983; Marengo et al., 1985).

Our results on positive types of thought disorder, such as bizarre–idiosyncratic thinking, showed no age–related differences within either the continuous or intermittently hospitalized chronic schizophrenic groups. Both younger and older schizophrenics tended to demonstrate severe signs of bizarre–idiosyncratic thinking in each schizophrenic sample.

There was a tendency, significant on some measures and near significant on other measures, for more severe bizarre–idiosyncratic thinking to be found among the continuously institutionalized than among the intermittently hospitalized chronic schizophrenics.

In summary, our results indicate the following:

1. Very poor intellectual–cognitive functioning is pervasive in continuously institutionalized schizophrenics from both the pre– and postphenothiazine era.

2. Intellectual deficits are not simply a function of continuous institutionalization, but are also found in many chronic revolving-door schizophrenics.

3. In general, intellectual deficit does not worsen with age among chronic schizophrenics.

4. Concrete thinking and impaired abstraction are still important parts of the clinical picture in chronic schizophrenia. Even young, nonchronic schizophrenics show some limited impairment in this area.

5. Chronic schizophrenics show somewhat more pervasive concrete thinking with age.

6. Impaired abstract performance and concrete thinking in schizophrenia are influenced by intellectual impairment as well as by general levels of psychopathology.

7. In the postphenothiazine era, some schizophrenics are still showing Kraepelinian–type clinical declines with severe cognitive and social impairment.

In this study, neither chronological age nor difference in continuous versus periodic institutionalization bore a strong relationship to the cognitive deficits found in chronic schizophrenia. Long–term hospitalized as well as chronic revolving–door schizophrenics demonstrate severe intellectual deficits.

In contrast, our posthospital follow–up studies of young non-chronic schizophrenics showed only mild to moderate cognitive dysfunction in this group when assessed on the same measures. However, there may be a subgroup of young acute schizophrenics who will become chronic and whose posthospital course will be marked by a gradual decline in cognitive functioning. This remains an unresolved issue.

Overall, the current findings showed some similarity to those of Johnstone *et al.* (1981), suggesting that schizophrenic defect states are more likely due to some putative deteriorative process than to environmental impoverishment. We would add our hypothesis that the defect state features found in some schizophrenics are a consequence of low initial intellectual ability and poor initial integrative ability. Regardless of which factor is more important (schizophrenic deterioration or low initial ability), the data suggest that cognitive deficit in schizophrenia is not due, except in a very small way, to environmental factors or to the effects of continuous institutionalization.

Acknowledgments

This research was supported, in part, by Grant No. MH–26341–08 from the National Institute of Mental Health, Grant No. SIMH–8039–3 from the State of Illinois, DMH–DD, the John D. and Catherine T. MacArthur Foundation, and Four Winds Research Fund.

13 Clinical Neuropsychological Findings in Schizophrenia and Aging

Robert K. Heaton

Michael Drexler

University of Colorado School of Medicine

Previous literature reviews have concluded that patients in most psychiatric diagnostic groups typically do not show significant impairment on clinical neuropsychological tests; therefore, these tests have value in screening for brain disorders in psychiatric settings as well as in other treatment settings (Heaton, Baade, & Johnson, 1978; Heaton & Crowley, 1981). The major exception or complication to this conclusion is that schizophrenics, and particularly chronic schizophrenics, very often perform like brain damaged patients on neuropsychological testing (Goldstein, 1978; Malec, 1978). The reason chronic schizophrenics show organic–like cognitive impairment is still debated, although there is increasing evidence that their neuropsychological deficits are related to demonstrable abnormalities of brain structure and function.

We have reexamined available neuropsychological studies of schizophrenia, placing particular emphasis upon the possible interactions between cognitive impairment and aging. This task was approached with several questions in mind. First, what is the prevalence and nature (severity, pattern) of cognitive deficit in schizophrenia? When does it develop, and does it change in relation to the aging process, clinical status at times of testing, or the long–term course of the schizophrenic illness? Is the impairment related to premorbid factors, such as premorbid intellectual or psychosocial functioning, or to age of disease onset? Finally, to what degree is the deficit related to iatrogenic effects of somatic treatments (drugs, ECT) and to nonbehavioral evidence of abnormal brain structure and function (EEGs, CT scans, etc.)?

We located 100 studies that assessed schizophrenics' neuropsychological functioning at a single point in time. Gross "cross-sectional" comparisons of studies with different outcomes were used to explore possible effects of aging and the other intervening variables mentioned above. We also found 14 longitudinal studies that considered schizophrenics' test performances either before and after disease onset, or at two or more points during the course of their illness. Although small in number, these latter studies provide much more direct evidence of possible changes in cognitive functioning over time.

CROSS–SECTIONAL STUDIES

The 100 cross–sectional studies in this review included some 140 schizophrenic groups. For each of these groups the following information was recorded, if available: group n, mean age and education, sex distribution, chronic/process classification, inpatient/ outpatient status, medication status, whether the patients were in long–term treatment facilities, and the number of neuropsychological tests and test combinations on which they showed impairment or no impairment relative to various reference groups or norms. In addition, because of our interest in patterns of schizophrenics' abilities, if a study used the WAIS or Wechsler Bellevue we recorded mean IQs and subtest scores. We intended to review patterns of results on the Halstead–Reitan Battery as well; however, it was difficult to compare the relevant studies because of inconsistencies in subtest inclusion (partial batteries) and in reporting the results (raw scores versus two "impairment rating" systems).

It should be noted that most studies failed to specify how the subjects were selected or whether the groups were representative of the general population in the treatment setting or the population of patients sent for testing because of suspicion of neurological impairment. The criteria for psychiatric diagnoses usually were not mentioned, and clinically relevant subtypes of schizophrenics rarely were identified and considered separately. Usually inadequate or unspecified criteria were used to ensure that the psychiatric patients did not have a neurological disorder. Neurological comparison groups often were poorly described and/or irrelevant to the differential diagnosis of schizophrenia versus dementia due to other causes.

Mean age was not reported for 29 of the schizophrenic groups. Reported ages for the remaining groups ranged from 15 to 73 years, but only 13 groups had a mean age of 50 or older. The fact that so few older groups were represented obviously precludes any firm conclusions about cognitive functioning of schizophrenics in old age.

Only about half of the schizophrenic groups ($n=74$) had their mean years of education reported. Two–thirds of these groups averaged 9 to 11 years, suggesting that many patients studied were somewhat below average in general intelligence.

Sex distribution was not given for 38 schizophrenic groups, and most of the remaining groups were either all males ($n=60$) or mostly males ($n=22$). This reflects the fact that many of the studies were conducted in Veterans Administration facilities and further limits the generalizability of the findings.

Table 13-1
Clinical/Treatment Status of Schizophrenic Groups
Involved in 100 Neuropsychological Studies

	Chronic groups	100% inpatient groups (n)	Groups in long-term facilities (n)	Groups taking medications (n)
Yes	66	122	74	40
No	18	7	33	4
Not reported	56	11	33	96

Table 13-1 summarizes what was reported about the clinical and treatment status of the schizophrenic groups studied. These studies did not use any consistent definition of chronicity, and many of the groups called "acute" or "recent admissions" were *not* being tested shortly after the onset of their illness. Several studies defined length of hospitalization as time at the particular institution where the study was being done, apparently ignoring any previous hospitalizations elsewhere. It is probably fair to say that the 66 groups called chronic were in fact chronic, but that many of the other groups were fairly chronic as well. Almost all subjects were inpatients, and most of the studies were conducted in long-term facilities. Since relatively few schizophrenics require long-term institutionalization, it is unlikely that the test results of such convenience samples in hospitals accurately represent the neuropsychological functioning of schizophrenics generally considered. Finally, Table 13-1 shows that medication status was not reported for almost 70% of the groups, and only 37% were said to be tested off medication. When somatic treatments were mentioned, most studies simply stated that the patients were "on drugs."

In the 100 studies reviewed, the neuropsychological results of schizophrenic groups were compared either with norms for brain damage or with the results of various reference groups: brain damaged groups, nonschizophrenic psychiatric groups, or normals. We classified each schizophrenic group as impaired, not impaired, or as having equivocal results, based upon the percentage of tests on which it showed impairment relative to the reference group or norm. Studies also were categorized according to whether their goal was to characterize average functioning of the schizophrenic groups (group mean comparison) or to place individual subjects into diagnostic categories (discrimination attempts).

Table 13-2 summarizes the results of these studies. Perhaps not surprisingly, the table shows a modest tendency for more schizophrenic groups to be found impaired relative to normals and unimpaired relative to brain damaged groups. However, it is clear that the

Table 13-2

Summary of 100 Neuropsychological Studies Comparing Schizophrenic Groups with Reference Groups or with Norms for Brain Damage

Schizophrenics' outcome	Studies of group mean comparisons			Studies of discrimination attempts		
	Schizophrenic groups (n)	Tests used (n)	Test combinations used (n)	Schizophrenic groups (n)	Tests used (n)	Test combinations used (n)
Impaired vs. normals	31	82	0	2	1	1
Equivocal	3	11	0	0	0	0
Unimpaired vs. normals	18	92	1	1	0	1
Impaired vs. other psychiatric	7	14	0	2	4	10
Equivocal	3	6	0	0	0	0
Unimpaired vs. other psychiatric	7	18	3	1	3	0
Same as brain damaged	24	127	0	11	25	8
Equivocal	2	17	0	0	0	0
Better than brain damaged	33	141	13	35	81	23
Impaired vs. norms	9	13	0	6	9	1
Unimpaired vs. norms	13	18	0	2	2	0

Note. Schizophrenic samples involved in group mean comparisons were classified as "impaired" if at least 60% of test comparisons had that outcome (41 to 59% = equivocal; ≤ 40% = unimpaired). For studies of discrimination attempts, schizophrenic samples were considered "impaired" if fewer than 60% of the schizophrenic subjects were classified by the tests as neurologically normal.

overall results in these studies were quite mixed, with sizable percentages of groups being impaired and unimpaired in each type of comparison. This raises the question of why some schizophrenic groups show neuropsychological impairment and others do not. Several studies failed to control for factors that might be related to impairment, such as age, education (which is a gross estimate of premorbid intelligence), premorbid psychosocial functioning (the process–reactive dimension), chronicity, amount of lifetime hospitalization, clinical condition (including type and severity of symptoms), medication status, and nonbehavioral evidence of cerebral abnormalities.

To explore the possible effects of demographic and clinical/treatment status variables, we divided and compared the 140 schizophrenic groups according to whether they were impaired or unimpaired in relation to *any* reference group or norm. Considered in this way, there were 60 impaired groups and 74 unimpaired ones. Six groups that had equivocal test findings were excluded. Also, it should be recalled that there was a considerable amount of unreported (missing) demographic and clinical/treatment status data in these studies, so the ns in the comparisons fluctuate accordingly.

The impaired groups had an average age of 39.3 years ($n=44$) and an average of 11.0 years of education ($n=26$). The corresponding figures for the unimpaired groups were essentially the same: 38.8 ($n=62$) for age and 11.1 ($n=46$) for education. These results do not suggest an increasing likelihood of impairment for older schizophrenic groups, as might be expected with a progressive neurologic disorder; also consistent with this finding is the Foulds and Dixon (1962*a*) report that large groups of schizophrenics and neurotics showed equivalent inverse relationships between age and performances on Raven's Progressive Matrices. Furthermore, although studies have shown that poor school performance and low IQ in childhood are poor prognostic signs in schizophrenia (Jones & Offord, 1975; Offord, 1974; Offord & Cross, 1971), the present results regarding educational background do not suggest that premorbid intellectual functioning was a major contributor to the group differences in neuropsychological outcome.

Premorbid psychosocial functioning and rapidity of disease onset were considered in relatively few of the neuropsychological studies. Their results provide only inconsistent support for the hypothesis that process schizophrenics with poor premorbid adjustment show greater cognitive impairment (Davis, DeWolfe, & Gustafson, 1972; Herron, 1962*b*; Horine & Fulkerson, 1973; McDonough, 1960; Parsons & Klein, 1970; Tutko & Spence, 1962; Tyrell, Struve, & Schwartz, 1965). In addition to the problem of different process–reactive rating systems, evaluating these results was complicated by the fact that this dimension is often confounded with other potentially important factors such as chronicity and duration of hospitalization. One study documented this association, but also found that amount of lifetime hospitalization was much more related to neuropsychological impairment than were process–reactive ratings (Tyrell *et al.*, 1965). Another study restricted its sample to fairly acute cases and failed to find a significant relationship between neuropsychological impairment and the process–reactive dimension (Halperin, 1975).

In considering the possible effects of chronicity and length of hospitalization, we were limited by the fact that very few studies used schizophrenic groups described as being acute or in short–term hospitals (see Table 13–1). Also, chronicity and length of hospitalization undoubtedly were confounded in most studies, and these are not truly dichotomous variables; across studies there was an unknown amount of overlap among samples called chronic and relatively acute. Still, these crude classifications appear to have some limited relationship with neuropsychological outcome. Some 88% of impaired groups (*n*=40) were called chronic, as compared to 68% of the unimpaired groups (*n*=40); percentages of groups in long–term facilities were 80 for the impaired category (*n*=46) and 62 for unimpaired (*n*=55).

Patients' clinical status at the times of testing was rarely mentioned in the neuropsychological studies. Only a few studies even reported that they excluded patients who were uncooperative or unable to put forth adequate effort. The potential magnitude of this problem is illustrated by some interesting figures provided by Foulds, Dixon, McClelland, and McClelland (1962): 11% to 37% of patients in six schizophrenic groups were considered untestable due to uncooperativeness or gross confusion.

The literature contained limited and inconsistent support for the hypothesis that paranoid patients tend to be less neuropsychologically impaired than nonparanoid patients (Foulds & Dixon, 1962*a*; Goldstein & Halperin, 1977; Heaton, Vogt, Hoehn, Lewis, Crowley, & Stallings, 1979; Horine & Fulkerson, 1973; Kay, S., 1979; Krynicki & Nahas, 1979; Smith, 1964). Somewhat more intriguing to us were two studies that found significantly less cognitive impairment in patients who were behaviorally active and showed more affect than in patients who were withdrawn and apathetic (Depue, Dubicki, & McCarthy, 1975; Lilliston, 1973). There were indications that withdrawn patients with blunted affect also tend to have an earlier disease onset and more malignant clinical course, and one recent CT scan study found that these so–called "negative" schizophrenic symptoms were associated with an increased probability of enlarged cerebral ventricles (Andreasen, Olsen, Dennert, & Smith, 1982; a nonsignificant trend in the same direction was reported earlier by Johnstone *et al.*, 1978).

Schizophrenics' medication status tended to be confounded with clinical condition and inpatient versus ambulatory status. In evaluating their cognitive impairment, therefore, it was difficult to separate any iatrogenic drug effects from effects of disease severity. Only four of the 140 patient groups were tested off drugs, and two of these showed neuropsychological impairment. Several other studies found little or no correlation between neuroleptic drug doses and degree of cognitive impairment, no change in neuropsychological test performance after withdrawal from neuroleptics, and either no change or slight improvement in neuropsychological performance (especially on tests of attention) after courses of neuroleptic treatment (see review by Heaton & Crowley, 1981). Considered together, these findings make it unlikely that the cognitive impairment associated with schizophrenia is primarily due to acute adverse effects of drug treatment. However, it is unknown whether any cognitive changes are caused by long-term neuroleptic treatment, and to our knowledge there have been no formal neuropsychological studies of tardive dyskinesia.

It was mentioned above that the neuropsychological impairment observed in many schizophrenics may be secondary to demonstrable abnormalities of brain structure and/or function. There are numerous reports in the literature that schizophrenic groups show a greater incidence of cerebral abnormalities than do normals and other psychiatric diagnostic groups not only on neuropsychological tests, but also on clinical neurological examinations, electroencephalograms, regional cerebral blood flow studies, CT scans, and histopathologic studies of the brain (see Heaton & Crowley, 1981). Recent CT scan studies have shown enlarged cerebral ventricles in 30% to 60% of the chronic schizophrenics evaluated, and sulcal enlargement in 20% to 30% (Andreasen et al., 1982; Golden, et al., 1982, 1980; Rieder, Donnelly, Herdt, & Waldman, 1979; Weinberger, Torrey, Neophytides, & Wyatt, 1979a, 1979b). This CT scan evidence of brain atrophy could not be explained on the bases of age, duration of illness, institutionalization, or previous drug treatment or ECT (Golden et al., 1980; Weinberger et al., 1979a, 1979b). Furthermore, several studies have now found significant correlations between neuropsychological impairment and cerebral ventricular size or sulcal prominence (Donnelly, Weinberger, Waldman, & Wyatt, 1980; Golden et al., 1980; Golden et al., 1982; Johnstone, Crow, Frith, Husband, & Kreel, 1976; Rieder et al., 1979). Another study found that neuropsychological impairment in a schizophrenic group was more related to degree of EEG abnormality than to degree of psychosis, disease chronicity, or ratings of premorbid psychosocial adjustment (Heaton et al., 1978).

The foregoing studies suggest than nonbehavioral neurodiagnostic procedures are apt to be helpful in understanding the neuropsychological impairment seen in many schizophrenics. Also relevant to these associations are some recent proposals by Crow (1980) regarding two major schizophrenic syndromes. The first is an acute syndrome characterized by so-called "positive" schizophrenic symptoms, changes in dopaminergic transmission in the brain, and a relatively good response to neuroleptic medications. The second syndrome is described as a chronic "defect state" that is less related to changes in dopaminergic transmission and is characterized by more "negative" schizophrenic symptoms, relatively poor response to neuroleptic medications, and increased probability of enlarged cerebral ventricles

Table 13-3

Mean Age, Education, and Wechsler Intelligence Scale Results for Ten Schizophrenic Groups

	Wehler & Hofemann (1978)	Kay (1979)	Smith (1964)	Holland & Watson (1980)	Goldstein & Halperin (1977)	Holland & Watson (1980)	Smith (1964)	Heaton et al. (1979)	Rieder et al. (1979)	Donnelly et al. (1980)
Age	61	25	34	42	38	42	53	29	25	28
Education	9	—	—	11	12	11	—	13	12	—
Information	7	8	8	11	10	11	9	11	13	12
Comprehension	4	7	5	9	10	10	8	11	9	11
Arithmetic	6	7	6	9	9	9	9	10	12	10
Similarities	4	9	6	9	10	10	8	13	12	12
Digit Span	7	8	9	9	9	9	9	10	9	12
Vocabulary	6	8	8	10	10	11	10	12	10	13
Verbal IQ	81	87	89	96	98	100	100	106	104	110
Digit Symbol	2	6	6	7	7	7	6	8	9	7
Picture Completion	5	6	6	9	9	9	8	10	10	10
Block Design	5	7	5	9	9	9	8	11	13	11
Picture Arrangement	4	7	5	8	8	8	6	9	10	10
Object Assembly	5	6	7	8	9	9	10	11	8	10
Performance IQ	81	77	85	93	93	95	100	100	103	100
Full Scale IQ	80	83	86	94	96	97	103	104	104	106

Note. The groups are presented in the order of their FSIQs. The Reider et al. (1979) and Donnelly et al. (1980) groups presented here are those with normal CT scans.

and neuropsychological impairment. The above-mentioned correlations between negative symptoms, CT scan abnormalities, and cognitive deficits would be consistent with this view, as would a recent report of higher inverse correlations between positive symptoms and plasma prolactin concentrations (a peripheral measure of CNS dopaminergic activity) in schizophrenics with *normal* cerebral ventricles (Kleinman *et al.*, 1982). It would seem worthwhile, therefore, for future neuropsychological studies of schizophrenia to focus more on the clinical, neuroradiological, and biochemical variables that appear to distinguish these two syndromes.

Most neuropsychological studies of schizophrenia used no more than a few tests, and these tended to be relatively complex "screening tests." Such studies do not permit inferences about the relative status of specific abilities. However, several studies presented mean subtest scores on the Wechsler Intelligence Scales and/or the Halstead-Reitan Battery, and there have been a few attempts to compare various diagnostic groups with respect to pattern of performance on these batteries.

Wechsler IQ values were reported for 16 of our 140 schizophrenic groups. Group mean Full Scale IQs were *not* inversely related to age. In fact, there was a slight tendency for the older groups to have higher IQs, again arguing against any consistent progression of intellectual deficit in schizophrenia. Although Verbal IQ exceeded Performance IQ for most of the schizophrenic groups, the discrepancy was not pronounced: the two IQs were within five points of each other for 10 groups, and only two groups had a fairly sizable mean Verbal-Performance "split" of 10 points.

Wechsler subtest scores were reported for 10 of the schizophrenic groups. Table 13-3 shows that, in general, these groups did best on tests of past accumulated knowledge (Information, Vocabulary) and worst on a test of learning and psychomotor speed (Digit Symbol); this pattern of results is fairly typical of brain damaged samples as well. Unlike brain damaged groups, however, schizophrenics have tended to do relatively poorly on a verbal test assessing appreciation of social "common sense" relationships (Comprehension). A comparison of the schizophrenics' scores on the Performance subtests further revealed that these groups did relatively well on measures of spatial analysis and visuoconstructional skills (Block Design and Object Assembly). The latter finding also tended to differ for brain damaged groups (Davis *et al.*, 1972). Nevertheless, attempts to discriminate schizophrenics from diffusely brain damaged patients by relying strictly upon Wechsler subtest patterns have yielded inconsistent and ultimately disappointing results (Chelune, Heaton, Lehman, & Robinson, 1979; DeWolfe, 1971; Watson, 1972).

Factor analytic studies of Wechsler subtest scores have shown very similar factorial structures for groups of neurotics, brain damaged patients, and acute and chronic schizophrenics (Berger, Bernstein, Klein, Cohen, & Lucas, 1964; Cohen, 1952). In considering the relatively minor differences among diagnostic groups, Berger *et al.* (1964) also noted that their brain damaged group was most similar to the chronic schizophrenics. This again suggests that the patterns and interrelationships among Wechsler subtest scores are not likely to be helpful clinically in differentiating brain damaged patients from schizophrenics (particularly chronic schizophrenics).

In the studies we reviewed, subtest scores on most parts of the Halstead–Reitan Battery were reported for eight schizophrenic groups. These groups tended to do worst on measures of logical analysis and new concept formation (Category Test) and incidental memory for aspects of a recently completed problem–solving task (Location component of Tactual Performance Test). They tended to be unimpaired on the Spatial Relations error score (consistent with the Wechsler results) and also on the Aphasia Screening Exam and Sensory–Perceptual Exam. However, as with the Wechsler results mentioned above, patterns of subtest scores on the Halstead–Reitan Battery have not been helpful in distinguishing individual schizophrenics from brain damaged patients. When this neuropsychological discrimination was possible, overall *level* of impairment on the Wechsler and Reitan Batteries appeared to be a much more powerful indicator than any specific pattern of strengths and deficits (Chelune *et al.*, 1979).

LONGITUDINAL STUDIES

Several recent publications have described results of intermediate or long–term clinical follow–up of schizophrenic subject groups (Bland, Parker, & Orn, 1976; Bridge *et al.*, 1978; Ciompi, 1980; Duckworth, Kedward, & Bailey, 1979; Stephens, 1970). These provide a useful context in which to consider the neuropsychological studies below. In general, the longitudinal clinical studies showed a surprisingly high percentage of favorable outcomes over the course of the schizophrenic illness. Although mortality rates tended to be somewhat higher than in the general population and in groups of patients with other psychiatric disorders, the majority of surviving schizophrenics (60–70%) did not require very long–term hospitalization. Moreover, as chronic schizophrenics became older, their specific psychotic symptoms often receded or even disappeared. Psychiatric evaluations of overall psychosocial adjustment revealed that some 50% to 60% of older schizophrenics had either recovered or were significantly improved, and about the same percentage showed either no organic-like deterioration of mental functions or very mild deterioration. Ciompi (1980) also has shown that rapid disease onset and undulating course of the illness (related to the process–reactive dimension) tend to be associated with favorable prognostic indicators. These aspects of premorbid adjustment, disease onset, and clinical course have not been adequately studied in relation to changes in neuropsychological functioning over the course of the schizophrenic illness; this appears to be an important goal for future longitudinal research.

Table 13-4 summarizes the major findings of the longitudinal neuropsychological studies. Of the four studies that compared premorbid test results with testing after hospitalization for schizophrenia, the first (Rappaport & Webb, 1950) is considered invalid because the majority of subjects were uncooperative and gave grossly impaired performances during their second evaluations. Some invalid results may be included in other studies as well, but usually this problem was not mentioned.

The other three studies that directly assessed cognitive impairment associated with the onset of schizophrenia used various military classification tests; scores on these have been shown to correlate well with results of more traditional intelligence testing (Lubin, Giesking, & Williams, 1962). These longitudinal studies found that schizophrenics lost the equivalent of about 5 to 10 IQ points compared to their own premorbid results, whereas normal controls showed some improvement on follow-up testing. The net loss associated with disease onset was somewhat variable across studies, but appeared to average around 10 IQ points. To put this in another perspective, Lubin *et al.* (1962) also reported that the deficit associated with the onset of schizophrenia was substantially less than that shown by subjects who had suffered brain injuries between baseline and follow-up testing.

Although most of the subtests in the military classification batteries revealed some deficit with the onset of schizophrenia, a review of the deficit score patterns in these studies suggests that skill in spatial organization tasks was relatively spared. Also, Schwartzman and Douglas (1962) found that subjects with an acute onset of schizophrenia tended to show less cognitive decrement (from premorbid baseline) than did those with gradual onset, and that ambulatory (clinically improved?) subjects were generally less impaired than those who were hospitalized at the times of their follow-up evaluations.

The remaining 10 studies listed in Table 13-4 did baseline testing after the onset of schizophrenia and follow-up testing from 1 to 14 years later. In addition to using a variety of tests and follow-up periods, these studies considered subject groups that differed with respect to clinical condition, inpatient versus ambulatory status, and medication status. Some of the groups showed IQ *increases*, usually of about 5 to 10 points, over several years of schizophrenic illness. Improved groups include the Schwartzman, Douglas, and Muir (1962) ambulatory group; the Klonoff, Fibiger, and Hutton (1970) group (mostly ambulatory); the Foulds and Dixon (1962a) short-term hospitalized groups; the Haywood and Moelis (1963) clinically improved group; and the Smith (1964), Hamilton (1963), and Hamlin (1969) groups that appear to have been chronically hospitalized (Hamlin noted that the clinically improved subjects made the greatest gains, however, and the Hamilton subjects appear to have improved clinically as well). A mostly ambulatory group of Martin, Friedmeyer, and Sterne (1977) showed no significant change in

Table 13–4
Longitudinal Studies of Neuropsychological Functioning in Schizophrenia

Study	Group(s)	Initial test condition	Follow-up test condition	Mean test-retest interval	Mean age at follow-up	Test(s)	Test-retest outcome
Rappaport & Webb (1950)	10 chronic schizophrenics	Pre-illness (Jr. or Sr. high school)	Hospitalized 2–18 months; 7 Ss gave poor or marginal cooperation	Not reported	22 years	Different group IQ tests	9 of 10 Ss had large IQ drops (mean = 34 points)
Schwartzman & Douglas (1962)	A:30 hospitalized schizophrenics B:20 ambulatory schizophrenics C:30 normals. All groups matched for baseline IQ	Pre-illness (at induction into Canadian military)	Patients had been diagnosed schizophrenic for 2–3 years	9 years	32 years	Military classification exam (8 subtests)	Combined patient group lost 6 IQ points (avg.) whereas controls gained 6 points. Hospitalized Ss had significant decrease on 5 subtests, ambulatory Ss on only 2.
Schwartzman, Douglas, & Muir (1962)	All from Schwartzman & Douglas (1962) above: 10 hospitalized and 20 ambulatory	See Schwartzman & Douglas (1962) above	Diagnosed schizophrenic for 10–11 years	17 years from first testing	40 years	Same as above	Hospitalized group showed additional IQ decrease about same size as that between pre-illness and first follow-up (above). Ambulatory group gained a similar amount.
Lubin, Giesking, & Williams (1962)	A:159 schizophrenics B: 64 brain damaged C:162 normals	Pre-illness (at induction into U.S. military)	Patients retested 1–3 months after hospitalization	2 years	26 years	Military classification exam (5 subtests)	Normals made gains on all subtests (probably significant on 2). Schizophrenics showed significant decrement on 4 of 5 subtests (1/3 to 1/6 S.D. loss).

Kingsley & Struening (1966)	A:50 acute schizophrenics B:30 chronic schizophrenics C:50 normals	Pre-illness (at induction into U.S. military)	A: acutely hospitalized (1 week) B: total of 3 years in short-term hospital and/or multiple admissions C: active duty military	Not recorded but varied from 2 weeks to 20 years.	A:23 years B:33 years C:23 years	Military classification exam	Overall results A: decrease 0.4 S.D. B: decrease 0.2 S.D. C: increase 0.9 S.D.	Performance decrements of brain damaged Ss were significantly worse than those of the schizophrenics.
Moran, Gorham, & Holtzman (1960)	30 chronic paranoid schizophrenics	Hospitalized from 1–19 years	Still hospitalized	6 years	47 years	WB–I vocabulary subtest and 7 special word meaning tests	No significant change on any of the measures	
Ginett & Moran (1964)	67 chronic schizophrenics	Hospitalized	Still hospitalized	13 years	Not reported	WB–I vocabulary subtest	No significant change	
Foulds & Dixon (1962b)	59 paranoids 61 catatonics 66 hebephrenics Further categorized in subgroups based upon total hospitalization	Not reported (probably hospitalized)	Most in hospital (ns not given)	2 years	41 years	Progressive Matrices (PM) Mill–Hill Vocabulary (MHV)	MHV more stable than PM scores. Short-term hospitalized Ss tended to get worse. Catatonics improved on both PM & MHV. Paranoids started higher, got slightly worse on PM. Hebephrenics started low, changed little.	

Table 13–4 (continued)

Study	Group(s)	Initial test condition	Follow-up test condition	Mean test-retest interval	Mean age at follow-up	Test(s)	Test-retest outcome
Smith (1964)	All judged "clinically deteriorated". A:11 younger earlier onset nonparanoids B:13 older, late onset (after age 40) paranoids	Hospitalized mean of 8 years (Group A) and 9 years (Group B)	Still hospitalized	8 years	A:42 years B:61 years	WB-I Porteus Mazes, Capps Homographs, Weigl sorting	Older group baseline scores higher; with baselines covaried, no group differences in change scores. FSIQ increased 6 points (avg.) for younger group and 2 points for older. Virtually no changes on Capps and Porteus. On Weigl, 17 Ss were able to shift at baseline; 10 of these unable to follow-up.
Hamlin (1969)	24 from Smith (1969) plus 5 others A:13 younger, earlier onset nonparanoids B: 16 older, later onset paranoids	Hospitalized	Most hospitalized (ns not reported)	14 years	A:47 years B:65 years	WB-I	FSIQ increased 10 points (avg.) for younger group and 3 points for older. Clinically improved Ss showed largest IQ gains.
Haywood & Moelis (1963)	A:20 schizophrenics clinically improved at follow-up. B:20 schizophrenics unimproved at follow-up. Groups matched for age and baseline IQ.	Shortly after hospital admission	Still in hospital	A:5 years B:6 years	A:46 years B:45 years	Various combinations of WB-I	Improved group gained 7 FSIQ points (avg.) but unimproved group lost 3 points. 16 improved Ss made IQ gains and 13 unimproved Ss showed IQ losses.

Study	Subjects	Setting	Test timing	Follow-up interval	Age	Test	Results
Klonoff, Fibiger, & Hutton (1970)	A:42 chronic schizophrenics	About 1/2 of group hospitalized	Most ambulatory (ns not reported)	A:8 years	47 years	WAIS	Average gains: 5 VIQ points, 8 PIQ points, 7 FSIQ points.
	B:35 chronic schizophrenics	Not reported	All ambulatory	B:1 year	Not reported (about 47 years)	Halstead–Reitan Battery	Some "improvement (practice effect not controlled) on Category Test, Tactual Performance Test, and Finger Tapping. Little change on Seashore Rhythm, Speech Perception and Trails–B.
Martin, Friedmeyer, & Sterne (1977)	211 schizophrenics: 172 had ≤ 2 previous admissions ("acute") and 39 had > 2 previous admissions ("chronic").	Tested during week of hospital admission. Initial mean IQs above average, with chronics > acutes.	#1: the week before discharge #2: 12 months after admission (most were outpatients) #3: 24 months after admission (most were outpatients)	See Follow-up test condition	#1:31 years #2:32 years #3:33 years	Shipley–Hartford: age, education, and baseline Gorham Proverbs; scores were covaried.	(Difficult to assess due to covariance procedures.) Total group did not change significantly over 24 months. Nonsignificant trend for clinically improved patients to have more positive IQ changes.
Hamilton (1963)	36 chronic nonparanoid schizophrenics; most were involved in activity programs.	Hospitalized	Hospitalized	2 years	Not reported	Mill-Hill Vocabulary, Raven's Progressive Matrices	Gained an average of 5.3 IQ points (p <.10) on the MHVT and 12.1 IQ points (p< .01 on the RPMT.

Shipley IQ after a 24-month period; however, a clinically improved subgroup had a slight increase in mean IQ (2 points), whereas an unimproved subgroup had a slight decrease (3 points). The Schwartzman *et al.* (1962) hospitalized group showed continued intellectual decline, as did the Foulds and Dixon (1962*b*) long-term hospitalization groups and the Haywood and Moelis (1963) group that failed to show clinical improvement after a lengthy period of treatment. Two studies showed no change in vocabulary test performances after many years of hospitalization for schizophrenia (Moran, Gorham, & Holtzman, 1962; Ginett & Moran, 1964). Although Smith's (1964) chronically hospitalized subjects showed IQ increases over an 8-year period, their performances on the Porteus Mazes and Capps Homographs remained stable, and they showed increased perseveration on the Weigl sorting task. In a group that was ambulatory (clinically improved?) at follow-up, Klonoff *et al.* (1970) found improvement in performance on the Halstead-Reitan Battery after 1 year; the mean scores at follow-up were still in the "impaired" range, however. (Findings such as these, showing that ambulatory subjects remain cognitively impaired, argue against the possibility that the impairment is primarily due to hospitalization or institutionalization *per se*.)

The above studies suggest that the cognitive impairment associated with the onset of schizophrenia is at least partially reversible in many subjects, but in some others it is probably progressive. Schizophrenics who remain chronically hospitalized and fail to show clinical improvement appear to be at greatest risk for unremitting impairment or progressive cognitive decline.

Smith (1964) and Hamlin (1969) did long-term follow-up evaluations of younger and older schizophrenic groups. Although the younger, earlier onset group had lower baseline IQs, when baseline level of performance was covaried the groups did not differ significantly in their amounts of IQ change (improvement). As noted above, Foulds and Dixon (1962*a*, 1962*b*) found no evidence of steeper cognitive declines associated with aging for schizophrenics than for neurotics or normals.

The older and younger schizophrenic groups of Smith (1964) and Hamlin (1969) also differed in terms of the paranoid/nonparanoid distinction; the younger nonparanoids had much lower IQs at baseline, gained a little more over the course of the study, but remained an average of 10 IQ points lower than the older paranoids. Lubin *et al.* (1962) reported that their paranoids were not significantly different from their nonparanoids in premorbid IQ or in degree or pattern of intellectual deficit after becoming schizophrenic. Foulds and Dixon (1962*b*) considered separately groups of paranoids, catatonics, and hebephrenics; the hebephrenics had lower baseline scores on the Mill Hill Vocabulary and Progressive Matrices tests, and the catatonics made the greatest gains over the 2-year follow-up period.

SUMMARY AND CONCLUSIONS

To briefly summarize the neuropsychological research findings, it appears that some cognitive deficit is associated with the onset of schizophrenia. The deficit is at least partially reversible in many patients, but others show stable or progressive impairment. Continuing or progressive cognitive impairment tends to be associated with unfavorable clinical course of the schizophrenic illness, although the relevant clinical correlates have not been thoroughly investigated.

The limited evidence available suggests that cognitive functioning in schizophrenia is not dramatically or abnormally affected by aging *per se*. Recent clinical studies suggest that some patients improve symptomatically in old age, but there have been no neuropsychological studies of this phenomenon.

Although patients requiring long–term hospitalization are likely to show cognitive impairment, significant impairment has been noted in ambulatory groups as well; this suggests that hospitalization *per se* is not the major cause of the deficits, even though the isolated and unstimulating institutional environment may be a secondary contributing factor.

The cognitive impairment observed in schizophrenic groups cannot be explained on the basis of ECT or acute drug effects, although the neuropsychological effects of long–term neuroleptic therapy have not been studied adequately. The nature of the cognitive deficit in schizophrenia does not appear to differ much from that shown by neurological patients with diffuse brain disorders, and the reported correlations of cognitive impairment with nonbehavioral evidence of cerebral abnormalities suggest that some schizophrenics do have organic dementias. Given the sampling biases in the available neuropsychological studies, however, the true prevalence of this phenomenon cannot be established at the present time.

Finally, to our knowledge, the *effects* of neuropsychological deficits on schizophrenics' everyday functioning and long–term prognosis have not been investigated. In future research, otherwise clinically comparable patients with and without significant cognitive deficits should be compared longitudinally with respect to a variety of outcome variables; these would include capacity for independent living, social and vocational adjustment, need for hospitalization, and ability to profit from psychotherapy as well as medication.

14 Schizophrenia and Aging: Information Processing Patterns

George Niederehe

University of Texas Medical School at Houston

Michele J. Rusin

Emory University School of Medicine

Since both aging and schizophrenia are associated with cognitive changes, one might wonder about the joint impact of the two factors. Inasmuch as schizophrenic illness typically develops in early adulthood, whatever patterns of cognitive change occur in affected individuals in their later years might be attributed to either the aging process or the progressive course of the psychiatric disorder. Yet we know little about the typical course of cognitive change across the life span in chronic schizophrenia. Similarly, the cognitive features of late–onset schizophrenia, in individuals who have already experienced cognitive changes due to the normal aging process, have received little attention. Clinically, of course, we have the images of both a progressively dementing course in some schizophrenic patients and of a remitting course or "burn–out" process with age in many others (Bridge *et al.*, 1978).

At a theoretical level, at least four potential patterns of cognitive change can be hypothesized, depending upon how schizophrenia and the aging process may interact.

- Older schizophrenics might show more severe cognitive deficits than either younger patients or normal age–peers, if aging further impairs the same dimensions of cognitive functioning affected in schizophrenia, in an additive or synergistic way.
- If the changes produced by aging and schizophrenia, respectively, are "orthogonal" and affect qualitatively distinct facets of cognition, then the deficits shown by the older schizophrenic may not be more severe, but simply more numerous.
- Even if both processes produce similar deficits, no further change may occur with aging if schizophrenia is in fact a form

of "premature aging," and if the affected functions are altered to an asymptotic degree.

- If the effects of aging somehow counteract or balance off those of schizophrenia, older patients might show less decrement in cognitive functioning relative to age–peer normals than do younger schizophrenics, and the effects of aging might be no worse than in the normal elderly.

The differentiation of these various theoretical possibilities would require considerable psychological experimentation that simply has not been attempted thus far. This chapter represents an attempt to survey the status of the experimental literature on cognitive functioning, and to comment on what it indicates about the age–related time course of cognitive changes in schizophrenia.

COGNITIVE–EXPERIMENTAL STUDIES AND LATE–LIFE SCHIZOPHRENIA

The term "cognitive functioning" is used here in a more limited and formal sense than the "cognitive" or "thought" disorder label often given to overt clinical symptoms in schizophrenia, such as delusions or hallucinations. The focus is on specific patterns of intelligent behavior, assessed by performance on experimental procedures and/or on standardized ability tests, which are hypothesized to reflect specific components within an overall model of general intellectual operations.

This chapter focuses specifically on the experimental literature on cognitive functioning to the exclusion of clinical neuropsychological studies. Although both research fields define cognitive functioning similarly as a set of operations underlying overt behavior, the two literatures are distinguished primarily by their assessment techniques and general approach to research. Neuropsychological studies assess performance on standardized psychological and neuropsychological tests, whereas experimental studies typically utilize unnormed procedures designed to operationalize specific constructs of theoretical interest. Although such distinctions are far from assured, neuropsychological studies are more apt to assess naturally available clinical groupings of patients for purposes of comparing profiles; experimental studies are (or should be) more apt to use narrower samples, carefully selected so as to reflect diagnostic categories of particular theoretical interest and to rule out extraneous variables needing to be "controlled." Whereas neuropsychological studies can legitimately be exploratory or descriptive, experimental procedures are typically guided by more explicit hypotheses and models of the underlying cognitive mechanisms.

For the past 20 years or more, the dominant paradigm for cognitive experimentation in psychology has been an information processing perspective. Information processing studies have also been extensively pursued in applied research on schizophrenia. Thus, although it was a tenuous undertaking (given some debate whether reliable findings about schizophrenia have emerged from this literature), there was some reason to hope that promising trends might be identified as to the cognitive aging of schizophrenics.

Sadly, however, our literature search indicates almost no information processing reports relevant to this topic. Although minimal longitudinal research of any sort has been undertaken to chart cognitive changes in schizophrenics into their late life, and although cognition in late–onset schizophrenia had not been studied in any systematic way, we anticipated finding some experimental literature on chronic schizophrenia that had taken at least a cross–sectional look at the age dimension. Such is not the case. There have been few cognitive investigations of chronic schizophrenia where the mean age of the sample was greater than 50, and almost all of these seem to fit better in the neuropsychological than the cognitive–experimental category in terms of the testing procedures (e.g., Chaikelson & Schwartzman, 1983; Frith, 1977).

In general, published experimental studies in the area tend to report only the mean ages and age ranges of their samples. They fail to specify the number of older schizophrenic subjects included. A majority of the studies appear to focus on young, acute schizo–phrenics, adopting the reasoning that such samples provide the cleanest look at basic properties of the disorder, uncontaminated by the effects of long–term medication use and institutionalization. Experimental investigators typically view age as a variable to be controlled. Thus, they usually match the ages of the various groups compared, but the contribution of age to intragroup variation on the cognitive tasks studied is rarely analyzed. Reviews of the cognitive literature on schizophrenia never mention the topic of age, except as a nuisance variable. In short, age and the aged seem to be system–atically excluded from the experimental research on schizophrenia.

Lacking direct experimental evidence about information processing in aging schizophrenics, an alternative approach to the topic may be to examine the separate literatures on information processing in schizophrenia research and in gerontology, looking for points of similarity and of difference. Cameron (1939) expressed the idea that schizophrenics might be usefully compared with the elderly. He later retracted this notion, however, noting that the similarities consisted only of a series of deficits or "negative" symptoms, whereas the "positive" schizophrenic symptoms, such as disordered associations, were not typical of aging.

Saccuzzo (1977), in a similar vein, pointed out numerous similarities between the types of deficits found among the aged and among schizophrenic patients, most prominently their slowed reaction times and distractibility. Viewing the value of an informa–tion processing approach as its differentiation of specific areas of deficit, he suggested that systematic comparisons between schizo–

phrenics and the normal aged could be particularly useful in identifying the point(s) at which their profiles of deficit differ, as well as where they are similar. From this perspective, aging is viewed as a form of pathology or deterioration of function, and interest is directed at how schizophrenic deficits appear unique in comparison.

Such a comparison indeed is feasible, since considerable information processing research has been done with the normal aged as well as with schizophrenics. Comparing findings may serve to suggest relevant questions for research. Before proceeding to compare findings from the two fields of research, it would be useful to briefly clarify some of the basic assumptions of an information processing perspective.

INFORMATION PROCESSING MODELS

No single or universal information processing model exists, but rather a multiplicity of models are extant, each attempting to explicate the steps a subject must implicitly go through in performing a given type of task. Most centrally, all such models are built on the premise that the intelligent behavior of a human subject can be viewed as the operation of a symbol–manipulating system. This general paradigm has evolved from the traditions of verbal learning, neobehaviorism, and human engineering within psychology, and from related traditions within the communication engineering, computer science, and psycholinguistics fields (Lachman, Lachman, & Butterfield, 1979). More complete reviews of the essential elements of the information processing paradigm in cognitive psychology can be found in other sources (Lachman *et al.,* 1979; Neisser, 1967).

Because of the multiplicity of models, it may be useful to review some of the common denominators and organizing principles characteristic of information processing studies. First, an information processing approach views all observable behavioral performance as complex, comprising a combination of multiple, simpler psychological operations. Second, by experimental manipulation, presumably performance can be arranged so as to decompose it, "decoupling" or isolating these simpler components. Third, these basic psychological operations occur in real time, requiring a measurable duration in which to transpire, and typically are assumed to be sequential. Time then becomes a primary metric by which cognitive operations can be measured. Operations that take longer to complete are viewed as requiring more of the intervening simple operations, i.e., as more complex or as involving more information to be processed. Reaction times occupy a central role as measurements in this research, and comparison of latencies required for one sequence of steps (e.g., ABCD) versus a similar sequence that lacks one step (e.g., ACD) becomes a prominent method for decoupling that step from the larger complex.

A fourth characteristic of information processing research is that, typically, very briefly exposed, highly discrete stimuli are used as inputs in order to trace the sequence of stages a piece of information goes through as it is processed. Such laboratory situations are not very representative of the continuous flow of information typical of "real life" situations. However, information processing research has been less concerned with the ecological validity of its tasks than with their internal validity, or power to isolate component constructs within a theoretical model of the activity that subjects are performing. Thus, although the system it traces is nonphysiological, the objectives of information processing research are similar to those of cerebral angiography, in which certain tracer elements are tracked through the brain to delineate the cerebrovascular pathways followed.

A fifth characteristic is particularly relevant to information processing studies in schizophrenia. The basic objective in information processing studies is to specify the series of operational steps that must be traversed in order to complete a particular response—in other words, to spell out the "program" for that behavior. In modeling the cognitive behavior of normal adults, the experimenter is not concerned with the physiological substrate necessary to carry out the operations, but simply with specification of the necessary steps in the program. However, in research that applies an information processing approach to studying a clinical problem area (such as schizophrenia or aging), researchers have an obvious interest in going beyond the abstract model to the physiological substrate. Akin to the computer technician who times a machine's operations to analyze its "hard wiring," most schizophrenia researchers utilizing information processing techniques tend to be very concerned as well with the neurological and/or psychophysiological dimensions of behavior, and usually measure these concomitantly in their research. They probably would not employ an information processing model unless they thought its various components quite directly reflected processes considered to be of potential clinical importance in the etiology of schizophrenia.

In order to understand trends in this research field, it is useful to note one final characteristic. Although both temporal and spatial metaphors have always had their place in information processing conceptualizations (Hoyer & Plude, 1980), in recent years notions of processing space have gained increasing prominence, largely in conjunction with a growing emphasis on the concept of attention. The notion of limited channel capacity has been one basic, spatial construct, and has been used to emphasize the limitations on mental activities that require focal attention for enactment. In large part, spatial dimensions within an information processing model are used in analyzing how various processes may interfere with each other; procedures for overloading the system thus may provide a means of studying internal organization and complexity. Important here is the distinction between serial and parallel processes (Neisser, 1967). Although any single process is viewed as a sequential series of steps, some processes must operate serially (usually those requiring focal attention). Others appear capable of proceeding in parallel and thus are less subject to decomposition by overall measures of the temporal duration they require (usually those that are overlearned or habitual and can operate outside awareness). The work of Kahneman (1973) on attention and mental effort has been an influential source of ideas about these aspects of information processing.

Along lines suggested by Hoyer and Plude (1980), we might distinguish three general types of information processing models. The first emphasizes the time dimension and represents information processing as a continuous flow of input through various stages to some output or response. Such flowcharts can depict the movement of information from peripheral receptors to the brain, but are perhaps best exemplified in "storage bin" models of memory, showing how information moves to successive stages of encoding over time (Atkinson & Shiffrin, 1968; Sternberg, 1966; Waugh & Norman, 1965).

A second type of model emphasizes a hierarchy of functions or processes within the processing of information, such as rehearsing, encoding, selecting, and retrieving. A prominent example is the levels–of–processing model for memory, which postulates that information will be memorable in accordance with the semantic "depth" or degree to which it has been encoded (Craik & Lockhart, 1977). Many models encompass elements of both the first and second type, since they have both structure and process components, and are differentiated only by the degree to which they emphasize one or the other.

The third type of model emphasizes processing capacity aspects of the system, such as the amount of information that can be handled at once, the interference of simultaneous processes, measures of task difficulty or mental "effort," and other ways of examining how an individual allocates fixed–capacity resources. This viewpoint is based on a spatial metaphor.

In the discussions that follow, we shall refer primarily to the first type of model, of information processing stages, but one that incorporates various features of the second type (process emphasis) as well. This will be useful because it helps to organize the material and has been the type of model behind much of the research conducted to date. We shall also allude to capacity theory viewpoints, however, since these may offer alternative interpretations of the empirical data when evaluating whether a specific area of deficit exists.

The information processing model shown in Figure 14–1 represents a composite of the most common features in various generally accepted and used models. Note that it contains both structural and fluid components. The conventional information stores are indicated by boxes, and the processes that transform information along its flow are shown by arrows. Whereas the individual's behavior can be viewed from either vantage point, adopting one or the other viewpoint leads to different emphases. Thinking in terms of structures leads toward viewing the individual as passive, and toward an emphasis on automatic and unconscious processing. Emphasizing processes leads one

Figure 14-1
Composite Information Processing Model

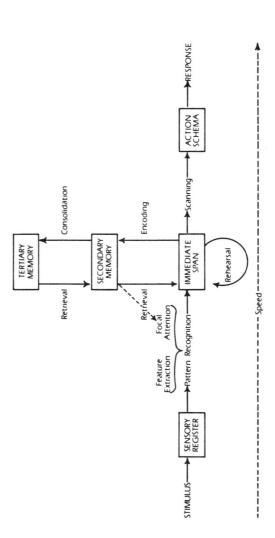

toward viewing the individual as an active participant in the processing of information and toward understanding how information arrives
at any given point in the chain. Research trends have favored the
investigation of processes in recent years.

The rest of this chapter discusses various components of the
model in Figure 14-1, starting at the earliest information processing
stages. In each area, comparisons will be made between the changes
that characteristically appear to occur due to aging and due to
schizophrenia.

SENSORY PROCESSES

Information processing begins with the arrival of stimulus information at the sensory end organs. No evidence suggests that schizophrenic patients show impairments in basic sensory acuity to receive
this information in visual, auditory, tactile, or other modalities
(Maher, 1966). Sensory deficits are well documented in the elderly,
however. Not only do sensory receptors become less sensitive with
age, but structural changes in the end organs may also introduce
distortion at the initial reception of information. In the elderly,
reductions in sensory acuity have been demonstrated in vision
(Fozard, Wolf, Bell, McFarland, & Podolsky, 1977) audition (Corso,
1971, 1977), smell and taste (Engen, 1977) and tactile sensitivity
(Kenshalo, 1977; Thornbury & Mistretta, 1981). On the average, then,
the older individual begins information-processing tasks with
somewhat degraded stimulus information.

The model in Figure 14-1 refers to a "sensory register" because,
in each sensory modality, the information from a stimulus seems to
persist once the stimulus has ended and to continue to be available
for use in a brief sensory "afterimage" or "very short-term memory
(VSTM)." In the sensory register, the information still retains the
original properties of its sensory modality and thus may be referred
to as an "auditory echoic store" or as "iconic memory" in vision.
Studies operationalizing this register generally present a stimulus
array for a brief duration and then cue the subject to report on, or to
otherwise utilize information from, the afterimage only after the
original stimulus is already absent.

A variety of procedures have been used to define the properties
of this very early, and brief, stage of information processing. These
include full report of whatever is perceived, partial (or selective)
report, forced-choice recognition, stimulus integration methods, and
backward masking. Since the greatest amount of research has been
done in the visual modality, the findings discussed here all refer to
the icon, or iconic afterimage.

In general, schizophrenic patients and the elderly tend to perform more poorly than comparison groups on tasks designed to
operationalize their sensory registers. When briefly presented with a
stimulus array, both groups appear deficient at detecting items and

tend to process fewer items from the display, totally (Brody, Saccuzzo, & Braff, 1980; Neale, McIntyre, Fox, & Cromwell, 1969). Such findings merely describe performance levels, however, and do not adequately specify the underlying reasons for the performance deficits.

Three questions appear to be paramount. First, do schizophrenic subjects (or the aged) form images in the sensory register as readily (at the same rate) as do others? Second, do their images persist for the same amount of time, or decay more rapidly? Third, can schizophrenic subjects (or aged subjects) read information off the icon as effectively and efficiently as others?

Backward masking studies have been used to demonstrate the length of time that it takes for the icon to develop. In this type of study, a stimulus array is briefly flashed on a screen followed after an interval by a "noise" pattern, or mask, that stops or interferes with further development of the icon. The interval between the presentation of the stimulus and of the mask (interstimulus interval or ISI) is varied, and the results obtained at different ISI provide a measure of how long it takes the icon to develop to its full strength. A number of studies have indicated that schizophrenic subjects require lengthier stimulus exposures and longer ISI in order to perform comparably to normal individuals (Braff & Saccuzzo, 1981; Saccuzzo, Hirt, & Spencer, 1974; Saccuzzo & Miller, 1977). When formation of the icon has not been limited by masking, schizophrenic groups have performed comparably to psychiatric controls (Cash, Neale, & Cromwell, 1972; Knight, Sherer, & Shapiro, 1977). Although these studies suggest an inefficiency in icon formation, some of the already cited studies indicated that schizophrenics performed poorly even when there was no masking and an indefinite amount of time was allowed for icon formation (Brody et al., 1980; Neale et al., 1969). Such results suggest that slow icon formation is not a sufficient explanation for the schizophrenic perceptual performance deficit.

With regard to the sensory register in the normal elderly, "there is a definite age-associated slowing in the rate of processing visual information" (Hoyer & Plude, 1980, p. 230). Like schizophrenics, the elderly require longer stimulus presentation times to achieve a given accuracy of performance. Exposure times must be even longer than those required by young schizophrenics (Brody, et al., 1980). Older adults need longer ISI in order to escape the effects of backward masking (Kline & Birren, 1975; Kline & Szafran, 1975; Till, 1978; Walsh, 1976; Walsh, Till, & Williams, 1978). In some situations, younger subjects continue to outperform older ones at all ISI (Kline & Baffa, 1976).

The finding that schizophrenic subjects report fewer items from iconic memory has often been interpreted as meaning that their icons decay more rapidly. However, when only a single stimulus item is presented, the performance of schizophrenics is equivalent to that of controls (Neale et al., 1969). Issues of icon decay have been investigated using stimulus integration tasks in which the ISI between two stimuli presented in rapid succession is varied to determine whether they appear as a single stimulus. Schizophrenics usually perform such tasks comparably to control subjects (Knight, Sherer, Putchat, & Carter, 1978; Spaulding, Rosenzweig, Huntzinger, Cromwell, Briggs, & Hayes, 1980). When they have been shown deficient, it has been at relatively briefer ISI. If the icon decayed too rapidly, one would expect impaired schizophrenic performance on stimulus integration tasks at the longer, rather than the shorter, ISI.

In gerontological research, several studies have found that older individuals were able to see successive stimuli as continuous over longer ISI than younger subjects, suggesting that the icon actually persisted longer in the aged (Kline & Orme-Rogers, 1978; Walsh & Thompson, 1978).

If the icon can be assumed to form and persist normally, then the observed impairments in schizophrenics' perceptual performance might be attributed to impaired ability to further process information contained in the icon. Such an explanation is consistent with the observation that as stimulus complexity increases, the performance of schizophrenics (and the aged) falls off. The notion of defective read-off of information from the icon might be related also to findings from sensory integration experiments. Schizophrenics do not appear to summate sensory stimuli as others do. Whereas normal individuals respond the same to two brief flashes of light presented in rapid succession as they do to a single flash whose intensity equals the sum of the two brief bursts, to schizophrenics the successive stimuli appear weaker (Collins, Kietzman, Sutton, & Shapiro, 1978).

Summarizing the findings on the iconic store, it appears most likely that schizophrenics have normally persisting icons, but slowed or otherwise deficient processing of iconic information (e.g., improper summation). The findings are inconclusive on whether their icons form at a slowed rate. Elderly individuals, meanwhile, appear to show slowed processes in all aspects of this stage—slow icon formation, slowed processing from the icon, and even prolonged persistence (slow decay) of the iconic information. From a qualitative standpoint, it is noteworthy that the elderly seem to process information at this stage more accurately than schizophrenics, even if more slowly (Brody et al., 1980).

PATTERN RECOGNITION

The next information store generally identified after the sensory register is the immediate span of memory, or primary memory. In between, processes operate that serve to extract features of the sensory information contained in the iconic or echoic image and to identify items vis-a-vis the individual's already existing stores of information ("knowledge systems"). Feature extraction is generally considered to be an automatic, "preattentive" process, not under the

172 / COGNITIVE AND PSYCHOLOGICAL VARIABLES

individual's conscious control. The available information is partially processed, with a focus on features (e.g., angles, shape) sufficient to establish a figure–ground discrimination but yielding a relatively crude, general formulation of the stimulus. For example, feature extraction might lead to the determination that a given stimulus was a letter of the alphabet with sharp angles, without determining that it was an "M".

Schizophrenics differ in their degree of dependence on, and skill at, automatic processing. The available research evidence suggests that both nonparanoid schizophrenics and the elderly show some deficits in these preattentive processes, whereas paranoid schizophrenics appear capable of using them effectively. Studies by Russell and Knight (1977) suggest that nonparanoid schizophrenics typically adopt global processing styles that ignore available, relevant information. The poor levels of accuracy that they achieve tend to improve when salient features are highlighted (Cox & Leventhal, 1978; Magaro, 1981). Paranoid schizophrenics showed greater accuracy on various tasks reflecting preattentive processing (Cox & Leventhal, 1978).

Although preattentive processes in the elderly have not been investigated to any great extent, one study suggested that the elderly may show mild impairments. Young, middle–aged, and elderly subjects were shown displays that contained irrelevant information. Only the elderly subjects were slowed by the presence of items oriented in a different direction from the target characters, suggesting reduced ability to attend solely to relevant perceptual features (Farkus & Hoyer, 1980).

Focal attention, sometimes referred to as selective attention or controlled processing, is a complex phenomenon in which the subject directs processing toward a particular subset of the stimulus array while avoiding further processing of other stimulus information. Such processing is considered to be under conscious control and is that step at which the subject completes a thorough analysis of the item so that its identity is established. Maintenance of attention entails both sustained concentration on the focal item(s) and avoidance of distraction by irrelevant information.

In visual search tasks, paranoid schizophrenics show effective use of focal attention. Nonparanoid schizophrenics usually do not, and their responses appear to continue relying on preattentive processing. They thus tend to make more errors when the task requires more detailed examination of features (Pic'l et al., 1979; Russell & Knight, 1977).

The elderly also may have deficits in their use of focal attention. They appear to have difficulty separating relevant from irrelevant information (Hoyer & Plude, 1980; Hoyer et al., 1979; Kausler & Kleim, 1978; Rabbitt, 1965). Yet, when given a choice, the elderly may prefer a strategy emphasizing controlled processing over one emphasizing automatic processing. A number of studies indicate that older adults adopt a more cautious style, requiring greater certainty about accuracy before making a response (Botwinick, 1966; Silverman, 1963). Despite this cautious style, however, the aged generally do not achieve a greater accuracy of response than do younger subjects.

MEMORY PROCESSES

Almost every cognitive operation in the information processing system can be construed as a "memory" function, if one wishes to highlight the preservation of information over time that is involved. The longer the time or preservation, or the more events intervening during the retention interval, the more apt we are to refer to "memory." Information processing researchers distinguish primarily between short-term or primary memory, and long-term or secondary memory. The important points, for our purposes, are that primary memory has a limited capacity, whereas secondary memory does not, and that information is retained at the point of primary memory only so long as actively rehearsed or otherwise kept in the focus of attention. Further processing or "encoding" of the information must occur for it to enter secondary memory. Thereafter, active attention is no longer necessary for retaining access to the information. Since much information does tend to fade from secondary memory when it is no longer relevant to the individual's ongoing activities (at least after days or weeks), sometimes a stage of "tertiary" memory is distinguished to represent the relatively permanent retention of other kinds of information.

Retrieval of information can occur at any point in the sequence. Less extensive searching and matching of internal cues is thought to be required to recognize past inputs than to recall such inputs.

Most memory studies have suggested that schizophrenic patients learn or acquire information more slowly, form memory traces that are more forgettable from trial to trial, show relatively greater deficits in recall than in recognition, and show less organized recall responses (Traupmann, 1980). Many similar findings have been reported in memory studies of the aged.

Despite their slower acquisition of new learning or memories, the deficit in schizophrenics does not seem to be due to structural limitations on the capacity of primary memory (which might limit the rate of input of information into longer term memory). The amount of information that can be handled in primary memory, or the "immediate span" as we have termed it in Figure 14-1, does not appear altered. The ability of schizophrenics to utilize basic rehearsal strategies does not appear impaired. In general, the rate of automatic search and scanning processes within primary memory, as reflected in the Sternberg memory scanning task, has also appeared to be normal in schizophrenics (Checkosky, cited in Sternberg, 1975; Koh *et al.*, 1977; Neufeld, 1977; Neufeld & Broga, 1981; Russell *et al.*, 1980), although Pharr and Connor (1980) have reported finding a prolonged scanning rate in schizophrenics.

According to Koh (1978), schizophrenics do not show impaired structural aspects of the memory system, but are deficient in memory performance insofar as it reflects their inefficiency in terms of organizational processes within memory. Many short-term memory processes are either automatic (e.g., scanning) or require little conscious effort (e.g., rote rehearsal), and Koh suggests that these tend to be unimpaired. If, however, high-level organization or elaboration is required, schizophrenics may show deficiencies even at short-term memory stages. Actually, the "constructive coding" described by Koh as occurring within short-term memory is equivalent to the encoding processes by which information is transferred into secondary memory. A variety of studies indicating that the performance deficits of schizophrenics can be attributed to ineffective encoding, or what Koh terms "mnemonic organization," include an extensive series of published reports reviewed by Koh (1978), as well as others indicating that schizophrenics encode over-inclusively (Weinberger & Cermak, 1973), show less organization or clustering of responses in free recall (Koh et al., 1973; Russell et al., 1975; Russell & Beekhuis, 1976), and the like. At the same time, other studies suggest that the performance decrements are not due to simple distractibility, slowness of information processing, or inability to utilize the meaningful elements of the stimulus material (Berg & Leventhal, 1977; Straube et al., 1979). In fact, extensive experimentation indicates that schizophrenic subjects respond normally to major aspects of the stimulus material, employ similar semantic rules, and are capable of using the same memory strategies employed by normal subjects (Koh et al., 1980; Marusarz & Koh, 1980; Straube et al., 1979; Traupmann, 1980). Koh (1978) concludes that schizophrenics employ normal mnemonic strategies, but apparently in an inefficient way or without sufficient active effort, since they fail to spontaneously and fully utilize these potential strategies and, consequently, show subnormal performance in free recall tasks (i.e., manifesting a "production deficiency").

Most research has indicated that recognition memory is intact in schizophrenics (Bauman & Murray, 1968; Koh et al., 1973; Nachmani & Cohen, 1969). Thus, their deficiencies in free recall have been taken as evidence for deficits in the additional search and retrieval processes required in free recall. Russell et al. (1975), however, found both recognition and free recall memory impaired, as did Traupmann (1975), but only in process schizophrenics, not in reactive schizophrenics.

The general pattern of findings in gerontological memory research is strikingly parallel. It is generally felt that primary memory is not impaired with aging except "when the task demands reorganization of the material or a division of attention between two or more mental operations" (Craik, 1977 p. 395). Production deficiencies in encoding have also been shown to be a prominent factor that may account for many of the performance deficits characteristic of older adults. The aged are capable of utilizing effective encoding strategies (e.g., organization, stimulus elaboration, visual imagery), but often fail to do so, or at least do not use them effectively (Hultsch, 1969, 1971; Perlmutter, 1978; Poon et al., 1980). The reasons for these changes are unclear, though executive–level processing seems to be involved. Thus, the memory changes associated with aging appear to be located most centrally in the encoding of new information into secondary memory (Craik, 1977).

The picture is also mixed regarding the extent to which recognition memory is affected by aging, though it is clear that age differences are most prominent in free recall (Smith, 1980). Craik (1977) suggests that retrieval as well as encoding processes are involved in age changes in memory.

Whereas the profiles of information processing aspects affected by aging and by schizophrenia are similar, one major difference emerges. Various researchers have reported that schizophrenics tend to show greater cognitive deficits, the more meaningful the stimulus material involved (Collins, 1978; Koh, 1978; Russell et al., 1975). In contrast, the memory performance of the elderly (and of normal individuals in general) tends to be aided by greater meaningfulness. Such findings reinforce the viewpoint that, in schizophrenia, the disruption of information processing may occur primarily within the associative and organizational processes that must occur when new information is encoded (integrated with preexisting schemas) or when retrieved and integrated into responses.

Such a conclusion is very much in line with an overview of information processing research in schizophrenia (Callaway & Naghdi, 1982). These authors suggest that in schizophrenics those cognitive processes are normal which are automatic, unconscious, parallel, or unlimited in capacity, whereas the deficiencies are seen in conscious, serial, and limited–capacity processes.

The overall suggestion in this research that schizophrenics primarily show deficits at the encoding and response organization points in the information–processing chain may seem contradictory to the widespread impression that schizophrenics suffer from an attentional dysfunction. Attention has been seen as operating early in the information processing chain, and the attentional difficulties of schizophrenics have generally been attributed to defective filtering out of irrelevant information even earlier in the chain. This viewpoint has been in keeping with a linear perspective on the sequence of cognitive operations. Viewed in this fashion, it is always the case that early–stage components have the greatest explanatory potential, and a breakdown at any point in the sequence cannot be accepted as specific or meaningful unless deficits at prior points have been ruled out.

While not discounting the general notion of attentional difficulties in schizophrenia, recent cognitive theories suggest that breakdowns in filtering need not be attributed to faulty preattentive mechanisms, but can occur as a by–product of deficient organization of information at later processing stages (Magaro, 1980). The reason why "later" stages can influence seemingly earlier ones is that actually cognitive processes are not linear but operate in a cyclic or feedback fashion. The current idea is that selectivity is imposed on incoming information by the cognitive and other purposive activities in which the individual is engaged at the time. Failure to filter can thus result from disruptions of the purposive and associative processes that appear to be later in the schema, but which actually are in progress at all times. No independent filter need be postulated at a preattentive stage.

In this regard, it is noteworthy that relatively little information processing research has investigated the output or response–oriented side of the processing chain in schizophrenia. The research has been directed primarily toward early–stage input events, possibly reflecting the overall linear model of information processing that has been in use. Various lines of evidence, however, link the disorganization of behavior seen in schizophrenia more directly to the output than to the input side, e.g., studies indicating intact language reception versus impaired language production (Cohen & Camhi, 1967). Much of the research in the area of response organization has dealt with motoric behavior rather than the verbal/symbolic tasks characteristic of the information processing approach. There is, of course, considerable evidence of disturbances in the organization of reaction time responses and other motoric behavior in schizophrenia (Holzman *et al.*, 1976; Manschreck *et al.*, 1981; Nuechterlein, 1977).

Since schizophrenic impairments seem to involve primarily executive–level or control processes that govern the flow of information from stage to stage, such as the use of encoding strategies and the allocation of attention, it is tempting to speculate that these may be connected with abnormalities of the frontal lobes, or perhaps with what Luria (1974) termed the tertiary association areas of the brain. This thought, of course, rests on the presupposition that these brain areas form the anatomical substrate for such executive functions, and considerable research would be required to establish an empirical basis for such speculations in schizophrenia.

CAPACITY THEORY VIEWPOINTS

Before accepting stage–specific interpretations of the findings from information processing studies, it is essential to consider alternate explanations that may account more parsimoniously for the same pattern of results. In particular, both a methodological critique and an alternate theoretical framework suggest possible reasons why a particular information processing stage may appear more impaired than others, when actually that aspect of cognitive operations is not specifically impaired.

The methodological critique insists that the various tasks or tests used to operationalize the different information processing stages must first be equated for difficulty levels before differential results on them can be accepted as evidence of real differences (Chapman & Chapman, 1973). The criticism is that such methodological groundwork has rarely been attempted, much less demonstrated, with the tasks used in information processing studies. Thus, all the conclusions drawn about specific deficits must be questioned as possibly being mere artifacts of the unequated tasks used.

The more theoretical critiques of information processing studies also incorporate considerations of varying task difficulty, but more basically suggest that the variations in performance seen in schizophrenia (or in aging) can be accounted for by more generalized factors that pervade the entire processing sequence. Currently, there is great interest in what might be termed "capacity theory," or the notion that the individual has only a fixed amount of resources to allocate for information processing (Kahneman, 1973). In this view, the primary effect of conditions like schizophrenia or aging is assumed to globally reduce the amount of "processing resource" available. The inefficiency subsequently shown by schizophrenics or by the aged might then show up on just about any task, or at any stage of information processing, provided the task required more resources than are readily available. Tasks are assumed to vary inherently in the amount of resources they require, and this notion becomes another way of speaking about task difficulty, complexity of cognitive operations, mental effort, etc. The degree of focal attention required for completing a task becomes one metric for gauging the processing resource required. Rather than trying to equate for them, variations in task difficulty are manipulated. The underlying premise, however, is the same as that in the methodological critique, namely, that performance deficits will show up first, or most measurably, on tasks that are the most difficult or place the greatest demands on the limited resources available. A number of researchers have suggested that global reductions in overall capacity may be the best way to account for the empirical variations seen on cognitive tasks both in gerontological research (Craik, 1977; Wright, 1981) and in the schizophrenia field (Gjerde, 1983; Knight & Russell, 1978).

Although markers for capacity reductions can be of many sorts, one of the most commonly suggested variants in the clinical literature suggests a central role for changes in the speed of behavior. One of the most reliable findings in both elderly and schizophrenic populations is slowed speed of behavior (Nuechterlein, 1977; Welford, 1977). There has been considerable debate in both fields about whether the slowing reflects breakdowns in the information processing sequence or constitutes an underlying factor that can account for information processing reductions (e.g., Gottsdanker, 1982; Salthouse & Somberg, 1982). Most prominently among gerontologists, Birren and his colleagues (Birren, 1965; Birren, Woods, & Williams, 1980; Botwinick, 1978) have suggested that generalized slowing at the neurological level may place limits on older individuals' ability to handle information. Rabbitt (1977) suggests that some tasks, if not done quickly, cannot be done at all. Certainly this is true in terms of processing information that decays rapidly. There have been similar theories that the cognitive deficits in schizophrenia can be accounted for by slowness of information processing (Korboot & Yates, 1973; Yates, 1966; Yates & Korboot, 1970).

Although consensus has yet to be reached on the validity and utility of the various information processing viewpoints, one cannot help but note the seeming generality and diffuseness of the cognitive inefficiencies and deficits seen in both the aged and schizophrenic populations. Also striking are the overall similarities, rather than differences, in the profiles of the two populations generated by information processing studies. Both observations lead toward questioning the value of an information processing approach for identifying areas of specific deficit in either population.

Perhaps the strongest suggestion in the data reviewed is that organizational schemas involved in information storage and response formation are critical determinants of the performance deficiencies shown by aged and by schizophrenic subjects. We have discussed how the organization of information in both memory and action schemas may affect what is perceived and the way the data are subsequently processed. One might wonder whether the remission of schizophrenic symptoms with advancing age may not result partly from life experiences that shape the individual's cognitive schemas and bring them more into line with consensual reality.

RESEARCH RECOMMENDATIONS

The information processing literature sheds little light on the cognitive status of aging schizophrenics. The available data do not permit inferences about what is likely to change from an information processing viewpoint as a schizophrenic individual ages. We cannot gauge whether the aging changes are likely to add to the schizophrenic deficits, to have little further effect, or in some way to counterbalance the cognitive deficits seen earlier. Comparisons between young schizophrenics and the normal aged are more likely to indicate something about young schizophrenics than about aged ones.

The first step in researching cognitive aging among schizophrenics needs to be the gathering of better descriptive data on the cognitive functioning of schizophrenic individuals in later life, using neuropsychological and other psychometric methods on available samples. The most immediate use of these data is apt to be analyses of the cross-sectional age differences seen between young and old schizophrenics on various measures, as compared with patterns seen within normal groups. The sparse information available to date would suggest that the age differences for schizophrenic samples very much parallel those for normal subjects and are essentially additive to the performance deficits associated with schizophrenia (Chaikelson & Schwartzman, 1983; Collins, 1978).

The value of an information processing approach will come

somewhat later, in attempts to specify a particular locus for whatever deficits are observed in the psychometric findings. If such experimental studies heed the lessons learned in other gerontological research, numerous complicating factors will have to be taken into account before any cognitive dysfunctions that are isolated can be attributed to the aging process *per se* (or to interactions between aging and schizophrenia). Particular care must be taken to examine and rule out the effects of sensory losses, physical health status (especially cardiovascular illness), institutionalism, and the individual's emotional or other negative reactions to being tested (Crook, 1979). Similar cautions would need to be observed about nuisance factors that are problematic for schizophrenia studies, such as the diagnostic heterogeneity apt to be present within schizophrenic samples, complications associated with psychotropic medications, and the effects of chronic institutionalization and labeling as abnormal.

Even without conducting whole studies on age changes, however, our knowledge about cognitive aging in schizophrenics would be enhanced substantially if schizophrenia researchers would simply begin analyzing the meaning of the age dimension within the samples they have available. For instance, it would be helpful to know how much of the variance on the cognitive measures used in various studies is attributable to age differences within the sample. In the future it is hoped that some researchers will take an interest in following their samples over time to determine what age changes take place longitudinally within the life course of the individual.

Research in this area should also shift away from focusing on single dependent variables toward studying broad profiles of the patient's cognitive functioning. This calls for comprehensive assessment programs, so that various aspects and stages of information processing can be compared within the same individuals. If, as a consequence of spending more time per individual, the number of individuals has to be reduced, it is hoped that samples will be selected more rigorously.

Finally, if we are able to get a developmental look at what is happening with aging in schizophrenia, research should focus not just on cognition, but on dimensions of change in cognitive processes. This implies selecting samples most apt to illustrate processes of change. The two target groups that would appear to be of greatest interest, on the basis of clinical observations, would be schizophrenics who progress toward a severely demented state and those who show a pattern of "burn-out" in their clinical symptoms. Studies of the latter group may be particularly useful since there appears to be substantial evidence for the burn-out phenomenon, the patients should remain readily testable, and the intriguing possibility exists that something about aging in these individuals might be identified as a process running counter to their schizophrenic characteristics.

P A R T

V

SOCIAL ADAPTATION
AND FUNCTION

Social adaptation to schizophrenia depends somewhat on whether the syndrome is florid or negative. Florid conditions are worsened by overstimulation while negative syndromes are worsened by an impoverished social environment. This may be compounded by age at onset, with earlier onset correlating with less adequate social skills.

Observing schizophrenia from the point of view of life course social science points out the stresses caused by being off-time, or out of synch with one's peers in life events such as completing school or getting married. The interruption of multiple hospitalizations often place the patient off-time in reference to others, adding to his stress in living in the community. Similarly, off-time events could be stressful enough to precipitate episodes in the vulnerable. With normal advancing age, the influence of peers is typically reduced, and the off-timeness tends to be less critical, which may help account for the apparent remission in so many schizophrenics.

Some patients adapt in later life, while others with no prior sign of illness break down. Some schizophrenics succeed in achieving a comfortable aloof homeostasis in life despite weak ego strength and lack of ability to withstand stress or form meaningful interpersonal relationships. Still others in structured and semistructured living environments, such as board and care homes or single room occupancy hotels, adapt by lessening the pressures on themselves. Vulnerable persons predisposed to mental illness may have found similar support systems with family or spouse, such that loss of this structure (e.g., through the death of the head of the family) may precipitate a late-onset illness. Similarly, pressures for more intimacy, such as are brought about by the retirement of a spouse, may be stressful enough to elicit overt symptoms of mental distress.

15 Long-Term Social Adaptation in Schizophrenia

J.K. Wing

Institute of Psychiatry, London

Three recent follow-up studies (Bleuler, 1972, 1978; Ciompi, this volume; Huber, 1975, 1976) have demonstrated that some 20%–25% of schizophrenic disorders clear up relatively quickly, although the short-term course can be stormy, while a similar proportion result in severe long-term disability. These proportions have probably not been affected by the introduction of modern methods of social and pharmacological treatment.

On the other hand, 50%–60% of cases run a fluctuating long-term course, which might well be influenced by medication and by factors in the social environment. If this were true, it would be inappropriate to speak of the natural history of schizophrenia (Wing, 1978a). It would also be inappropriate to discuss the relevance of a complex concept such as aging without taking into account the long-term adjustments that people with chronically disabling conditions commonly make anyway.

The following review, therefore, begins with a consideration of three hypotheses concerning the relationship between schizophrenia and the social environment (Wing & Brown, 1970; Wing, Leff, & Hirsch, 1973). The first states that at least two schizophrenic syndromes can be distinguished, each with its own characteristics and implications for course and outcome. The second states that these two syndromes are precipitated or made worse by different kinds of environmental factors. The third states that secondary handicaps (adverse personal reactions to disability and the circumstances associated with it) can be as important in determining social outcome as primary or intrinsic impairment.

CLINICAL SYNDROMES

The two schizophrenic syndromes considered here are commonly designated "florid" (or positive or productive) and "negative" (or defect or deficit). Conditions that have, or appear to have, a specific organic etiology, are not included.

Symptoms of the florid syndrome include the first rank phenomena of Kurt Schneider and hallucinations and explanatory delusions based on them. Hallucinations and delusions not affectively based that have apparently never been associated with first rank symptoms are usually also included in the florid syndrome. According to the International Pilot Study of Schizophrenia (WHO, 1973), such conditions are relatively uncommon among acute nonorganic psychoses.

The negative syndrome includes symptoms such as flatness of affect, slowness, underactivity, poverty of speech, and inability to use nonverbal means of communication. This group of symptoms is highly intercorrelated and, in long–stay inpatients, stable over long periods of time; social withdrawal is the most obvious behavioral correlate (Wing, 1961; Wing & Brown, 1970).

The relationship between the two syndromes is not well understood. An analogy could be drawn with the damage and release symptoms interpreted by Jackson in terms of a hierarchy of levels of the nervous system. Several attempts have been made to apply these ideas to schizophrenia without, in my view, stimulating useful empirical investigations (e.g., Ey, 1975). Each syndrome can appear, at any particular time, by itself or together with the other, and each can be made more or less severe. However, the florid syndrome is often dramatic in its appearance and disappearance, while it is more difficult to say at what point the negative syndrome is present or absent.

If the florid syndrome occurs alone, without much evidence of negative symptoms except during acute attacks, the prognosis tends to be relatively good. There is some evidence that such attacks are particularly likely to be precipitated by toxic substances or cerebral pathology (Connell, 1958; Davison & Bagley, 1969; Slater, Beard, & Glithero, 1963).

When the two syndromes occur together, as they commonly do, the negative syndrome is more important for prognosis of the social outcome, since it tends to antedate and to follow the more acute florid symptoms; i.e., the negative syndrome is associated with an insidious onset and a chronic course (WHO, 1979).

This has led to suggestions that the negative syndrome is more important for diagnosis than the florid. In the absence of external criteria to substantiate such a conclusion, I can see no justification for acting upon it. The negative syndrome, particularly in its milder manifestations, is much harder to recognize reliably. Slowness, underactivity, and social withdrawal have many other causes, among them Asperger's syndrome (Asperger, 1944; Wing, L., 1981), the aftereffects of encephalitis, chronic depression, and personality disorder.

In most of the research with which I have been associated, the selection of cases of schizophrenia has been based on the presence of the florid syndrome at some time during the clinical history, irrespective of whether a defect syndrome has supervened. This operational criterion has the merit of a fair degree of replicability as well as including most cases that psychiatrists all over the world call schizophrenic (Wing, Cooper & Sartorius, 1974, chapter 7).

Many epidemiological studies have demonstrated that onset (which usually means florid onset) occurs earlier in men than in women. An early onset is likely to be insidious, that is, associated with antecedent negative symptoms, a lack of personality development, and poor acquisition of social and occupational skills. It is not surprising, therefore, that relatively few men with schizophrenia marry and their fertility is low (Stevens, 1969). A later onset, commoner in women, is associated with a predominance of florid symptoms and occurs in people who have already developed their personal and social skills to some extent. Aging therefore has to be considered in relation not only to the length of time that various kinds of symptoms have been present but also to the age of onset.

REACTIVITY OF THE SCHIZOPHRENIC SYNDROMES

Evidence that the severity of the negative syndrome is dependent, to some extent and in some cases, on the quality of the social environment, was presented in a series of investigations carried out during the 1960s (Wing & Brown, 1970; Wing & Freudenberg, 1961). The theory was put forward that poverty of the social environment tended to increase slowness, underactivity, flatness of affect, poverty of speech, and social withdrawal and that a socially rich environment tended to decrease these symptoms. No claim was made for complete restitution. Rehabilitation and follow–up studies suggested that patients varied in the level of functioning attained but that most did continue to show some apparently irreducible impairment (Brown, Bone, Dalison, & Wing, 1966; Wing, 1960; Wing, Bennett, & Denham, 1964). Moreover, the principle was thought to hold for all types of social settings, not just for long–stay hospital wards (Brown et al., 1966).

One of the rehabilitation studies showed that too vigorous attempts at social stimulation, in patients who had not been sufficiently prepared for rehabilitation, could lead to relapse of florid symptoms that had not been apparent for years previously (Wing, Bennett, & Denham, 1964). Other studies suggested that life events that most people take in their stride appeared to precipitate an acute onset of florid symptoms, including a first onset (Brown & Birley, 1968). Finally, a series of investigations showed that some schizophrenic patients, particularly those whose relatives were critical of aspects of behavior that were not recognized as part of an illness, were at high risk of relapse following discharge from hospital. The risk was highest in patients who did not take the medication prescribed and who were constantly in face–to–face contact with the critical relative (Brown, Birley, & Wing, 1972; Brown, Monck, Carstairs, & Wing, 1962; Vaughan & Leff, 1976b). A controlled study of intervention, based on these principles, has demonstrated that the relapse rate can be significantly reduced (Leff, Kuipers, Berkowitz, Eberlein–Fries, & Sturgeon, 1982).

The original sketch of a theory linking these two sets of observations was based on the hypothesis that "thought disorder" was a key intermediary (Wing & Brown, 1970, pp. 22 & 181). Subsequent results have led to refinements but no essential change (Wing, 1977; Wing et al., 1973). Schizophrenic patients find it difficult, even painful, to communicate, because of the thought disorder that lies behind poverty of speech and derailment and because of their impaired use of nonverbal means of communication. This, together with slowness and underactivity (which must have a nonsocial component), makes social withdrawal a natural means of protection, but the process can go too far, particularly in understimulating surroundings. A socially intrusive environment, on the other hand, whether at home or in an over–optimistic rehabilitation unit, means that the patient cannot withdraw into a protective shell but is forced to interact and try to communicate. Florid symptoms then manifest themselves more openly, and the resulting speech and behavior abnormalities often lead to a crisis.

Somewhere between the two extremes lies the optimum social environment, in which the expectations of others are clearly evident, predictable, and consonant with the patient's actual abilities. However, in schizophrenia, as in any other chronically disabling condition, much depends on other factors that affect the ability to cope.

ADVERSE SECONDARY REACTIONS

The third hypothesis has something in common with Lemert's concept of secondary deviation (Lemert, 1951; Wing, 1978b, pp. 140–166; Wing & Brown, 1970, pp. 22–24). Institutionalism, the gradual acceptance of the values and routines of the institution so that an inmate eventually no longer wishes to live any other sort of life (Goffman, 1961), is an extreme example of the development of handicapping attitudes. We found that schizophrenic patients were less likely to say they wanted to leave hospital the longer they had been resident, and this remained true when age at admission was taken into account (Wing, 1961; Wing & Brown, 1970).

Subsequent experiments showed that certain adverse attitudes could be changed by training in specific environments, but there was no "transfer of training." For example, a change in attitude toward work, following experience in an industrial rehabilitation unit, did not carry with it a change in attitude toward discharge (Wing, 1960; Wing et al., 1964).

The more severe the clinical impairment, the less room there is for improvement due to a reduction in secondary reactions. An attitude of indifference may be a negative symptom that can only be reduced to a limited extent by environmental treatments. Similarly, unrealistic attitudes may be part of a delusional system that is unresponsive to social measures.

INTERACTION BETWEEN CLINICAL AND
PSYCHOSOCIAL FACTORS

The factors discussed above interact with each other and with all the other circumstances that make each individual's life unique. Someone with schizophrenia who comes into Manfred Bleuler's large inter-mediate group, where the course depends a good deal on the social environment, has to walk a tightrope with different kinds of danger on each side. Too much and too little social stimulation carry different kinds of risk. The extraordinary thing is that many patients do learn to cope, usually through trial and error and after a long period of suffering. They do not necessarily express this in so many words or even recognize how they are coping. The most articulate have to speak for the rest (Wing, 1975b). The same is true of many relatives, who learn to understand that social withdrawal is not necessarily unfriendliness, nor slowness laziness. Very few patients or relatives are given much long–term help by professionals, although some basic principles can now be formulated (Wing, 1975a, 1977).

In considering the course from this point of view, it appears that most families experience an early turbulent phase. Some patients and/or relatives learn, eventually, how to deal with the various problems they encounter and work out how to live with schizophrenia. Others do not. Family ties may be broken and the patient becomes institutionalized or vagrant, or family life continues in an atmosphere of tension and pain. Even in the latter case, however, many families do settle down. This may not occur for many years, until the patient is middle–aged, siblings have long left home, and the parents (or, more likely, the widowed mother) have become elderly. The florid symptoms become less evident and, although the negative ones tend to persist, they are often less severe than they would be in a completely unstimulating social environment such as an old–fashioned back ward.

Such a change could be due to a coming to terms, over a period of years, with a set of chronic disabilities. If so, it is particularly difficult in schizophrenia, but it is not essentially different from the process that occurs with physical handicaps. Most of us learn to live with ourselves as we grow older. Is aging in schizophrenia anything more?

There may, of course, be biological interactions. Kraepelin's designation dementia praecox may turn out to have been prescient. Early cognitive deficit in schizophrenia may herald greater risk of premature aging or of presenile or senile dementia. There are analogies in some forms of mental retardation. Long–term medication might accelerate biological aging in schizophrenia. None of these hypotheses has been disproved. But what we ordinarily mean by aging is more than this. We think of psychosocial adaptations to failing powers and diminishing opportunities. Disabled people have to anticipate such adaptations, and it is even possible that they could thereby become better prepared for them. At the very least, this hypothesis is worth considering with the others.

SUMMARY

Several recent follow–up studies have suggested that a substantial proportion of schizophrenic disorders run a fluctuating course, determined to a substantial extent by factors in the psychosocial environment as well as by medication. The epidemiological evidence points to an earlier onset, with a predominance of negative over florid symptoms (although both are present), in men than in women. An early and insidious onset of negative symptoms, often antedating a florid onset, is associated with a poor prognosis.

The two kinds of syndrome are differentially affected by environmental pressures. Poverty of the social environment increases negative symptoms; overstimulation precipitates a florid breakdown. Medication helps prevent the latter, at least in the short run, but not the former.

A third factor is personal reaction to adversity. Some patients and relatives cope with schizophrenia better than others, even allowing for severity of disability and pressure of other circumstances. This is also true over time, but eventually there is a tendency toward learning to live with schizophrenia. Normal aging, as a psychosocial as well as a biological process, involves similar adjustments. There may, of course, be an interaction between cognitive deficit and biological factors in aging, as in some forms of mental retardation, and the effects of very long–term medication have yet to be assessed. But no consideration of aging and schizophrenia is complete without taking into account what is known about long–term psychosocial adaptation.

16 Schizophrenia and the Adult Life-Course

Bertram J. Cohler

Carlton L. Ferrono

The University of Chicago

Advances in the treatment of schizophrenia across the past three decades have led to dramatic changes in the lives of patients and in the prognosis for this disturbance, which particularly disrupts continuity in sense of self and perceived place within the expected life course. While former cohorts of psychiatric patients remained in hospitals across much of their adult lives, most patients today are able to participate in the community, at least to a limited extent. These changes highlight the importance of understanding the impact of vulnerability, episode, and recovery, together with the effects of age itself, upon the life course of the schizophrenic patient.

All too often, schizophrenia is viewed as a disturbance of young adults. Little is known about the long-term course of life among these patients, first hospitalized in young adulthood, particularly across their middle and later years. Yet even less is known about the life course of those who first develop symptoms of schizophrenia in middle or late life. Some reports have suggested that intrinsic personality changes associated with aging dampen the expression of the most virulent schizophrenic symptoms (Bridge *et al.*, 1978; Ciompi, 1980a; Davis, 1974; Ehrentheil, 1964; Muller, 1963). On the other hand, these same intrinsic personality changes may intensify symptoms among those persons who first become schizophrenic in the second half of life, as portrayed in Freud's (1911) review of Schreber's memoirs (1903).

This chapter reviews findings on the lives of schizophrenic patients in terms of life-course social science, which emphasizes the dialectical relationship between social-historical processes and aspects of individual development (Buhler, 1968; Clausen, 1972; Elder, 1979; Elder & Rockwell, 1979; Perun & Bielby, 1980; Riegel, 1979). From a life-course perspective: (1) individual development and processes of aging take place in particular social and historical contexts; (2) shared understandings of both expected life events and performance of characteristic roles at particular stages of adulthood lead to a sense of being more or less "on-time"—with morale or life satisfaction being largely determined by congruence between place in the life course and expected place among persons of a particular age (Cohler & Boxer, 1984); and (3) shared understanding of the limits of the expectable duration of life, which means that with the advent of middle age less time is left to be lived than has been lived already, altering both presently construed meanings of the personal past and hopes and fears regarding the future (Cohler, 1982; Jaques, 1965; Munnichs, 1966).

The course of life of a schizophrenic is affected not only by constitutionally determined vulnerability and episodes that disrupt personal continuity and performance of expected adult roles, but also by the stigma attributed by self and others to the diagnosis itself, to its characteristic symptoms and, typically, to periods of hospitalization (Clausen, 1981). Study of schizophrenia across adulthood from a life-course perspective may clarify some of the issues faced by the aging schizophrenic.

TIME, AGE, AND THE LIFE COURSE

Since Durkheim's (1915) pioneering analysis of the social origins of thought, much interest has been shown in the interrelationship between experiences of particular persons and the social order that structures and organizes these individual experiences (Berger & Luckman, 1966; Geertz, 1973; Sorokin & Merton, 1937), including changing meanings of time and aging over the course of life. Precisely this social definition of the individual life (Van Gennep, 1960) transforms the study of the life span or life cycle into study of the life course. As Elder and Rockwell (1979) note:

> The life-course perspective locates individuals in age cohorts and thus in historical context, depicts their age-differentiated life patterns in relation to this context, and illuminates the continual interplay between the social course of lives and development . . . (it) directs inquiry toward understanding the process by which lives are lived. Through an understanding of the life course and its consequences for development, we are able to explain the process by which early life events are related to later events. Age relates history and social structure in the human biography, and it is through age differentiation that we find the implications of time and place for development. (p. 34)

Chronological age, itself, is important only to the extent that it refers to both expectable events and salient roles to be performed at particular points in the course of fe, within particular cohorts.

These cohorts are differentiated by social-historical events, such as the Great Depression (Elder, 1974), experienced by persons at a particular age, which lead to a communality of experience beyond that conveyed by place in the life course (Cain, 1964, 1967; Elder, 1974, 1979; Riley, 1971,1973, 1976; Ryder, 1965). Despite problems in the definition and use of the concept of cohort in social science research (Baltes, Cornelius, & Nesselroade, 1979; Cain, 1967; Rosow, 1976, 1978), this concept reflects real differences across "generations" in the understanding of self and others (Elder, 1975, 1979).

A particular cohort shares expectations of the bounds of the life course and the ages at which events are most likely to occur and roles are to be performed, including progression across roles and statuses (Fiske, 1980; Neugarten & Peterson, 1957; Neugarten, Moore, & Lowe, 1965; Neugarten & Moore, 1968; Neugarten & Hagestad, 1976). Considerable variation across both societies and cohorts within societies may be caused by factors such as gender, social status, or changing life expectancy (Fallo-Mitchell & Ryff, 1982; Hareven, 1980; Neugarten & Hagestad, 1976).

Age norms represent both explicit and implicit social proscriptions for particular actions and also provide the basis for standards or expectations that persons apply to their own lives. Neugarten (1979) has observed that:

> Adults carry around in their heads, whether or not they can easily verbalize it, a set of anticipations of the normal, expectable life cycle. They internalize expectations of the consensually validated sequences of major life events—not only what those events should be, but when they should occur. They make plans and set goals along a time line shaped by these expectations. (p. 125)

As Smith (1961) and Roth (1963) have noted, these socially defined expectations constitute the "timetables" by which persons evaluate their own lives, determining whether they are roughly on schedule. Within any particular cohort, events such as school entry and leaving, career changes, marriage, parenthood and grandparenthood, retirement, and death, all are experienced and evaluated as taking place roughly at the expectable point, as defined by prevailing age norms, or as happening too "early" or "late" relative to others of the same age within the same cohort. Precisely because progression of roles and statuses at expectable times is an internalized standard, failure to attain a particular status on time may lead to lowered morale (Bradburn, 1969; Brim & Ryff, 1980; Cohler & Boxer, 1984).

Distress resulting from being "off-time" may be intensified by a lack of support from significant others. For example, if widowhood occurs too early in the life course, few role colleagues may be available for support and anticipatory socialization. Events taking place too late, such as leaving school or getting married, may be regarded both by self and significant others as evidence of some personal failure or lack of social competence.

While being off-time is not unusual, persistent and extreme asynchronization (Cain, 1964) in many different spheres of life may cause time relationships to become dislocated and time disordered (Seltzer, 1976), making it increasingly difficult to catch up. This problem is particularly significant among multiply hospitalized psychiatric patients for whom both symptoms and hospitalization itself affect social timing across adulthood. Society allocates "idiosyncrasy credits" (Hollander, 1964; Neugarten & Hagestad, 1976) for such factors as social privation, disaster, or illness. As these credits are used up, as occurs among persons with multiple psychiatric hospitalizations, the sense of temporal dislocation increases. The lowered morale associated with role and timing asynchrony often interacts with symptoms of illness in a reciprocal fashion, each exacerbating the effects of the other.

Among the most significant socially determined expectations of the course of life concerns the length of the life span itself. While shared understandings on length of life vary somewhat with gender, social status, and cohort, persons living on into their eighties begin to feel that they are survivors. As Neugarten (1973, 1979) has noted, with the onset of middle-age, many persons first become aware of their mortality, (Cohler, 1982; Jaques, 1965; Jung, 1933; Munnichs, 1966), which leads to particular changes in understanding of self and of place in the life course that appear to be intrinsic to the process of normative aging. There is a shift toward increased reminiscence, first in the service of problem solving but later in life, with the goal of settling accounts prior to death—the so-called "life review" (Butler, 1963).

Accompanying this process of coming to terms with the finitude of life, there is a shift from an outer world orientation to increased preoccupation with the inner world, termed "interiority" by Neugarten (1973, 1979), together with lessened interest in impersonal cultural institutions (Erikson, 1968). This increased interiority may lead to marked changes in sources of life satisfaction. For example, loneliness and lack of meaningful social contact appear to cause much more personal distress among younger persons than among older persons. These personality changes across the second half of life have particular significance for the schizophrenic: older adults may experience both the onset of and recovery from psychotic episodes quite differently from younger adults.

CONTINUITY IN SCHIZOPHRENIC SYMPTOMS
ACROSS ADULTHOOD

Although it had been assumed that schizophrenic patients remained in hospitals throughout much of their adult lives, studies carried out over the past three decades suggest that only 10–20% of persons first hospitalized in early adulthood remain hospitalized over long periods of time (Bleuler, 1968, 1978; Bridge *et al.*, 1978; Ciompi, 1980*a*; Huber, Gross, & Schuttler, 1975; Huber, Gross, Schuttler, & Linz, 1980; Stephens, 1970).

The view of schizophrenia as an episodic disturbance among persons capable of at least limited community participation (Clausen, 1985) is consistent with the perspective on vulnerability portrayed by Zubin (1977, 1978), Zubin and Spring (1977), Spring and Zubin (1977), and Zubin and Steinhauer (1981). Central to this view, as Zubin (1978) noted, is the assumption that:

> . . . the permanent characteristic of schizophrenia is not the disorder but the vulnerability to the disorder, and that the episodes of the disorder are time limited. . . . vulnerability is the proneness to develop an episode when sufficient stress-producing life events (external as well as internal) occur that exceed the stress–tolerance of the person. (p. 641)

The syndrome of chronic hospitalism, all too often viewed as synonymous with the disturbance, must be differentiated from the disturbance itself, as expressed in particular episodes.

Vulnerability to schizophrenia appears to be constitutionally determined, with both monogenetic (Kidd, 1978; Matthysse & Kidd, 1976) and polygenetic (Gottesman & Shields, 1976; Rosenthal, 1963) theories of transmission providing plausible accounts of it's pathogenesis (Heston, 1970). The extent of vulnerability varies, with those more vulnerable more likely to experience subsequent episodes. According to this view, strains associated with performing adult roles, particularly role transitions, as well as stresses resulting from adverse life events, including those perceived as idiosyncratically stressful (Beck & Worthen, 1972), become significant for the timing of particular episodes, although not necessarily for the etiology of the disturbance (Brown, Harris, & Peto, 1973).

It is important to note that vulnerability or risk for schizophrenia extends throughout life (Hanson, Gottesman, & Heston, 1976; Hanson, Gottesman, & Meehl, 1977). Persons genetically more vulnerable may experience schizophrenic episodes earlier in life, and accordingly, less stress and strain may be required to precipitate an episode. Among less vulnerable persons, a greater number of stressful events may be required to precipitate an episode, thus delaying the manifestation of any overt symptoms until later in life. Also, some highly vulnerable persons may not be exposed in early life to those particular events which, for them, are capable of precipitating an episode (Bandura, 1982; Gergen, 1977, 1980).

From the perspective of risk and vulnerability, schizophrenic episodes may occur at any time from adolescence to oldest age. Prevalence and incidence studies focusing on rates of schizophrenia among older persons are particularly difficult to interpret because of cross–national variations in both diagnosis and reporting, and also because of problems in locating housebound elderly. Further, as Yolles and Kramer (1969) noted, distinctions must be made between treated and untreated prevalence. Using essentially untreated prevalence figures, Neugebauer (1980) estimated a rate of .32 for schizophrenics among persons over age 60, based on European reports, as contrasted with a rate of .60 for all adults, based primarily on U.S. data (Neugebauer, 1980). Reviewing incidence statistics, Adelstein and colleagues (1968) and Kramer (1978) both noted new referrals for schizophrenia even after age 60. Kay and Bergman (1980), reviewing earlier figures by Helgason, suggested that 15% of the risk in men and 37% of the risk in women remains after age 50.

Comparative studies of older persons admitted to psychiatric hospitals in England and Sweden (Kay, 1959, 1963; Kay & Roth, 1961, 1963; Kay & Beamish, 1964; Roth, 1955) noted a disorder with hallucinations, thought disorder, and lack of insight, in spite of intact memory and good intelligence. While some patients were married, most were single women who had lived alone most of their lives. Many patients had led particularly isolated and withdrawn lives, even prior to the appearance of symptoms. Life events associated with such major role transitions as retirement and widowhood were not clearly associated with the onset of symptoms. Detailed review of the symptoms of this disorder of later life led Kay (1963), Kay and Roth (1961, 1963), and Post (1980) to conclude that paraphrenias of later life must be considered as forms of schizophrenia.

THE COURSE OF SCHIZOPHRENIA ACROSS THE
SECOND HALF OF LIFE

The study of schizophrenia across the second half of life involves two separate clinical problems: (1) the course of life of persons whose first episode occurred in young adulthood and (2) patterns of episode, recovery, and subsequent life course of persons whose initial episode occurred in middle or late life. Most studies of schizophrenia and aging have addressed primarily the first question, although some, particularly those of Huber, Gross and Schuttler (1975) and Huber *et al.* (1980), have included patients initially hospitalized at any point from adolescence to old age.

Central to the discussion of subsequent life course is the distinction between positive (active) and negative (passive or residual) symptoms. Positive symptoms, the characteristic cognitive dysfunctions such as hallucinations, delusions, and thought disorder, are often controlled by medication. Negative symptoms—flattened affect, poverty of speech, and loss of drive—are probably more effectively controlled by psychotherapy. These distinctions are important when considering the course of schizophrenia across adulthood.

Positive symptoms may be time limited, although patients continue to show residual or negative symptoms that may increase the likelihood of subsequent episodes. Study of negative symptoms is particularly complex (Strauss & Carpenter, 1979; Strauss, Carpenter, & Bartko, 1974). Expression of negative symptoms may be affected by such social factors as prolonged hospital stay, leading to institutionalization (Goffman, 1962), labeling (Scheff, 1966), and stigma (Clausen, 1981). Prolonged hospital stay disrupts the patient's life, making it increasingly off–time; negative symptoms reciprocally contribute to feelings of being off–time, leading to further pessimism about the future and lack of energy.

Evaluation of negative symptoms is more likely to be confused with particular cohort effect (Baltes, Cornelius, & Nesselroad, 1979; Riley, 1973; Ryder, 1965) than the evaluation of positive symptoms. Schizophrenic patients hospitalized prior to the late 1950s remained far longer in psychiatric hospitals than more recent cohorts, who have benefited from both medication and increased understanding of the psychiatric hospital as a treatment modality (Caudill, 1958; Goffman, 1962; Greenblatt, Levinson, & Williams, 1957; Stanton & Schwartz, 1954). In addition, increased concern with aftercare as a means of reducing the length of hospitalization has made it possible for otherwise vulnerable persons to spend more of their adult lives as effective members of the community (Cohler & Grunebaum, 1981).

Relatively few studies have addressed the second half of life of persons with early onset schizophrenia, and even fewer have covered the subsequent life course of late onset schizophrenics. The relationships among symptom, episode, and subsequent life course may be quite different for patients first hospitalized in young adulthood and those first hospitalized in middle or old age, reflecting apparent lack of continuity in the dynamics of lives over time (Cohler, 1982; Neugarten, 1969, 1979).

Much of the interest in the long–term study of formerly hospitalized persons has been in determination of prognosis. Although some investigators note a pessimistic outcome (Harrow, Grinker, Silverstein, & Holzman, 1978), and although definitions of diagnosis vary across studies and over time, studies across two and three decades have been interpreted as both supporting the concept of episode and vulnerability and showing a generally good prognosis for recovery from particular episodes. These conclusions appear particularly warranted as a result of recent reports by European investigators who were able to follow cohorts of patients, using a narrow definition of schizophrenia, excluding course as a criterion for diagnosis, over more than two decades (Bleuler, 1968, 1978; Ciompi, 1980a; Huber, Gross, & Schuttler, 1975; Huber et al., 1980).

Those few studies using concepts from normative aging in understanding the lives of older schizophrenic patients, primarily those first hospitalized in the first half of life, have suggested discontinuity in adjustment over time, with marked diminution of both positive and negative symptoms after mid–life. Muller and leDinh (1976), following up patients in Bleuler's (1968) study, reported that effects of aging led to diminution of symptoms among approximately half these patients, with about a quarter of the total group showing marked increase in accommodation to the social surround, and reduction in delusional ideas. These reports, and Lawton's (1972) review of older patients studied at least 30 years after hospitalization, showed an increase in communality of Rorshach percepts, suggesting increased ability to understand the world in the same terms as nonhospitalized persons of the same age. Such changes can be accounted for either by assuming intrinsic psychological changes across the second half of life, or by learning acceptable behavior (although this latter explanation does not account for the inability to accept such communality at younger ages). Ehrentheil (1964; Ehrentheil et al., 1962) also noted marked reduction of psychotic symptoms among older schizophrenic patients. However, those patients more withdrawn at time of first hospitalization, 30 years earlier, remained more withdrawn, and also showed less reduction in thought disorder.

More recently, Bridge et al. (1978) reviewed findings from a number of long-term studies, some extending as long as 40 years following initial hospitalization, and including reports from a number of Russian investigators not elsewhere accessible in the English literature. Review of these studies supports assumption of a marked decrease among schizophrenic patients with the advent of mid-life. While both diagnosis and outcome measures varied across these studies and, while cohort effects further complicate interpre- tation of these findings, symptoms may "burn out" with attainment of mid-life (Davis, 1974).

Detailed reports from a number of European studies provide additional support for the assumption of an association between psychosocial changes in mid-life, together with diminution of symptoms, generally among patients first hospitalized in young adulthood. Bleuler (1968, 1978), reporting on a follow-up study of schizophrenic patients across more than two decades, noted that more than half of these patients showed a complete recovery when followed-up in mid-life. Only 10% of the patients in the original study were permanently hospitalized. Ciompi (1980a), reporting on a follow-up study of as long as 50 years, noted that more than two-thirds of persons initially hospitalized in young adulthood were functioning effectively in the community as older persons. An additional group of about 20% of persons initially hospitalized up to 50 years earlier, in young adulthood, were able to function effectively in the community, but were occasionally rehospitalized for schizophrenic episodes.

Huber, Gross, and Schuttler (1975) and Huber, Gross, Schuttler, and Linz (1980) followed a group of formerly hospitalized patients across more than two decades, and observed that only 13% of patients remained permanently hospitalized. As in Ciompi's report, more than half of all patients were fully recovered, while virtually all patients not permanently hospitalized were able to remain in the community. Of particular interest in the research of Huber and his colleagues was the inclusion of patients hospitalized both initially in young adulthood and initially after mid–life. A somewhat larger proportion (30%) of patients initially hospitalized in the fourth and fifth decades of life showed complete remission than those initially hospitalized in late adolescence and early adulthood (21%). However, a greater number of patients initially hospitalized later in life also showed continuing negative symptoms.

SCHREBER'S MEMOIRS AND LIFE–COURSE PERSPECTIVES
ON SCHIZOPHRENIA

Many of the problems involved in study of schizophrenia across the second half of life, particularly initial hospitalization at mid–life, may be seen in the case of Schreber, made famous as a result of Freud's (1911) analysis of his memoirs. Schreber's first episode, in his early forties, occurred when he was a county judge, just after failing to win election to the Reichstag. Hospitalized for 7 months, he was treated by Professor Paul Flechsig (1847–1929) of Leipzig for what was described as a serious attack of hypochondria. Schreber's second illness, precipitated by his appointment as Chief Judge of the Dres-den Superior Court, occurred at age 52 and was of psychotic propor-tions including suicidal intent, visual and auditory hallucinations, and persecutory and grandiose delusions. He was hospitalized for 9 years, until he won a court–ordered release in 1902. The third illness, also a psychotic break, came in 1909, occasioned by the death of his wife and mother. He remained hospitalized until his death 2 years later. Given these three episodes, and the stressful life events that precipi-tated them, Schreber provides ample evidence of "enduring vulner-ability" in schizophrenia.

Several significant off–time transitions were evident in Schre-ber's life: his father, a famous physician and pedagogue, underwent a major personality change after a gymnasium accident at the age of 51 and died 2 years later, when his son was 19. His older brother committed suicide at age 38. Schreber was married in his mid–thirties to a woman who, by all accounts, was his social and intellectual inferior. Further, the couple was unable to have children, and Schreber writes of their "repeated disappointment" in this regard.

Schreber's second illness provided the basis for his *Memoirs*, the doctor's reports, court proceedings regarding his release, Freud's (1911) investigation, and subsequent psychoanalytic reports (Bau-meyer, 1956; Katan, 1949; Niederland, 1974). Schreber himself vividly portrays the stress and off–time nature of his appointment as Chief Judge, where he presided over judges much his senior in age and court experience.

Since the genetic component in schizophrenia of later life appears to be less of a factor than in the schizophrenias of early adulthood (Kay & Roth, 1961, 1963), the impact of both early life experiences and later adult development must be considered. In the first instance, because of detailed accounts of the father's child-rearing practices, it is possible to understand Schreber's early life environment, including the norms, expectations, and ideals with which he was inculcated. Many of the father's methods and ideas may be seen in a transformed state in the son's later delusions and hallucinations (Schatzman, 1973).

Freud's view of the significance of intrinsic psychological changes accompanying the transition to mid–life, for the course of schizophrenia, is markedly different from that of more recent investigators in psychiatry and social sciences. Indeed, for Freud, such changes at mid–life may lead to intensification rather than reduction of positive symptoms:

> At the time of this illness Dr. Schreber was fifty–one years of age, and he had therefore reached a time of life which is of critical importance in sexual development. It is a period . . . of far–reaching involution . . . men as well as women are subject to a 'climacteric' and to the special susceptibility to disease which goes along with it. (p. 46)

Gutmann (1975, 1977) noted the increased passivity and sensu-ality among men in later life. Schreber's symptoms represented almost a parody of such expectable changes among older men in Western society: he believed he was being turned into a woman and experienced periods of voluptuousness, during which he caressed his own body and adorned himself in women's clothing and jewelry. At the same time, delusions of being transformed into a woman by God, providing for the renewal of mankind, represented an effort at deal-ing with his feelings of failure to realize the parental role, certainly one of the most significant of adult roles.

Consistent with concepts of increased interiority in later life, Schreber became increasingly preoccupied with his own thoughts, ultimately developing his own religious system in an effort to deal with the problem of the finitude of life, and proclaiming his immor-tality. However, the concern expressed in postscripts to his memoirs, dealing with such issues as cremation and the future beyond his own life, show a continuing awareness of issues of living and dying.

CONCLUSION

Consideration of schizophrenia from a life–course perspective raises important questions for subsequent study. In the first place, consid-eration of cohort effects has been neglected in the study of the life course among former patients over periods of two and three decades. Patients hospitalized prior to the development of neuroleptic medi-cation and the emphasis upon the psychiatric hospital as a thera-peutic milieu may have perceptions of the significance of symptoms and long-term prognosis quite different from those of patients hospitalized more recently. Expression of residual or negative symptoms is particularly likely to be influenced by such cohort effects.

Study is also required of the continuity of the schizophrenic disturbance itself across the course of life, including possible changes in the expression of both positive and negative symptoms associated with point in the life course of the first episode, as well as changes in the content and intensity of symptoms subsequent to the first episode. It is particularly important to delineate the role of developmental changes in personality across middle and later life, as these changes are related to both timing of the initial schizophrenic episode and the subsequent course of the patient's life. Prospective longitudinal studies would be particularly important in understanding the course of life on vulnerability, episode, and recovery in schizophrenia.

17 Predisposition to Schizophrenia: Breakdown or Adaptation in Later Life

H. Richard Lamb

University of Southern California School of Medicine

Research increasingly suggests the operation of genetic and bio-chemical factors in the predisposition to mental illness. The adoption studies of Kety and associates (1976) indicate that schizophrenia is in large part genetically determined, and similar evidence has been found for the major affective disorders (Cadoret, 1978). This paper discusses those environmental factors that determine how persons predisposed to mental illness adapt or fail to adapt and function in later life. The discussion includes those whose level of functioning has been low since adolescence and early adulthood as well as those who have functioned well, either continuously or intermittently, before decompensating in their fifties or sixties.

DECOMPENSATION AND ADAPTATION SINCE YOUTH

A recent study of long-term severely disabled psychiatric patients (in a board and care home in Los Angeles) showed that significantly more patients under the age of 30 had goals to change *anything* in their lives, compared to patients over 30 years old (Lamb, 1979). How can we interpret this finding? Perhaps, as these persons with limited capabilities became older, they experienced more failures in dealing with life's demands and in striving toward their earlier goals. They had more time to lower or set aside their goals and to accept a low level of functioning that did not exceed their capabilities. By the time they entered middle life, many may have adopted such a lifestyle and in this way adapted to their illness. In the same study, a strong relationship was found between age and history of hospitali-zation—three-fourths of those under 30 had been hospitalized during the preceding year, compared to only one-fifth over age 30.

When people are still young, mentally ill or not, and just beginning to deal with life's demands and making their way in the world, they struggle to achieve some measure of independence, to choose and succeed at a vocation, to establish satisfying inter-personal relationships and attain a degree of intimacy, and to acquire some sense of identity. Lacking ego strength, the ability to withstand stress, and the ability to form meaningful interpersonal relationships, the mentally ill person's efforts often lead only to failure in this ubiquitous search for independence, identity, and intimacy (Lamb, 1982). The result may be a still more determined, even frantic effort with a greatly increased level of anxiety that begins to border on feelings of desperation. Ultimately, this process may lead to further failure accompanied by feelings of despair. For a person predisposed to retreats into psychosis, the result is predictably a stormy course with acute psychotic breaks and repeated hospitalizations often related to these desperate attempts to achieve. The situation becomes even worse when such persons are in a high expectancy environment, that is, where the high expectations not only emanate from within the person, but also from family members and mental health professionals.

Some chronically dysfunctional and mentally disordered indi-viduals gradually, over a period of years, succeed in their strivings for independence, a vocation, intimacy, and a sense of identity. Many others, however, eventually give up the struggle and find face–saving rationalizations. For instance, a middle–aged woman says, "I would have raised my children, but the judge was lied to and took them away from me." Or a person in his middle years says, "I am retired now on Social Security," referring to his SSI monies, which in fact are given for his disabling psychiatric disorder. Many similar face–saving, ego–defending rationalizations are heard from chronically dysfunc-tional persons who have come to feel they must passively submit to overwhelming forces that control their destinies and impede their progress. Often, one hears no rationalizations at all but finds only a constricted passive stance on life, as in the case of the patient who looks no further than his next cigarette.

On the other hand, many patients reach an adjustment similar to successful retirement—they spend their time reading, puttering about, and interacting with their families. Either way, much of the pressure that in their younger years had resulted in psychotic decompensations is removed, and middle and later life is often characterized by a relative stabilization of illness. Maturation also seems a factor, since age makes a person less impulsive and more philosophical in the face of adversity and disappointment.

Board and care homes exemplify one kind of adaptation in a protected, low pressure setting of persons predisposed to mental illness. Board and care homes for psychiatric patients in California are unlocked and provide a shared room, three meals a day, super-vision of medications, and minimal staff supervision.

Psychiatrists come to the facility and prescribe psychotropic drugs for the majority of the residents. The better members of the staff are reasonably aware of residents who are becoming symptomatic or more floridly symptomatic and convey this to the visiting psychiatrists, who may adjust medications accordingly. In addition, the staff often sees what is causing the residents to be symptomatic and may intervene by manipulating the patients' environment to ease the pressures on them.

Additional structure is provided by supervising the residents' money and disbursing it according to the staff's estimate of the residents' ability to handle their finances. Some residents may be overprotected by this, but the staff generally tries to give residents as much responsibility as they can handle. Serving meals at fixed times not only adds structure but ensures that the residents eat on a regular basis. Many residents reported that when living alone their eating habits were erratic, often to the point of undermining their physical health and certainly their sense of well-being. Although having all their meals prepared may be more than some of the residents require, most of them feel taken care of and relieved of a major responsibility. For a large proportion of long-term psychiatric patients, the board and care home has not only replaced but taken over the functions of the state hospital.

Despite this type of structure, residents have a great deal of freedom. In many such facilities, they are free to come and go as they please. Although some never leave the building, the great majority (95% in one study) use community resources to varying degrees, mostly by visiting local supermarkets and eating places and by taking walks in the neighborhood.

Persons in their middle or later years who have sought refuge in such facilities consistently recount an early inability to cope with social and vocational demands, an inability to withstand life's pressures, and a poverty of interpersonal relationships (Lamb, 1979). A small minority of such persons are particularly aware and insightful—they recognize that they become anxious and overwhelmed in social or vocational situations. With varying degrees of reluctance, they have made conscious decisions to limit their exposure to pressure and in some cases to avoid pressure of any kind.

Persons in such environments have come to what one might call adaptation by decompression. They have found a place of asylum from life's pressures, but at the same time a place with support, structure, and some treatment, especially in the form of psychotropic medications. Many, of course, probably could and should do more, and these persons might well be functioning at a higher level if social and vocational rehabilitation had been made available early on by persons skilled in working with residents with limited ego strength. But for those who cannot benefit from rehabilitation efforts, it may be that an inactive, sometimes even seclusive lifestyle in a pressureless setting may be the highest level at which they can function for any sustained period of time without decompensation (Murphy, Engelsmann, & Tcheng-Laroche, 1976). All that has just been said applies equally well to living with families. It may be correct but misleading to refer to these persons as "regressed" or "institutionalized"; one may be seeing not just the results of their living environment but also the results of their inherent limitations and lack of capabilities.

DECOMPENSATION IN LATER LIFE

Many persons predisposed to mental illness may have shown little indication of it in their youth and middle years. They may have found community support systems or sheltered environments, such as living with parents or with a supportive spouse. Their levels of functioning may have varied over a wide range. Those living with parents may have been able to hold full-time or part-time jobs, or at least to have assumed some responsibility around the home. On the other hand, they may have remained essentially in the role of child. The same is true for those living with supportive spouses. A man may have been able to hold a relatively undemanding job, or at least to have taken care of the gardening and perhaps assumed the role of house-husband while his wife worked. Similarly, a wife may have taken varying degrees of responsibility as a homemaker with much assistance and support from the husband.

In many cases, the person first decompensates only in middle or later life when these supports are lost. For instance, a 55-year-old women had, at age 26, gone directly from living with her very protective parents into marriage. The husband had not only worked, but assumed most of the responsibility for the household and the children. The patient was first hospitalized at age 54 following the sudden death of her husband. She was withdrawn, hallucinating, and her associations were extremely loose. She reconstituted in the hospital but needed a sister to come and live with her as head of the household. A year later the sister announced that she was no longer willing to continue in this role. The patient again decompensated, and finally the teenage children were placed with relatives and the patient placed in a board and care home, where she has led an inactive existence but remained in remission. As the social worker involved in the case said, "Dying was the worst thing that the husband could have done to this patient."

A 57-year-old man, never married, had always lived with his parents. His father had died several years before. Though he had led an inactive and seclusive life and tended to have rambling speech, he was not overtly psychotic. When his 76-year-old mother became seriously ill he decompensated and was found aimlessly walking the streets, hallucinating and incoherent, and was hospitalized for the first time. Even while still psychotic, he was able to say, "What will I do when my mother dies?"

Another example is a 58-year-old divorced woman who had never been known to be mentally ill until her husband left her at age 52. At that time her parents found her paranoid, delusional, hearing voices, and talking incoherently, though these symptoms subsided after several months without any psychiatric intervention. When she was 53 her son, an only child, died from a narcotics overdose. She again manifested the same psychotic symptoms, and again they subsided after a few months, only to appear again on each anniversary of the son's death. She continued to live alone, though with considerable support from her aging parents. On the fifth anniversary of the son's death, while psychotic, she set fire to some newspapers in the lobby of her apartment building. There was little damage, but she was taken to jail and from there sent to a hospital for the first time. Psychiatric evaluation revealed her to be delusional, hallucinating, and to have a marked thought disorder. An important factor appeared to be the rapidly failing health of her parents.

Research has indicated that if persons predisposed to schizophrenia encounter stimulating environments in the home or the work place or even in treatment settings, relapse rates increase (Wing, 1978; Anderson, Hogarty, & Reiss, 1981; Schooler & Spohn, 1982). In the same vein, many schizophrenics have only a limited tolerance for interpersonal closeness. This can be a factor at retirement. For 30 years, a 58–year–old woman had led a marginal, somewhat seclusive life as a housewife in a childless marriage where the husband was absorbed in his work, leaving her alone with her household chores. Though she was disorganized in her activities and her thinking and intermittently paranoid, her husband seemed satisfied. When the husband retired, they were constantly together, with the husband, now home most of the day, seeking ways to use his energies, and looking to his wife for companionship and much more of a relationship than they had had before. Her first blatantly psychotic decompensation and psychiatric hospitalization occurred within several months. Work with this patient centered around helping the husband involve himself with outside activities and restoring a semblance of their previous relationship.

A late onset psychosis is not infrequently seen in women in their middle years whose identity has been primarily that of parent. When the children are grown, many persons find other interests, perhaps involvement with grandchildren including babysitting, or a vocation and another identity, or a rich and more rewarding marital relationship. For those who do not, an overt psychosis can be precipitated in a person so predisposed.

But even adapting to the stresses of this period may leave other perils ahead. A 66–year–old woman had received much help from a very supportive husband in raising their two children. At age 31 she had had what was diagnosed as a catatonic schizophrenic (schizophreniform) episode just after the death of her mother; she went into remission after a 1–month hospitalization and apparently remained free of overt psychotic symptoms for the next 35 years. When the children had grown and left home, she had become involved in undemanding volunteer work requiring almost no interaction with people and had also continued in her role as housewife. Shortly after the death of her husband, she was hospitalized for the second time with a psychotic episode characterized by inappropriate affect and disorganization of her thought processes. She also appeared to be responding to internal stimuli. Work in the hospital with her and her married daughter resulted in such major decisions as selling the house, locating an apartment, and finding a low–risk investment for the insurance money. A major factor was the daughter's decision to become more involved with her mother on an ongoing basis.

CONCLUSION

Generally, persons who first decompensate in later life have limited amounts of ego strength (the ability to cope with stress). They have met life's demands, but often only with the aid of a strong and consistent support system specific to their needs, such as a very dependent relationship. In a similar category are persons with so–called schizophreniform disorders with a decompensation in later life—perhaps whose functioning over the years has for the most part been adequate, though punctuated by decompensations of 2 weeks to 6 months in duration. Persons in this group usually have more ego strength than those who decompensated in youth and early adulthood and have been low functioning since. Persons who functioned adequately before a late–life psychosis can probably regain their previous level of functioning, or something close to it, if they can find another support system.

Some who decompensate early in life may also achieve a low–level adaptation by the time they reach middle and later life. But whenever decompensation occurs, the key to helping these patients adapt is to provide supports appropriate to their needs, to reduce pressures they cannot handle, and to provide treatment and rehabilitation that will maximize their potential without pushing them beyond their capabilities.

Some of the major challenges of our day include finding ways to enlist mental health professionals in the treatment of elderly psychotic patients and securing funding to develop day treatment centers, a range of residential treatment facilities, and other resources needed to provide adequate community support systems for these patients. The mental health professions tend to focus on the problems of younger psychotic patients, and this is certainly an important task. It may well be, however, that we need community support programs at the federal and state levels to specifically address the problems of the elderly who are predisposed to major mental illness.

18 Elderly Schizophrenics and Paranoiacs Living in Single-Room Occupancy Hotels

Carl I. Cohen

S.U.N.Y. Downstate Medical Center

No detailed descriptions are available of those aging schizophrenics who have become ensconced within the dilapidated walls of the single–room occupancy (SRO) hotels that dot America's cities. What little is known about them tends to contravene the popular myth that they are representative of the elderly population living in SRO hotels. Of 201 individuals aged 60 and over surveyed as part of a larger study of SRO hotels in Manhattan, only 7% reported previous psychiatric hospitalization (New York State Department of Social Services, 1980). Unfortunately, this survey failed to provide any descriptive data about the demographic, health, psychiatric, and behavioral characteristics of these former mental patients. In order to redress this deficiency and to confirm the finding that SRO hotels house proportionately few elderly schizophrenics, data derived from a longitudinal study of 162 individuals aged 60 and over living in midtown Manhattan SRO hotels were examined. The principal aim was to provide a more detailed picture of those respondents who met DSM–III criteria for schizophrenia or paranoia, or who had been previously hospitalized for these conditions. Their demographic, health, and social characteristics were compared with other elderly SRO residents and with a general sample of the elderly living in New York City.

METHOD

A cluster sampling design (Van Dalen, 1973) was used, in which 18 hotels were randomly selected from a universe of 22 SRO hotels in a midtown sector of Manhattan. Within selected hotels, an effort was made to interview all residents aged 60 and over on a roster furnished by the management. Respondents received $5 for the interview, which averaged 4 hours and was completed in one or two sessions.

Initial interviews were conducted during 1978–79, and follow–up interviews were conducted over the subsequent year. The final sample consisted of 162 residents (72 men, 90 women), which represented slightly more than 20% of the elderly population within the sampling universe. The mean age of the sample was 73 (range: 60 to 95 years). Racial distribution was 93% white, 4% black, and 1% hispanic.

Physical and mental health and social functioning were determined by the Comprehensive Assessment and Referral Evaluation (CARE) developed by Gurland and associates (1977–78). The interrater reliability was .85. Measures of social interaction were obtained from the Network Analysis Profile (NAP), which was developed in previous work with inner city populations (Sokolovsky & Cohen, 1981). The NAP comprised six fields of interaction: ego–hotel contact, ego–outside nonkin, ego–kin, ego–hotel staff, ego–agency staff, and ego–social institution. The interrater reliability ranged from .83 to .92 on various subsections of the profile.

Numerous criteria have been employed to examine the multifaceted aspects of social networks (Barnes, 1954; Boissevain, 1974; Mitchell, 1969). For use here, morphological and interactional characteristics of networks were examined. The morphological characteristics measured were:

1. Size: The number of linkages in respondents' networks
2. Density: The ratio of actual links to potential ones
3. Configuration: A graphic measure of network interconnectivity

The following interactional network characteristics were studied:

1. Frequency and duration of interaction: number of contacts per unit time and length of acquaintance.
2. Transactional content: the material and nonmaterial elements (e.g., visiting, conversation, loans, and health assistance) exchanged between two persons. The material exchanges were divided into "uniplex" relationships, in which links contained only one type of content, and "multiplex" relationships that contained more than one content. Linkages were also differentiated as to whether sustenance items (viz., food, money, and medical assistance) were exchanged.
3. Directionality: the direction in which aid in a dyadic relationship flowed—"instrumentally," from ego to other; "reciprocally," in equal measure between ego and other; or "dependently," from other to ego. In this analysis, the directional flow was determined for each content area of a dyadic relationship, and then an overall directionality score was calculated.

Persons were selected for the "S" group if they met any of the following:

1. DSM–III criteria for schizophrenia
2. DSM–III criteria for paranoia

3. Previous psychiatric hospitalization for schizophrenia or paranoia.

A total of 18 individuals, 11% of the sample, met these criteria; 15 were schizophrenic and 3 were paranoiac. No individual with a primary diagnosis of organic brain syndrome was included.

RESULTS

For selected variables, the mean values between the S group and the remaining SRO residents (N group) were compared. Statistical differences were determined using the Mann–Whitney U Test. For some variables, comparison data with the New York City sample of the Cross–National Survey were available (Gurland *et al.*, 1977–78). A summary of the findings are presented in Tables 18–1 and 18–2.

Demographics

The S and N groups did not differ in age, residential stability, or income. However, both groups were only slightly above the poverty level of $3,300 for 1978 (United States Bureau of Census, 1979).

Statistically significant differences were found between the two groups in gender and marital history. Nearly three–fourths of the S group were women, compared to slightly more than half of the N group. Although both groups had substantially lower rates of marriage than the general elderly population, the N group exceeded the rate of the S group by 7 percentage points.

Health Status

Except for schizophrenic symptoms and psychiatric hospitalization rates, the two groups were not significantly different in health status. Only 22% of the S group were receiving neuroleptic medication; an additional 17% were taking benzodiazepines. Interestingly, despite showing no differences in physical symptoms, the S group spent more than twice as many days in general hospitals than did the N group (ns). Also noteworthy was the fact that the SRO group as a whole reported significantly more physical symptoms than did the NYC sample, although none of the differences were very great, i.e., only one–half symptom per person.

Needs

The neediness of the S group was one of the most prominent differences between the two groups. Despite having approximately the same income as the N group, the members of the S group reported significantly more financial hardship. Moreover, the SRO group as a whole reported more financial hardship than did the NYC sample. The

Table 18–1
Comparison of S Group and N Group on Selected Variables[a]

Variable	S group (n=18)	N group (n=144)	p
M age	72.1	73.1	ns
Percent females	72	54	.05
M annual income[b]	4.5	4.9	ns
M years in neighborhood	13.2	16.8	ns
M years in SRO hotels	18.8	16.1	ns
Percent previously married	39	46	.05
M Schizophrenia Scale	2.6	0.3	.01
M Organic Brain Syndrome Scale	1.6	1.0	ns
M Depression Scale	5.1	3.9	ns
M Physical Symptom Scale	4.2	3.3	ns
M Activity Limitation Scale	5.9	4.7	ns
M days in general hospital	137	58	ns
M days in psychiatric hospital	107	2.1	.01
M Total Needs Scale	6.3	4.4	.05
M Service Needs Scale	3.1	2.0	ns
M Financial Hardship Scale	1.9	0.8	.05
M total network size	6.4	8.0	ns
M informal network size	5.2	6.7	ns
M total multiplex links	5.8	7.1	ns
M total sustenance links	2.9	3.5	ns
M number of clusters	1.1	2.3	.01
M density of informal network	40.8	24.2	.05
M Revised Social Isolation Scale	3.7	2.8	.05

Note. S group = schizophrenics and paranoiacs; N group = residents without history of schizophrenia or paranoia.
[a] Mann–Whitney U Test
[b] Income category 4=$2,600–3,899; income category 5=$3,900–5,199

Table 18–2
Comparison of SRO Sample as a Whole with the
NYC Sample of the Cross–National Study
on Selected Variables[a]

Variable	SRO sample (n=162)	NYC sample (n=445)	p
M annual income[b]	4.9	5.4	.01
M Organic Brain Syndrome Scale	1.1	1.4	ns
M Depression Scale	4.0	4.3	ns
M Physical Symptom Scale	3.4	3.1	.01
M Activity Limitation Scale	4.9	4.5	.01
M Service Needs Scale	2.2	1.6	.01
M Financial Hardship Scale	0.9	0.8	ns
M Social Isolation Scale	11.0	7.4	.01

[a] Mann–Whitney U Test
[b] Income category 4=$2,600–3,899, 5=$3,900–5,199, 6=$5,200–6,499

S group also scored significantly higher than the N group on a 40–item total needs scale based on their ability to meet health, nutritional, financial, hygienic, and social requirements of daily life. The S group had important gender differences that were not found within the N group. S group men manifested considerably more difficulty than the women in meeting their overall needs ($r=.44$).

Social Supports

There were significant differences between the S and N group on a revised version of the Social Isolation Scale of the CARE. The revised scale is an indicator of the subjective difficulty respondents report in making contact with friends, neighbors, and kin; this may not correspond with the actual number of linkages. A detailed analysis of the actual linkages revealed no significant differences in the number, frequency, and complexity of interactions, although the N group had approximately 20% more linkages (uniplex and multiplex) within their informal network sectors (hotel, outside nonkin, kin). Within the formal sector (agency and hotel staff), the groups had an equal number of linkages.

The two groups varied significantly in the structural configurations of their networks. The S group had an average of only one cluster formation, whereas the N group had a mean of two clusters. Because of the lack of linkages between these clusters, individuals in the N group had significantly less dense network structures than those in the S group.

It should be underscored that both the S and N groups had

relatively small networks. Their informal networks were one-half the size of middle-class elderly (unpublished data) and of younger SRO residents (Cohen & Sokolovsky, 1978). Moreover, the SRO group as a whole showed significantly more isolation than the NYC sample on the original version of the Social Isolation Scale of the CARE. Finally, the size of their formal networks (1.2 linkages) did not suggest that SRO residents used this kind of support to compensate for the smallness of their informal networks.

DISCUSSION

The findings confirmed an earlier report that SRO hotels are *not* havens for proportionately large numbers of elderly who are former mental patients or who are in need of psychiatric hospitalization. Indeed, only 11% of the sample evidenced symptoms of schizophrenia or paranoia, or had been previously hospitalized for these conditions. The SRO group as a whole was more indigent, somewhat more physically impaired, more needy, and more socially isolated than their counterparts in the general population. However, it should be underscored that despite these deficiencies, the SRO residents were able to meet 89% of their needs.

Within the SRO sample, the S group showed important differences vis-a-vis the N group with respect to their inability to meet needs, their greater use of hospitals (medical and psychiatric), and their more impoverished social network structures. Furthermore, although there were no appreciable disparities in income between the two groups, the S group reported more financial hardship. Here again it must be emphasized that members of the S group were still meeting 84% of their total needs.

What was most striking was that despite relatively high levels of psychopathology, near-poverty level income, and few social supports, the S group managed to survive in the community. In fact, they did so without manifesting any substantially higher levels of depression than other SRO residents or NYC elderly. The low prevalence of neuroleptic use suggested that medication was not a major explanatory factor in community survival. Several other factors did contribute to the ability of S group members to survive in the community. For one thing, although their networks were small, 91% of all their contacts involved multicontent (multiplex) relationships. Moreover, 45% of their contacts involved the exchange of sustenance items, i.e., food, money, or medical assistance. The high density of the network structure indicated that members were in contact with each other and thereby could complement each other's assistance. In short, members of the S group made the most of what they had.

Nevertheless, their survival system was not without breakdown. Their rates of medical as well as psychiatric hospitalization were higher than those of the N group, but it was not clear whether medical hospitalization was a substitute for psychiatric hospitalization, a result of an inability to obtain adequate medical and social services in the community, or a result of medical conditions that would necessitate hospitalization under any circumstances. Notably, on 1-year follow-up the S group showed no higher mortality rates than the N group.

Finally, despite the hardships of living in an SRO environment, the low-expectation ethos found in these settings may alleviate much of the social pressure and stigma that schizophrenics experience in the outside world. SRO hotels are havens for those with physical and mental pathology, poor employment histories, and the elderly (Shapiro, 1971). Most of the people receive some form of governmental assistance. As Lamb (1982) found among those former mental patients living in board and care homes, there is an "adaptation by decompression." Residents have found asylum from many of life's pressures. Although the social world of the hotel does not offer the concomitant structure and support of a board and care facility, it does provide sufficient material and emotional supports for survival.

Despite considerable idiosyncratic behavior, two patterns of survival appeared prominent among S group members. One pattern employed the indigenous support system of the hotel, and the other relied on formal agency support. The following case illustrates the first pattern:

EW is a 64-year-old white woman with a long history of residual schizophrenia. Thirty-five years ago she had a frontal lobotomy. As a consequence of her illness her family severed ties with her. Although EW still exhibits some bizarre ideation and flattened affect, she has attempted to meet her material and emotional needs by doing errands and providing meals to other hotel residents. In return, they offer emotional girding and provide material assistance when she is ill.

The ability to engage in reciprocal transactions is probably the best way to ensure future support within the hotel social system, but it is not the only way. In our previous investigative work (Cohen & Sokolovsky, 1979b) and that of Shapiro (1971), it was common to find several indigenous helpers within each SRO hotel. These helpers often formed the nidus of a quasi-family for 6-10 residents who met in their room for meals, socialization, and the like. Other helpers served individuals separately by delivering meals, escorting persons to the hospital, and lending money. Not uncommonly, former mental patients were members of these helpers' networks.

A second case illustrates how formal agency resources can assist in maintaining individuals in the community: MM is a 72-year-old white woman with a long history of multiple psychiatric hospitalizations for paranoid schizophrenia. Following the death of her boyfriend, she was left with only a few single-content (uniplex) relationships. An outreach program from a local senior citizen agency was able to engage her by offering a free lunch at their center. At the center, staff assisted her in obtaining entitlements, she participated in various group activities, and she was seen monthly by a psychiatrist. During periods of psychiatric decompensation, staff encouraged her to take medication, provided additional supportive therapy, and made visits to her hotel as necessary. Consequently, several hospitalizations were aborted.

This case is an excellent example of how vigorous outreach programs to SRO hotels have succeeded in providing supports to former mental patients. Without such programs, persons such as MM would have continued to experience frequent rehospitalizations.

In closing, it should be underscored that the small size of the S group must preclude any definitive generalizations. Nonetheless, this study does provide some clues as to how markedly impaired individuals are able to survive in the community. It is hoped that this report will serve as a stimulus for future research.

Acknowledgments

Funding for this research was provided by the NIMH Center for the Studies of the Mental Health of the Aging, Grant No. 1–RO1–MH31745. The author thanks Community Research Applications (Drs. Teresi and Holmes) and Mr. Henry Rajkowski for their assistance.

PARANOIA AND LATE ONSET SCHIZOPHRENIA: PHENOMENOLOGY, ETIOLOGY, AND TREATMENT

Paraphrenia, a mental disorder occurring in later life, exemplifies with particular clarity both the unity and diversity of schizophrenic illnesses. It is similar to schizophrenia in many ways, yet is different enough to merit investigation in its own right.

A study of late–onset mental illness showed that about 10% of the patients over 45 admitted to psychiatric hospitals met the criteria for schizophrenia. Such studies have already led to a redefinition of schizophrenia as an illness no longer restricted to the young.

The high incidence of deafness among paraphrenics led to a study of deafness as precursor. Examining the relationship between deafness and indicators of suspiciousness and isolation among the elderly revealed that, contrary to predictions, isolation was reduced significantly in those with greater hearing loss. Mild hearing loss appeared to generate more stress than severe loss, but was not sufficient to explain paraphrenia. Difficulty with intimacy seemed to be a necessary concomitant.

Computed tomography scans of the brains of patients with late onset schizophrenia showed larger ventricle to brain ratios in patients than in normal controls. However, where controls' ventricles enlarged with age, paraphrenics showed a significant negative linear relationship. This surprising finding suggests the possibility that different processes are involved. Younger paraphrenics could represent the end of a continuum of classic schizophrenia, while the others may owe their symptomatic onset to another process.

Autopsy results from adult psychiatric patients whose clinical records showed a paranoid syndrome revealed a significant excess of pathology in the brain compared to other psychiatric patients, suggesting some association between brain injury and paranoia. Clinically, those with delusional disorders manifested a higher incidence of chronic physical illness and higher rates of mortality.

Late Paraphrenia: Phenomenology and Etiological Factors and Their Bearing Upon Problems of the Schizophrenic Family of Disorders

Sir Martin Roth

Addenbrooke's Hospital, University of Cambridge

HISTORICAL BACKGROUND

The term "paraphrenia" first appeared in the 8th edition of Kraepelin's textbook (1909–13). It referred to a group of chronic paranoid
psychoses marked by florid and fantastic symptoms associated with
hallucinations in clear consciousness. The four main features of
paraphrenia judged by Kraepelin to differentiate it from dementia
praecox were the preservation of volition, the absence of impoverishment of emotion or of loss of initiative, the coherence and
integration of the delusional ideas, and the lively, passionate manner
in which they were expressed. The capacity to apply ordinary logic
and reason outside the scope of the delusions and the preservation of
basic personality, which was found to be intact even after long
periods of observation, were additional discriminating features.

"Presenile delusional insanity," described by Kraepelin in his 7th
edition as occurring after the age of 55, differed from this concept in
the absence of hallucinations. These cases were subsumed within the
concept of "paranoia," a chronic psychosis without auditory or other
hallucinations in which, in some cases, full remission could occur.

Influenced by psychoanalysis, Eugen Bleuler, who coined the
term "schizophrenia," emphasized the primary character of certain
symptoms such as dissociation of thinking, weakening of willpower,
emotional poverty, and ambivalence. Symptoms such as delusions,
hallucinations, and catatonic features were regarded as secondary.
Believing that the same fundamental psychological disturbance could
be detected in paraphrenia and paranoia, he concluded that both
these syndromes (with the exception of some rare paranoiac states)
that Kraepelin judged as distinct from dementia praecox, should be
included within the schizophrenic group of disorders. This broad
concept of schizophrenic illness was to prove widely influential,
paving the way for the work of Kretschmer and later shaping the

development of the Scandinavian concept of psychogenic paranoid psychosis, which includes some disorders diagnosed elsewhere as paraphrenia and paranoia.

This wider view appeared to derive support from the follow-up study of paraphrenic patients by one of Kraepelin's coworkers (Mayer, 1921) which revealed that 30 of 78 patients diagnosed as paraphrenic by Kraepelin himself developed into typical schizophrenics with other signs of the disease besides the delusions.

The concept of paranoia appeared to suffer a similar fate. Kraepelin described this disorder as "the insidious development of a permanent and unshakable delusional system arising from internal causes, which is accompanied by perfect preservation of clear and orderly thinking, willing and acting." Hallucinations were absent and, although the disease ran a chronic course, deterioration of personality did not occur.

However, Kolle (1931) selected 66 cases which fulfilled Kraepelin's definition of "paranoia," including 19 diagnosed as such by Kraepelin himself. On follow-up, Kolle found that in all but four of the cases primary delusions had subsequently developed. Moreover, he inferred some genetic association with schizophrenia since the incidence of this disorder in the families of paranoiacs was higher than in the general population. Although both Kolle and Mayer interpreted their observations as favoring a unitary view of schizophrenia, it is doubtful whether refutation of the ideas originally expressed by Kraepelin about paraphrenia and paranoia were as conclusive as has been generally supposed. Neither study, for example, was controlled with comparable observations on schizophrenic subjects and it is difficult to evaluate Kolle's finding in the follow-up study that 24% of patients with paranoia "required permanent hospital care." The degree of deterioration of personality as compared with that found in schizophrenia was not described. Although emphasis is laid on the genetic relationship with schizophrenia, the incidence of this disorder among relatives of paranoiacs was only half that recorded in the families of schizophrenics; a result comparable with recent findings in "late paraphrenia." Nor does the view that all paraphrenics show progressive schizophrenic deterioration appear well supported. In late paraphrenia, for example, the symptomatology is indubitably schizophrenic, but follow-up studies (Kay & Roth, 1961) have shown that the deterioration of personality does not occur for many years. From a clinical descriptive point of view this disorder therefore belongs with schizophrenia. But in its heredity and pattern of outcome it is not wholly uniform with it. Thus, while Kolle and Mayer favored a unitary view of schizophrenia, their findings appear in retrospect to have been more consistent with a view intermediate between the original standpoint of Kraepelin, who set paraphrenia apart from dementia praecox, and that of his critics.

At the other extreme from the school that regards all chronic paranoid psychoses as schizophrenic is the group of psychiatrists who have held that paranoia and similar disorders are psychogenic. This view drew some inspiration from the contributions of Kretschmer who investigated a group of paranoid psychoses he named "Der sensitive Beziehungswahn" (1918). Despite the indubitable "nuclear" symptoms in a substantial proportion of patients, Kretschmer considered that the illness was understandable in light of their sensitive, tender, high-minded personalities in which a sense of humiliation and moral failure had been engendered by life events of a specific nature. With subtle psychological perception he traced the development of the delusional illness as the inescapable outcome of a patient's history and personal experience; his ideas, emotions, aspirations, and the content of his mental life were disclosed with delicate comprehension. In that the psychosis could be shown to evolve as an understandable development, it failed to satisfy the central criterion of a break in the continuity of psychic life and its qualitative transformation, adopted by Jaspers as the distinctive hallmark of a schizophrenic "process."

Kretschmer's findings had relatively little influence on the evolution of the concept of schizophrenia within Germany, but the concept of "psychogenic psychosis" took a firm hold in Scandinavia, as exemplified in the work of Wimmer (1916), Strömgren (1948), Welner and Strömgren (1958), and in more recent years, Faergeman (1963) and Retterstöl (1966, 1970).

The wide range of disorders subscribed by this concept was conveyed by the text and case summaries in Retterstöl's publications (1972). If disorders such as the "erotic jealousy syndrome of old maids" in which vivid somatic hallucinations of sexual interference and rape by occult forces, as also paraphrenic and paranoic syndromes are included, then the limits of schizophrenia proper must be circumscribed by a more narrow and strict definition than is accepted in most countries. The psychosis of old maids to which reference has been made would probably be regarded as schizophrenic by most psychiatrists.

The contributions of Kretschmer, Strömgren, (1945, 1974) and Retterstöl, among others have been important in establishing that some paranoid and schizophrenic-like psychoses evolve in the context of a life situation that renders the emergence of symptoms and their content partly understandable. There are some strands of continuity between the patient's previous personality and psychic life and certain elements of the illness. However, the form of the psychotic disorders cannot be so explained. Ordinary psychological mechanisms will not account for the topsy-turvy private logic pursued, nor the total absence of insight. The impressive character of the adverse life events at onset is deceptive, because in the great majority of cases with indubitable delusional symptoms, they are neither necessary or sufficient. Identical syndromes appear in a stepwise fashion in the absence of precipitants, and identical adversities will in other cases be followed by neurotic illness or transient emotional distress. The term 'psychogenic' oversimplifies the etiological basis of such conditions, for it is the special meaning of the stressful event for the individual and its interaction with his personality that appear but only in a limited proportion of cases are impressively associated with the onset of symptoms. The extent of the contribution made to the etiology of illness by heredity, adverse life circumstance, and their interplay with constitutional and personality factors remains to be determined. 'Psychogenic' describes only a strand within a web of causation. But when these concepts were evolving, the over–emphasis of the term psychogenic was perhaps justifiable.

Late paraphrenia was first described some three decades ago (Roth & Morrisey, 1952; Mayer–Gross, Slater, & Roth, 1954; Roth, 1955). Its kinship with schizophrenic illness was recognized from the outset, but it differed in a number of features from paraphrenia and from the senile paranoid psychosis of Kraepelin. The clinical profile and the maintenance of emotional response broadly conformed to the description of ordinary paraphrenia given by Kraepelin. However, a number of features had not figured in previous accounts of late paranoid psychoses. The illness occurred predominantly in women, and in 80% of those admitted to hospital, the first attack occurred after the age of 60. Premorbid personality was conspicuously abnormal in a high proportion of patients. Deafness and visual impairment were excessively prevalent, and sensory deficits appeared, from the results of comparisons with control subjects (Cooper *et al.*, 1974, 1975) to have contributed to the causation of the illness. Because such deficits increased social isolation and thus engendered emotional distress, a proportion of the cases could have been regarded as psychogenic by some psychiatrists. However in most cases the illness was of sudden onset and, when onerous life situations were present at onset, they appeared to be mere claps that had brought down an avalanche. The majority of cases had neither sensory defects nor antecedent stresses to render the disorder understandable.

As the condition is responsible for approximately 9–10% of those admitted to mental hospitals after the age of 65 and has been found in 1–2% of a community sample of elderly people (Williamson *et al.*, 1964), paraphrenia merits investigation in its own right. It also offers some opportunities for shedding light upon the classification and etiological basis of schizophrenic illness and the penumbra of syndromes that bear an uncertain relation to it. The sections that follow discuss the phenomenology, classification, and what is known about the etiology of the disorder, as well as the implications of late paraphrenia for clinical diagnosis and for certain scientific enquiries into schizophrenia.

CLINICAL FEATURES

At the time late paraphrenia was first described, two hypotheses regarding the etiological basis and nosological status of paranoid disorders of late life were widely held. According to the first, any paranoid psychosis appearing for the first time after the age of 60 was to be regarded as organic in origin regardless of its psychiatric features. According to the second hypothesis, all paraphrenic syndromes (in the sense of Kraepelin) were to be judged as homologous with schizophrenia of early life. Each was an all–or–none hypothesis, and they were mutually incompatible. In light of the evidence, the first hypothesis now stands refuted; the second is consistent with some of the data relating to late paraphrenia but cannot be validated in its all–or–none form. Data from the Newcastle study of aged in the community (Kay, Beamish, & Roth, 1964a,b) revealed median age of onset to be 66 years, in persons who had previously worked to support themselves in an independent life.

In the majority of cases, two main stages could be defined in the development of the illness. In the first, which lasted 6–18 months, a gradually increasing accentuation of certain personality traits was to be observed. Suspiciousness, irritability, and hostile attitudes grow more prominent. Patients become more seclusive, developed shifting ideas of reference in relation to others, and made querulous complaints to the police or threatened legal action against neighbors.

The second stage usually began in a steplike manner, often with the sudden eruption of auditory hallucinations in clear consciousness. Voices cajoled, commanded, or threatened, addressing the patient in the second or third person. Comments were critical, derisory, at times obscene, and in some cases had an imperative quality causing the patient to respond in a hostile or aggressive manner.

The clinical picture had a distinctively florid character: There were rappings on the wall, or a chorus of criminals singing aloud in the adjacent house determined to oust the patient; men and boys were reported to enter freely through the bedroom walls. Electrical sensations were felt in the perineum, and acts of rape were felt to be committed nightly by occult means—by spirits, influential politicians, or acquaintances, erotically interested in the patient. The air was heavy with fumes or the stench of decomposing bodies. Patients complained of being pursued and persecuted by Communists, Freemasons, and would–be assassins. Their bodies were played upon by means of 'atomic apparatus', television, X–rays, or 'astral bodies'. Torture machines were used to keep them awake at night and submit them to shameful insults. Noxious gases descended from the ceiling and poisonous fluids were sprayed through the window. They were photographed in the bathroom by means of special cameras which could be heard clicking in the adjacent houses. Their thoughts were read and sometimes anticipated by the hallucinatory voices.

The delusions appeared to arise in primary fashion, in some cases out of an entirely clear sky. A man who had never shown interest in the patient is suddenly accused of entering her bed at night and interfering with her sexually. A recent patient introduced at a social gathering to a man who had been superficially acquainted with her many years ago suddenly inferred from his manner of looking at her, that the man was in love with her and had infected her by some unknown means with "virulent syphilis."

Schneiderian first-rank symptoms were present in a high proportion of cases. They included auditory hallucinations of voices that referred to the patient in the third person, feelings of passivity, or primary delusions that emerged as a flash of insight from a normal perception. Thought broadcasting occurred in a proportion of cases, but thought insertion, withdrawal, and derailment were rare. Thought disorder, in a strict sense, was absent. Patients were generally lucid and coherent in discussing subjects outside the realm of their psychotic experiences, but incoherent or inconsequential when delusional symptoms were described.

Depressive features rarely created difficulties in diagnosis. In paraphrenia, the scope of paranoid symptoms extends well beyond themes consistent with a diagnosis of affective psychosis. However, a small minority of cases begin as affective psychoses, with unusually pronounced and wide-ranging paranoid-hallucinatory features that dominate the clinical picture to an increasing extent in successive attacks. The areas of consciousness, memory, orientation, capacity for reasoning outside the scope of the psychosis, personal appearance, and sphincter control remain well-preserved and intact over many years of observation, usually until near the end of life (Roth, 1980). Differentiation of paraphrenia from organic psychoses with prominent paranoid features rarely gives rise to difficultly.

COURSE

In the early years of investigation, it became clear that late paraphrenia was rarely accompanied by the personality deterioration characteristic of chronic unremitting schizophrenia, namely, growing poverty of emotion, apathy, autism, incoherence of thought and speech, and inertia. After years of increasing preoccupation with delusional and hallucinatory phenomena, the effects of age—including limited cognitive impariment and withdrawal caused by gradual sensory loss—the picture in some cases bore a resemblance to personality deterioration. It was difficult to determine to what degree this was a coloring lent by the premorbid personality with its emotional coldness, suspicion, eccentricity and tendency to self-segregation, and to what degree the result of normal senescence, or the effects of an unremitting chronic psychosis. Recent advances in the treatment of schizophrenia have modified the course of the disorder. Although the condition remains chronic and liable to relapse on withdrawal of medication, deterioration of a kind observed in schizophrenia of early life is very rare. Progressive deterioration of an organic type caused by senile or multi-infarct dementia supervenes in only a small proportion of cases, typically appearing at least 5 years after the onset of the paraphrenic illness.

Life expectancy in paraphrenic patients is not significantly shortened, the ratio observed to expc ted deaths being 0.97 in women and 0.81 in men (Kay, 1963b), in contrast to the lifespan of those with organic psychoses in which the ratio is less than 0.30. A small proportion of cases die from cerebral disease, as in the general population. The causes of death in the Stockholm material (Kay, 1963b) proved to be closely similar to those recorded in the general population, age for age, in contrast to the vague, nonspecific causes of death recorded in a high proportion of patients with dementia.

Although the overall prognosis is now favorable with a high proportion of good remissions, outcome has an element of indeterminacy, and predictions in the individual case cannot be made with confidence. Good premorbid social adaptation, marriage, onset before the age of 70, and an early and favorable response to treatment augur well for outcome.

VARIETIES OF PARAPHRENIA

Three main varieties of paraphrenia were described on the basis of the original enquiries (Kay & Roth, 1961). The syndromes described by other workers (Post, 1966) are similar.

Late Paranoia

The first group, comprising 15–20% of patients, develops as an insidious paranoid illness based on lifelong personality traits that inhibit relationships with others and give rise to increasing isolation. The onset of the illness is difficult to date precisely as the psychosis evolves initially in the form of a growing parody of lifelong personality traits. The delusional convictions of theft and harassment are understandable, up to a point, but some of the delusions, such as poisoning or infection with disease from a distance, are bizarre and penetrated by no shred of insight. Hallucinations are absent, and in earlier life such conditions are usually described under the heading of paranoia.

Late Paraphrenia with 'Reactive' Features

The second variety usually has a clearly defined onset following a prodromal period in which shifting ideas of reference are manifest. The disorder is more florid, and hallucinations as well as delusions are present. Some of the latter can be related in part to sociofamilial circumstances such as isolation, desolation, sexual conflict, or familial disputes over possessions or the Will of a relative. Neighbors wish to evict the patient from her home and can be heard plotting to do so. However, delusional beliefs extend beyond such commonplace themes to include persecutory ideas of being recorded and controlled by machines or being bombed, machine-gunned, or fumed out of the house. The patients fail to respond to changes in their environment and their symptoms cannot be explained in terms of reactions to adversity.

'Endogenous' Late Paraphrenia

This group makes up about two–thirds of the cases. There is a steplike onset out of a clear sky or following life events of a trivial nature. The delusions and hallucinations are variable, often fantastic, and systematized to varying degrees. The persecutory and erotic delusions, persistent auditory hallucinations, and passivity feelings combine to form a picture similar to that of paranoid schizophrenia in earlier life. However, although the disorder is chronic and demands long–term treatment, personality is well preserved, and deterioration is not observed even after many years of illness.

The florid and fantastic nature of the psychotic disorder is exemplified by the case of a woman of 65 who fell ill suddenly a year after her son's accidental death. There were strange feelings "like electricity" in her stomach caused by two men in an adjoining flat and also by cars and passers–by. She felt compelled to watch films of naked men and women having sexual intercourse, heard obscene words shouted, and complained of being tortured, hypnotized, and submitted to violent assault. She believed she had given birth to a child in the night and later asserted that her bed was full of small children. Her psychotic experiences were often described in an incoherent manner, but at other times, her talk was lucid and logical.

The disorders are linked by broadly similar premorbid person-alities, the prevalence of deafness in all groups, the chronic course pursued, and the mode of response to treatment. There are no sharp lines of clinical distinction between the three syndromes; they merge insensibly with each other.

ETIOLOGY

A number of findings have established a close kinship between late paraphrenia and schizophrenia of earlier life, though there are cer-tain differences. Comparison of cases of early and late onset schizophrenia poses certain new hypotheses for investigation.

Hereditary factors almost certainly contribute to the causation of late paraphrenia in that, in approximately one–fifth of patients, at least one first–degree relative has suffered from an indubitable schizophrenic illness. For example, taking only hospitalized cases of paraphrenia and a risk period of 18 to 50 years, Kay (1959, 1963b) found the morbid risk for schizophrenia in siblings to be $2.5 \pm 1.2\%$, in children $7.3 \pm 4.2\%$, in parents 0, and among nephews and nieces $3.1 \pm 1.1\%$. As 40 of the siblings of paraphrenic probands out of the 206 who had reached the age of 18 had emigrated in early life, the num-ber of cases of schizophrenia recorded in first–degree relatives in this study very likely depicted the minimum morbid risk, possibly short of the true expectation. Notwithstanding this, one fifth of the probands had at least one first–degree relation with schizophrenia. There were some relatives whose state was strongly suggestive of schizophrenia, but the diagnosis could not be made with confidence. If these cases had been included, the revised morbid risks would have been higher. It is noteworthy also that among the affected relatives, the schizophrenic illness had in the majority of cases begun before the age of 40, although one sister and one nephew had developed psychoses requiring hospital care after the age of 60. There was no increase in the expectation of either manic depressive illness or organic dementia.

Findings similar in certain respects have been recorded by other workers. Herbert and Jacobsen (1967) found that 23 relatives of 47 paraphrenics had suffered from mental illness. Eight had been schizophrenic, three depressed, six psychopathic, two alcoholic, and four undiagnosed. The family history was negative in 24 cases. Funding (1961) found a morbid risk of 2.5% in siblings of schizophrenics (uncorrected). Though significantly greater than the normal risk (0.9%), it was far lower than that of younger schizophrenics (7.4%). The 43 relatives of 93 patients with a positive family history in Post's material (Post, 1966) included 5 schizophrenics, 16 with affective disorders, 27 with personality disorders and alcoholism, and 8 with organic disorders including epilepsy. As paranoid states of indubitably organic etiology were included in this material, the findings are not comparable with those quoted from other studies. Nevertheless, the full genetic predisposition underlying schizophrenia is lacking, since the morbid risk among first–degree relatives is substantially lower than among first–degree relatives of patients with schizophrenia of early onset.

The mean age of onset of late paraphrenia is about 66 years. As the rates of admission in relation to the population at risk do not vary in the different age groups above 60 years, a feature in striking contrast to dementia, there is not likely to be any significant connection between late paraphrenia and cerebral degenerative change (Roth et al., 1967; Blessed et al., 1968).

The excess of women and the over–representation of unmarried patients are characteristic. Late paraphrenia resembles schizophrenia in the low marriage rate and low fertility rate of affected subjects, these features probably being associated with the abnormal prepsychotic personality. For example, the fertility of female paraphrenics studied in Sweden by Kay proved to be significantly less (an average of 1.2 children per patient) than that of Swedish women of comparable age (3.8 children). Even married patients had an average of 1.9 children per marriage compared with an average of 3.0 children born to affective cases and 2.72 to organic patients. This low fertility rate is similar to that found in schizophrenia of earlier life. The importance of these observations resides in the fact that they provide evidence regarding abnormal reproductive behavior in a variant of schizophrenic disorder decades before the appearance of symptoms.

This behavior could not have been a consequence of psychosis; it could have arisen only from lifelong personality traits, influencing adjustment long before symptoms of illness made their appearance.

Premorbid Personality and Interaction with Other Features

Personality characteristics of a paranoid and schizoid nature are commonly found in paraphrenia. Systematic inquiry shows the patients have limited interests, are serious, solitary, reserved, hostile to relatives, unsympathetic, suspicious, eccentric, quarrelsome, cold, and often affiliated with minority religious sects (Kay & Roth, 1961). A number of these traits may well militate against marriage, and such marriages as do occur tend to be complicated by the patient's lack of warmth and tenderness—they prove unhappy as well as infertile and are frequently disrupted by divorce. One patient remained with her newly wed husband for a week, then left him and reverted to her maiden name by deed poll.

Although the single state may reflect nonselection for marriage (Odegaard, 1953), its failure to materialize over so many decades suggests that deprivation of intimate personal relationships and emotional bonds may also play some part in causing emotional breakdown. Up to a certain point, a life without personal contacts may prove protective. But in old age the severance of the few lasting ties through death and bereavement appear in a small number of cases to play a part in precipitating a breakdown. The closeness of the relationship between premorbid personality and illness was demonstrated by a study of Kay, Cooper, Garside, and Roth (1976) using a stepwise regression analysis to define the features other than those manifest during illness that best predicted schizophrenic disorder on the one hand and affective illness in a group of comparison cases on the other. Six independent variables predicted 40% of the variance. The characteristics that predicted paranoid psychosis were, in order of their discriminating value, (1) schizoid premorbid personality, (2) few surviving children, (3) deafness, and (4) low social class. The two features predictive of affective psychosis were (1) precipitating factors, and (2) family history of affective disorder. Of these six variables, schizoid premorbid personality had the highest predictive value.

Sensory Impairment

The lower genetic loading in paraphrenic patients appears to be offset by a higher prevalence of exogenous factors than those found in patients suffering from schizophrenia with early onset. The evidence suggests that these make some contribution to causation. In inquiries undertaken in cooperation with otologists and ophthalmologists in Newcastle, paraphrenic patients were shown to have a higher prevalence of disabling deafness and blindness than age-matched controls with affective disorders (Cooper *et al.*, 1974; Cooper & Porter, 1975; Cooper, Garside, & Kay, 1976).

A number of features of the deafness suggests that it may contribute to causation.

1. The onset of the sensory defect precedes the commencement of the psychosis by many years.
2. The character of the defect differs from that found in control cases, conductive deafness being more common among patients with paraphrenic illness.
3. In addition to a difference in social deafness, the hearing defect was confirmed by independent otological and audiometric examination.
4. Anomalies of personality were found to be somewhat less pronounced in patients with deafness than in those with normal hearing, although they were qualitatively similar (Cooper *et al.*, 1976). This suggests an interaction between sensory deficits and personality factors in the creation of the rift from reality reflected by the psychosis.

Cerebral Disease

As far as the pathology of senile dementia of Alzheimers type is concerned, the brains of patients with late paraphrenia do not differ from those of subjects with affective disorder or normal controls. Senile plaques and neurofibrillary tangles, for example, fall within the normal range (Blessed *et al.*, 1968). However, approximately 5 to 10% of patients have stationary cerebral lesions mainly due to solitary cerebrovascular accidents, and these may contribute to a limited extent to causation. This minority of cases represents a counterpart of the fringe group of patients with schizophreniform disorders in earlier life caused by organic factors such as amphetamine intoxication and lesions in the temporal lobes and diencephalon (Davison and Bagley, 1969). However, follow-up studies show that paraphrenia is quite distinct in course and outcome from senile and multi-infarct dementia (Roth, 1955; Kay, 1959).

TREATMENT

The response of paraphrenia patients to treatment with neuroleptic drugs supports the hypothesis that they represent a special form of schizophrenic illness. Only an outline of management can be sketched in here.

As many patients have been ridiculed, rejected, and reviled prior to their appearance in the psychiatric clinic, special pains have to be taken to establish a full therapeutic relationship. A friendly, supportive, tolerant, and sympathetic attitude is of paramount importance. Understanding and acceptance of the patient's individual needs, problems, and idiosyncrasies have to be made manifest in positive ways.

Neuroleptic drugs are of central importance in management. As compliance may be difficult to secure initially, it is desirable to admit patients to Hospital for the early stages of treatment. Compliance will usually be secured when symptoms have been relieved, usually in 4 to 6 weeks after the initiation of therapy. Oral treatment is on the whole preferable to depot medication in late paraphrenics. A flexible regime of medication should be instituted whenever this is possible, and treatment should therefore be initially attempted with 15 mg to 25 mg of Trifluoperazine or 100 mg to 300 mg of Thioridazine. For maintenance, the lowest possible dose shown by close observation to suffice should be employed.

If depot medication has to be employed, Flupenthixol decanoate in a 20 mg dose monthly (after a trial dose of 10 mg) should suffice in the majority of cases. The disadvantages are that extrapyramidal side effects such as Parkinsonism and tardive dyskinesia are rather common, and arterial hypotension and the falls that result from it are all too liable to be complicated by fractures. Where compliance proves satisfactory or administration of drugs can be supervised by a reliable relative, treatment by means of oral medication is strongly to be preferred.

In most cases, associated depressive symptoms subside as the schizophrenic illness recedes. In a minority of patients, tricyclic compounds may need to be added, although no therapeutic trials have tested their value in this condition. In that minority of patients with the complete symptomatic profile of an endogenous depressive illness in addition to prominent paranoid features, a course of ECT may be indicated. But it is wise to continue with a maintenance course of neuroleptics where a firm diagnosis of paraphrenia has been made.

The response to treatment is more favorable than that in schizophrenia of earlier life. Very few treated paraphrenics become chronic hospitalized patients as they certainly did before neuroleptic drugs were employed in treatment.

In Post's study of 71 paraphrenic patients, 14 (20%) made a full recovery, 29 (41%) recovered without insight, 22 (31%) achieved social recovery but some abnormal ideas survived, and 6 (8%) made no response. Outcome over a 3-year period was closely related to the maintenance of drug treatment, which could be discontinued in only seven patients.

FUTURE PERSPECTIVES

This section will draw together the main findings relating to phenomenology and course of late paraphrenia, as well as to genetic, environmental and exogenous factors that have been shown to contribute to its causation.

Implications for clinical practice and scientific inquiry into the nature of schizophrenia in early and late life will be considered by posing a number of questions in relation to these main issues.

What Is the Relationship Between Late Paraphrenia and Schizophrenia in Other Stages of the Lifespan?

The standpoint adopted in this paper has been that schizophrenia is primarily a phenomenological concept comprising a number of co-varying features derived from observations relating to the evolution and clinical presentation of the disorder. Progress often follows the initial description of such a syndrome as a result of subdivisions initially prompted by clinical observation. The advantages that flow from such a refinement of description and classification lead to a greater homogeneity of patient populations. This may in turn accelerate progress in the prediction of outcome, the discovery of etiologic factors, and the development of more effective treatments.

A strong body of evidence favors the view that late paraphrenia is a form of schizophrenic illness. For example, the clinical profile of the presenting illness satisfies the criteria set for schizophrenia both in DSM-III and in the Mental Disorders section of the Ninth Revision of the International Classification of Diseases. The findings summarized here might therefore appear to support Mayer (1921) and Kolle (1931) in their refutation of the claim by Kraepelin that paraphrenia constituted a syndrome distinct from schizophrenia. Such a reading would misconstrue the evidence. Although kinship with schizophrenia is upheld by observations derived from phenomenology, genetics, and treatment response among other features, the data also provide some vindication for Kraepelin's insight. Within the schizophrenias, late paraphrenia deserves a distinct place of its own for the following reasons:

1. Emotional response and volition as observed in the presenting clinical picture are consistently well preserved.
2. Although the disease pursues a chronic course, the deterioration of the personality in the sense of the "dementia" of dementia praecox does not develop in the majority of cases.
3. Hereditary factors, though homologous with those underlying schizophrenia, make a smaller contribution to causation.
4. A number of exogenous factors (of which deafness, found in some 40% of cases, is the most conspicuous) play some part in etiology.
5. Lifetime premorbid personality features are more sharply delineated than in the case of schizophrenia of earlier life.

Prior to breakdown a relatively high proportion of individuals have been unmarried, shown low fertility, had unstable marriages, and consistent failures in interpersonal relationships, in addition to being emotionally distant, cool, suspicious, eccentric and relatively incapable of intimacy, tenderness and affection. This line of demarcation within schizophrenia therefore provides opportunities for certain lines of inquiry. These will be considered in the sections that follow.

What Causes Can Be Defined for Late Manifestation?

Those who first develop schizophrenic illness in advanced age enjoy the boon of a lifetime spent for the greater part in the community often in productive, self-fulfilling, and at times distinguished work. Beds in mental hospitals are left unoccupied during a latent period of decades. Women constitute the majority of late paraphrenics in contrast to the male predominance of schizophrenia of early life. They tend to suffer their first attack of schizophrenia later than men, but only a small proportion of illnesses commence in senescence. If those with late paraphrenia are predisposed to schizophrenic illness in terms of both genetic factors and previous personality and pattern of adjustment, how do they escape breakdown until they reach old age? One possibility suggested by recent observation is that the mental integrity of paraphrenic patients during most of their span of life may be due to the success with which their personality features have enabled them to avoid exposure to emotionally taxing personal relationships. That the social situation of these patients is due in part to self-isolation is suggested by certain findings (Kay & Roth, 1961). The possible role of isolation receives support from clinical observation of that small proportion of patients who break down rapidly after they are bereaved through the death of or separation from the few surviving human contacts who have given them some measure of support. One patient used to visit a sister every 2 weeks. She would take her meals at this sister's home, bring her washing to be laundered, make little conversation, and depart without a word of thanks. Although she had been growing more suspicious and withdrawn for some 2 years, she first broke down with a florid paraphrenic illness 2 days after the sister's sudden death from a stroke.

However, the relationship between isolation and personality is called in question by other evidence. In a consecutive sample of 69 schizophrenic patients (Kay *et al.*, 1976) no significant associations or interactions were found between a personality score of schizoid and paranoid features on the one hand and low social class, the unmarried state, or living alone on the other. The direction of causality as between premorbid personality, which may be most closely related to what is transmitted by heredity, and the social predicament of paraphrenic patients before illness is therefore uncertain.

Further investigation may resolve some of the paradoxes posed by these lines of evidence. More detailed analysis both of retrospective data in late life cases and of the findings in prospective investigation of elderly persons with prominent paranoid or schizoid traits identified in the community should yield more precise information regarding the weight to be attached to the different factors in causation.

What Is the Relative Importance of Hereditary and Environmental Factors in Schizophrenias of Late and Early Life?

Kay and Roth (1961) advanced a polygenic theory for the underlying hereditary basis of late paraphrenia. According to this theory the predisposition for this form of illness is quantitatively graded and determined by many genes, each with a small effect. The continuous variation of the traits determined by such polygenes can be reconciled with the abrupt development of psychoses in some of those predisposed by postulating threshold effects, similar to those defined in diabetes, epilepsy, hypertension, and probably Alzheimers disease. Such a theory provides scope for the influence of nongenetic factors such as deafness, social isolation, and the influence of limited cerebral lesions in a proportion of cases. Their contribution would be expected overall to be inversely proportional to that made by genetic features. In their authoritative text Gottesman and Shields (1982) favored a polygenic theory of schizophrenia along similar lines and showed it to be consistent with a large body of genetic and theoretical evidence.

The theory makes use of a threshold concept and proposes that schizophrenia may be caused by a combination of genes together with a variety of environmental contributory factors, such that vulnerability to exogenous factors would be expected to vary as a function of the degree of genetic loading. Their theory does not exclude the contribution by rare single genes in a small proportion of schizophrenics, but regards polygenes in interaction with environmental factors as the cause of the majority of cases. The theory has the merit of accounting for schizophrenia in late as well as early life. Those with schizophrenia first manifest in old age would be expected to be weakly predisposed genetically. This is confirmed by the lower morbid risk for schizophrenia in first-degree relatives of late paraphrenias, together with the significant contribution to causation made by exogenous factors such as deafness, which are not manifest in schizophrenia of earlier life.

Further evidence in favor of the theory has emerged from inquiries into the association between deafness and personality deviation in late paraphrenic patients (Cooper *et al.*, 1976). Among those who had become deaf some decades before the onset of psychoses, personality as measured by a schizoid personality scale was found to be less abnormal than in patients in whom deafness had arisen within a relatively short period before the onset of psychosis. These findings are consistent with predictions implicit in the polygenic diathesis-stressor theory of Gottesman and Shields. However, as Kay *et al.* (1976) have indicated, further investigation is needed to disentangle the effects of patients' personality traits from coincidental factors over which these could have exerted little or no influence. If late paraphrenia is accepted as a variant of schizophrenia manifest in late life, the contribution of hereditary factors to its causation will need to be re-estimated. Morbid risks might be of a different order when calculated on the basis of an age of risk of 15 to 75 or 80 years rather than of 15 to 40 or 50 years, the accepted practice in most previous inquiries into the heredity of schizophrenia.

To sum up, hereditary factors appear to exert less influence in late paraphrenia and exogenous factors to make a greater contribution to causation than in schizophrenia of earlier life. But the differences are matters of degree rather than qualitative in character.

How Does Paraphrenia Bear on the Problem of Unity or Diversity of Schizophrenic Illness?

Perhaps paraphrenia and the evidence regarding its phenomenology, course, treatment response, and etiological basis is important above all for the implications it carries for the problem of unity or diversity of schizophrenic illness. This issue has, in turn, a bearing upon the conceptual framework and the strategy appropriate for scientific inquiry and clinical practice. The concept implicit in the title of Eugen Bleuler's monograph "Dementia Praecox or the Group of Schizophrenias," has often been interpreted as a radical departure from Kraepelin's concept of schizophrenia. Such a view misconceives the nature of Bleuler's teaching. He advanced a broad unitary concept on the basis of the disturbances of psychological functioning he regarded as the fundamental starting point of all the schizophrenias. His concept embraced "unclear" cases as also paranoid psychoses and conditions of similar phenomenology such as alcoholic hallucinosis in which organic factors make some contribution. What he did call into question was the premature assumption that the schizophrenic syndrome had to be etiologically homogenous to pass muster as a valid concept. This view has been responsible for much circular reasoning regarding the classification of schizophrenia and the manner in which its causes and origins need to be investigated. The evidence accumulated over the past few decades shows phenomenology to be the best substantiated and most logical foundation for the concept of schizophrenia. Whether there is unity or diversity of etiology within the clinical territory so defined must be determined by empirical investigation.

The phenomenologic unity and etiologic diversity found in late paraphrenia constitute a close parallel to the situation that prevails in relation to schizophrenia in early life. There are "idiopathic" cases with no known cause other than a genetic basis and other groups of cases in which deafness, limited cerebral lesion, adverse life circumstances, or a combination of such factors can be judged as contributing to causation. These are the "symptomatic" cases. In early life they have their counterparts in some of the disorders that have been described in association with intoxication with alcohol and amphetamine among other substances, cerebral lesions (Davison & Bagley, 1969), and psychological stress of a severe or overwhelming character (Labhardt, 1963; McCabe, 1975; Strömgren, 1958).

The evidence that argues against excluding conditions such as amphetamine psychosis from the family of schizophrenic disorders has been given in detail elsewhere (Davison & Bagley, 1969; Davison, 1976). The phenomenology includes not only auditory and other hallucinations in clear consciousness, but, in some cases, thought disorder (Angrist & Gershon, 1972), blunting of affect, and some first–rank symptoms of Schneider (Panse & Klages, 1964). In a proportion of cases of long–standing LSD addiction, a chronic course identical with a schizophrenic defect state has been described. As the genetic factors found in schizophrenia make a more limited contribution in those syndromes which have been investigated, the organic factors have to be regarded as being among the causal agents possibly interacting with hereditary and personality factors. The existence of such symptomatic cases is consistent with the genetic theory of schizophrenia advanced by Gottesman and Shields (1982).

A recent investigation of the syndrome of alcoholic hallucinosis (Cutting, 1981) lends further support to the argument pursued here. Of 114 patients originally diagnosed as suffering from alcoholic hallucinosis, only 12 satisfied the strict criteria for this condition. Seven had delusions that were more complex than would have been expected from the hallucinations. One man heard voices calling him a "white–hearted Nancy boy" and believed he had "black syphilis." Another thought that someone had taken out his brain and tampered with it. Fifty percent of patients were given a 'Catego' diagnosis of schizophrenia and a further 9% of doubtful schizophrenia. Of 46% of patients followed up, 26 had a further episode and 16 of these were judged to have a schizophrenic or paranoid psychosis; only 7 had a typical alcoholic hallucinosis. The symptomatology clearly ranged far more widely than had been previously supposed. In terms of heredity, the situation is similar to that defined in late paraphrenia. For though the morbid risk for schizophrenia in the first–degree relatives of patients with such alcoholic psychoses is smaller than that found in the families of schizophrenics, it is significantly in excess of the risk in normal subjects (Reveley & Reveley, 1986, personal communication). There must therefore be an interaction between alcoholic addiction, heredity, and personality factors in the causation of these schizophrenia–like psychoses.

In the schizophrenia–like syndromes that follow severe emotional stress as described by Labhardt (1961) and some of the paranoid states studied by Retterstöl (1966) and Johanson (1964), the condition may prove relatively benign and of brief duration. Here, again, hereditary predisposition seems to be increased above normal expectation judging from the data of McCabe (1975) and Kringlen (1967), and it probably contributes to causation (Roth & McClelland, 1978).

Late paraphrenia, the schizophrenic disorder of late life, is for the greater part idiopathic in that only genetic factors are known to contribute to causation. Exogenous factors contribute to a limited extent in a proportion of cases, the most important being deafness in approximately 40%, social isolation, and in a small minority of 5–10%

of cases a limited cerebral lesion. These latter cases may be regarded as kindred counterparts of the "symptomatic" schizophrenias of earlier life.

The unity of all these syndromes is established through their common phenomenology and, to some extent, their response to neuroleptic drugs and other treatments in respect of which they resemble each other. Within this unity of the schizophrenias, diversity is created by a variety of contributory etiologic factors. The genetic factors and the other etiologic factors appear to be inversely correlated in the contribution they make to causation in the range of disorders subsumed within schizophrenia. The more clear the evidence in certain syndromes that closely resemble schizophrenia that exogenous factors play some limited role in causation the smaller the contribution of genetic factors and vice versa. But the same hereditary factors appear to contribute to causation along a wide spectrum of schizophrenic and paranoid psychoses, late paraphrenia included. That such variety and gradation in the contribution of etiologic factors finds expression in a similar clinical syndrome suggests that they exert their effects through a common pathway.

Late paraphrenia therefore exemplifies with particular clarity both the unity and diversity of schizophrenic illness. It makes a powerful case for the view that comparing schizophrenic syndromes whose etiology (apart from the contribution of heredity) is unknown with other schizophrenia–like disorders whose causation has been partly defined may prove fruitful for the formulation of hypotheses about the final common pathway that mediates the clinical phenomena. Late paraphrenia is also important on account of the questions regarding the factors responsible for differences between the schizophrenias of early life—with their indeterminate outcome and relatively high rate of chronicity, negative symptoms, and deterioration—and the disorders of late life, with their benign course, favorable treatment response, and integrity of personality after years of illness. That one and the same predisposition can find expression in such different destinies constitutes a major challenge to scientific inquiry.

20 The Clinical Features of Late Onset Schizophrenia

Peter Rabins

Paul R. McHugh

Susan Pauker

Joseph Thomas

Johns Hopkins School of Medicine

In their recent review of paranoid and paraphrenic disorders of late life, Bridge and Wyatt (1980*a*, 1980*b*) noted a dearth of American studies. They rejected the conclusion that the condition does not exist in this country and suggested it was more likely that American psychiatrists were much less interested in the condition than their European colleagues. The present study was therefore undertaken to determine the prevalence of such patients in an American psychiatric hospital and to examine the symptoms, signs, and treatment responses of a group of patients with schizophrenic symptoms beginning after age 44. Its goal was to determine whether patients similar to those described in the European literature are seen in this country.

METHOD

The criteria for diagnosing paraphrenia (the term late–onset schizophrenia will be used interchangeably) were derived from Kay and Roth (1961). They included (1) the presence of a persistent delusional state, (2) onset after age 44, and (3) absence of mood disorder and cognitive disorder. The age of onset was chosen as 45 since DSM–III excluded the diagnosis of schizophrenia when symptoms began after 45. Kay and Roth (1961) also commented that the disorder "usually (arises) in the fourth or fifth decade."

Patients were ascertained in two ways. Twenty–five patients 60 and over were examined prospectively between April 1, 1978 and March 30, 1982. Ten patients between the ages of 45 and 59 were ascertained by a retrospective chart review of patients hospitalized during the same period. The results combine these two groups.

Absence of cognitive disorder was determined by the use of the Mini–Mental State Exam (Folstein, Folstein, & McHugh, 1975). This is a reliable and valid structured cognitive exam with a maximum of 30 points. Patients scoring below 24 on discharge were excluded except for one 94–year–old woman. Her MMSE had remained stable at 17 for an 11–month period. She had never learned to read or write and was not socially deteriorated. Patients who fulfilled the criteria but had MMSE scores less than 24 on admission were included if they scored greater than 24 on discharge. Patients fulfilling DSM–III criteria for major depressive disorder were excluded.

RESULTS

A total of 35 patients meeting the criteria were hospitalized during the 4 years of the study. Table 20–1 shows their demographic characteristics. Twenty–five patients (71%) were over age 59 when first examined. This was 3.7% of all admissions over 59 years old. The patients aged 45 to 59 when examined represented 1.4% of admissions in that age group. Mean age at onset of symptoms was 61.1 ± 10.3 (*SD*). Most subjects had been or were married, but almost half were childless. At the time of the hospitalization 12 patients (34%) were living alone.

Table 20–1
Demographic Characteristics (*n*=35)

	45–59 years old	≥ 60 years old	Total
Male	0	3	3
Female	16	16	32
Age at onset (number)	16	19	
Age at ascertainment (number)	10	25	
Marital status			
Currently married			10
Widowed			15
Divorced or separated			7
Never married			3
Biological children			22
No biological children			12[a]
No information			1

[a] Includes three never married.

Table 20-2
Symptoms (n=35)

Delusions	35	
Hallucinations	28	(80%)
Auditory only	11	(31%)
Auditory and other modality	13	(37%)
Nonauditory only[a]	4	(11%)
None	7	(20%)
First rank symptom(s)	22	(63%)

[a]1 visual, 2 tactile, 1 olfactory.

By definition, all patients suffered from delusions (Table 20-2). Twenty-four (69%) had auditory hallucinations, but hallucinations in other sensory modalities were also frequent. Visual hallucinations were present in 10 (29%) individuals, and tactile hallucinations in 9 (26%). It should be emphasized, however, that most subjects who had tactile, visual, olfactory, or gustatory hallucinations also had auditory hallucinations. Nonauditory hallucinations were more common in those with onset after 59 (X^2=7.17, p<.01).

Twenty-one patients met all DSM-III criteria for schizophrenia except that requiring age of onset before 45. Eleven other patients met the DSM-III criteria for schizophreniform disorder, except for age of onset. That is, their symptoms lasted longer than 2 weeks but less than 6 months. Three patients met DSM-III criteria for paranoia.

Eight patients were reported to have hearing loss; five of these individuals were also visually impaired. Two other patients had visual impairment without hearing loss. We did not systematically study the patient's hearing and vision.

All patients were hospitalized. They received milieu and social therapy as befitted their needs, as well as appropriate neuroleptic pharmacotherapy.

To determine response to treatment, two examiners blindly reviewed all charts and placed patients in categories of (1) symptom free, (2) symptomatically improved but not symptom free, and (3) significantly symptomatic upon discharge. Twenty patients (57%) were judged to be symptom free on discharge, while 29% were improved but still symptomatic. Fourteen percent had debilitating, persistent symptoms.

Table 20-3 reports the status 2 years later of the 14 patients in the study who were 60 years of age or older when ascertained and had been hospitalized at least 2 years previously. A majority of the patients had had a relapse or remained symptomatic since discharge. One had died and one had been institutionalized following a stroke. The others were living with family or alone, suggesting that the prognosis for full recovery is not good but that most patients could live at home and lead functional lives.

Table 20-3
2-Year Follow-Up of Patients over 60 (*n*=14)

Symptom free	4
Relapses with symptom-free period(s)	5
Chronic symptoms	3
No follow-up	
Symptom free on discharge	1
Symptomatic on discharge	1

DISCUSSION

The patients studied here were quite similar to patients diagnosed as suffering from paraphrenia, late-onset paraphrenia, or late-onset schizophrenia by Roth (this volume), Kay and Roth (1961), Post (1978), and Herbert and Jacobson (1967). The patients they studied were primarily female, tended to be socially isolated, and had low fertility rates. Many had hallucinations in modalities other than hearing. Herbert and Jacobson, for example, reported hallucinations in all sensory modalities in many late-onset female paraphrenics. Eighteen of their patients (40%) had visual hallucinations.

The frequency of this diagnosis on our inpatient service was similar, although lower, than the 10% prevalence estimated by Bridge (1980a). Other American authors have described experience with such patients. Madden and coworkers (1952) reported that 8% of 300 patients over 45 admitted to a psychiatry service had a paranoid psychosis or schizophrenic psychosis. Raskind, Alvarez, Pietrzyk, Westerland, and Herlin (1976), in describing a geriatric outreach program in Seattle, stated that paranoid psychosis was the second most common psychiatric disorder found. Therefore, Bridge's conclusion that the lack of American studies of this disorder most likely results from a lack of interest rather than a difference in the incidence or prevalence of the condition is supported.

These data support the conclusion that a disorder with the symptoms and course of schizophrenia does begin after 45. The present study and previous follow-up studies of similarly diagnosed patients (Kay, 1975) have shown that the disorder often becomes chronic and socially disabling. Furthermore, others (Kay, 1975) have found a genetic relationship, albeit a weak one, with schizophrenia. We believe that schizophrenia is a syndrome and that late-onset patients should not be diagnosed as suffering a different disorder until meaningful clinical or biologically distinct subtypes can be delineated. The recognition that schizophrenic symptoms can begin in late life should lead to research that capitalizes on the difference in the early and late forms of the disorder. A prospective study of the many psychiatric, social, epidemiologic, and possible etiologic questions raised by retrospective studies seems in order.

21

Deafness as a Precursor to Paraphrenia

Barry J. Gurland

Carol Wilder

Columbia University

One of the key questions about the etiology of paraphrenia (late onset schizophrenia) is the role of aging. A causal relationship could be expected for several reasons, particularly the frequent history of relatively adequate mental and social functioning until the onset of paraphrenia in old age, and the lower genetic loading (family history) for paraphrenia than for early onset schizophrenia (Eisdorfer, 1980; Kay and Roth, 1961; Post, 1966).

A variety of aging changes have been studied to determine whether they occur more frequently than expected by chance in cases of paraphrenia (Kay *et al.*, 1976; Kay, 1972; Post, 1978). One of the most interesting relationships to emerge is that with hearing impairment (Cooper *et al.*, 1976; Cooper, Kay, Curry, Garside, & Roth, 1974). Elderly patients with paranoid psychosis have been reported to have a more severe degree of hearing loss and to be more often 'socially deaf' than patients with affective illness. The hearing loss has been the conductive type, coming on before age 45, due to middle ear disease, and with a latent interval of 6 years (often much longer) before the onset of paranoid symptoms. Paraphrenics with a history of deafness may tend not to have primary (process) symptoms nor as strong a family history of schizophrenia as those who are not hearing impaired.

Duration rather than quality of hearing impairment appears to be the crucial stress. A decrease in self-esteem (Rousey, 1971) and an increased tendency to withdraw (Havighurst & Albrecht, 1953) or misinterpret events (Wilford, 1971), as well as a reduction of corrective feedback from others about exaggerated or false beliefs have been reported.

Most of the evidence relating possible precursors to paraphrenia has come from studies conducted in clinical settings where the design is typically a case–control comparison. Under these conditions, data

Professor J.R.M. Copeland directed the study in London.

on precursors must usually be retrospective and the manifestations of the precursors and the early or prodromal symptoms of paraphrenia may be confounded. To cast further light on the possible role of hearing loss as a precursor to paraphrenia, we examined the relationship between impaired hearing and some indicators of suspiciousness and isolation among representative samples of the elderly in the community.

Although the relationships under study are of interest in their own right, the rationale for the relevance to the etiology of paraphrenia is the assumption that if hearing loss promotes suspiciousness and isolation it will also predispose to paraphrenia. There is ample clinical evidence (Post, 1978) that suspiciousness and isolation are symptoms and probably precedents of paraphrenia, although longitudinal studies demonstrating the sequence of events are lacking.

The model we initially had in mind is shown in Figure 21-1: suspiciousness and isolation over a long period of time, in the presence of constitutional vulnerability and with the addition of stress, leads to the development of paraphrenia.

METHOD

The data were collected under the auspices of the United States–United Kingdom Cross–National Project in the course of a study of the health and social problems of the elderly in the communities of New York and London (Gurland *et al.*, 1983). Randomly selected subjects 65 years and older were examined by semi-structured

Figure 21-1
Initial Model of Hearing Loss as a Precursor to Paraphrenia

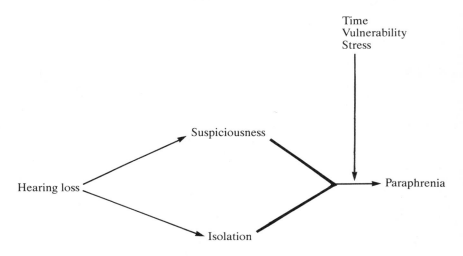

interview techniques. Response rates were 71% and 81%, respectively. Psychiatrists interviewed all 396 subjects in London and a random half of the 445 subjects in New York.

The interview items on hearing loss, suspiciousness, and isolation are shown in Table 21–1. They are a subset of a lengthy series in each of these three content areas (there were many other content areas, 22 homogeneous scales, and over 1500 items in the interview). The global rating of hearing impairment was based on self–report and interviewer's observations; audiometric testing was not done.

The items on suspiciousness covered aspects of referential and persecutory ideas; analysis of relationship to hearing impairment was made item by item and also with reference to persons classified as suspicious on the grounds of a positive rating on any one of this subset of items. The social isolation items that were selected for this analysis concerned the number of interpersonal contacts made by the individual during the previous month.

RESULTS

The cross–national comparison showed higher rates of both hearing loss and suspiciousness in London than in New York. The results on hearing impairment have been discussed more fully elsewhere (Gurland *et al.*, 1983) and probably reflect true differences between the elderly populations in the two cities. The results on suspiciousness are more debatable. Possible explanations include: in New York more than in London (1) suspicious elderly persons are likely to refuse interviews, (2) suspiciousness is likely to be regarded as normal, or (3) suspicious persons tend to leave the cities. It is also possible that (4) higher rates of deafness are causally associated with the higher rates of suspiciousness in London compared with New York. Curiously enough, Bridge and Wyatt (1980*b*) ask, "Does the striking lack of research [in the U.S. compared with Europe] mean that there are no late–life paranoid patients in the United States?"

As a practical matter, 49 individuals could be classified as suspicious in London and only 22 in New York; and 127 cases of hearing loss were reported in London but only 80 in New York. Because the greater numbers make the analysis simpler, this presentation of findings is restricted to the London sample. Even in London, only one case of paraphrenia was strongly suspected (although not firmly diagnosed); that person was also classified as impaired in hearing, suspicious, and isolated.

Suspiciousness was found at increased rates in persons complaining of hearing impairment. The difference between those without hearing impairment (rate of suspiciousness 7.3%) and those with mild hearing loss (rate of suspiciousness 15.8%) was significant at the .05 level. Surprisingly, the severest hearing impairment had a 10.3% rate of suspiciousness. This analysis was based on the first of the items listed for suspiciousness (feels criticized, laughed at, or

Table 21–1
Interview Items on Hearing Loss,
Suspiciousness, and Social Isolation
(US–UK Cross–National Geriatric Community Study)

Hearing loss

None
- Hearing is adequate for all purposes.

Mild
- Hearing is a slight inconvenience at times (e.g., can't hear in groups).

Severe
- Hearing is a definite inconvenience (e.g., people must speak up).
- Hearing is a serious handicap (e.g., can't carry on a normal conversation).
- Virtually or completely deaf.

Suspiciousness

- Feels people criticize or laugh at him or talk about him.
- Suspicious of, or puzzled by, behavior of others toward him.
- Believes that he has been attacked, harassed, cheated, or persecuted when the circumstances make it almost certainly not true.
- Suspects that people spy on him or eavesdrop.
- Has the unjustified feeling that people treat him unfairly.
- Looks or sounds suspicious.

Social isolation

- Number of children seen in past month.
- Number of siblings seen in past month.
- Number of relatives seen in past month.
- Number of friends seen in past month.
- Number of clubs to which subject belongs.

talked about). Frequencies on the other items were lower and thus less satisfactory for analysis, but similar results were obtained when subjects were classified as suspicious on the basis of a positive rating on any one of the 6 items on suspiciousness.

Contrary to our predictions, isolation was not higher in cases of impaired hearing; in fact, it was reduced to a significant degree in cases of severe hearing loss (frequency of isolation = 60.5% for no hearing loss, 64.9% for mild, and 40% for severe hearing impairment).

The relationship between scores of social isolation and suspiciousness was also examined and found to be not statistically significant (X^2=1.56, V=.0148, p=ns). However, a significant relationship was found between suspiciousness and two items not included in the concept and scale of current isolation, namely 21% "never been married" (were suspicious versus 9% for the presently married and 15.5 for the widowed group, p<.05); and "not feeling close to anyone" (40% were suspicious versus 11% for the rest, p<.0001).

Suspiciousness was also tested against a variety of self-report and observational scales of mental, physical, and social problems. Statistically significant relationships were found with depression (positive) and dementia (negative). The suspicious group also tended to have raised scores on a number of scales of physical conditions; in particular, a curvilinear relationship was found between suspiciousness and visual impairment, similar though weaker than that noted for hearing impairment.

DISCUSSION

The findings were not entirely consistent with our initial model of deafness as a precursor to paraphrenia. That model would be best supported by a positive association between degrees of hearing loss and both suspiciousness and current isolation, and also between suspiciousness and current isolation. Instead we found this only for *mild* hearing loss and suspiciousness.

We did, however, find a significant relationship between suspiciousness and never having been married and not feeling close to anyone. The first of these items may reflect a lifelong difficulty in forming intimate partnerships, and the second item may indicate current difficulty with intimacy.

Several reservations should be made prior to interpreting these data: These data are cross sectional and thus limited for testing a causal model; a single interview largely restricted to information obtained directly from the subject is not always adequate for detecting suspiciousness; the measures (including those of hearing impairment, suspiciousness, and isolation) were not assessed independently, and suspiciousness may not be a precursor to paraphrenia. The most important caution about these data is that the assessment of hearing impairment was largely dependent on the self-report of the subject. Although the rater's observations influenced the global

Figure 21-2
A Revised Model of Hearing Loss as a Precursor to Paraphrenia

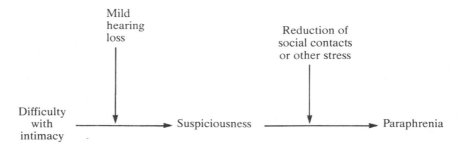

ratings, audiometry and physical examination were not employed. Nevertheless, these findings can be applied to development of an improved model for explaining the way deafness predisposes to paraphrenia.

We would now postulate that there is a group of elderly, with a lifelong tendency toward difficulty with intimate relationships, but with an adequate level of social contacts. This group is vulnerable to suspiciousness, but their social support network aids their adaptation until mild hearing loss supervenes, strains their tenuous interpersonal relationships, and precipitates the symptoms of suspiciousness. Nevertheless, the symptoms of suspiciousness do not degenerate into a paraphrenic state until social contacts drop away or other stressors arise (Figure 21-2).

Some of the reported contributing factors to paraphrenia do speak to the importance of increasing isolation with age, for example, being the last of the children in a family or having fewer surviving children of one's own (Kay & Roth, 1961). It is notable that severe hearing loss is not associated with suspiciousness and is related to less isolation. Possibly the reduced isolation of severe hearing loss is supportive and compensatory or, alternatively, the *ambiguity* of communication associated with mild hearing loss is a specific stress for this group of elderly. Some have suggested (Barker *et al.*, 1953) that where impaired hearing is of a lesser degree and less obvious to the person or others, greater potential conflict is occasioned by attempts to appear and function as normal.

These data may suggest an opportunity for preventive intervention. Nevertheless, it is notable that only 15 out of 95 cases with impaired hearing showed suspiciousness, and only 1 out of 49 cases of suspiciousness were diagnosed as probably paraphrenic. Greater specification of the group vulnerable to paraphrenia is needed to efficiently introduce preventive measures.

In making our model of the genesis of paraphrenia more consistent with our data on hearing loss, suspiciousness, and isolation we have imputed a causal sequence which is, of course, speculative. Further research is needed to longitudinally trace the evolution of paraphrenia (or other psychiatric problems) in cohorts of elderly with hearing impairment. Cross-section data and case-control studies offer an efficient means of identifying possible precursors to paraphrenia, but this approach is necessarily retrospective and thus subject to biased reporting. Moreover, it is especially difficult under those conditions to distinguish the characteristics of precursors from the prodromal symptoms of a disorder.

Further studies should take into account at least the following factors with respect to deafness as a stressor:

1. The role of lifelong vulnerability to paraphrenia such as is suggested by family history or manifested by difficulties with intimate relationships.

2. The nature and degree of chronic stress as exemplified by the different mental effects of mild (as opposed to severe) deafness.

3. The combinations of stressors that may be particularly damaging to the individual (e.g., when social supports are withdrawn from one who finds interpersonal relations difficult and is under a chronic handicap in communicating with people).

4. The age and developmental stage at which a potentially stressful event occurs: a person who, despite a vulnerability, has adapted by drawing strength from social contacts may react differently to middle-age hearing loss (which complicates social interaction) than someone whose early deafness forced a different mode of adaptation or whose later impairment is more socially acceptable as an age-related norm.

5. The duration of the stress: sudden hearing loss may precipitate dependency and depression, while prolonged or insidious onset hearing loss may elicit more complex adaptive and maladaptive responses.

Hearing loss is undoubtedly better measured within the broader context of communication impairment and by objective (e.g., audiometric) as well as self-report techniques. The confident classification of symptoms of suspiciousness or other prolonged mental abnormalities requires finding and interviewing informants. Despite the formidable difficulties of such a study, the findings on predisposition to late onset schizophrenia or paraphrenia would be of great importance for understanding the development of schizophrenia at any age and the stressful nature of age-related events and for determining preventive intervention.

22

Lateral Cerebral Ventricular Size in Late Onset Schizophrenia

Godfrey D. Pearlson

David Garbacz

Rhett H. Tompkins

Hyo S. Ahn

Peter V. Rabins

Johns Hopkins School of Medicine

Cerebral ventricular changes have been described in association with the form of schizophrenia that begins in early adulthood. CT scans of patients with the first onset of schizophrenic symptoms in late life were examined to determine whether similar changes were present.

METHOD

Using the criteria of Kay and Roth (1961), eight patients admitted to the Henry Phipps Psychiatric Clinic of the Johns Hopkins Hospital were identified as suffering from "late paraphrenia." The mean age for this patient group was 71.6±10.4 years. The patients had been symptomatic for a mean of 3.0±2.1 years, five were currently receiving neuroleptic medications, and an additional one had previously been treated with such agents. None of the patients had received ECT, none had a past history of head injury sufficiently severe to have led to unconsciousness, two had possible past histories of alcoholism, and two had positive serum syphilis serology (one had a negative spinal fluid VDRL; the second had been treated adequately in the past for syphilis). Cognitively, none of the subjects had Mini-Mental State scores (Folstein *et al.*, 1975) in the abnormal range, i.e., all scored 24 or above at the time of discharge from hospital.

Fourteen normal controls with a mean age of 72.9±9.0 years were chosen from the files of the Department of Neuroradiology of the Johns Hopkins Hospital. These individuals had been referred for

CT evaluation of headaches and/or dizziness. All had normal neuro-logical examinations, negative serum VDRLs, and no past history of major mental illnesses, head injuries, or alcohol or drug abuse. All subjects and controls gave informed consent.

All late paraphrenic subjects received a noncontrast CT scan on the AS&E 500 CT Scanner of the Johns Hopkins Hospital Department of Neuroradiology using standardized 10–mm cuts. The CT slice was selected that showed bodies of the lateral ventricles at their broad-est. The CT slices of the subjects and controls were enlarged to approximately life–size using an overhead projector and traced onto sheets of paper. Ventricle–to–brain ratio (VBR) was then calculated by a single individual blind to diagnosis using a computer–linked planimeter. The reliability of this procedure has been previously demonstrated (Pearlson, Veroff, & McHugh, 1981), as has its validity (Penn, Belanger, & Yasnoff, 1978).

RESULTS

The ages and VBRs of the paraphrenic and normal control groups are shown in Table 22–1. Although the paraphrenic patients had larger VBRs than the control group, this difference was not statistically significant. While normal controls, as predicted, demonstrated a moderately low but positive correlation between age and VBR ($r=0.45$, p=ns), paraphrenics exhibited a statistically significant neg-ative linear relationship ($r=-0.73$, $p<.05$).

DISCUSSION

A number of studies have reported CT changes in some early onset chronic schizophrenia patients (Weinberger, Torrey, Neophytides, & Wyatt, 1979a). These changes have included lateral cerebral ventric-

Table 22–1
Comparison of Late Onset Paraphrenics and Normal Controls

	Late onset paraphrenics n=8 (1 male)	Normal controls n=14 (3 males)
Mean age ± SD	71.6 ± 10.4	72.9 ± 9.0
Mean VBR ± SD	12.3 ± 2.4	10.8 ± 3.0
Correlation of VBR with age	r=0.73*	r=+0.45

*$p<.05$

ular enlargement (as demonstrated by increased VBRs) when compared to age–matched normal controls. One study (Johnstone, Crow, Frith, Husband, & Kreel, 1979) demonstrated significant lateral ventricular enlargement in a group of elderly schizophrenic patients whose illnesses had begun in early life. In the current study, although late paraphrenic subjects and normal controls were comparable in terms of age, the patient group exhibited only a slightly larger (and not statistically significant) mean VBR. When the relationship of VBR to age was examined, a significant negative linear trend was noted among the paraphrenic patients, which contrasted strongly with the expected opposite tendency in the normal controls.

These findings could be interpreted as the effects of two different processes. The younger late paraphrenic patients (i.e., those with the largest VBRs) could represent the furthest end of a continuum of "classic" schizophrenia, which traditionally has its onset in early life but may not find clinical expression until much later in some individuals. This group of schizophrenics might exhibit larger VBRs than controls. A second cluster of patients, who bear a phenomenological resemblance to the first group, may in fact owe their symptomatic onset to a separate process.

This hypothesis can be tested by collecting a larger series of patients with late onset paraphrenia and attempting to replicate the present VBR findings and to demonstrate significant differences between the two postulated groups on a number of variables. The most relevant of these would include presence or absence of a family history of schizophrenia, premorbid schizotypal personality (both of which would be expected to be positive more often in the younger but not the older onset patients), and response to treatment. The second group of late paraphrenics might be expected to show their clinical symptomatology on the basis of coarse brain disease having its onset in late life. The current study provided no evidence for such a phenomenon, either from Mini–Mental State score differences between the two groups or from careful examination of the CT scan slices for signs of abnormalities.

Acknowledgment

This work was supported by a Johns Hopkins University Institutional Research Grant.

23

The Paranoid Syndrome After Mid-Life

L.L. Heston

University of Minnesota

This report concerns the natural history of psychiatric disorders that feature paranoid signs, with emphasis on conditions beginning in middle age or later. The main paranoid signs are delusions of persecution or reference, suspiciousness, sensitivity, sullenness, jealousy, guardedness, and litigiousness. Because these manifestations of disturbance often occur together, they have been regarded as a syndrome through the modern history of psychiatry.

The paranoid syndrome, which is delimited by the presence of typical paranoid delusions, is a central feature of many con-ditions—schizophrenia of course, but also affective illness, toxic conditions, diffuse brain damage, and several metabolic disorders. Indeed, the paranoid syndrome, like anxiety or depression, is one of the cornerstones of psychopathology. The paranoid syndrome also occurs alone; "paranoia" or "paranoid state" are typical diagnostic terms used for such cases. Whether this disorder should be classified as one entity, or subdivided, or considered as a variant of some other disorder, usually schizophrenia, is arguable. This "pure" paranoid syndrome, which usually has its onset in later adult life, is the main concern of this paper.

METHOD

The starting point for this study was 1,849 autopsies done on adult psychiatric patients who died in Minnesota State Hospitals and nursing homes between 1952 and 1972. The cases appeared to have been unselected in any material respect except that dying in a psychiatric hospital implies unusually severe illness. Reports of the general autopsy, the neuropathological examination, and an abbre-viated clinical record, generally amounting to a death summary, were available along with the original pathology slides and brain tissues in paraffin blocks.

Table 23–1
Paranoid Syndrome Among Four Major Diagnostic Groups

Diagnostic group	Total	Number with paranoid syndrome	%
Affective illness	410	83	20.2
Schizophrenia	142	67	47.2
Brain injury	193	54	28.0
Paranoid only (or delusional disorder)	35	35	100.0

The first step was to review the clinical summaries to identify all cases where the paranoid syndrome appeared prominently in the presenting signs and symptoms. For these cases, the complete clinical record compiled by the hospital where the patient was cared for while alive was reviewed. All patients who had delusions of persecution, jealousy, or reference, or mixtures of such delusions were selected as subjects for this study.

Among the 1,849 autopsy records, 239 (13%) exhibited the paranoid syndrome. This was probably a substantial underestimate of the true proportion, as 203 clinical summaries were inadequate for scoring the paranoid syndrome as present or absent. For example, Freedman and Schwab (1978) observed 21% of 264 admissions to have paranoid delusions or ideas of reference. The final estimate from this study will be comparable.

The paranoid cases were divided into four groups (Table 23–1). If disorder of mood dominated the clinical picture, an affective illness was assumed. Bizarre fragmented thinking or an hallucinosis that dominated the clinical picture was considered schizophrenia. Cases were placed in the injured brain group if brain injury or brain disorder was associated with subsequent change in personality sufficient to constitute a paranoid syndrome.

Despite the fact that they were selected by an exclusionary process, all remaining cases, the "paranoid only" category, met the criteria for paranoid disorder or paranoia in DSM–III, or for paranoid state or paranoia in ICD 9. Hallucinations, if present, were transient. The delusions tended to be long–lived and to revolve about a central theme. Nearly all would be regarded by clinicians as "systematized," although the exact denotation of that term is unclear. This group will henceforth be called "delusional disorder" and abbreviated "DD." Kendler and Tsuang (1981) have reviewed the classification of paranoid disorder; with minor variances, the denotation of delusional disorder in this study seems consistent with theirs.

RESULTS

Age at Onset

First admissions for the paranoid syndrome were fairly constant from age 30 to 70 (Table 23–2). Affective illness accounted for 34.7% of admissions, more than any other single category. Affective illness with admission at earlier ages were mainly bipolars; later, unipolar depressions dominated. Schizophrenia, rarely present among younger admissions, peaked between ages 30 and 39 and then tailed off, continuing through age 70. The later onset admissions were regarded clinically as late onset paraphrenias as described by Sir Martin Roth and his colleagues (Roth, 1955; Kay & Roth, 1961).

The ages at admission among the brain injured group exhibited a bimodal distribution; the frequency peaked between ages 40 and 49 and again between 60 and 69. The early admission group was composed mainly of seizure disorders, but included Huntington's disease (3), hereditary ataxia (1), alcoholism (7), and blunt trauma (2). (The autopsy series was largely compiled before the drug abuse epidemic of the 1960s; the category would be larger today.) Later onset cases in this group were mainly associated with alcoholism, vascular disease, and trauma.

The delusional disorder group showed up in significant proportions between ages 40 and 49; actually, the first cases in this interval were at age 45. After that, the proportionate contribution of DD became substantial. The eventual total of 15% of all paranoid syndrome cases seems high. One reason may be this group's relative

Table 23–2
Percentage Distribution of Paranoid Syndrome by
Age at First Admission and Diagnostic Group

Age interval	Affective illness	Schizophrenia	Injured brain	Delusional disorder	Total
<20	1.3	0.8	—	—	2.1
20–29	7.9	1.7	0.8	0.8	11.2
30–39	7.1	10.0	2.9	0.4	20.4
40–49	3.3	7.1	8.8	6.7	25.9
50–59	6.7	5.4	2.9	3.8	18.8
60–69	5.9	2.9	7.1	7.5	18.4
>69	2.5	—	—	0.8	3.3
Total	34.7	27.9	22.5	15.0	100.0

Table 23–3
Cases of Delusional Disorder With Onset Over Age 45

	Females	Males	Totals
Number	13	19	32
Mean Age Onset ± *SE*	53.8 ± 2.2	60.5 ± 3.1	57.8 ± 2.1
Range	45–69	45–78	
Mean Age Admission ± *SE*	58.8 ± 2.8	61.9 ± 2.6	60.6 ± 2.4
Range	45–77	45–80	
Mean Age Death + *SE*	68.8 ± 3.6	70.5 ± 2.7	69.8 ± 2.9

intractability to treatment, with consequent long admissions and increased risk for death in hospital and autopsy.

Demographic Data

Table 23–3 displays the ages of onset, first admission, and death for the 32 cases of DD with onset at or over age 45. This series differed from most others in that males constituted a large majority of the Minnesota cases. No ready explanation was apparent for this finding. Most artifacts of ascertainment among older psychiatric subjects favor female admissions. Females are generally the younger partner in marriages and live longer than males. Therefore, an ill male is more likely than an ill female to have a spouse available to provide care. On the other hand, males with DD may be more difficult to manage than females, and hence more likely to be found in psychiatric hospitals. This was supported by the fact that males were admitted sooner after onset than females were.

Nonetheless, the main difference between this series and others must be presumed to lie in essential structure; the Minnesota study

Table 23–4
Social Factor

	Delusional disorder *n*=32	Controls *n*=32
Never married	7	14
Hearing loss	3	0
Vision loss	1	0
Eccentric premorbid	4	1

was a 20–year incidence study, the incident being death and autopsy in psychiatric hospital. The only other study population comparable on most points was Retterstol's (1966), which found 63% males among 83 "pure paranoids" and "paranoiacs". Overall, whether gender affects the frequency of DD is a question best regarded as unsettled.

Control Subjects

In order to provide comparison or control groups, 32 cases of affective illness and a like number of schizophrenia were found in the records that matched the DD subjects on gender and age at admission. Cases where paranoid features were prominent were excluded. At this time, only the affective controls have been investigated and compared to the DD cases.

In view of the natural history of the two disorders, it was not surprising that the affective cases were younger on average at onset of illness. The affective group had three suicides compared to none among the DD cases. When those cases were excluded, the age at death was the same; apart from suicide, delusional disorder did not affect longevity.

The literature suggests several other factors associated with DD (Kay *et al.*, 1976; also, review by Kendler, 1980). Studies of DD subjects have been reported to contain large proportions of unmarried persons. The Minnesota group had seven subjects who were never married (Table 23–4). This was, however, half the rate of the affective controls and in this sample, remaining single was characteristic of psychiatric patients generally. A small excess of DD subjects had impaired hearing or vision, which is consistent with the report of Kay *et al.* (1976).

An attempt was made to classify the DD cases as having or not having characteristics often seen in relatives of schizophrenics, i.e., "eccentric premorbid adjustment." These characteristics have been called "schizoid" or "schizophrenia spectrum" or "schizotypical" by researchers and have some features in common with the borderline personality. No excess of such personality disorders was found among DD subjects.

Medical Conditions

Table 23–5 compares DDs with controls with respect to medical illnesses present before onset of the psychiatric condition but not regarded by the attending physicians as associated with that condition. That conclusion was reaffirmed by the review of case material done at the start of this study. However, despite those negative clinical judgments, more chronic illness appeared in the DD group— 60% of the DD group compared with 20% of controls. No specific illnesses set the two groups apart, but the total pathology was significantly greater in the DD group.

Table 23–5
Pre–Onset Medical Illnesses

Illnesses	Number ill[a]	
	Delusional disorder $n=19$	Controls $n=7$
Hypertension	7	4
Rheumatic valvular disease	2	—
Tuberculosis	2	1
Chronic obstructive pulmonary disease	2	1
CVA (thrombosis)	1	—
Pernicious anemia	1	—
Seizures	1	—
Diabetes M.	2	—
Cancer (breast)	1	—
Alcohol abuse (no incidence of brain injury)	7	3
Chronic cholecystitis	0	1

[a] Some subjects had more than one illness

Family History

Affective illness appeared in two relatives of DDs and five relatives of controls, but these were not significant numbers. Schizophrenia was present in three DD families and no control families, while other psychiatric illnesses occurred in nine DD and two control relatives. There was an excess of psychiatric disorder generally among relatives of the DD group, mainly personality disorders; four were addictive alcoholics. The family history was from records only and hence is incomplete. Experience in Minnesota has been that about 60% of severe psychiatric illness in first–degree relatives of patients is not recorded in medical charts. Field investigations would be required, and the results in hand suggest that the work would be worth doing.

It is hard to know how these preliminary results would compare to those in the literature, because the diagnostic criteria applied to probands varied widely. Kendler and Davis (1981) have reviewed the subject, and Kendler and Hayes (1981) presented new data. However, they did not report the estimate of most interest, the frequency of DD among relatives of DD probands. They did not find an excess of schizophrenia or affective illness among those relatives. Winokur (1977) did find an excess of schizophrenia among relatives of pro–bands with paranoia. Kendler and his coauthors regard some of the schizophrenic cases discovered by Winokur as actually being "para–noid psychosis," not schizophrenia. In fact, the point is moot; even if making such fine diagnostic distinctions among relatives were pos–

Table 23-6
Underlying Cause of Death

	Delusional disorder $n=19$	Affective controls $n=7$
Cancer	10	2
Ischemic heart	7	10
Rheumatic valvular	2	0
Cerebral thrombus	4	4
Cerebral hemorrhage	2	4
Chronic obstructive pulmonary disease	3	1
Pulmonary infarction	2	2
Accident (hip fracture)	1	0
Intestinal obstruction	0	2
Biliary obstruction	0	1
Abdominal aneurysm	0	2
Pyelonephritis	0	1
Suicide	0	3
Unknown	1	0

sible, which is doubtful, especially since field investigations were not done, the presence of either paranoid psychosis or schizophrenia could be interpreted from a genetic viewpoint; one would only have to posit that "paranoid psychosis" was a less severe form of schizophrenia, which is certainly reasonable. Thus Winokur's result, which is consistent with previous evidence, should stand.

Results of Treatment

The DD group in this study was utterly refractory to treatment. The controls clearly did benefit from treatment—11 of 17 improved with electroshock, 2 of 5 improved with phenothiazines, and 3 of 7 responded well to antidepressants. Most of them had been discharged and readmitted one or more times.

The DD group tended to stay about the same with respect to psychiatric status from the time they entered the hospital. Treatments had no appreciable effect, although compliance may have been a major cause of the complete failure of phenothiazines. Seven members were discharged, but they tended to return quickly; the longest stay outside of the hospital was 5 months. Their psychiatric problems were quite homogeneous. They had persistent delusions, developed no insight, and tended to behave in response to their delusions in ways that made it impossible for them to live outside of the hospital. However, they made excellent adjustments in hospital,

Table 23-7
Brain Pathology
(including direct causes of death)

	Delusional disorder	Controls
Cystic lesions	2	1
Metastatic cancer	3	—
Small strokes	5	1
Alzheimer's pathology	2	1
Degeneration, occipital lobe	1	—
Old hemorrhage	1	—
Pontine venous malformation	—	1

tending to settle in, cause little problem for staffs, and become valued as "good workers."

Autopsy Results

The underlying causes of death as discovered during autopsy differed little between the two groups (Table 23-6). More chronic disease occurred in the DD group, but the finding is of uncertain significance. However, there was an apparent difference in the total amount of pathology found in the brains of subjects (Table 23-7). Overall, a significant excess of pathology was discovered in the DD group. However, no particular pathological entity could be singled out as distinguishing the two groups. One negative finding was interesting; there would seem to be no association between progressive dementia and the paranoid syndrome.

DISCUSSION

A study of this kind can only hint at hypotheses to be tested. An association between the paranoid syndrome and brain injury was suggested by the evidence. This was especially pronounced in more youthful subjects, as has long been known, but the relationship may extend throughout the life span in more subtle form.

Paranoid states in more elderly subjects may be related to chronic disease, suggesting that vigorous search for and treatment of chronic disease is most important in elderly persons showing signs of psychiatric disorder. However, this finding cannot take us far toward etiological explanations. The diseases that may distinguish the DD groups from affective controls in this study are extremely common in the population, whereas DD, by any measure, is rare. Few persons with those chronic illnesses develop DD, so some special vulnerability must be posited. One predisposing factor is likely genetic, and weak evidence does suggest a link to a less severe form of schizophrenia with relative preservation of the personality. Such a finding would be consistent with general experience in medical genetics.

In general, the later the age at onset, the less dramatic the manifestations of illness, the less severe the course, and the lower the recurrence risk to relatives. The relationship between schizophrenia and DD is consistent with those general expectations. This reasoning suggests that a logical program for the investigation of paranoid syndromes would be progressively more refined family studies.

TREATMENT PERSPECTIVES

Physicians need to take great care when prescribing neuroleptics for the elderly. Initial doses should be ¼ or less that prescribed for healthy adults. Anticholinergic medications should not be used prophylatically. Combining neuroleptics with other psychotropic drugs can lead to unwanted effects.

A serious complication of long–term administration of neuroleptics is tardive dyskinesia, a neurologic condition that is potentially irreversible. Studies have shown a direct relationship between aging and susceptibility to tardive dyskinesia, even with short–term administration of these drugs. The likelihood of reversal of tardive dyskinesia also decreases with age.

Heightened risks of side effects from neuroleptics should lead clinicians working with older schizophrenic patients to consider other treatment modalities, particularly psychotherapy, as well. While symptoms may be seen by others in the community as normal concomitants of aging, leading to a more accepting social milieu for the older schizophrenic than for his younger counterpart, this can also lead to various treatment options being overlooked. Their social isolation is also less obvious since older persons in general tend to live alone. The need for health care because of the aging process creates opportunities for psychiatric intervention and continuity of care. Thus, with aging, psychotherapeutic interventions through direct care and consultation can become significant.

Long–term psychotherapy with a specific schizophrenic patient has contributed greater understanding of the transitions between psychotic and nonpsychotic states, and the role of the therapist and particular interventions during these changes. Evidence that brief hospitalizations emphasizing pharmacological treatment may contribute to an increase rather than a decrease in chronicity underscores the need to integrate psychotherapy into the treatment plan.

24 Neuroleptic Use in the Elderly

Ben Gierl

Rush Medical College

Maurice Dysken

University of Minneapolis

GREEC V.A., Minneapolis

John M. Davis

University of Illinois at Chicago

Jary M. Lesser

University of Texas at Houston

The purpose of this paper is to review the use of neuroleptic medication in the elderly. This topic has become increasingly important with the rise in the number of elderly with organic and functional impairments.

Pfeiffer (1977) estimated that 10% to 25% of the more than 20 million elderly have moderate to severe mental disorders. Goldfarb (1962) estimated that 50% to 80% of nursing home residents have psychiatric disorders. Organic causes represent about 45% of all mental disorders among the elderly, if mild to severe cases are included, based on admission records in an assortment of psychiatric treatment facilities (Pfeiffer, 1977). A survey of 12 Veterans Administration hospitals revealed that 55% of patients with organic brain syndromes were receiving psychotropic medication (Prien, Haber, & Caffey, 1975). Of the 900,000 seriously demented elderly in the United States a decade ago, an estimated 600,000 were suffering from Alzheimers disease, as judged from a study of brains of demented old people (Terry & Wisniewski, 1975).

Because of the behavioral changes due to impairment in cognitive abilities, patients may be unable to control their noisiness, assaultiveness, wandering, and inappropriate social behavior. Loss of intellectual and cognitive skills is thought to lead to an inability to integrate sensory stimuli and a misinterpretation of reality. The illness may progress to paranoid ideation with hostile accusations and visual and auditory hallucinations and require antipsychotic medication.

Empirically, neuroleptics are of great help because of their particular property of relieving the symptoms of agitation, violent and irrational behavior, and typical perceptual disturbances (Eisdorfer, 1975). In these circumstances, the antianxiety agents are of little value, especially in the cognitively impaired, as they depress cognitive abilities further, which may exacerbate the initial symptoms. It is most important to avoid giving psychotropic medication to control uncooperative patients before they are diagnosed. While some refer to antipsychotics as "chemical strait jackets" (Covert, Rodrigues, & Solomon, 1977), this concept is not useful. If a drug is used to treat clear-cut symptoms rather than socially disruptive behavior, it cannot be considered a restraint. Neuroleptics normalize all aspects of behavior and do not have a nonspecific taming effect.

Before prescribing a neuroleptic, or psychotropic of any kind, a comprehensive medical, psychiatric, and psychosocial evaluation, including information about past and present medication, is essential. Symptoms may be due to a physical or mental disease or to drug toxicity. The history may be difficult to obtain if the patient has trouble communicating and if other sources give conflicting histories and descriptions. Also, the patient may be too uncooperative to be examined adequately. One must look for evidence indicating reversible medical factors that may be contributing to the agitation and psychosis.

The elderly patient or his family should bring in all current medications, including over-the-counter preparations. Some of these drugs, such as sleep compounds and antihypertensives, may be contributing to the patient's depression, agitation, or confusion. Learoyd (1972) noted that 16% of 236 patients who were receiving psychotropic drugs and had abnormal behavior prior to admission to a psychogeriatric unit had disorders directly attributable to the deleterious effects of psychotropic drugs. Their symptoms abated after discontinuation of the medication.

A recent stressor, such as a birth or death in the family or a move to an unfamiliar surrounding, may explain a sudden change in the elderly patient's behavior. The patient's symptoms in some cases may respond to psychotherapeutic intervention or environmental change without the need for neuroleptics.

A correct psychiatric diagnosis may be difficult to establish. For example, symptoms in the elderly patient of agitation, social withdrawal, night wandering, confusion, crying, and incontinence may erroneously lead to a diagnosis of dementia and the use of a neuroleptic, whereas the correct diagnosis is a major depressive disorder. The agitated, psychotic, demented patient suffering primarily from depression may benefit from a neuroleptic, but this medication may further obscure the diagnosis. Markedly agitated behavior which the patient cannot control should be considered a psychotic equivalent in the elderly, analogous to a delusion, which cannot be abandoned when confronted with a realistic need to do so. Such agitation may be more similar to agitation seen in functional psychoses than to simple organicity.

We propose the following five diagnostic groups in the differential diagnosis of agitation and psychosis in the elderly:

1. Psychosis secondary to organic mental disorder presenting predominantly with dementia.
2. Psychosis secondary to organic mental disorder presenting predominantly with delirium.
3. Late life paranoid disorder (paraphrenia).
4. Chronic schizophrenia.
5. Major affective disorder—manic or depressed episode.

Of course, some patients may have symptoms due to two or more of these diagnostic possibilities, a situation that calls for a combined-treatment approach.

ORGANIC MENTAL DISORDER WITH DEMENTIA

Dementia is diagnosed when the clinician finds evidence of a decline in previously held intellectual skills. Using DSM–III (APA, 1980) criteria, organic mental disorder is used when the etiology is known or presumed for a particular organic brain syndrome. The most common etiology for a dementing illness is Alzheimers disease, called primary degenerative dementia in DSM–III, which is characterized by insidious onset and uniformly progressive deterioration. Far less frequent is multi–infarct dementia, which has a stepwise deterioration in intellectual functioning. Substance–induced dementias, such as alcoholic dementia, are quite common. Potentially reversible cases comprise 10%–15% of dementias, including: normal pressure hydrocephalus, benign intracranial masses, drug toxicity, hypothyroidism, hyperthyroidism, pernicious anemia, infections, epilepsy, liver disease, depression, mania, and hysteria. The reversibility of these conditions is usually time limited; if treatment is delayed too long, irreversible brain damage may supervene and nullify therapeutic efforts (Wells, 1979). Despite the DSM–III diagnostic exclusion, one should not fail to diagnose and treat a coexisting major depression in demented patients as it may greatly improve the quality of their lives and result in some cognitive improvement.

These patients may be unable to comprehend the need to care for themselves and may engage in nonpurposeful physical acts in a dangerous, unpredictable fashion. Neuroleptic medication can relieve such agitated and psychotic symptoms, which may reach a life-threatening level. Obviously, anxiolytics will not control the psychotic symptoms, although a short half–life soporific can be beneficial in reestablishing a nocturnal sleep pattern.

Alzheimers disease is receiving much attention as researchers attempt to decrease the rate of cognitive decline, but once it has advanced, no correction of the cognitive deficit seems possible. Although symptomatic treatment with neuroleptics is often beneficial, this does nothing to halt the primary dementing process. A psychiatrist should continue to evaluate the need for medication, as it may change as the primary disease process evolves. Not all patients with these diagnoses need psychotropic medication; clinical judgment and experience are necessary to weigh the potential risks and benefits. Once symptoms have been controlled, the neuroleptic may be decreased in many cases without loss of efficacy.

ORGANIC MENTAL DISORDER WITH DELIRIUM

Delirium as an organic mental disorder is diagnosed when the etiology of the delirium is known or presumed (APA, 1980). Delirium is a floridly abnormal mental state characterized by disorientation, fear, irritability, misperception of sensory stimuli, frightening delusions, and visual and other sensory hallucinations. Full–blown delirium states are said to come on rapidly and can alternate with lucid periods. The causes of these are usually metabolic or toxic disorders affecting the nervous system, e.g., acute poisoning with atropine, the alcohol–barbiturate withdrawal syndrome, acute prophyria, uremia, acute hepatic failure, encephalitis, collagen vascular disorders, and a legion of other causes (Plum & Posner, 1980). The exacerbation of a preexisting chronic illness or the onset of a new acute medical illness can cause a delirium. For example, an older patient with hypoxia from congestive heart failure secondary to a silent myocardial infarct or pneumonia may present with delirium. It is most important to look for the cause of the delirious state and correct this whenever possible. Plum and Posner provide a reference table of causes of delirium that, if uncorrected, may proceed to stupor and coma.

The elderly are especially at risk for developing toxic delirium states, often with accompanying psychotic symptoms, as approximately half of all persons over age 65 are on medications for two or more chronic illnesses. Elderly patients often take multiple drugs, sometimes unbeknownst to several of their physicians, making them more likely to develop drug–drug interactions, which can lead to a toxic delirium. The elderly are especially sensitive to the side effects of commonly used medical and psychiatric drugs. Seidl and colleagues (1966) found that the incidence of adverse reactions to common medications was 12% in patients between ages 41 and 50 and 25% in those over age 80.

Davis, Fann, El–Yousef, and Janowsky (1973) described a toxic confusional state resulting from the combined anticholinergic properties of drugs with CNS anticholinergic properties, such as antipsychotic drugs, antiparkinsonian drugs, and tricyclic antidepressants. This toxic confusional state, also referred to as a "central anticholinergic syndrome," is characterized by a marked disturbance in short-term memory, impaired attention, and concurrent peripheral anticholinergic signs, such as dry mouth, constipation, paralytic ileus, vertigo, urinary retention, increased intraocular pressure, and cardiac arhythmias (Dysken, Merry, & Davis, 1978). It may seem surprising, but this syndrome is sometimes difficult to recognize in the elderly psychotic patient who may have been intermittently psychotic, confused, and agitated before the onset of this drug-induced anticholinergic syndrome. At onset, this disorder may seem like a worsening of the preexisting psychosis by the addition of toxic symptoms to the preexisting psychotic symptomatology. If erroneously attributed to a worsening of the psychosis, the offending psychotropic drug may be increased with a predictable worsening of symptoms. The correct diagnosis probably will not be made unless the clinician has a high index of suspicion and acts quickly to perform a mental status examination to detect evidence of a toxic brain syndrome and a physical examination to find evidence of peripheral anticholinergic signs. Discontinuation of all potentially offending drugs will usually resolve the confusional state within 1 or 2 days, after which a smaller amount of anticholinergic medication might be resumed. Phenothiazines should not be given to any patient who is experiencing hallucinations secondary to alcohol or barbiturate withdrawal because of the risk of lowering the seizure threshold (Goldfrank & Bresnitz, 1974).

LATE LIFE PARAPHRENIA

Late life paraphrenia has not yet been specified as a separate entity in DSM-III, but it is often helped by neuroleptics. The syndrome begins in the 6th or 7th decade and is characterized by paranoid delusions and by auditory and sometimes visual hallucinations in the absence of cognitive impairment or significant affective disturbance. The delusional idea is usually encapsulated and focused on one principal theme, such as poisoning. Patients with paraphrenia frequently get into disputes with community figures who are objects of their paranoid accusations and are thus referred to psychiatrists (Raskind, Alvarez, & Herlin, 1979).

Late paraphrenia accounts for about 10% of first psychiatric hospitalizations of the elderly. Kay and Roth (1961) studied 99 inpatients with this disorder and found them to be a relatively homogeneous group, separate from affective disorder; this finding suggests that late paraphrenia should be considered as a separate diagnostic category. Although paraphrenia occurs in patients without previous psychotic illness, the majority have premorbid schizoid or eccentric personality traits. The disorder is notably more frequent in women (7:1), in individuals who live alone, and in elderly people with hearing impairment (20% have a hearing impairment). Women with this disorder often have never married and are childless.

Late paraphrenia differs from paranoid symptoms associated with organic mental disorders in that the sensorium is intact. In organic mental disorders, the paranoid symptoms accompany cognitive dysfunction and a history of intellectual decline. In contrast to paraphrenic patients, elderly patients with chronic paranoid schizophrenia have a long history of severe incapacitating psychiatric disturbance.

In the treatment of late paraphrenia, Kay (1963a) noted that prior to the introduction of phenothiazines, recovery or lasting remission of psychotic symptoms was considered rare. Results with antipsychotic drug treatment are good. Patients with this syndrome have, in general, a better prognosis for social recovery than patients with schizophrenia, primarily because they have usually maintained a better social adjustment with few, if any, of the personality, volitional, affective, and coping disabilities found in chronic schizophrenics. Most of the limited data on somatic therapy involves neuroleptics, although Klages (1961) reports use of insulin coma, continuous sleep, and ECT in late onset schizophrenic subjects with 33 out of 51 cases showing marked remission. However, many of these patients had affective features, and all had become psychotic before age 60, which suggests they were psychotically depressed, not paraphrenics.

The first systematic investigation of neuroleptics with these patients was a small trifluoperazine–placebo study that demonstrated that no patient treated with placebo improved, whereas most drug–treated patients did improve (Post, 1962). Post (1966) later studied 93 inpatients with this syndrome admitted between 1954 and 1961 with follow–up care for 1 to 3 years. Organic brain damage was confirmed at autopsy in 16 patients and was suspected in another 17. Affective symptoms occurred in 53 patients and were severe in 20. Most patients treated with medications were found to respond to daily ingestion of 15–25 mg of trifluoperazine or 150–600 mg of thioridazine. Twenty–four patients in the total sample of 93 received no antipsychotic medication, and all of these patients remained psychotic throughout the 3 years of observation. Seventy–one patients had an adequate initial course of treatment, with only 6 judged as complete nonresponders, whereas 43 had complete loss of their psychotic symptoms. Very few of those 43 responders actually achieved insight into previous delusional beliefs. There was a relative preservation of interpersonal skills and relationships in these patients. Interestingly, clinical outcome was only weakly correlated with occupational status in the follow–up period, and only slightly positive correlation was found between symptom resolution and general adjustment. Degree of response to initial drug treatment, establishment of insight, and success in maintaining drug therapy were all positively correlated with ultimate prognosis at follow–up. Sex, age, and type of delusion were not related to prognosis.

There have been no subsequent studies of treatment of late paraphrenia of this magnitude. Herbert and Jacobson (1967) reported equally successful phenothiazine treatment in female paraphrenic inpatients, but no attempt was made to follow these cases after discharge. Raskind *et al.* (1979) studied the response of late paraphrenics to either oral haloperidol or intramuscular fluphenazine enanthate. Both courses of treatment were administered by an outreach team visiting patients in their own homes. As might be expected, the fluphenazine group did significantly better as rated by the BPRS and CGI. The implication, as in Post's study, was that since such patients rarely go on to develop insight despite improvement in symptoms with medication, the most important prognostic limiting factor may be medication compliance, which often is a problem. These few studies show that antipsychotic medication is effective in the majority of late paraphrenic patients, but this effectiveness only rarely extends to development of insight, and the major impediment to continued remission is medication noncompliance.

A few words should be said about psychotherapeutic treatment, which may increase the patient's compliance with pharmacotherapy. Although no systematic studies have been reported, in our experience such patients relate best to the helping professional who is concerned and empathic, and tries to help the patient cope with the stress created by voices, jealous neighbors, and the like. Delusions should not be confronted, and the patient must be allowed to maintain a degree of interpersonal and physical distance. These patients, like many psychiatrically hospitalized elderly, seem to form treatment relationships more easily when the therapist offers them concrete help with social and medical problems.

Another important aspect of treatment is evaluation and correction (where possible) of contributing sensory and perceptual deficits. Deafness may contribute to suspiciousness, misinterpretation, and attribution of hostile intent to others by the patient (Eisdorfer, 1980). This principle can be broadened to include correction of physical defects producing weakness or immobility, since these problems increase the patient's feelings of vulnerability and perception of the environment as inimical.

CHRONIC SCHIZOPHRENIA

Although schizophrenia is usually regarded as an illness of youth or early maturity, many schizophrenics carry their characteristic behavioral and thought symptoms into old age. In some cases, the more obvious schizophrenic symptomatology is replaced by a combination of paranoid and depressive symptoms (Stotsky, 1975).

Although neuroleptics are used frequently in the treatment of the elderly psychiatrically impaired, there have been few recent well-controlled comparative studies that would allow neuroleptic selection to be based on other than clinical grounds. In one carefully done double-blind study, haloperidol was found to be equally as effective as thioridazine in the aged population (Tsuang, Lo, Stotsky, & Cole, 1971). Compared to haloperidol, thioridazine produces a lower incidence of extrapyramidal side effects. This difference in side effects illustrates an important contrast between high and low potency neuroleptics and is usually the basis on which a particular antipsychotic agent is chosen. There is little doubt that neuroleptics, when compared to placebo, are very effective in treating psychoses in the elderly (Sugarman, William, & Alderstein, 1964; Tobin, Brousseau, & Lorenz, 1970). Thioridazine was shown by Lehman and Ban (1970) to be effective in controlling psychoses in the elderly. One should judge the need for long-term maintenance by the patient's own clinical history. Those with a history of psychoses that relapse off medications are candidates for maintenance therapy. However, a patient without relapses may be taken off neuroleptic medication (Prien *et al.*, 1975).

A severely catatonic patient who might by history be chronically schizophrenic may reach a serious medical condition from starvation, dehydration, immobility, and infection. In this situation ECT may be necessary if the neuroleptics do not produce improvement.

As in younger schizophrenics, a postpsychotic depression may occur requiring additional treatment with an antidepressant. Again, the risks of inducing an anticholinergic psychosis must be borne in mind when a high anticholinergic drug is added, especially if a low potency, highly anticholinergic neuroleptic is being used. High potency neuroleptics have considerable extrapyramidal side effects, and the differentiation of agitation from akathisia may be difficult, especially in a patient with a peculiar communication style.

MAJOR AFFECTIVE DISORDER—MANIC

OR DEPRESSED EPISODE

Major depressions are common in the elderly even when a first episode occurs in a patient over 65. The patient may present with somatic complaints and deny depression but have neuro-vegetative symptoms that meet DSM-III criteria for major depressive episodes. Elderly depressed patients may present in an atypical fashion. Symptoms of agitation, somatic delusions, and delusions of poverty, pseudo-dementia, apathy, and failure to thrive may erroneously lead to a diagnosis of organic mental disorder rather than depression. In depression, the mood disturbance predominates, and feelings of worthlessness, hopelessness, and helplessness are expressed verbally or nonverbally. The cognitively impaired elderly are especially vulnerable to depression, and often the two diagnoses coexist

(Reifler, Larson, & Hanley, 1982). Therefore, physicians should maintain a high index of suspicion for depression in elderly patients with brain impairment. The rate of successful suicide increases dramatically with increasing age (Murphy & Wetzel, 1980).

Newer antidepressants and monoamine oxidase inhibitors (MAOIs) are often used in the pharmacotherapy of depression in the elderly. Any medication that has been effective for a particular patient should be reinstituted, if possible, for recurrent episodes later in life. For an agitated or psychotic depressive episode, ECT is often the treatment of choice and may be more rapidly effective in a seriously ill patient as well as being one of the safest forms of therapy. The alternative treatment choice is combined neuroleptic and antidepressant, as either of these treatments alone has low effectiveness. Bearing in mind the central anticholinergic syndrome, this risk might be reduced by using low anticholinergic medications, e.g., perphenazine and desipramine, with gradual dosage increases. Thioridazine is advertised as being one of the only neuroleptics with antidepressant efficacy, but this drug is highly anticholinergic and is known to cause EKG changes that some believe may lead to serious arrhythmias and sudden death (Levenson, Beard, & Murphy, 1980).

Antidepressant choice frequently involves cardiac risk considerations, and the same is true for neuroleptics in the elderly. Levenson and associates (1980) list absolute contraindication to major tranquilizers: symptomatic orthostatic hypotension, idiopathic hypertrophic subaortic stenosis, hypertensive vascular disease treated with guanethidine, history of Stokes–Adams attacks, patients scheduled to have general anesthesia or exercise training, and patients requiring epinephrine or ephedrine. In many other cases, the clinician must consider the risk of the psychiatric problem in relationship to the risk of treatment. ECT can be given safely to many patients with the above listed neuroleptic contraindication and may succeed when other treatments have failed to bring a depressive episode into remission.

Manic episodes are not uncommon among the elderly, but generally the clinician will find a history of previous hypomanic or manic episodes if the patient has a major affective disorder–bipolar type. One must look closely for organic, toxic, and metabolic causes if the patient has a first episode of mania in old age. Bear in mind that antidepressant use may precipitate a manic episode, which can be controlled by stopping the antidepressant and adding a neuroleptic.

Treatment of mania in the elderly may be similar to treatment for adults except that the lithium dose to achieve the same blood level will probably be lower because of decreased renal function. Significant toxicity from lithium may be seen at lower blood levels in elderly patients. The lithium half–life may be greater (Davis, 1974), which suggests the possibility of once–daily dosage in the maintenance of a patient with frequently recurring manic and depressive episodes. More acute control of a floridly manic patient may require a neuroleptic, since lithium alone may take 1 to 3 weeks to take effect (Davis, 1974). When neuroleptics are given, the psychiatrist should watch for side effects and taper the medication if necessary. A few weeks after the mania is controlled, the psychiatrist should take the patient off the neuroleptic to remove the patient from unnecessary drug–exposure risk. Carbamazepine has been effective for refractory manic episodes (Ballenger & Post, 1980), and ECT may be rapidly beneficial if the acute manic behavior is endangering the patient's health, e.g., decompensating cardiac functioning, which raises the toxicity risks of neuroleptics and lithium.

For follow–up of depressive episodes, neuroleptics can frequently be tapered or discontinued within weeks, especially if the patient is maintained on an antidepressant after a psychotic depression treated with a combined neuroleptic and antidepressant. Discontinuation of the neuroleptic would minimize possible long–term side effects such as tardive dyskinesia. Generally, the antidepressant should be continued for as long as the depressive episode had gone on before treatment, with 6 months as the minimum maintenance time.

GUIDELINES FOR TREATING THE ELDERLY
WITH NEUROLEPTICS

A number of age–related physiological changes result in potentially higher plasma levels of neuroleptic agents in the elderly. A standard adult dosage given to an elderly patient may produce dangerous and at times life–threatening side effects. Triggs and Nation (1975) summarized these physiological changes as follows: (1) cardiac output decreased by 30%–40% with renal and hepatic flow also decreasing; (2) glomerular filtration rate (GFR) decreases; (3) hepatic–enzyme activity decreases; (4) albumin concentration relative to globulin decreases; (5) drug distribution is altered as fat replaces functional tissue during the aging process. The pharmacokinetic effects of these changes can be increased drug half–life because of reduction in total drug clearance, increased unbound drug concentration, and decreased renal clearance.

Elderly patients may also be more sensitive to drug effects because of increased receptor sensitivity. One study found that a lower blood level of diazepam is needed in older persons to achieve a given degree of CNS depression (Reidenberg et al., 1978). The elderly are more susceptible to the toxic effects of flurazepam (drowsiness, confusion, or ataxia), and for this reason a low initial dose (15 mg) is recommended (Greenblatt et al., 1977).

Extensively metabolized neuroleptics such as chlorpromazine and thioridazine show differing metabolic patterns from individual to individual (Cohen, Herschel, & Soba, 1980), and can produce an array of psychoactive metabolites, varying greatly in potency, all from the same compound. The same agent given to different individuals might, on this basis, be expected to produce varying clinical effects.

TARDIVE DYSKINESIA

A potential risk of using neuroleptics that increases with length of use is tardive dyskinesia, which is characterized by involuntary buccal, lingual, and masticatory movements and may include lip smacking and sucking, lateral jaw movements and chewing, and 'fly–catcher' tongue thrusting. Less likely are choreiform and athetoid movements of the extremities or truncal involvement. These movements are worse during emotional stress or activity and disappear completely during sleep.

Tardive dyskinesia was first described in elderly chronic female mental patients who had received prolonged treatment with phenothiazines and antiparkinson agents. Many of these patients also had received ECT or leucotomy (Hunter, Earl, & Thornicroft, 1964). It is now well established that this syndrome can occur in younger patients with no evidence of brain damage following only short periods of neuroleptic exposure, but the elderly have about three times the prevalence of tardive dyskinesia as patients under 40 (Jeste & Wyatt, 1981). Patients over 60 years of age are particularly at risk for tardive dyskinesia, which may occur in over 30% of those treated with neuroleptics. Women have a higher incidence, which may be related to their longer average life span or perhaps to treatment difference or biological factors. Thus far, there is no strong evidence that different antipsychotic agents vary in their tendency to cause this side effect.

Dyskinetic movements can develop spontaneously in the elderly in the absence of drugs. These spontaneous movement disorders were found to occur in 18% of elderly subjects studied by Bourgeois, Bouilh, Tignol, and Yesavage (1980), compared with 42% of neuroleptic treated patients. This difference is highly significant ($p<.0001$, X^2 test). Spontaneous orofacial dyskinesias may be associated with neurological diseases such as Huntington's chorea, encephalitis, and Wilson's disease (Granacher *et al.*, 1981). Spontaneous dyskinesias probably do not account for more than one–fourth of the orofacial dyskinesias that make their appearance during antipsychotic therapy (Bourgeois *et al.*, 1980).

In nearly 40% of initially asymptomatic patients, tardive dyskinesia is first noticed during neuroleptic withdrawal, especially after the abrupt discontinuation of unusually large doses. The interval between discontinuation of neuroleptics and the first signs range from one day to several weeks. A significant percentage of these withdrawal dyskinesias (up to one–third) seems to be reversible, remitting within 3 months of drug withdrawal. Generally, increasing the neuroleptic dose results in a short–lasting remission, but symptoms tend to return.

The pathophysiology of tardive dyskinesia involves the development of supersensitive postsynaptic dopaminergic receptors in the nigrostriatal area as a compensatory effect of prolonged dopaminergic blockade. This results in an override of the blockade, and with dopamine stimulation the supersensitive receptors overrespond, causing the tardive dyskinesia syndrome, which is similar to what is seen with dopamine excess. Although supersensitivity has been demonstrated at the biochemical and behavioral level, histological studies of animal and human brain have shown no marked changes after chronic neuroleptic administration.

As yet no effective treatment has been found for tardive dyskinesia, although a number of agents have been tried: phenytoin, antihistamines, lecithin, choline, vasodilators, amantadine, lithium, apomorphine, Hydergine, and antipsychotic agents. The emphasis, then must be on prophylaxis to prevent tardive dyskinesia. Elderly patients should be carefully monitored, every 3 months or so, for early signs such as rhythmical vermicular movements of the tongue. Since there is some evidence that early diagnosis makes reversibility more likely, early discontinuation of neuroleptics should be considered whenever possible.

OTHER SIDE EFFECTS OF NEUROLEPTICS

Geriatric patients are often sensitive to the side effects and therapeutic effects of neuroleptics, sedation being one of the most common adverse effects. The high potency antipsychotic drugs, such as haloperidol, generally have minimal sedating effects but may be oversedative because of the sensitivity of geriatric patients to central sedative effects. When sedation is a problem and causes confusion, agitation, and injuries from falls, the dosage of the offending medication should be lowered or discontinued and a less sedative neuroleptic restarted if necessary.

Acute extrapyramidal side effects include dystonias, akathisia, and pseudo–parkinsonism, which occur in 15%–50% of patients given neuroleptics. Dystonic reactions can occur within hours of a single dose of an antipsychotic drug and generally will occur before other extrapyramidal side effects. Dystonias usually present as spasms of the face, neck (torticollis), back, or extraocular muscles (oculogyric crisis). These painful spasms can be relieved by anticholinergic drugs such as benztropine mesylate (Cogentin) or an antihistamine such as diphenhydramine (Benadryl) administered either intravenously or intramuscularly. Oral anticholinergic medication is the standard treatment for less acute side effects. Akathisia is experienced as a compulsion to move. Patients constantly pace and move their legs in a restless manner that is difficult to differentiate from psychotic agitation, but is often described as "feeling like you want to crawl out of your skin." Drug–induced pseudo–parkinsonism is characterized by akinesia, muscle rigidity, tremor, drooling, mask–like facies, shuffling gait, and loss of associated movements. Patients with underlying parkinsonism worsen dramatically with this syndrome, which greatly limits their use of high potency neuroleptics.

Low potency neuroleptics are most likely to produce alpha–

adrenergic blockade and anticholinergic side effects. After several weeks of treatment, these effects tend to diminish. An especially important autonomic effect in the aged is postural hypotension. Most hypotensive episodes occur early in treatment, especially after intramuscular low potency neuroleptics are given (Man & Chen, 1973). Patients and their families should be cautioned against rapid postural change to guard against falls, which in this population can cause devastating injuries like broken hips, skull fractures, and subdural hematomas. Significant atropine–like side effects include dry mouth, blurred vision, nasal congestion, constipation, urinary retention, and paralytic ileus. Urinary retention is a particular concern in elderly males with prostatic hypertrophy and may require catheterization for relief. Itil and Soldatus (1980), in a review of epileptogenic effects of psychotropics, state that low potency neuroleptics are more likely to cause these symptoms, with seizures being more likely in those with preexisting brain damage.

Antipsychotic agents can produce nonspecific T–wave changes on the electrocardiogram. Rare cases of sudden death have been associated with antipsychotic administration, but no evidence suggests any causal relationship with these EKG changes (Levenson *et al.*, 1980). As with many treatment modalities, the potential gain must be weighed against the risk.

SUMMARY

When neuroleptic medication is the treatment of choice, the clinician should inform the patient or family of the potential risk. There are advantages in physicians using neuroleptics with which they have the most knowledge and experience. In general, one should begin with dosages one–quarter that prescribed to healthy adults and even lower dosages for more debilitated patients. The dosage is then gradually increased or decreased according to clinical response and the development of side effects. It is a good idea to give antipsychotic drugs to elderly patients in divided doses two or three times a day to minimize adverse cardiovascular effects. For the elderly patient with nighttime agitation, giving a larger proportion of the daily dosage in the late afternoon or 1 or 2 hours before the agitation begins maximizes the therapeutic effect when it is most needed. Liquid preparations are useful for elderly patients who cannot or refuse to swallow tablets. Avoid giving low potency neuroleptics IM because of the high risk of a hypotensive crisis.

Anticholinergic medication should not be prescribed prophylactically but should be started when cogwheel rigidity or other extrapyramidal symptoms are detected. Combining a neuroleptic with other psychotropic drugs can lead to unwanted effects of oversedation, anticholinergic symptoms, and cardiotoxicity. Elderly patients with CNS dysfunction are especially sensitive to CNS depressant drugs such as benzodiazepines, narcotics, and analgesics. A combination of such drugs may lead to increased agitation, confusion, and combativeness, and increasing the dosage of such drugs will only further increase these signs and symptoms. Only one medication at a time should be adjusted, allowing several days for the effect to be seen while checking closely for adverse effects. Soporifics and antianxiety agents should be used only when necessary and for brief periods of time.

Clinicians should carefully assess the etiology of agitation and psychosis in each elderly patient, keeping in mind that organic mental disorders, affective disorders, and late life paraphrenia are most likely in this order of frequency, and that treatment should be symptom-oriented after establishing the diagnosis. The choice of a neuroleptic might best be guided by evaluating the potential side effects and relative risks in light of the patient's other problems.

25 Aging and Tardive Dyskinesia

Dilip V. Jeste

University of California at San Diego

Richard Jed Wyatt

National Institute of Mental Health

Saint Elizabeths Hospital

Neuroleptics constitute our most effective form of treatment for schizophrenia. Yet long–term administration of these antipsychotic agents is fraught with the risk of inducing complications such as tardive dyskinesia, which may be potentially irreversible. This danger is much greater in the elderly than in the young. The risk of tardive dyskinesia is high in patients diagnosed as having schizophrenia in early adulthood who have continued receiving neuroleptics through old age, and persons who first develop psychosis in old age and are then placed on neuroleptic treatment. In this chapter, we discuss the problem of tardive dyskinesia with particular reference to the elderly.

DEFINITION

Tardive dyskinesia may be defined as a syndrome consisting of abnormal, stereotyped involuntary movements, usually of choreo–athetoid type, principally affecting the mouth, face, limbs, and trunk, which occurs relatively late in the course of drug treatment and for which drug treatment is a necessary factor. While tardive dyskinesia occurs following treatment with various drugs, neuroleptics are by far the commonest cause of iatrogenic tardive dyskinesias.

HISTORICAL BACKGROUND

The first neuroleptic, chlorpromazine, was introduced into psychiatry in 1952. In 1957, tardive dyskinesia made its first appearance in the literature. In a German article, whose title may be translated as "A Peculiar Syndrome in Oral Region as a Result of Administration of Megaphen," Schonecker described three women with cerebral arteriosclerosis who started lip smacking after 2 to 8 weeks of Megaphen (chlorpromazine) treatment and did not improve with the antiparkinsonian drug Akineton (biperiden hydrochloride). The dyskinesia persisted for weeks or months until neuroleptic use was reduced or discontinued.

Sigwald, Bouttier, and Raymondeaud (1959) described four patients in France in whom chronic dyskinesia persisted for months after neuroleptics were discontinued. All four patients were non-schizophrenic women between 54 and 69 years of age. The primary diagnoses included anxiety state, obsessive–compulsive neurosis, trigeminal neuralgia, and herpatic neuralgia.

Uhrbrand and Faurbye (1960) from Denmark published the first epidemiologic study of "Reversible and Irreversible Dyskinesias After Treatment with Perphenazine, Chlorpromazine, Reserpine and Electroconvulsive Therapy." The investigators reported that prolonged use of neuroleptics was likely to induce dyskinesias in some patients, especially the elderly and those with brain damage, and that these dyskinesias were irreversible in certain cases.

The number of articles on tardive dyskinesia has increased over the years in an exponential manner. Today probably no major journal covering neuropsychiatry has not published papers on this subject.

DIAGNOSTIC CRITERIA

We have proposed a set of diagnostic criteria for tardive dyskinesia (Jeste & Wyatt, 1982a). These include phenomenology, history, treatment response, and differential diagnosis.

Phenomenology

- The abnormal movements are choreiform (i.e., nonrepetitive, rapid, jerky, quasi–purposive movements), or athetoid (i.e., continuous, slow, sinuous, purposeless movements), or rhythmic abnormal involuntary movements in certain areas of the body that are reduced by voluntary movements of the affected parts and increased by voluntary movements of the unaffected parts.
- The abnormal movements are increased by stress and reduced when the person is relaxed. They may be temporarily controlled by volitional effort. The movements are absent during sleep.
- One or more of the following three areas are usually involved in tardive dyskinesia: tongue, jaw, and extremities. Isolated involvement of other body parts (in the absence of dyskinesias of tongue, jaw, or extremity movement) is rare.

- Tremors, acute dystonias, myoclonus, mannerisms, and compulsions are not part of the dyskinesia syndrome. Some of these may, however, coexist with dyskinesias.

History

- The movement disorder should be present for at least 4 weeks before tardive dyskinesia is diagnosed. Although symptom severity may vary, the dyskinesia should be present continually over that period. (Acute and withdrawal–emergent dyskinesias usually disappear within 1 to 4 weeks of stopping the drug treatment.)
- The patient should have a history of administration of neuroleptics (for neuroleptic–induced dyskinesia) for at least 3 continuous months.
- The same movements should have been absent before treatment with neuroleptics. The dyskinesia should have appeared either while the patient was on neuroleptics or within a few weeks of drug withdrawal.

Treatment Response

- Antiparkinsonian agents usually have no effect or may worsen tardive dyskinesia.
- Increasing the dose of a neuroleptic usually reduces severity of dyskinesia. Dose reduction or withdrawal of neuroleptics aggravates the symptoms, at least temporarily.
- Some catecholaminergic agents such as L–dopa and amphetamine make tardive dyskinesia worse.

Differential Diagnosis

Ill–fitting dentures, use of drugs such as L–dopa or amphetamine, and Huntington's chorea are among the major causes of movement disorders that may mimic neuroleptic–induced tardive dyskinesia. Other conditions in differential diagnosis include heavy metal intoxication, liver and kidney damage, parathyroid disorders, and several other rare neurologic syndromes (Baldessarini *et al.*, 1980; Granacher, 1981). The mere presence of one of the conditions does not necessarily exclude a diagnosis of tardive dyskinesia, but its role in the patient's dyskinesia must be determined.

Several conditions figure prominently in the differential diagnosis of tardive dyskinesia among the middle–aged and the elderly:

- Denture or dental problems are probably the most common cause of nontardive dyskinesias in this age group. In patients with dental problems or ill–fitting dentures, proper dental treatment results in alleviation of the oral dyskinesia. Usually, dyskinesias of dental origin are mild.

Table 25-1
Comparative Prevalence of Dyskinesias Among Middle–Aged and Elderly
Neuroleptic–Treated Versus Nonneuroleptic–Treated Psychiatric Inpatients

Authors	Population	Neuroleptic		Nonneuroleptic		Ratio of % tardive dyskinesia to % spontaneous dyskinesia
		n	% with dyskinesia	n	% with dyskinesia	
Siede and Muller (1967)	Elderly patients	404	11.4	160	1.3	8.8
Greenblatt, Stotsky, and DiMascio (1968)	Elderly residents of nursing homes	52	38.4	101	2.0	19.3
Jones and Hunter (1969)	Patients over 40 years with abnormal mouth movements	82	30.5	45	6.7	4.6
Jeste, Potkin, Sinha, et al. (1979)	Patients over 50 years	88	23.9	198	4.5	5.3
Bourgeois, Bouilh, Tignol, (1980)	Residents of a retirement home or hospital	59	42.4	211	18.0	2.4
Total (5 studies)						8.1 ± 6.7 (mean ± SD)

- Disorders of the basal ganglia, such as demyelination (as in multiple sclerosis), degeneration (e.g., Alzheimers disease), neoplasms, and vascular pathology (e.g., arteriosclerosis) may occasionally result in orofacial dyskinesias.
- Nonneuroleptic drugs, especially L–dopa, used in the treatment of Parkinsons disease may produce dyskinesias.
- Spontaneous persistent dyskinesias occurring in the absence of any known cause of such abnormal movements occur, but are rare (Altrocchi, 1972; Marsden, Tarsy, & Baldessarini, 1975). They are similar in appearance to the tardive dyskinesias but are generally mild.

A proper clinical evaluation should help in the different diagnosis.

Comparative Prevalence of Spontaneous and Tardive Dyskinesias in the Elderly

We have found no systematic studies on the prevalence of dyskinesias in the elderly done prior to 1960. During the last 20 years, five studies comparing the prevalence of spontaneous and persistent dyskinesias in middle–aged and elderly patient populations have been published (Table 25-1). In each of these studies, the prevalence of dyskinesia was higher in the neuroleptic–treated group. The mean ($\pm SD$) ratio of percent prevalence of tardive dyskinesia (among neuroleptic–treated patients) to that of spontaneous dyskinesia (among nonneuroleptic–treated patients) was 8.1 ± 6.7.

Two other reports show low prevalence of spontaneous dyskinesia among residents of homes for the elderly. Heinrich, Wagener, and Bender (1968) found dyskinesia in only 2 of 110 such persons. Degkwitz's (1969) figures were 6 of 750 men and 6 of 750 women (0.8% each) who were not demented.

Two studies, which were not restricted to elderly patients, found no significant difference in the prevalence of dyskinesia among neuroleptic–treated versus nonneuroleptic–treated patients (Demars, 1966; Owens, Johnstone, & Frith, 1982). In both of these studies, however, the investigators looked at different types of abnormal involuntary movements rather than those specific to tardive dyskinesia. Also, the nonneuroleptic–treated groups were about 10 years older than the drug–treated samples.

Thus, the combined evidence strongly suggests that prolonged neuroleptic use markedly increases the chances of developing dyskinesia. According to neurologists such as Baker (1969) and Altrocchi (1972), spontaneous orofacial dyskinesia that is not secondary to a known neurological disease is quite rare.

Table 25-2
Prevalence of Tardive Dyskinesia by Age

Authors	Age											
	Under 40		41-50		51-60		61-70		>70		Total	
	n	%TD	n	%TD	n	%TD	n	%TD	n	%TD	n	%TD
Crane and Paulson (1967)	46	4	34	21	49	8	31	19	22	36	182	15
Degkwitz and Wenzel (1967)	255	5	148	9	197	19	113	42	53	32	766	17
Jones and Hunter (1969)	—	—	3	0	26	38	38	21	23	43	90	31
Brandon, McClelland, and Protheroe (1971)[a]	106	2	122	13	157	17	223	34	302	31	910	23
Fann, Davis, Janowsky (1972)[b]	29	17	34	26	50	34	40	45	40	45	193	35
Jeste (unpublished data)	38	13	16	25	14	43	13	46	33	45	114	32
Total	474	6	357	14	493	20	458	35	473	34	2,255	22

Note. n indicates total number of patients, while % TD refers to the percentage of patients with tardive dyskinesia.
[a] These investigators gave figures for combined prevalence of tardive and spontaneous dyskinesias.
[b] These investigators gave a figure for prevalence of tardive dyskinesia in patients over the age of 60 (45% prevalence among 80 patients). For the sake of uniformity, we divided this n into 40 patients between 61 and 70 years and 40 patients over the age of 70.

AGING AND PREVALENCE OF TARDIVE DYSKINESIA

There is a general consensus among most clinicians and researchers that the prevalence of neuroleptic–induced tardive dyskinesia increases with aging. Hunter, Earl, and Thornicroff (1964), Demars (1966), Edwards (1970), Fann, Davis, and Janowsky (1972), and Jeste, Kleinman, and Potkin (1982) reported that the mean age of patients with tardive dyskinesia was considerably higher than that of non–dyskinetic patients. Most of the studies comparing the prevalence of tardive dyskinesia in patients under 40 with that in patients over 40 found that the older patients had 50% to 2,200% higher prevalence. The overall weighted mean prevalence of tardive dyskinesia in patients over 40 was nearly three times that in patients under 40 (Jeste & Wyatt, 1982a).

Table 25–2 shows prevalence of tardive dyskinesia in different age groups, as reported in six studies. The maximum proportion of patients with tardive dyskinesia (46%) was in the 61– to 70–year–old group.

Figure 25–1 shows predicted probability of tardive dyskinesia in various age groups, based on our study of a chronically ill schizophrenic inpatient population (unpublished data). Using the statistical method of logistic regression (BMDP–LR program, Dixon, 1981), we obtained a good fit for our data. The following formula was employed for computing probability of having tardive dyskinesia (T).

$$T = \frac{e^{-5.137320 + 0.140985x - 0.000980x^2}}{1+e^{-5.137320 + 0.140985x - 0.000980x^2}}$$

For patients 65 years and older, the probability of having tardive dyskinesia was greater than 0.4. (We should add that no attempt was made to match our patients from different age groups with respect to the length or total amount of neuroleptic treatment).

One study did report a different type of a relationship between age and prevalence of tardive dyskinesia. In a state hospital near Bombay, India, Doongaji, Jeste, and Jape (1982) found that tardive dyskinesia was most common in the 41– to 50–year–old group. The reasons for the relative drop in prevalence after the age of 50 are unclear. However, the overall prevalence of tardive dyskinesia in the Indian patient population (9.7%) was much lower than that in the western countries. This seemed to be related, at least partly, to the use of relatively small daily doses of neuroleptics (198 mg chlorpromazine equivalents) in India.

A study by Smith, Oswald, and Kucharski (1978) concluded that the prevalence of tardive dyskinesia increased linearly with age in women while the prevalence in men decreased after age 70. Such a gender difference has not been found consistently in other investigations.

IS THE AGE–DEPENDENCE OF TARDIVE DYSKINESIA
AN ARTIFACT?

It may be argued that the increased prevalence of tardive dyskinesia associated with aging may be an artifact of greater amounts of neuroleptics received by the elderly. Yet in our patient population, we found that the mean daily doses of neuroleptics given to patients over 50 were several times lower than those prescribed for younger patients. Similarly, the greater prevalence of tardive dyskinesia in the aged cannot be explained on the basis of longer history of neuroleptic treatment. A number of studies (reviewed by Jeste & Wyatt, 1982a) reported a lack of a significant correlation between prevalence of tardive dyskinesia and length of neuroleptic treatment. Furthermore, at least two groups of investigators (Jus *et al.*, 1976; Jeste, Kleinman, & Potkin, 1982) found that age at onset of neuroleptic treatment was one of the most significant variables for discriminating between dyskinetic and nondyskinetic patient groups. It therefore appears unlikely that the association between aging and tardive dyskinesia is secondary to neuroleptic–treatment–related variables. It is, of course, conceivable that the elderly may receive polypharmacy for their multiple physical ailments. Some of these

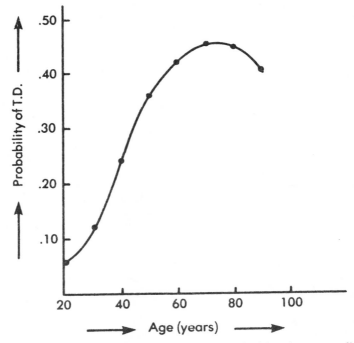

Figure 25–1. Probability of having tardive dyskinesia according to age. (See text for explanation.)

drugs (e.g., anticholinergic and antihistamine agents) may predispose to dyskinesia. The overall evidence suggests, however, that any contribution of such drugs to the etiology of tardive dyskinesia is probably minimal.

We can thus conclude that some direct relationship probably exists between aging and susceptibility to tardive dyskinesia.

HOW DOES AGING PREDISPOSE TO TARDIVE DYSKINESIA?

The mechanisms by which aging increases the liability to develop tardive dyskinesia are unclear. Several possibilities, which are not mutually exclusive, exist.

Pharmacokinetic mechanisms. Absorption, metabolism, and excretion of drugs are often altered in the elderly, resulting in their increased accumulation. Martensson and Roos (1973) reported that among patients receiving thioridazine, the elderly had much higher serum concentrations of the neuroleptic than younger patients. We (Jeste, Delisi, & Zalcman, 1981) found threefold higher serum neuroleptic activity in patients over 50 years compared with younger patients receiving comparable doses of similar neuroleptics. Recently, Yesavage, Holman, and Cohn (1981) reported a positive correlation (Pearson's $r=.41$; $p<.05$) between age and serum concentrations of thiothixene following oral administration of an acute single test dose (10 or 20 mg of the drug). Although there is no evidence for increased absorption of neuroleptics, other pharmacokinetic processes might possibly account for such a difference in serum concentrations of neuroleptics. Hypoalbuminemia resulting in reduced protein binding and increased concentrations of unbound drug, and liver and kidney damage causing impaired metabolism and excretion of neuroleptics may be among such mechanisms.

Another possibility to be considered is that central effects of a drug may be related to concentrations of that drug in specific areas of the brain. Hicks, Strong, and Schoolar (1980) found that old mice had a longer latency and a longer duration of compulsive-gnawing response to amphetamine. Whereas the plasma concentrations of amphetamine in younger and older mice were similar, the older mice had a longer elimination half-life from the striatum. Such studies are needed with respect to neuroleptics.

Central mechanisms. Neuronal damage, changes in the number and sensitivity of receptors, and reduced efficiency of homeostatic processes may all increase the risk of neurologic side effects of drugs in the elderly. Significant neuronal loss in various areas of the brain, including the nigrostriatal system, is undoubtedly a part of the aging process. A loss of presynaptic neurons may result in denervation supersensitivity of postsynaptic dopamine receptors in the basal ganglia. The available evidence, however, questions this dopamine hypothesis. Makman, Ahn, and Thal (1979) and Weiss, Greenberg, and Cantor (1979) have presented data that suggest selective decreases, with aging, in the number of biogenic receptors as well as in the receptor capacity to develop supersensitivity in animals.

Several other objections arise to the theory of postsynaptic dopamine receptor supersensitivity in tardive dyskinesia (Jeste & Wyatt, 1981; Kaufmann *et al.*, in press). Noradrenergic and pre-synaptic catecholaminergic mechanisms are likely to be implicated, at least in subtypes of tardive dyskinesia. Neuronal damage in the nigrostriatal system of the aged may involve alteration of presynap-tic mechanisms (e.g., diminished reuptake—Pradhan, 1980), pre-disposing to the development of tardive dyskinesia. Interestingly, Tanner and Domino (1977) reported increased effects of d–ampheta-mine (with predominantly presynaptic action), but not of apomorphine (presumed to be a postsynaptic receptor agonist) in aged gerbils.

Impaired capacity of homeostatic mechanisms is seen in geri-atric patients. The nature of such mechanisms is not fully understood. Various physical diseases (e.g., hypertension) that accompany old age may, in unknown ways, predispose to complications such as tardive dyskinesia. There is some evidence that spontaneous dyskinesia occurs more frequently in the aged. Casey (1982) has reported a high prevalence of spontaneous dyskinesias in older monkeys.

AGING AND LOCALIZATION OF TARDIVE DYSKINESIA

Orofacial dyskinesias are more common in the elderly compared with younger patients, while the reverse is true for limb dyskinesias. We (Jeste & Wyatt, 1982a) compared the localization of moderate to severe tardive dyskinesia in 54 patients over 50 years of age with that in 24 patients under age 50. The involvement of the lips was three times as frequent in the older patients, possibly reflecting a contribution of edentulous state and dental problems to dyskinetic manifestations. In contrast, upper extremities and limbs were affected about twice as often in the young. No such differences appeared between the two groups for dyskinesias of other body parts.

Tardive dyskinesia tends to become more severe with aging (Smith & Baldessarini, 1980). This may be because dyskinesias spread to previously uninvolved body parts. The reasons for the differences in localization and severity of tardive dyskinesia in the young versus old patients are not known.

AGING AND PERSISTENCE OF TARDIVE DYSKINESIA

The likelihood of reversal of tardive dyskinesia after neuroleptic withdrawal decreases with aging. A number of investigators have found aging to be an important factor associated with persistence of dyskinesia (Uhrbrand & Faurbye, 1960; Degkwitz, 1969; Yagi, Ogita,

Ohtsuka, 1976; Itoh & Yagi, 1979; Jeste & Wyatt, 1982*a*). Smith and Baldessarini (1980) concluded from their review of literature that there was a significant negative correlation between rates of spontaneous remission of tardive dyskinesia and age (*r*=-.62, *p*<.001). The rate of improvement was 83% for patients younger than the median age of 54.5 years versus 46% for older patients.

CLINICAL IMPLICATIONS

Tardive dyskinesia is not only common in the elderly (with prevalence figures in excess of 40% for inpatients with a history of prolonged neuroleptic treatment), but also tends to be severe and persistent (the rate of persistence after neuroleptic withdrawal is greater than 50%). Although a number of therapeutic strategies have been tried in dyskinetic patients, no satisfactory method has yet been found for treating this disorder.

Use of neuroleptics in the elderly should be restricted to specific indications such as those outlined in the American Psychiatric Association Task Force on Tardive Dyskinesia (Baldessarini *et al.*, 1980). There is little justification for prescribing neuroleptics as sedatives. Even relatively short-term administration of these drugs to geriatric patients carries a risk of producing persistent tardive dyskinesia. The following is a list of suggested guidelines for using neuroleptics in the elderly.

- Neuroleptics should be prescribed only for well-justified indications, in smallest effective doses, and for the shortest possible periods. The dosage requirements for older patients are often much smaller than the standard doses for younger adults given in the Physician's Desk Reference (1982). The available data do not support a blanket recommendation for drug-free periods to prevent tardive dyskinesia (Jeste & Wyatt, 1982*b*).
- The risk of tardive dyskinesia should be discussed with the patients and their families.
- Both the need for neuroleptics and the fact of having discussed the risk of tardive dyskinesia with patients and families should be documented.
- Patients should be examined for the presence of dyskinesia before, and at regular intervals after, starting neuroleptics. The findings should be documented.
- Anticholingeric and antihistamine drugs should not be prescribed unless specifically indicated.
- At the first signs of tardive dyskinesia, neuroleptics should be discontinued or, at least, their doses should be reduced. If these drugs must be continued, the reasons for doing so should be documented and consent should be obtained from the patient and his or her guardian. Preferably, the type of drug

may be switched. Although most of the commonly used neuro-leptics are similar in terms of the risk of tardive dyskinesia, individual drugs may be better or worse for given patients.

RESEARCH IMPLICATIONS

One cannot stress too strongly the need for developing newer anti-psychotic agents that are free of neurologic side effects. Continued work on the neurochemical mechanisms underlying tardive dyskinesia is warranted. A strategy of considerable clinical relevance is to determine risk factors for tardive dyskinesia by conducting long-term prospective studies of patients treated with neuroleptics (Kane, S. M., Woerner, M., Lieberman, J., & Kinon, B. 1984). The possible contribution of subcortical brain damage and noradrenergic hyperactivity (Kaufmann *et al.*, in press) as well as other neurochemical abnormalities to the pathophysiology of tardive dyskinesia needs to be studied further.

Acknowledgments

We thank Robert Rawlings, Chief, Statistics and Mathematical Applications Branch, Alcohol, Drug Abuse, and Mental Health Administration, Room 6C–12, Parklawn Building, 5600 Fishers Lane, Rockville, Maryland 20857 for his help with statistical analysis of data. We also thank Theresa Hoffman for secretarial assistance.

26 Psychotherapeutic Approaches to Schizophrenia in Later Life

Gene D. Cohen

National Institute of Mental Health

Psychotherapeutic approaches to the treatment of schizophrenia in later life should take into consideration intrapsychic, behavioral, and psychosocial dynamics. The literature, though, is noticeably sparse in this area (Butler, 1960; Cohen, 1982; Eisdorfer, 1980; LaRue, Dessonville, & Jarvik, 1985; Linden, 1955; Pfeiffer, 1976; Post, 1980). Before expanding on such approaches, three particular perspectives should be kept in mind. First, pharmacotherapy for schizophrenia is such an important component of an overall treatment plan that it has to be strongly considered in most cases, independent of the patient's age; it is not an issue of somatic versus nonsomatic approaches to the older schizophrenic, but how both interventions are used in combination and how each influences the effective utilization of the other. Second, varying classification schemes have been proposed based on different paranoid and schizophreniform symptom clusters in later life (Post, 1980); while these are useful in efforts to expand the ways we attempt to understand psychosis in the elderly, it is important not to overlook crosscutting treatment techniques, applicable to a variety of psychotic states in older adults. Third, the phenomenology of aging can temper the course, treatment, and prognosis of schizophrenia in later life; this must be considered in treating late onset schizophrenics as well as those with an earlier onset who have grown old with the disorder.

Much of this discussion is based on data from a descriptive longitudinal study of mentally ill elderly living in the community. This study, in progress since 1971, has been conducted in an independent–living senior housing building, with a population of approximately 300 individuals, most between 60 and 100 years of age (Cohen, 1979). Nearly 25% of the building's residents have experienced significant mental health problems, covering a full spectrum of disorders. Individuals with schizophreniform symptoms vary considerably as to age of onset, including persons diagnosed before age 45, others between 45 and 60, and some after 60 years of age; 23 older adults with such symptoms have been followed. Those with onset of illness before age 45 include some who moved into the building following discharge from a psychiatric hospital. Subjects are seen in their apartments, with considerable opportunity to observe them in relation to their families, neighbors, and everyday environment.

Social, interpersonal, and physiological aspects of aging appear to influence the course of illness for the patient as well as psychotherapeutic treatment considerations. For example, part of a person's acceptance in the community is based on how he or she is perceived by others, and these perceptions vary with the age of the individual being viewed. Symptoms in general are much more likely to be regarded as manifestations of illness in the younger adult than in the older one; in the latter, they may be dismissed as normal or inevitable concomitants of growing old. On the one hand, this can result in various treatment options for the older person being overlooked. On the other hand, bizarre behavior may be much more easily tolerated in an elderly person than a younger one, resulting in a more accepting social milieu for the older schizophrenic.

With aging, these older schizophrenics also seem to experience less threat to their self-esteem in terms of performance expectations. With a peer group more likely to be retired than working, elderly schizophrenics no longer have the same pressure to perform, and because of social security, the consequences of not performing are lessened. In a related sense, the older schizophrenic can fit in better, standing out less in terms of task-oriented difficulties. Similarly, in the face of the greater likelihood of older persons in general to be living alone (one in seven men over age 65 lives alone; one in three women in this age group lives by herself—USDHEW, 1978), social isolation on the part of the schizophrenic in later life appears less in relief.

From a physiological standpoint, the motivation of the clinician to consider psychosocial interventions is greater for the older patient because of increased concerns about the consequences of neuroleptic medication. The higher risk of side effects, drug-drug interactions, impact on coexisting physical disorders, and tardive dyskinesia all heighten this tendency. Interestingly though, because of more frequent physical illness in older schizophrenics than younger ones, the former may be more likely or find it easier to seek help—problems of soma rather than psyche stirring them to act. This need for increased contact with health care providers because of the aging process creates additional opportunities for interventions and continuity of care. The physical problems of older schizophrenics often make it easier for the families to bring them for help as well.

It is interesting to look at situations where social, interpersonal, and other phenomenologic aspects of aging converge on the clinical course of schizophrenia and how psychotherapeutic interventions through direct care and consultation can become significant.

Case Example

A 66–year old man was discussed with the new resident manager of the independent–living senior citizens building where I had just started to provide consultation and direct care. She described the man as being very bizarre and provocative. The manager expressed the belief that it would perhaps be better for everyone if the man no longer remained in the building because his behavior so disturbed other residents. For example, he would spray air freshener or sprinkle powders on himself, tape pennies to his wrist, and touch a Bible and a bar of soap to his lips. When I asked the manager whether the man actually physically engaged anyone, she only then realized he had not. His disturbance was, in effect, mainly a visual one. No one had been either threatened or harmed by him. Moreover, on closer review it appeared to me that the concern about this man may have been more on the part of the manager and only a few of his neighbors, with many tolerating him, given that his symptoms did not appear new and that he had been living there for about 3 years.

I suggested to the manager that the bizarre traits of this man were in actuality symptoms, that symptoms are usually signals of underlying problems, and that people experiencing severe stress or different types of illness sometimes indirectly give out messages seeking help in the form of symptoms quite varied in nature. I further suggested that the next time the manager met the man in the building she ask him how he is doing, and tell him she had been concerned about him and wondered if he would like to talk to a doctor who comes to the clinic in the building to help people with their worries and other problems. To her surprise, when she carried out the suggestion, the man accepted her recommendation to see a doctor who she knew he realized was a psychiatrist.

When interviewed, the man, Mr. NQ, presented the previously described appearance and demeanor. Not long into the interview the meaning of some of his symptoms became clear. He described horrible hallucinations of smell, which he attempted to dilute by applying chemicals and powders to himself, much the way one would use an air freshener to rid bad odors in a room. In addition, he expressed considerable guilt about sexual fantasies he had about women other than his wife, who had become bed–bound with illness, physically less able and emotionally less available for love making. Mr. NQ's bizarre way of dealing with this guilt was to attempt to control and cleanse his thoughts with the Bible and the soap, as if his mental images were dirty words on his lips. Understanding the significance of the pennies taped to Mr. NQ's wrists was considerably more difficult and challenging. I noticed, however, that whenever he talked about the terrible odors he smelled, he rubbed the pennies. I began to see the association and to recognize the significance of this symptom: Another name for a penny is a cent, which in the primary process (magical) thinking to which he had regressed was equated to the homonym "scent." The patient's primitive symbolic approach to gain control over his olfactory hallucinations was to smother these scents (cents) under tape on his wrists, while using the perfumes and powders as adjuncts.

Meanwhile, comprehensive medical evaluation disclosed no physical or organic basis for his symptoms. It became apparent that Mr. NQ was suffering from a schizophreniform disorder. As best as could be determined from history obtained from the patient and his family, he did not begin to develop apparent abnormal behavior until his 50s. In an effort to better understand possible deeper psychodynamic influences on Mr. NQ's behavior, I eventually pieced together the following information: When 11 years of age, Mr. NQ was burned severely in a kerosene fire. He vividly and painfully recalled smelling his own burning flesh along with the subsequent horror and disgust he felt viewing his distorted appearance in the mirror; he felt like a pariah, ashamed of his looks at that young, critical age. Despite his clothes covering most of the burned areas of his body, with his face fortunately only minimally affected, Mr. NQ remained very sensitive about how he looked for many years to follow. In the midst of all the normal upheaval of adolescence, Mr. NQ carried the extra burden of a traumatized body image. He became somewhat of a loner, acquiring work as a chef after completing high school, a job he stayed with until the last restaurant he worked in went out of business. Afterward, he was not able to get a comparably good job and retired with further damaged self-esteem. It was apparently during his troubled later life job search that he started to become more symptomatic. His symptoms took on paranoid delusional qualities in combination with the olfactory hallucinations; he felt external forces were manipulating the "putrid" smells about him.

In the complex and disconcerting nature of the paranoid condition, the delusional individual commonly effects a scenario where his perception that those around him are against him gets fueled. If a paranoid person looks threatening—even though not intending to hurt anyone—others may become frightened of the individual and respond in a negative or constraining manner. The paranoid person can then feel, "Aha, they *are* against me," even though he himself has unconsciously set up the tense interaction. In an extraordinary way, Mr. NQ created a situation where others were appalled by his disturbing visual and odorous presence. With creative pathology, so to speak, he had symbolically reenacted a situation that confirmed that others, too, were disgusted by the horrible smells and appearance of his burns, substituting a myriad of sprays and powders for the smells, and the taped pennies, soap, and Bible for the appearance. While the sprays canceled out his olfactory hallucinations, on the other hand they were unconsciously used to create bothersome odors for others. In his paranoid frame of mind, he knew the "real" reason why people shunned him. There was meaning to his madness.

While the details of these therapeutic discussions were not shared with the manager of the building, early on she was told that this deeply troubled man was tormented by his terribly distressing hallucinations of smell, which he tried to control in the ways described above. I attempted to help her understand that he did not will these actions, but was driven to them in desperation. I used the example of a diabetic, who when hypoglycemic can behave as if he were drunk and yet whose problem is due to a chemical imbalance (of insulin) in the pancreas; in much the same way, many scientists theorized that disturbing behavior like that of Mr. NQ could be explained by a chemical imbalance (of neurotransmitters) in the brain. Similarly, just as the diabetic's condition is managed by a combination of behavioral (e.g., diet and weight control) and pharmacologic approaches, so too behavioral and pharmacologic interventions would probably benefit Mr. NQ. She was also advised that just as diabetes is a chronic problem that can usually be controlled, Mr. NQ's problem was also likely to be chronic and similarly capable of being controlled. Her uneasiness about the man, largely due to her fear of the unknown, was replaced by compassion and concern. Through a new understanding of part of the nature of mental illness, her own emotions evolved from fear to curiosity to empathy. She was able to recognize her tenant's problem as a chronic psychosis and came to understand his need for and the impact of long-term treatment.

Over the subsequent 14 years, the management of the building changed six times. Each new manager "rediscovered" this man, seeing him as an urgent problem who would probably require placement in another setting. In each instance I intervened in the same way, with the same outcome of altered perceptions in the respective managers. Mr. NQ continued to experience exacerbations and remissions of his illness until his death from prostatic carcinoma at the age of 80, but was better understood and tolerated by his neighbors with the progression of time.

During this period, treatment combined psychotherapy with neuroleptic medication. Drug treatment, though, proved to be a problem, as it can be with many paranoid patients. Despite a good working relationship with the patient, he continued to be very resistant to taking his medication regularly. Interestingly, when his symptoms were particularly severe, causing a significant increase in his level of agitation, he would be more amenable to taking the medication; the psychotherapeutic relationship was strong enough to gain his cooperation at these times. But he consistently refused long-acting neuroleptics and hospitalization, rationalizing the latter by saying that his sick wife needed him to be maximally accessible, with a paranoid rebuff for the former. Up until his death, his degree of symptomatology stayed within fairly consistent boundaries—becoming a little more stable, definitely not worse.

Psychotherapy was essentially supportive in nature. It provided a structure for reality testing and an outlet for Mr. NQ's paranoid concerns. He agreed to try to restrict the expression of his paranoid concerns to our meetings, recognizing that others could not understand them; this strategy proved reasonably successful, as his discussions of delusional ideas with neighbors lessened. The frequency and visibility of his spraying deodorants also diminished, making him appear less bizarre.

Mr. NQ seemed to derive a sense of personal value from our meetings. Psychotherapy appeared to enhance his self-esteem, as he began to talk about some of his accomplishments in the past and possible new interests in his present situation, with more time being spent on these topics than on his delusions in our discussions.

The psychotherapeutic and psychodynamic considerations in this case have several aspects. Attention to psychodynamics helped give meaning to Mr. NQ's symptoms, which in turn provided a basis for meaningful consultation that stabilized the patient's social situation. In a related sense, attention to psychological dynamics in the patient's interpersonal interactions had a major impact on his life course with the disorder, preventing major crises over a considerable period of time. Supportive psychotherapy engendered a therapeutic alliance with the patient that facilitated drug treatment. The psychotherapy, in its own right, appeared to mitigate the patient's symptomatology by enhancing his sense of reality and of self.

The case of Mr. NQ also illustrates what can happen to an older person with schizophreniform symptoms, not only as a result of the natural history of the illness, but as determined by the influence of significant others who interact with the ill individual. Significant others can be helpers, or they can aggravate the situation. Though Mr. NQ's disorder persisted, it did not get worse; nonetheless, six crises occurred where the *perception* of his illness by others almost resulted in unnecessary and major deterioration in his overall living situation.

The goal of health care is not just to prevent or cure illness, but at times to keep a serious disorder from deteriorating. Mr. NQ's mental illness reached a relative stability; it was the social milieu that was uncertain and caused the biggest challenges to his life course. Moreover, chronic mental illness is often seen differently from chronic physical illness. Physicians, families, and friends know that many severe chronic physical disorders can flare up, causing great distress and management problems in getting the illness back under control. They also understand that flare-ups and remissions can be part of the clinical course of such diseases, that proper treatment will very likely bring even a major exacerbation back under control. Those with labile diabetes and congestive heart failure represent common examples of this phenomenon. Unfortunately, similar understanding about the clinical course of severe chronic mental disorders, as with schizophrenia, is frequently absent among physicians, families and friends—especially if the patient is elderly. But when these disorders reappear, they too can typically be brought back under control—no matter how late in the life cycle. Furthermore, with an exacerbation of physical illness, those close to the patient do not feel that the preceding interval of remission was wasted; they redouble their efforts to help the patient back into remission. Too often with a flare-up of psychiatric symptoms, shoulders shrug and sighs abound from those around the patient, as if previous efforts that brought about a symptom-free period were for naught. In reality, the course of chronic mental illness with aging closely resembles that of chronic physical illness, and, often, mental disorders in the elderly—including schizophrenia—are even more responsive to treatment.

Case Example

Mrs. EM, a 72-year-old woman, divorced for more than 25 years and childless, complained of disturbing visual symptoms and had been seen in her apartment by a public health nurse. Struck by the delusional quality of her complaints, the nurse suggested that the patient undergo further evaluation. Mrs. EM consented, and a comprehensive evaluation followed, including internal medicine, ophthalmologic, and psychiatric examinations. The patient initially ignored the suggestion to see the psychiatrist, but when she was introduced to me in the waiting room of the clinic while waiting to see the internist, she agreed to get together with me since she "was already there." She began by asserting that she was not crazy. I responded by indicating that it was nonetheless clear that her concerns were taking a toll on her and that it would be important to try to reduce the impact of the stress on her. She tentatively agreed.

The results of her work-up revealed that Mrs. EM was a diabetic, controlled with insulin, had some visual problems associated with the diabetes, experienced hearing loss becoming more pronounced over the past few years, and suffered from delusions about the lighting in her apartment being altered by malevolent others along with ideas of reference about sounds in her environment. She dated the latter symptoms back 12–13 years when they had precipitated a move. She wondered whether it was time to move again.

Fourteen years later, the patient is still in treatment. She has been able to tolerate only low dosages of neuroleptics because of side effects interfering with ambulation and vulnerability to anticholinergic effects that limit benztropine administration as well. Psychotherapy has been supportive in nature and has served to relieve considerable anxiety. Treatment has been carried out in home visits. During this period the patient has alerted me to multiple potentially maladaptive plans, including frequent thoughts about moving, regular urges to contact the police about all the frightening things happening to her, and periodic intentions of confronting people in her building who she becomes convinced are involved in the plots against her. My reminding Mrs. EM about her long history of being able to come through many difficult situations usually is very reassuring to her and dissuades her from taking many actions that would have negative consequences. At times when her symptoms are particularly salient she will call my office. Even if I am unavailable and she can only talk at that moment to my secretary, her agitation is lightened.

At other times, she has berated me for not being able to do anything about all the people intent on harassing or hurting her and on several occasions has ordered me never to return, being adamant about this decision for varying intervals of time. I try to keep the channels of communication open during these episodes, suggesting that she should feel free to call me as needed and advising her that I will call her periodically to see how she is doing; usually, she responds by saying something like, "We'll see." I also have an arrangement with the public health nurse to drop by to see Mrs. EM whenever these episodes occur. This way, Mrs. EM is helped not to burn her bridges with significant others. These episodes also seem to represent a periodic need on her part to distance herself from people toward whom she is drawn close. It is uncommon, though, for more than 2 to 6 weeks to go by without Mrs. EM giving some signal—often via the nurse— for me to return. To save face, she usually has some external reason for wanting me to visit her again. On one occasion when I returned, curious as to what her stated reason for wanting me to come back would be, she said her light bulb had gone out and that she could not get anyone to come in to replace it. She then asked me if I would change her light bulb. My own associations were quite rich between the deeper meaning of her request and the public's repertoire of psychiatrist/light bulb jokes.

Establishing a therapeutic alliance was also important in guiding her to attend to her auditory and visual problems, given the association of the two—particularly hearing loss—with *late paraphrenia*, and paranoid symptoms in the elderly (Cooper & Porter, 1976; Cooper *et al.*, 1976). Whenever Mrs. EM was negligent about using her hearing aid over a period of a week or two she did appear more agitated and suspicious.

Encouragement as part of the supportive psychotherapeutic approach was helpful in two other ways as well. The effect of physical illness on Mrs. EM became greater over time, compounded by a general increase in frailty due to advanced old age. When she became more physically symptomatic, her delusions also intensified. This intensification was seen as more psychogenic, since when the discussion focused on the effect an exacerbation of her physical ills had on her, the delusional ideation diminished; these seemed to represent times when she was unable to separate stress emanating from the soma from that of the psyche. Our conversations, though, appeared to restore the separation in her mind. Similarly, these periods of increased physical distress reduced her already minimal social interactions outside her apartment. Increased seclusion also appeared to play a part in intensifying her psychotic symptoms. Reminders about the relief she experienced in getting out once in a while often succeeded in mobilizing her socially, with symptoms being somewhat curtailed in conjunction with her increased activity.

In this case, too, several points are illustrated. Psychological aspects of access to care are immediately apparent around Mrs. EM's entry into treatment, facilitated by a clinic set up to provide integrated physical and mental health care for the elderly. Intrapsychic tensions around closeness to a significant other can lead to conflict and the risk of burning interpersonal bridges as an expense of creating periodic distance. Awareness of such patterns can be translated into treatment planning involving a team where one member can be available to help another in keeping communication bridges open, as is occasionally the situation with Mrs. EM. A related phenomenologic finding in this study has been the tendency for most of those seen with schizophreniform symptoms to stay put in their present environment, with less *social drift*—not moving as often as they had at earlier ages. When a move did occur, it was almost always to join other family members or to a nursing home, apart from death. The result was an enhanced opportunity for service providers to furnish better continuity of care. This certainly applied to continuity in psychotherapy for Mrs. EM. The influence of sensory changes on intrapsychic processes and interpersonal relationships has surfaced as a management issue in psychotherapeutic work with Mrs. EM, as it does with a statistically significant number of older schizophrenics in general. Similarly, adverse intrapsychic consequences of increased physical limitations and social isolation are apparent, as is their response to supportive psychotherapeutic intervention in this elderly schizophrenic woman. The role of psychotherapy for both the "young-old" and the "old-old" with schizophrenia is illustrated in the same patient, as she aged from her early 70s to her late 80s during this period.

Case Example

The sister of Ms. JF, a 67-year-old woman with chronic schizophrenia, contacted me with a sense of urgency. She described Ms. JF as being diabetic and having developed an infected foot that was getting worse. But Ms. JF was refusing to seek medical attention, saying that God was in touch with her, assuring her that He would watch out for her. Her sister knew, however, that Ms. JF might eventually lose her foot if the infection was not treated. In the past, Ms. JF had received psychiatric treatment and neuroleptic medication, though neither had been utilized during the previous 10 years. Since Ms. JF would not go to the clinic, I was invited by the sister to meet with the two of them in Ms. JF's apartment. Upon being introduced to me, Ms. JF said there was no need for me to be there, that God was looking out for her. She said that I should go and not take up her time. But while so instructing me, she continued to talk about God in a manner that kept up the conversation with me. She then walked across the room and sat down in a chair, reciting that she had nothing else to say. She did not stop talking, however, and selected a chair that was next to an empty one, as if she positioned herself to have someone sit next to her.

Hypothesizing that this was a nonverbal message to me, I walked over to the chair and sat down next to her. When Ms. JF registered no nonverbal discomfort I sensed I was on sound footing, even though she reminded me that she did not need any help. Sticking with my hypothesis about her nonverbal invitation for me to stay, I operated on the assumption that while she was verbally uncooperative, she was listening. I proceeded to explain to her that her foot was badly infected and approaching an emergency situation. I suggested further that she allow her sister to bring her to the internist in the clinic and have treatment initiated. She resumed her litany about God's help, though without suggesting again that I leave.

After about an hour I left and later arranged to have a private consultation with the sister. I reviewed with her the scenario that had transpired. I pointed out that Ms. JF's words said one thing, her nonverbal behavior another. Verbally the patient protested, but not in action. I suggested that she try escorting her sister to the internist, tactfully ignoring verbal resistance; if Ms. JF physically resisted, not to try to force her. If she did not resist, then accompany her during the entire visit, gently removing Ms. JF's stocking for her foot to be examined, and so forth. To her amazement, the pattern of divergent verbal and nonverbal messages persisted, and the visit to the internist was successfully completed, with treatment initiated.

The sister was very relieved and wondered how to proceed from there in helping Ms. JF. Her initial request was not out of concern about Ms. JF's psychotic thoughts, but about her physical health. The whole episode, though, forced the sister to reevaluate the situation and to realize that things had deteriorated in the absence of regular psychiatric follow-up for the patient. What made things especially difficult was that Ms. JF simply refused to take pills, at least on a regular basis. She needed to be on medication.

The sister, who was widowed, was in the process of retiring and was discussing the pooling of resources with another sister, also widowed. The two had been thinking about sharing a place together, and now that the concern about Ms. JF was much greater they thought that they might try to get her to live with them as well. That way they could not only better watch out for Ms. JF, but they could all benefit by dividing the costs of a larger living arrangement among them. Ms. JF went along with the idea. Further consultation among Ms. JF's two sisters and myself resulted in a plan where I would see Ms. JF on periodic follow-ups, while attempting to have the patient take neuroleptics in liquid form; the idea again was that her nonverbal acquiescence might allow the patient to accept the medication in this less apparent manner.

The plan has worked fairly well. Eleven years later, the three are still living together, in reasonable compatibility. Ms. JF has become physically more frail, while her delusions have slightly diminished in intensity. She continues to say that she does not need to see me, but continues to accept my visits.

Though most of my work with Ms. JF has been in the form of brief follow-ups with medication management, it began with a psychotherapy orientation drawing upon knowledge of discrepancies between verbal and nonverbal expressions, between stated and unconscious desires. The ability to reinstitute and to maintain neuroleptic treatment has been enabled by the same orientation.

CONCLUSION

The opportunities and needs for research on the psychotherapy of schizophrenia in later life are clearly considerable. The directions for such research are similarly many. The role, course, and effect of psychotherapy should be compared between early onset schizophrenics who have grown old and those with a *de novo* onset of the syndrome in later life. We need to know more about the indications and optimal use of psychotherapy with elderly schizophrenics in conjunction with drug treatment, in those who cannot be treated with or do not respond well to neuroleptic medications, and in individuals with coexisting physical illness. Numerous questions arise around technique, including attention to the varied forms of psychotherapy that can be drawn upon with these patients, frequency and duration of treatment, and approaches to those with different symptom clusters and in different settings of care. With the dramatic increase in the number of elderly persons in general that will continue well into the 21st century, the number of schizophrenics in the over–65 age group with different treatment needs will also be increasing. This is the strongest reminder of the place and possibilities for research.

27 Long-Term Psychotherapy of a Schizophrenic Patient

John S. Kafka

George Washington University Medical School

Mrs. Dorothy L. has been studied and treated psychodynamically for more than 29 years. While long-term work with a number of patients has contributed to the formulation of my ideas, the psychotherapy with Mrs. L has lasted longer than any other I have undertaken. She recently told me that she is thinking of writing a book entitled, "How to Train One's Therapist." Certain emphases in my presentation are quite properly the result of her training activities. She has played a significant part in my formulation of a hypothesis linking schizo-phrenic thought disorder to perceptual processes, a hypothesis supported by observations of other schizophrenic patients, which has led to useful therapeutic strategies.

The personal fine tuning of an individual therapist by an individual patient can take a long time, and has the advantage of helping in the formulation of hypotheses about the disorder, which other approaches are not likely to generate. Patient and therapist age during such prolonged therapy, and not all issues related to this parallel development can be taken up here. Continuous observation during several decades, in any case, affords one a unique perspective on the effects of the patient's disorder on the course of her life.

PATIENT HISTORY

Mrs. L is married to a retired executive. She is in her late fifties and is the mother of two professionally successful children, who are married and have children. Mrs. L's father, Mr. K, was a prominent social science professor and her mother a rather eccentric illustrator of children's books. It is likely that Mrs. K, in late adolescence or in her early adult years, had a disturbed period, perhaps a psychotic episode during which she was cared for in an attic at home. Mrs. L has a brother 2 years her junior and an adoptive brother 7 years her junior. Both are successful in academic professions.

Dorothy L has often been told that she "tore something" in her mother when she was born. Always a tall, gawky child, she grew into a somewhat awkward adolescent, taller than most of her classmates, including the boys. Her mother's lack of interest in the household, particularly anything having to do with food preparation, was striking. Meals consisted of little more than bread and water whenever the maid was not there to prepare them. Mr. K's protectiveness of Mrs. K went very far, and once when one of Dorothy's brothers started to complain about a particularly inadequate meal, Mr. K silently picked him up and carried him out of the room. Early pictures of Dorothy generally show a depressed expression and neglected clothing and grooming. Throughout her childhood and into adolescence, however, an aunt and a grandfather regularly took Dorothy away from her parental home, especially during long summer months. She was the only child in this home, pampered, sometimes dressed up like a doll, but always the subject of much genuine attention and affection; the household staff, which included cook, maid, and chauffeur, acquiesced to all her requests and treated her like a little princess. (There are indications that different "ego-states" during the course of her treatment are related to her two "homes.")

Socially quite isolated in school, bossy with the brother closer in age, protective and affectionate with her younger brother, she became a hardworking and excellent student. She was consistently a teacher's pet, and her teachers' expressions of approval are important memories sustaining her at times of shattered self-esteem.

Some adolescent pictures show Dorothy as imitating elements of her father's clothing. She described some outings with her father during which she experienced what can only be called fulfillment. She sometimes came very close to experiencing herself as his only son and sometimes also as his caretaking wife.

Dorothy started attending college away from home but soon obeyed a call to return to the then maternal household because Mr. K had an important wartime assignment overseas. Dorothy felt that she was called home to counterbalance the mother's erratic behavior, perhaps to cook for the younger siblings whenever the maid was not available. The summons home also interrupted an important romantic relationship with a young man—a fellow student.

While at home, Dorothy was quite depressed, the level of her academic performance in some part-time courses dropped markedly, and she attempted to combat her marked isolation through brief contacts with young soldiers. She then enlisted in the women's corps of one of the armed services, where after a few months, at the age of 21, she experienced her first diagnosed schizophrenic episode. Withdrawal, neglect of her body and clothing, marked deterioration of her functioning and work, probably some delusions and paranoid ideation, and some grotesque overconscientiousness had been noticed. She precipitated her hospitalization by swallowing, in front of an officer, a medication intended for external treatment of a minor skin disorder. She was hospitalized briefly and then given a medical discharge from the service. During the next 10 years, prior to my contact with her, she sometimes functioned on a marginal, sometimes on a good level. She married and bore two children. She also had some psychotic episodes. Treatment modalities prior to my work with her included psychotherapy, insulin, and electroconvulsive shock.

COURSE OF ILLNESS

I have seen Dorothy L in almost continuous psychotherapy ranging in frequency from 5 hours to 1 hour per week, for almost 30 years. Occasionally I saw her only once every 2 weeks, but she rarely tolerated such a schedule because of mounting anxiety. During my longer absences, a psychiatrist she had also known during her longest hospitalization was available, and she usually contacted him at least once. During her lifetime she has had 15 hospitalizations, totaling about 9 years. No regularity or rhythmicity is noted in the psychiatric hospitalizations. The longest period of continuous hospitalization, in the early 1960s, was 4 years; the shortest, 1 week. Her time in halfway houses, day hospitals, or similar arrangements totaled 4 years. She has demonstrated a wide range of schizophrenic symptomatology, including systematized paranoid features and such catatonic features as waxy flexibility, mutism, refusal to eat, and retention of urine and feces of such severity that the consulting internist feared permanent bowel damage. It must be emphasized, however, that during "non-psychotic" periods the level of her intellectual and social functioning was frequently very high. She was actively involved in the raising of her children, had a moderately active social life, traveled abroad, studied languages and music, and was an appreciated volunteer in groups supporting artistic endeavors.

TREATMENT APPROACHES

The history of psychoanalytically oriented therapy with schizophrenic patients is complex and beyond the scope of this paper. In brief, however, Freud did not believe that psychoanalysis with this group of patients was possible because the schizophrenic individual was incapable of developing "transference" to the analyst. Frieda Fromm–Reichmann (1950) was foremost among those who believed that transference development was possible. The question hinges on the nature of schizophrenic object formation and differentiation.

The term object in psychoanalysis usually refers to the person with whom intense emotional relationship exists. The gist of my hypothesis is that the common sense notion that an individual, in the schizophrenic's mind, has more stability or consistency than a combination of characteristics and qualities, has to be abandoned. The therapist has to accept that transference to packages of character-istics supercede any attachment to the individual (including the therapist) as a person. This notion leads to changes in the therapeutic approach.

Although I was greatly influenced by the work of Paul Federn (1952), one of the first psychoanalysts—perhaps *the* first—to treat schizophrenic patients, my approach differed significantly from his in one respect from the very beginning. Federn had suggested that a therapist other than the one working with patients during the acute phases should treat schizophrenic patients in remission. For a variety of reasons, I wanted to explore the possibilities of bridge–building between these phases. Long hospitalizations were intended to allow the patient, during "nonpsychotic" phases, to deal with the content brought to the surface during the acute psychotic phase. This treat-ment approach was thought to be safer in a hospital setting. I have continued with the bridge–building approach, but since the patient, who initially fought violently against being hospitalized, became gradually more accepting of intermittent hospitalization, it became possible to treat her more intensively on an outpatient basis and hospitalize her when necessary.

Mrs. L's early admissions to hospitals could indeed be very dramatic. She was agitated and belligerent, arrived at the hospital in an ambulance with sirens blowing, and needed to be restrained by several strong attendants. Typical of more recent hospitalizations was her hallucinating my office in her vacation home at the beginning of decompensation. At that point, she obeyed my hallucinated sug-gestion to check into a hospital. The therapeutic strategies that led to this internalization of the therapist are discussed in a later section of this paper.

A word about medication: clinical observations of Mrs. L indi-cate that (1) remissions occur without the use of medication, (2) remissions which may have occurred more quickly because of pharm-acologic intervention were maintained for long periods when medi-cation was stopped, and (3) prolonged periods of medication use with this patient have never been fully effective prophylactically. Out-standing psychopharmacologists have been consulted in arriving at medication regimes, but thus far a limited use of medication at spe-cific times, which are determined by symptomatic fluctuations and variation in her response to psychotherapeutic intervention, seems to offer more advantages in her treatment.

A rather broad range of therapeutic techniques was employed:

1. Carefully timed introduction of "psychotic" material during "nonpsychotic" periods. When dealing with memories of her closeness to and identification with her father, for instance, the therapist reminded her that during a previous psychotic period she had the delusion that parts of her body—jaws and legs—had disappeared and been replaced by her father's bodily parts. She decided, for instance, not to shave her legs, because they were "father's legs."

2. Use of cold wet sheet packs during catatonic episodes at times

when she was not agitated, but absolutely mute. My crude rationale: Outer control should diminish need for inner control. The patient did, in effect, break her silence on several such occasions. Verbal therapy was used when the patient was in the sheet pack.

3. During nonpsychotic periods, a verbal therapy that at times could be described as close to classical psychoanalysis if this particular segment of treatment were seen outside the context of her overall treatment. I wish to emphasize that even the term modified psychoanalysis cannot be applied to the totality of a treatment during which the therapist is at times forcefully directive, protective, or confronting to the extent of showing her, during some "nonpsychotic" periods—when she denied the severity of her illness—photographs and films taken during her catatonic state. There were, however, segments of treatment in which what seemed typical neurotic conflicts were studied and approached with appropriate psychoanalytic methods.

4. Increasing use of interpretive, psychoanalytically based therapy during periods of transition between psychotic and nonpsychotic states. Here the combination of pharmacotherapy and psychotherapy can be particularly important, because the transition phases may be shortened and the patient can be confronted with material she produced very recently. It has been noted, for instance, that the content of psychotic episodes often finds expression in dreams many weeks— or months—after emergence from the episode (Kafka, 1980). With psychotropic medication such material may find its way into dreams within a few days after the end of a psychotic episode.

The following clinical notes from a session with Mrs. L illustrate the kind of psychoanalytically based therapy that can be done with a schizophrenic patient during phases transitional between overtly psychotic and nonpsychotic states.

> The patient experiences a big bowel movement as loss of her inner organs. She describes confusion between anal and vaginal orifices, feels that some skin is missing, and says she feels "something has been cut off." Direct interpretation of castration fear is made and related to her previously experienced delusional identification with men, particularly her father. I remind her of the photograph of herself in which she is wearing a tie and other male clothing.
>
> The patient asks me to hospitalize her. She tells me that previously she has denied that she is crazy but now she knows she is. She demonstrates this by a delusional preoccupation with dirt, which characterized many of her hospitalized periods. She has to wash every few minutes; she says the insulin with which she was treated many years ago is coming out of her hair and then tells me she has relapsed because she has masturbated. It is possible for her to accept the idea that her preoccupation with dirt is connected with masturbation. She makes clear to me that her view of the functioning society

lady is incompatible with her view of herself as someone who on rare occasions masturbates. She is visibly relieved when I tell her that sometimes she asks for hospitalization because she cannot live up to the idealized society role at all times. She is incredulous when I suggest that she go to one of her volunteer functions despite the fact that she has masturbated. She asks about the "aftereffects" of masturbation.

She describes a tightness in her lower abdomen which keeps her from sleeping. It becomes clear that the tightness now being discussed when she is an outpatient is related to the retention of feces during her previous hospitalization. It is an attempt to hold on tightly, to prevent loss of an imaginary penis. She interprets sexual flush as a punishing change in her body. As in other sessions, we discuss in minute detail bodily sensations and her interpretations of them. Her guilt feelings related to her having torn something in her mother are part of the picture.

At times it has been useful to classify and describe to Mrs. L resistances that manifest themselves in (1) not recognizing connections (e.g., masturbation and general dirt preoccupation) and (2) insisting on false connections (e.g., punishment and sexual flush). I have found that a rather "intellectual" approach does not necessarily lead to a strengthening of "intellectualizing" defenses in the usual sense, defenses that would hinder therapeutic progress. The patient can internalize to some extent the therapist's rational, respectful, and nonpunitive efforts to understand schizophrenic symptomatology.

THEORETICAL FORMULATIONS

The major conceptual themes that have emerged in connection with work of this kind (Kafka, 1964, 1977) have been described in a series of papers. They can only be briefly summarized here:

1. Reexamination of the very concept of schizophrenic thought disorder: The *constant objects* (often more "abstract," more "atmospheric," less related to individual persons) are different from those of nonschizophrenic patients. The thought operations *on* these *objects* are not characterized by a fundamentally *different* logic. Mrs. L, for example, during a period of remission, told me that she had not delusionally believed that the blonde nurse with a foreign accent whom she had called "Heidi" during a recent psychotic episode really was Heidi. She was able to explain to me that, since she had loved the book *Heidi*, having Heidi–like characteristics was much more important and more stable than being the same person. Neither she nor the others were experienced as having any continuity of existence, any identify as persons, at the time. The idea, the feeling of "Heidiness" did have some continuity. Heinrich Kluver's (1933) experimental work on objectively different stimuli that are treated as subjectively

equivalent, helped my understanding of the subjective equivalences which determine the formulation of such schizophrenic objects as "Heidiness." When a characteristic of an object has more constancy than a commonsense object itself, our usual notions of what is subject and what is predicate do not hold. This leads to a formulation of schizophrenic thought disorder that is radically different from that proposed by Arieti (Kafka, 1964).

Arieti, in discussing schizophrenic thought processes, quotes Von Domarus' principle which states: "whereas the normal person accepts identity only upon the basis of identical subjects, the schizophrenic may accept identity based on identical predicates . . . If, . . . "Arieti writes, "a schizophrenic happens to think, 'The Virgin Mary was a virgin, I am a virgin,' she may conclude 'I am the Virgin Mary.' For normal persons a class is a collection of objects to which a concept applies . . . In paleological thinking . . . a class is a collection of objects which have a predicate or part in common . . ." Arieti, however, fails to point out in this context that what is part and what is whole, what is subject and what is predicate, are not building blocks of, but are rather themselves the result of experience. When a patient has experienced a characteristic of a person as being more fundamental, more lasting, more "identical" than the person, this characteristic acquires qualities of the subject; and the person, then merely a personification of this more stable idea, acquires qualities of the predicate.

If patient and therapist operate with different logical principles, there is no hope for communication. If, however, the same logical operations are applied to different objects, communication becomes possible when the nature of schizophrenic object formation becomes understandable.

The "Heidiness" example illustrates the *phenomenology* of the schizophrenic object. My hypothesis concerning the *etiology* of such object formation—and thus of schizophrenic thought disorder—involves the experimentally supported notion (Stein, 1949; Westerlundh and Smith, 1983) that normal perceptual acts recapitulate the ontogeny of perception and are carried to relative completion. The degree to which perceptual acts are completed by schizophrenic patients, however, may be extremely variable. Dynamic or biological factors—or a combination of the two—could explain such inconsistency. In any case perceptual variability could account for idiosyncratic patterns of subjective equivalence of objects and thus for the characteristics of schizophrenic objects themselves (see Kafka, 1986, for details).

2. The notion that parental intolerance of ambiguity rather than paradoxical communication is pathogenic, is pertinent here. The therapist who attempts to help the patient from bridges between psychotic and nonpsychotic states cannot function if he is paralyzed by the paradoxes encountered. Such a therapeutic stance should not, however, be confused with calculated intentional paradoxical commands, which I do not find helpful.

3. The importance of bridge–building techniques during the "therapeutic window" of the transition from psychotic to nonpsychotic states has already been emphasized. A refinement of the concept of the therapeutic window involves the view that the patient goes in and out of psychotic states very rapidly, especially during these transitions, and that micro–changes occur within seconds. Therefore, the therapist who communicates on different levels of complexity at the same time is more likely to be heard by the patient.

4. It was particularly clear in my work with Mrs. L, but I have observed more generally, that as the patient decompensates and moves toward the psychotic state, the *last organization* available is often *oral*. The most consistent indicator in Mrs. L's case of impending decompensation was some reference to food, teeth, the intestinal tract. The communication may be veiled, for instance, as in a phone call that she has seen another of my patients on the street or that she was either gaining or losing too much weight. I have come to understand that the patient interprets the diminution of her functioning as punishment for something she has done or failed to do. Fear of being starved or of her starving someone else are interpreted by me as manifestations of her primitive oral aggression. She perceives her own diminished functioning as oral aggression directed toward her, and feels attacked by her illness, has an "attack" or psychosis. Alternately, the therapist's dealing with the psychotic material that she produces is perceived by her as an attack from me. My interpretation that she considers her own psychotic symptoms as punishment sometimes interrupts the vicious cycle if the interpretation is correctly timed during a "therapeutic window" between psychotic and nonpsychotic states, wherein psychotic thought and understanding of fairly complex formulations coexist. These observations support the notion of a connection between schizophrenic pathology and the early oral stage of psychosexual development.

What psychotherapists have learned about treatment and management of schizophrenic patients could easily be neglected at a time of rapid biological advances. We are beginning to see that brief hospitalizations with more or less exclusive emphasis on pharmacological treatments may contribute to an increase rather than a decrease in chronicity. Attempts to integrate psychoanalytically and biologically based modes of thinking about schizophrenia are essential.

SUMMARY

The clinician's investment can perhaps only be justified if he is also a clinical investigator hoping to use his observations to arrive at somewhat generalized hypotheses. I have often thought that I could explain relapse by understanding actual or intrapsychic conflicts or losses, but after three decades, I have come to the sobering conclusion that such understanding does not permit me to prevent the occurrence of psychotic episodes in this patient. It does seem that anticipated absences of some family members and of the therapist are periods of increased vulnerability. It is also true that there are early signs of threatened decompensation such as preoccupation with the intestinal tract, but the reasons, dynamic or biological, for an increase of such preoccupations are not clear.

When we consider the interaction of the schizophrenic disorder with the patient's life history, we must remind ourselves that we are dealing with a person whose overt psychosis is episodic. Is it, however, possible that other patients with apparently nonepisodic chronic psychosis would present as episodically psychotic patients if comparable therapeutic efforts were used?

I have often thought that Mrs. L could easily have become a chronic back ward patient. The nature of Mrs. L's psychotic episodes does not show a clearly developing pattern over the years. Paranoid and catatonic features, for instance, were present in early and late episodes during the 30-year span. Delusional jealousy, however, was present only in early episodes. "Benign paranoia," i.e., delusions that "helpers" were camped near the hospital, were also more prominent early. Later I was specifically labeled as a helper by her. The discouragement after psychotic episodes was greater in later phases, but the discouragement seemed rather short-lived, and her pleasure at returning to full functioning remains palpable. The denial of her psychotic episodes has diminished. When she recently, for instance, consulted a new internist for a routine physical exam, she gave him her psychotic history in rather complete detail.

During the course of treatment Mrs. L experienced the loss of both parents and of some other family members and friends. None of these events led to psychotic decompensation, but she discussed with me whether or not she should go to this or that funeral. She often decided not to go even when this was socially awkward, when she felt she could not tolerate it emotionally and/or might appear or behave inappropriately.

She did attend the weddings of both her children, but the regulation of how much focus should be on her on these occasions presented a problem. The normal roughhousing and fighting of young grandchildren is sometimes almost impossible to tolerate and could have been a precipitating factor of one psychotic episode. Since she once could tolerate the focus on grandchild so little that she tried to sit in the baby chair, she has become very careful in evaluating her condition before she visits or permits visits from grandchildren. Her delight with grandchildren is then considerable.

One cannot terminate the lifetime perspective story without emphasizing that after 30 years of psychotic illness, she is well functioning intellectually, has broad interests and activities. Her immediate family has learned that she returns to such a level of functioning after psychotic episodes, and this repeated experience has led to their having extremely supportive attitudes.

References

Abrams, R., & Taylor, M. A. (1978). A rating scale for emotional blunting. *American Journal of Psychiatry, 135,* 226–229.

Adelstein, A., Downham, D., Stein, Z., & Susser, M. (1968). The epidemiology of mental illness in an English city: Inceptions recognized by Salford Psychiatric Services. *Social Psychiatry, 3,* 47–59.

Adolffson, R., Gottfries, C. G., Roos, B. E., & Winblad, B. (1979a). Postmortem distribution of dopamine and homovanillic acid in human brain, variations related to age, and a review of the literature. *Journal of Neural Transmission, 45,* 81–105.

Adolffson, R., Gottfries, C. G., Roos, B. E., & Winblad, B. (1979b). Changes in brain catecholamines in patients with dementia of Alzheimer type. *British Journal of Psychiatry, 135,* 216–223.

Altrocchi, P. H. (1972). Spontaneous oral–facial dyskinesia. *Archives of Neurology, 26,* 506–512.

American Psychiatric Association (1980). *Diagnostic and statistical manual of mental disorders,* 3rd ed. Task Force on Nomenclature and Statistics, American Psychiatric Association, Washington, D. C.

Anderson, T. W. (1959). *An introduction to multivariate statistical analysis.* New York: John Wiley.

Andreasen, N. C. (1979). Affective flattening and the criteria for schizophrenia. *American Journal of Psychiatry, 136,* 944–947.

Andreasen, N. C., & Olsen, S. A. (1982). Negative *v* positive schizophrenia. *Archives of General Psychiatry, 39,* 784–788.

Andreasen, N. C., Olsen, S. A., Dennert, J. W., & Smith, M. R. (1982). Ventricular enlargement in schizophrenia: Relationship to positive and negative symptoms. *American Journal of Psychiatry, 139,* 297–302.

Andreason, N. C., Smith, M. R., Jacoby, C. G., Dennert, J. W., & Olson, S. A. (1982). Ventricular enlargement in schizophrenia: Definition and prevalence. *American Journal of Psychiatry, 139,* 292–296.

Angrist, B. M., & Gershon, S. (1972). Psychiatric sequelae of amphetamine use. In R. I. Shader (Ed.), *Psychiatric complications of medical drugs* (p. 175). New York: Raven Press.

Appel, S. H. (1981). A unifying hypothesis for the cause of amyothrophic lateral sclerosis, Parkinsonism, and Alzheimer disease. *Annals of Neurology, 10,* 499–505.

Asarnow, R. F., & MacCrimmon, D. J. (1978). Residual performance deficits in clinically remitted schizophrenics: A marker of schizophrenia? *Journal of Abnormal Psychology, 87,* 597–607.

Ascough, J. C., Smith, R. E., Strouf, M. J., & Cohn, C. (1971). Concurrent validity of the Mosaic Test for differential diagnosis between brain injury and schizophrenia. *Journal of Consulting and Clinical Psychology, 37,* 295–297.

Ascough, J. C., Strouf, M. J., Cohn, C. S., & Smith, R. F. (1971). Differential diagnosis of brain damage and schizophrenia by the Memory–for–Designs Test. *Journal of Clinical Psychology, 27,* 571–572.

Asperger, H. (1944). Die Austistischen Psychopathen im Kindesalter. *Archiv fur Psychiatrie und Nervenkrankheiten, 117,* 76–136.

Astrachan, B. M., Brauer, L., Harrow, M., & Schwartz, C. Symptomatic outcome in schizophrenia. (1974). *Archives of General Psychiatry, 31,* 155–160.

Astrachan, B. M., Harrow, M., Adler, D., Brauer, L., Schwartz, A., Schwartz, C., & Tucker, G. J. (1972). A checklist for the diagnosis of schizophrenia. *British Journal of Psychiatry, 121,* 529–539.

Atkinson, R. C., & Shiffrin, R. M. (1968). Human memory: A proposed system and its control processes. In K. W. Spence & J. T. Spence (Eds.), *The psychology of learning and motivation* (Vol. 2). New York: Academic Press.

Babigian, H. (1977). The impact of community mental health centers on the utilization of services. *Archives of General Psychiatry, 34,* 385–394.

Babigian, H., & Odoroff, C. (1969). The mortality experience of a population with psychiatric illness. *American Journal of Psychiatry, 126,* 470–480.

Bachrach, L. (1980). Model programs for chronic mental patients. *American Journal of Psychiatry, 137*(9), 1023–1031.

Bacrucci, M. (1955). a) La vecchiaia degli schizofrenici. Riv. Pat. nerv. ment *76:257.* b) La vecchiaia degli schizofrenici (reperti necrosopici) Rass. Studi psichiat. *64,* 1.

Baker, A. B. (1969). Discussion. In G. E. Crane & R. Gardner, Jr. (Eds.), *Psychotropic drugs and dysfunctions of the basal ganglia.* Washington, D.C.: U.S. Government Printing Office.

Baldessarini, R. J., Cole, J. O., Davis, M. Gardos, G., Preskorn, S. H., Simpson, G. M., & Tarsy, D. (1980). Tardive dykinesia: Task force report. Washington, D.C.: American Psychiatric Association.

Ballenger, J. C., & Post, R. M. (1980). Carbamazepine in manic depressive illness: A new treatment. *American Journal of Psychiatry, 137,* 782–790.

Baltes, P., Cornelius, S., & Nesselroade, J. (1979). Cohort effects in developmental psychology. In J. Nesselroade & P. Baltes (Eds.), *Longitudinal research in the study of behavior and development* (pp. 61–80). New York: Academic Press.

Bandura, A. (1982). The psychology of chance encounters and life paths. *American Psychologist, 37,* 747–755.

Barbeau, A. (1962). The pathogenesis of Parkinson's disease: A new hypothesis. *Canadian Medical Association Journal, 87,* 802–807.

Barden, N., Dupont, A., Labrie, F., Merand, Y., Rouleu, D., Vaudry, M., & Boisser, J. R. (1981). Age–dependent changes in the beta–endorphin content of discrete rat brain nuclei. *Brain Research, 208,* 209–212.

Barker, R. C., Wright, A. W., Myerson, E., and Gonick, M. (1953). *Adjustment to Physical Handicap and Illness. A Survey of the Social Psychology of Physique and Disability.* New York: Social Science Research Council.

Barnes, J. (1954). Class and committees in Norweigian island parish. *Human Relations, 7,* 39–58.

Barrett, E. T., Jr., & Logue, P. E. (1974). The use of the Spiral After-Effect Test to differentiate chronic schizophrenics from chronic organics. *Journal of Clinical Psychology, 30,* 513–516.

Barron, S. A., Jacobs, L., & Kinkel, W. R. (1976). Changes in size of normal lateral ventricles during aging determined by computerized tomography. *Neurology, 26,* 1011–1013.

Bauman, E., & Murray, D. J. (1968). Recognition versus recall in schizophrenia. *Canadian Journal of Psychology, 22,* 18–25.

Baumeyer, F. (1956). The Schreber case. *International Journal of Psychoanalysis, 37,* 61–74.

Beck, J., & Worthen, K. (1972). Precipitating stress, crisis theory, and hospitalization in schizophrenia and depression. *Archives of General Psychiatry, 26,* 123–129.

Beck, M. (1968). Twenty-five and thirty-five year follow-up of first admissions to mental hospital. *Canadian Psychiatric Association Journal, 13,* 219–229.

Bender, L., & Hirschmann, J. L. (1956). A longitudinal study of ninety schizophrenic women. *Journal of Nervous and Mental Disease, 124,* 337–343.

Benjamin, J. D. (1944). A method for distinguishing and evaluating formal thinking disorders in schizophrenia. In J. S. Kasanin (Ed.), *Language and thought in schizophrenia.* New York: W. W. Norton.

Berg, P. A., & Leventhal, D. B. (1977). The effect of distractor strength versus rate of item presentation on retention in schizophrenics. *British Journal of Social and Clinical Psychology, 16,* 147–152.

Berger, L., Berstein, A., Klein, E., Cohen, J., & Lucas, G. (1964). Effects of aging and pathology on the factorial structure of intelligence. *Journal of Consulting Psychology, 28,* 199–207.

Berger, P., & Luckman, T. (1966). *The social construction of reality.* New York: Doubleday.

Bernheimer, H., Birkmayer, W., Hornykiewicz, O., Jellinger, K., & Seitelberger, F. (1973). Brain dopamine and the syndromes of Parkinson and Huntington: Clinical, morphological and neurochemical correlations. *Journal of Neurological Science, 20,* 415–455.

Berstein, I. H. (1963). A comparison of schizophrenics and nonschizophrenics on two methods of administration of the Bender-Gestalt Test. *Perceptual and Motor Skills, 16,* 757–763.

Bird, E. D., & Iversen, L. L. (1974). Huntington's chorea: Post-mortem measurement of glutamic acid decarboxylase, choline acetyltransferase and dopamine in basal ganglia. *Brain, 97,* 457–472.

Birley, J. L., & Brown, G. W. (1970). Crises and life changes preceeding the outset of acute schizophrenia: Clinical aspects. *British Journal of Psychiatry, 116,* 327–333.

Birren, J. E. (1965). Age changes in speed of behavior: Its central nature and physiological correlates. In A. T. Welford & J. E. Birren (Eds.), *Behavior, aging and the nervous system.* Springfield, IL: Charles C. Thomas.

Birren, J. E., Woods, A. M., & Williams, M. V. (1980). Behavioral slowing with age: Causes, organization, and consequences. In L. W. Poon (Ed.), *Aging in the 1980's*. Washington, DC: American Psychological Association.

Bland, R. C., Parker, J. H., & Orn, H. (1976). Prognosis in schizophrenia. A ten–year follow–up of the first admissions. *Archives of General Psychiatry, 33,* 949–954.

Bland, R. C., Parker, J. H., & Orn, H. (1978). Prognosis in schizophrenia: Prognostic predictors and outcome. *Archives of General Psychiatry, 35,* 72–77.

Blessed, G., Tomlinson, B. E., & Roth, M. (1968). The association between quantitative measures of dementia and of senile change in the cerebral grey matter of elderly subjects. *British Journal of Psychiatry, 114,* 797–811.

Bleuler, E. (1911). Dementia praecox. In Aschaffenburg, *Handbuch der Psychiatrie*. Leipzig–Wien: Deutike.

Bleuler, E. (1950). *Dementia praecox or the group of schizophrenias*. New York: International University Press.

Bleuler, M. (1968). A 23–year longitudinal study of 208 schizophrenics and impressions in regard to the nature of schizophrenia. In D. Rosenthal (Ed.), *Transmission of schizophrenia*. Oxford: Per- gamon Press.

Bleuler, M. (1972). *Die Schizophrenen Geistesstörungen im Lichte Langjähriger Kranken—und Familiengeschiten*. Stuttgart. Georg Thieme Verlag (New York: Intercontinental Medical Book Corp., U. S. Distribution) pp. 673, as reviewed by Teschke, G. C. in *Schizophrenia Bulletin, 4*(1), 48–55.

Bleuler, M. (1972). *Die schizophrenen Geistestörungen im Lichte Langjähriger Kranken und Familiengeschichte*. Stuttgart: Thieme.

Bleuler, M. (1974). The long–term course of the schizophrenic psychoses. *Psychological Medicine, 4,* 244–254.

Bleuler, M. (1976). Long–term course of schizophrenic psychoses. *Annual Review of Schizophrenic Syndrome, 4,* 435–453.

Bleuler, M. (1978a). *The schizophrenic disorders: Long–term patient and family studies*. New Haven, CT: Yale University Press.

Bleuler, M. (1978b). The long–term course of schizophrenic psychoses. In L. Wynne, R. Cromwell, & S. Matthysse (Eds), *The nature of schizophrenia: New approaches to research and treatment (pp. 631–637)*. New York: Wiley–Interscience.

Bleuler, M. (1981). Einzelkrankheiten in der Schizophreniegruppe? In Huber, G. (Ed.), *Schizophrenie. Stand und Entwicklungstendenzen der Forschung*. Stuttgart–New York: Schattauer.

Boissevain, J. (1974). *Friends of friends*. New York: St. Martin's Press.

Boll, T. J. (1974). Psychological differentiation of patients with schizophrenia versus lateralized cerebrovascular, neuplastic, or traumatic brain injury. *Journal of Abnormal Psychology, 83,* 456–458.

Bondareff, W., Mountjoy, C. Q., & Roth, M. (1981). Selective loss of neurones of origin of adrenergic projection to cerebral cortex (nucleus locus ceruleus) in senile dementia. *The Lancet I,* 783– 784.

Botwinick, J. (1966). Cautiousness in old age. *Journal of Gerontology, 21,* 347–353.

Botwinick, J. (1978). *Aging and behavior* (2nd ed.). New York: Springer.

Bourgeois, M., Bouilh, P., Tignol, J., & Yesavage, J. (1980). Spontaneous dyskinesias vs. neuroleptic–induced dyskinesias in 270 elderly subjects. *Journal of Nervous and Mental Disease, 167,* 177–178.

Bowen, D. M., Smith, C. B., White, P., & Davison, A. N. (1976). Neurotransmitter–related indices of hypoxia in senile dementia and other abiotrophies. *Brain, 99,* 459–496.

Brackenridge, C. J. (1973). The relation of sex of the affected parent to the age at onset of Huntington's disease. *Journal of Medical Genetics, 10,* 333–336.

Bradburn, N. (1969). *The structure of psychological well–being.* Chicago: Aldine Publishing Company.

Braff, D., & Saccuzzo, D. P. (1981). Information processing dysfunction in paranoid schizophrenia: A two–factor deficit. *American Journal of Psychiatry, 138,* 1051–1056.

Brandon, S., McClelland, H. A., & Protheroe, C. (1971). A study of facial dyskinesia in a mental hospital population. *British Journal of Psychiatry, 118,* 171–184.

Breakefield, X. O., Giller, E. L., Nurnberger, J. I., Castiglione, C. M., Buchsbaum, M. S., & Gershon, E. S. (1980). Monoamine oxidase type A in fibroblasts from patients with biopolar depression illness. *Psychiatry Research, 2,* 307–314.

Breier, A. M., & Strauss, J. S. (1983). Self–control in psychotic disorders. *Archives of General Psychiatry, 40*(10), 1141–1145.

Bridge, T. P., Cannon–Spoor, H. E., & Wyatt, R. J. (1978). Burned out schizophrenia: Evidence for age effects on schizophrenic symptomatology. *Journal of Gerontology, 33,* 835–839.

Bridge, T. P., Wise, C. D., Potkin, S. G., Phelps, B. H., & Wyatt, R. J. (1981). Platelet monoamine oxidase: Studies of activity and thermolability in a general population. In E. Gersohn (Ed.), *Genetic strategies in psychopharmacology,* Pacific Grove, CA: Boxwood Press.

Bridge, T. P., & Wyatt, R. J. (1980a). Paraphrenia: Paranoid states of late life. I. European Research. *Journal of the American Geriatrics Society 28*(5), 193–200.

Bridge, T. P., & Wyatt, R. J. (1980b). Paraphrenia: Paranoid states of late life. II. American Research. *Journal of the American Geriatrics Society, 28,* 201–205.

Brim, O. G., Jr., & Ryff, C. (1980). On the properties of life events. In P. Baltes & O. G. Brim, Jr. (Eds.), *Life–span development and behavior* (pp. 368–388). New York: Academic Press.

Brody, H. (1976). An examination of cerebral cortex and brainstem aging. In R. D. Terry & S. Gershem (Eds.), *Neurobiology of aging* (pp. 177–181). New York: Raven Press.

Brody, D., Saccuzzo, D. P. & Braff, D. L. (1980). Information processing for masked and unmasked stimuli in schizophrenia and old age. *Journal of Abnormal Psychology, 89,* 617–622.

Bromet, E., Harrow, M., & Karl, S. (1974). Premorbid functioning and outcome in schizophrenics and nonschizophrenics. *Archives of General Psychiatry, 30,* 203–207.

Brown, G. W., & Birley, J. L. T. (1968). Crisis and life changes and the onset of schizophrenia. *Journal of Health and Human Behavior, 9,* 203–214.

Brown, G. W., Birley, J. T. L., & Wing, J. K. (1972). The influence of family life on the course of schizophrenic disorders: A replication. *British Journal of Psychiatry, 121,* 241–258.

Brown, G. W., Bone, M., Dalison, B., & Wing, J. K. (1966). Schizophrenia and social care. *Maudsley Monograph* (No. 17). London: Oxford University Press.

Brown, G. W., Monck, E., Carstairs, G. M., & Wing, J. K. (1962). Influence of family life on the course of schizophrenic illness. *British Journal of prev. soc. med. 16,* 55–68.

Brown, G., Harris, T., & Peto, J. (1973). Life–events and psychiatric disorders. Part II: Nature of causal link. *Psychological Medicine, 3,* 159–196.

Bruck, J., Heiss, W. D., & Trappl, R. (1968). Statistische Analyse chronisch schizophrener Verläufe bei mehrdimensionaler Diagnostik. *Schweizer Archiv fur Neurologie, Neurochirurgie und Psychiatrie, 102,* 407–429.

Bruyn, G. W. (1968). Huntington's chorea: Historical, clinical and laboratory synopsis. In P. J. Vinken & G. W. Bruyn (Eds.), *Handbook of clinical neurology* (pp. 298–378). New York: Wiley.

Buchsbaum, M. S., Mirsky, A. F., DeLisi, L. E., Morihisa, J., Karson, C. N., Mendelson, W. B., King, A. C., Johnson, J., & Kessler, R. (1984). The Genain quadruplets: Electrophysiological, positron emission and X–ray tomographic studies. *Psychiatry Research, 13,* 95–108.

Buckley–Marengo, J., & Harrow, M. (1979a). *Abstract and concrete thinking in early schizophrenia: Previous assumptions and current realities.* Presented to the 51st annual meeting of the Midwestern Psychological Association, Chicago, IL.

Buckley–Marengo, J., & Harrow, M. (1979b). *Abstract and concrete thinking in schozophrenia: A longitudinal approach.* Presented to the 87th annual meeting of the American Psychological Association, New York, NY.

Buell, S. J., & Coleman, P. D. (1979). Dendritic growth in the aged human brain and failure of growth in senile dementia. *Science, 206,* 854–856.

Bugiani, C., Salvariani, S., Perdelli, F., Mancardi, G. L., & Leonardi, A. (1978). Nerve cell loss with aging in the putamen. *European Neurology, 17,* 286–291.

Buhler, C. (1968). The course of human life as a psychological problem. *Human Development, 11,* 184–200.

Butler, R. N. (1960). Intensive psychotherapy for the hospitalized aged. *Geriatrics, 15,* 644–653.

Butler, R. N. (1963). The life–review: An interpretation of reminiscence in the aged. *Psychiatry, 26,* 65–75.

Bychowsky, G. (1952). Schizophrenia in the period of involution. *Disorders of the Nervous System, 13,* 150.

Cain, L. (1964). Life–course and social structure. In R. Faris (Ed.), *Handbook of modern sociology* (pp. 272–309). Chicago: Rand–McNally.

Cain, L. (1967). Age status and generational phenomena: The new old people in contemporary America. *The Gerontologist, 7,* 83–92.

Callaway, E., & Naghdi, S. (1982). An information processing model for schizophrenia. *Archives of General Psychiatry, 39,* 339–347.

Cameron, N. S. (1939). Deterioration and regression in schizophrenic thinking. *Journal of Abnormal and Social Psychology, 74,* 265–270.

Canter, A. (1971). A comparison of the background interference procedure effect in schizophrenic, nonschizophrenic, and organic patients. *Journal of Clinical Psychology, 27,* 473–474.

Caplan, G., (1964). *Principles of preventive psychiatry.* New York: Basic Books.

Carlsson, A., Adolfsson, R., Aquilonius, S. M., Gottfries, C. G., Oreland, L., Svennerholm, L., & Winblad, B. (1980). Biogenic amines in human brain in normal aging, senile dementia, and chronic alcoholism. In M. Goldstein (Ed.), *Ergot compounds and brain function: Neuroendocrine and neuropsychiatric aspects* (pp. 295–304).

Carlsson, A., & Winblad, B. (1976). The influence of age and time interval between death and autopsy on dopamine and 3–methoxy tyramine levels in human basal ganglia. *Journal of Neural Transmission, 38,* 271–276.

Carpenter, W. T., & Stephens, S. H. (1979). An attempted integration of information relevant to schizophrenic subtypes. *Schizophrenia Bulletin, 5,* 490–506.

Casey, D. E. (1982). *Spontaneous orofacial dyskinesias in rhesus monkeys: Age-related prevalence rates.* Presented at the 37th Annual Meeting of the Society of Biological Psychiatry, Toronto.

Cash, T. F., Neale, J. M., & Cromwell, R. L. (1972). Span of apprehension in acute schizophrenics: Full–report technique. *Journal of Abnormal Psychology, 79,* 322–326.

Caudill, W. (1958). *The psychiatric hospital as a small society.* Cambridge: Harvard University Press.

Chaconas, G., & Finch, C. E. (1973). The effect of aging on RNA/DNA ratios in brain regions of the C57BL/6J male mouse. *Journal of Neurochemistry, 21,* 1469–1473.

Chaikelson, J. S., & Schwartzman, A. E. (1983). Cognitive changes with aging in schizophrenia. *Journal of Clinical Psychology, 39,* 25–30.

Chapman, L. J., & Chapman, J. P. (1973). *Disordered thought in schizophrenia.* Englewood Cliffs, NJ: Prentice-Hall.

Chelune, G. J., Heaton, R. K., Lehman, R. A. W., & Robinson, A. (1979). Level versus pattern of neuropsychological performance among schizophrenic and diffusely brain–damaged patients. *Journal of Consulting and Clinical Psychology, 47,* 155–163.

Chittick, R. A., Brooks, G. W., Irons, F. S., & Deane, W. N. (1961). *The Vermont Story.* Burlington, VT: Queen City Printers.

Ciompi, L. (1969). A comprehensive review of geronto–psychiatric literature in the postwar period. The National Clearinghouse for Mental Health Information, NIMH, Chevy Chase, Maryland, No. 1811.

Ciompi, L. (1980). Catamnestic long–term study on the course of life and aging of schizophrenics. *Schizophrenia Bulletin, 6,* 606–618.

Ciompi, L. (1980). Ist die chronische Schizophrenie ein Artefakt––

Argumente und Gegenargumente. *Fortschritte der Neurologie und Psychiatrie, 48,* 237–248.

Ciompi, L. (1981a). Wie Können wir die Schizophrenen besser behandeln?—Ein Synethese neuer Krankheits—und Therapiekonzepte, *Nervenarzt, 52,* 506–515.

Ciompi, L. (1981b, September). *How to improve the treatment of schizophrenics?—A multi-causal illness concept and its therapeutic consequences.* Paper presented at the 7th International Symposium on the Psychotherapy of Schizophrenia, Heidelberg.

Ciompi, L. (1982). Affektlogik. Die Struktur der Psyche und ihre Entwicklung. Ein Beitrag zur Schizophrenieforschung. Stuttgart: Klett.

Ciompi, L., & Müller, C. (1976). *Lebensweg and Alter der Schizophrenen. Eine kata mnestische Langzeitstudie bis ins Senium.* Berlin–Heidelberg–New York: Springer.

Clausen, J. (1972). The life course of individuals. In M. Riley, M. Johnson, & A. Forner (Eds.), *Aging and society* (pp. 457–514). New York: Russell–Sage.

Clausen, J. (1981). Stigma and mental disorder: Phenomena and terminology. *Psychiatry, 44,* 287–296.

Clausen, J. (1985). A fifteen to twenty year follow–up of married adult psychiatric patients. In L. Erlenmeyer–Kimling and N. Miller (Eds.), *Life–span research on the prediction of psychopathology.* New York: Lawrence Erlbaum.

Clayton, P., & Hirschfeld, R. (1978). *Personal Resource Inventory* (PRI). St. Louis: Washington University.

Cohen, B. D., & Camhi, J. (1967). Schizophrenic performance in a word–communication task. *Journal of Abnormal Psychology, 72,* 240–246.

Cohen, B. M., Herschel, M., & Soba, A. (1980). Neuroleptic, antimuscarinic and antiadrenergic activity of chlorpromazine, thioridazine and their metabolites. *Psychiatry Research, 1,* 199–208.

Cohen, C., & Sokolovsky, J. (1978). Schizophrenia and social networks. *Schizophrenia Bulletin, 4,* 546–560.

Cohen, C., & Sokolovsky, J. (1979a). Health–seeking behavior and social networks of the aged living in single–room occupancy hotels. *Journal of the American Geriatrics Society, 27,* 270–277.

Cohen, C., & Sokolovsky, J. (1979b). Clinical use of network analysis for psychiatric and aged populations. *Community Mental Health Journal, 15,* 203–213.

Cohen, G. D. (1979/80, Fall/Winter). An alternative setting for community–based geropsychiatric care. *International Journal of Mental Health, 8,* 173–184.

Cohen, G. D. (1982). The older person, the older patient, and the mental health system. *Journal of Hospital and Community Psychiatry, 33,* 101–104.

Cohen, J. (1952). Factors underlying Wechsler–Bellevue performance of three neuropsychiatric groups. *Journal of Abnormal and Social Psychology, 47,* 359–365.

Cohler, B. (1982). Personal narrative and life–course. In P. Baltes & O. G. Brim, Jr. (Eds.), *Life–span development and behavior* (pp. 205–229). New York: Academic Press.

Cohler, B., & Boxer, A. (1984). Settling into the world: Person, time, and context during the middle adult years. In D. Offer & M. Sabshin (Eds.), *Normality and the life–course*. New York: Basic Books.

Cohler, B. & Grunebaum, H. (1981). *Mothers, grandmothers, and daughters*. New York: John Wiley.

Coleman, P. D., Kaplan, B. N., Osterburg, H. H., & Finch, C. E. (1980). Brain poly(A)RNA during aging: Stability of yield and sequence complexity in two rat strains. *Journal of Neurochemistry, 34,* 335–345.

Collins, J. L. (1978). Memory and aging in hospitalized and control adults. *Dissertation Abstracts International, 39*(5–B), 2489.

Collins, P., Kietzman, M., Sutton, S., & Shapiro, E. (1978). Visual temporal integration in psychiatric patients. In L. Wynne, R. Cromwell, & S. Matthysse (Eds.), *The nature of schizophrenia*. New York: Wiley.

Connell, P. (1958). *Amphetamine psychosis*. London: Chapman and Hall.

Cooper, A. F., Garside, R. F., & Kay, D. W. K. (1976). A comparison of deaf and non–deaf patients with paranoid and affective psychoses. *British Journal of Psychiatry, 129,* 532–538.

Cooper, A. F., Kay, D. W. K., Curry, A. R., Garside, R. F., & Roth, M. (1974, October 12). Hearing loss in paranoid and affective psychoses of the elderly, *The Lancet*.

Cooper, A. F., & Porter, R. (1976). Visual acuity and ocular pathology in the paranoid and affective psychoses of later life. *Journal of Psychosomatic Research, 20,* 107–114.

Corso, J. F. (1971). Sensory processes and age effects in normal adults. *Journal of Gerontology, 26,* 90–105.

Corso, J. F. (1977). Auditory perception and communication. In J. E. Birren & K. W. Schaie (Eds.), *Handbook of the psychology of aging*. New York: Van Nostrand Reinhold.

Cote, L. J., & Kremzner, L. T. (1974). Changes in neurotransmitter systems with increasing age in human brain. *Transactions of the American Society of Neurochemistry, 5,* 83.

Covert, A. B., Rodrigues, T., & Solomon, K. (1977). The use of mechanical and clinical restraints in nursing homes. *Journal of the American Geriatrics Society, 25,* 85–89.

Cox, M. D., & Leventhal, D. B. (1978). A multivariate analysis and modification of a preattentive, perceptual dysfunction in schizophrenia. *Journal of Nervous and Mental Disorders, 166,* 709–718.

Craig, R. J., & Verinis, J. S. (1979). Evidence for organicity in concrete vs. overinclusive thought–disordered schizophrenics. *Journal of Clinical Psychology, 35,* 696–703.

Craig, T., Goodman, A., & Haugland, G. (1982). Impact of DSM–III in clinical practice. *American Journal of Psychiatry 139*(7), 922–925.

Craik, F. I. Age differences in human memory. (1977). In J. E. Birren & K. W. Schaie (Eds.), *Handbook of the psychology of aging*. New York: Van Nostrand Reinhold.

Craik, F. I. M., & Lockhart, R. S. (1977) Levels of processing. A framework for memory research. *Journal of Verbal Learning and Verbal Behavior, 11,* 671–684.

Craik, F. I. M., & Tulving, E. (1975). Depth of processing and the retention of words in episodic memory. *Journal of Experimental Psychology: General, 104*, 269–294.

Crane, G. E., & Paulson, G. (1967). Involuntary movements in a sample of chronic mental patients and their relation to the treatment with neuroleptics. *International Journal of Neuropsychiatry, 3*, 286– 291.

Crook, T. H. (1979). Psychometric assesment in the elderly. In A. Raskin & L. F. Jarvik (Eds.), *Psychiatric symptoms and cognitive loss in the elderly: Evaluation and assessment techniques.* Washington, DC: Hemisphere Publishing.

Crow, T. J. (1980). Molecular pathology of schizophrenia: More than one disease process? *British Medical Journal, 780*, 66–68.

Curcio, C. A., Buell, S. J., & Coleman, P. D. (1982). Morphology of the aging central nervous system: Not all downhill. In F. J. Pirozollo (Ed.), *Aging Motor Systems.*

Cutting, J. (1978). A reappraisal of alcoholic psychoses. *Psychological Medicine, 8*, 285–295.

Daum (now Harding), C. M., Brooks, G. W., & Albee, G. W. (1977). Twenty–year follow–up of 253 schizophrenic patients originally selected for chronic disability: Pilot study. *The Psychiatric Journal of the University of Ottawa, 2*(3), 129–132.

Davis, A. E., Dinitz, S., & Pasamanick, B. (1974). *Schizophrenics in the new custodial community: Five years after the experiment.* Columbus, OH: Ohio State University Press.

Davis, J. M. (1974). Psychopharmacology in the aged. Use of psychotropic drugs in geriatric patients. *Journal of Geriatric Psychiatry, 7*, 145–164.

Davis, J. M., Fann, W. E., El–Yousef, M. K., & Janowsky, D. (1973). Clinical problems in treating the aged with psychotropic drugs. In C. Eisdorfer & W. E. Fann (Eds.), *Psychopharmacology and aging* (pp. 111–125). New York–London: Plenum Press.

Davis, W. E., DeWolfe, A. S., & Gustafson, R. C. (1972). Intellectual deficit in process and reactive schizophrenia and brain injury. *Journal of Consulting and Clinical Psychology, 38*, 146.

Davison, K. (1976). Drug–induced psychoses and their relationship to schizophrenia. In D. Kemali, G. Bartholine, & D. Richter (Eds.), *Schizophrenia Today.* Oxford: Pergamon Press.

Davison, K., & Bagley, C. R. (1969). Schizophrenia–like psychoses associated with organic disorders of the central nervous system. In R. N. Herrington (Ed.), *Current problems in neuropsychiatry.* London: R. M. P. A.

DeLisi, L. E., Mirsky, A. F., Buchsbaum, M. S., van Kammen, D. P., Berman, K. F., Caton, C., Kafka, M. S., Ninan, P. T., Phelps, B. H., Karoum, F., Ko, G. N., Korpi, E. R., Linnoila, M., Sheinan, M., & Wyatt, R. J. (1984). The Genain quadruplets 25 years later: A diagnostic and biochemical follow–up. *Psychiatry Research, 13*, 59–76.

DeLisi, L. E., Wise, C. D., Bridge, T. P., Rosenblatt, J. E., Wagner, R. L., Morihisa, J., Karson, C., Potkin, S. G., & Wyatt, R. J. (1981). A probable neuroleptic effect on platelet monoamine oxidase in chronic schizophrenic patients. *Psychiatry Research, 4*, 95–107.

DeWolfe, A. S. (1971). Differentiation of schizophrenia and brain damage with WAIS. *Journal of Clinical Psychology, 27,* 209–211.

DeWolfe, A. S., Barrell, R. P., Becker, B. C., & Spaner, F. E. (1971). Intellectual deficit in chronic schizophrenia and brain damage. *Journal of Consulting and Clinical Psychology, 36,* 197–204.

Deane, W. N., & Brooks, G. W. (1967, September). *Five–year follow–up of chronic hospitalized patients.* Report from Vermont State Hospital, Waterbury, Vermont.

Degkwitz, R. (1969). Extrapyramidal motor disorders following long-term treatment with neuroleptic drugs. In G. E. Crane & R. Gardner, Jr. (Eds.), *Psychotropic drugs and dysfunctions of the basal ganglia.* Washington, D.C.: U.S. Government Printing Office.

Degkwitz, R., & Wenzel, W. (1967). Persistent extrapyramidal side effects after long–term application of neuroleptics. In H. Brill (Ed.), *Neuropsychopharmacology.* Amsterdam: Excerpta Medica Foundation.

Demarest, K. T., & Moore K. E. (1979). Comparison of dopamine synthesis regulation in the terminals of nigrostriatal mesolimbic, tuberoinfundibular and tuberohypophyseal neurons. *Journal of Neural Transmission, 46,* 263–277.

Demars, J. C. A. (1966). Neuromuscular effects of long–term phenothiazine medication, electroconvulsive therapy and leucotomy. *Journal of Nervous and Mental Disease, 143,* 73–79.

Depue, R. A., Dubicki, M. D., & McCarthy, T. (1975). Differential recovery of intellectual, associational, and psychophysiological functioning in withdrawn and active schizophrenics. *Journal of Abnormal Psychology, 84,* 325–330.

Dimond, S. J., Scammell, R. E., Pryce, I. G., Huws, D., & Gray, C. (1979). Callosal transfer and left–hand anomia in schizophrenia. *Biological Psychiatry, 14,* 735–739.

Dimond, S. J., Scammell, R., Pryce, I. J., Huws, D., & Gray, C. (1980). Some failures of intermanual and cross–lateral transfer in chronic schizophrenia. *Journal of Abnormal Psychology, 89,* 505–509.

Dixon, W. J. (1981). *BMDP statistical software.* Los Angeles: University of California.

Dohrenwend, B. P., & Egri, G. (1981). Stressfull life events and schizophrenia. *Schizophrenia Bulletin, 7,* 12–23.

Donnelly, E. F., Weinberger, D. R., Waldman, I. N., & Wyatt, R. J. (1980). Cognitive impairment associated with morphological brain abnormalities on computed tomography in chronic schizophrenic patients. *Journal of Nervous and Mental Disease, 168,* 305–308.

Doongaji, D. R., Jeste, D. V., Jape, N. M., Sheth, A. S., Apte, J. S., Vahia, V. N., Desai, A. B., Parikh, R. M., Thatte, S., & Bharadwaj, J. (1982). Tardive dyskinesia in India: A prevalence study. *Journal of Clinical Psychopharmacology, 2,* 341–344.

Duckworth, G. S., Kedword, H. B., & Bailey, W. F. (1979). Prognosis of mental illness in old age. *Canadian Journal of Psychiatry, 24,* 674–682.

Durkheim, E. (1915). *The elementary forms of the religious life.* New York: Free Press.

Dysken, M. W., Merry, W., & Davis, J. M. (1978). Anticholinergic psychosis. *Psychiatric Annals, 8,* 452–456.

Earnest, M. P., Heaton, R. K., Wilkinson, W. E., & Manke, W. F. (1979). Cortical atrophy, ventricular enlargement and intellectual impairment in the aged. *Neurology, 29,* 1138–1143.

Eccles, J. C. (1973). *The understanding of the brain stem.* New York: McGraw–Hill.

Edwards, H. (1970). The significance of brain damage in persistent oral dyskinesia. *British Journal of Psychiatry, 116,* 271–275.

Ehrentheil, O. (1964). Behavioral changes of aging chronic psychotics. In R. Kastenbaum (Ed.), *New thoughts on old age* (pp. 99–115). New York: Springer Publishing Company.

Ehrentheil, O., Davis, E. T., Casey, T. M., & Alsenberg, R. B. (1962). Schizophrenic motor activity observed over thirty years. *Archives of General Psychiatry, 7,* 266–276.

Eisdorfer, C. (1975). Observations on the psychopharmacology of the aged. *Journal of the American Geriatrics Society, 23,* 53–57.

Eisdorfer, C. (1980). Paranoia and schizophrenic disorders in later life. In E. W. Busse & D. G. Blazer (Eds.), *Handbook of geriatric psychiatry* (pp. 329–337). New York: Van Nostrand Reinhold.

Eisdorfer, C., & Wilkie, F. (1977). Stress, disease, aging and behavior. In J. E. Birren & K. W. Schaie (Eds.), *Handbook of the psychology of aging.* New York: Van Nostrand Reinhold.

Elder, G. (1974). *Children of the Great Depression.* Chicago: The University of Chicago Press.

Elder, G. (1975). Age differentiation and the life course. *Annual Review of Sociology, 1,* 165–190.

Elder, G. (1979). Historical change in life patterns and personality. In P. Baltes & O. G. Brim, Jr. (Eds.), *Life–span development and behavior* (pp. 117–159). New York: Academic Press.

Elder, G., & Rockwell, R. (1979). The life–course and human development: An ecological perspective. *International Journal of Behavioral Development, 2,* 1–21.

Engen, T. (1977). Taste and smell. In J. E. Birren & K. W. Schaie (Eds.), *Handbook of the psychology of aging.* New York: Van Nostrand Reinhold.

Erickson, R. C. (1975). Outcome studies in mental hospitals: A review. *Psychological Bulletin, 82*(4), 519–540.

Erikson, E. (1968). *Identity, youth and crisis.* New York: Norton.

Ey, H. (1975). *Des idées de Jackson à un modèle organo–dynamique en psychiatrie.* Toulouse: Privat.

Faergeman, P. M. (1963). *Psychogenic psychoses: A description and follow–up of psychoses following psychological stress.* London: Butterworths.

Fallo–Mitchell, L., & Ryff, C. (1982). Preferred timing of female life–events. *Research on Aging, 4,* 249–268.

Fann, W. E., Davis, J. M., & Janowsky, D. S. (1972). The prevalence of tardive dyskinesia in mental hospital patients. *Diseases of the Nervous System, 33,* 182–186.

Farkus, M. S., & Hoyer, W. J. (1980). Processing consequences of perceptual grouping in selective attention. *Journal of Gerontology, 35,* 207–216.

Farley, I. F., Price, K. S., & McCullough, E. (1978). Norepinephrine in chronic paranoid schizophrenia: Above normal levels in limbic forebrain. *Science, 200,* 456–458.

Farquhar, M. N., Kosky, K. J., & Omenn, G. S. (1979). Gene expression in brain. In D. M. Bowden (Ed.), *Aging in nonhuman primates* (pp. 71–79). New York: Van Nostrand.

Favorina, V. N. (1965). Late remission in schizophrenia. *Zhurnal Nevropatologii I Psikhiatrii Imeni S. S. Korsakova, 65/1,* 8–87.

Federn, P. (1952). *Ego psychology and the psychoses.* New York: Basic Books.

Feighner, J. P., Robins, E., Guze, S. B., Woodruff, R. A., Winokur, G., & Munoz, R. (1972). Diagnostic criteria for use in psychiatric research. *Archives of General Psychiatry, 1972, 26,* 57–63.

Finch, C. E. (1977). Neuroendocrine and autonomic functions during aging. In C. E. Finch & L. Hayflick (Eds.), *Handbook of the biology of aging.* New York: Van Nostrand Reinhold.

Finch, C. E. (1980). Relationships of aging changes in the basal ganglia to manifestations of Huntington's chorea. *Annals of Neurology, 7,* 406–411.

Fiske, M. (1980). Tasks and crises of the second half of life: The interrelationship of commitment, coping and adaptation. In J. Birren & R. B. Sloan (Eds.), *Handbook of mental health and aging (pp. 337–373).* Englewood Cliffs, NJ: Prentice–Hall.

Fleck, N. (1928). Uber Beobachtungen bei Alten Fällen von Schizophrenie. *Archiv Fur Psychiatrie Und Nervenkrankheiten, 85,* 705–760.

Flekkoy, K., Lund, I., & Astrup, C. (1975). Prolonged clinical and experimental follow–up of hospitalized schizophrenics. *Neuropsychobiology, 1,* 47–58.

Folstein, M., Folstein, S., & McHugh, P. R. (1975). Mini–mental state: A practical method for grading the cognitive state of patients for the clinician. *Journal of Psychiatric Research, 12,* 189–198.

Forman, L. J., Sonntag, W. E., Van Vugt, D. A., & Meites, J. (1981). Immunoreactive B–endorphin in the plasma, pituitary and hypothalamus of young and old male rats. *Neurobiology of Aging, 2,* 281–284.

Foulds, G. A., & Dixon, P. (1962a). The nature of intellectual deficit in schizophrenia: Part I. A comparison of schizophrenics and neurotics. *British Journal of Social and Clinical Psychology, 1,* 7–19.

Foulds, G. A., & Dixon, P. (1962b). The nature of intellectual deficit in schizophrenia: Part III. A longitudinal study of the subgroups. *British Journal of Social and Clinical Psychology, 1,* 199–207.

Foulds, G. A., Dixon, P., McClelland, M., & McClelland, W. J. (1962). The nature of intellectual deficit in schizophrenia: Part II. A cross–sectional study of paranoid, catatonic, hebephrenic and simple schizophrenics. *British Journal of Social and Clinical Psychology, 1,* 141–149.

Fozard, J. L., Wolf, E., Bell, B., McFarland, R. A., & Podolsky, S. (1977). Visual perception and communication. In J. E. Birren & K. W. Schaie (Eds.), *Handbook of the psychology of aging.* New York: Van Nostrand Reinhold.

Fredericks, R. S., & Finkel, P. (1978). Schizophrenic performance on the Halstead–Reitan Battery. *Journal of Clinical Psychology, 34,* 26–30.

Freedman, R., & Schwab, P. J. (1978). Paranoid symptoms in patients on a general hospital psychiatric unit. *Archives of General Psychiatry, 35,* 387–390.

Freud, S. (1911). Psychoanalytic notes on an autobiographical account of a case of paranoia (Dementia Paranoides). In S. Freud, *The Complete Psychological Works of Sigmund Freud* (Volume 12). London: Hogarth Press.

Frith, C. D. (1977). Two kinds of cognitive deficit associated with chronic schizophrenia. *Psychological Medicine, 7,* 171–173.

Fromm–Reichmann, F. (1950). *Principles of intensive psychotherapy.* Chicago: University of Chicago Press.

Gambert, S. R. (1981). Interaction of age and thyroid hormone status on beta–endorphin content in rat corpus striatum and hypothalamus. *Neuroendocrinology, 32,* 114–117.

Gardner, E. A., Miles, H., Iker, H., & Romano, J. (1963). A cumulative register of psychiatric services in a community. *American Journal of Public Health, 53,* 1269–1277.

Garmezy, N. (1970, Fall). Process and reactive schizophrenia: Some conceptions and issues. *Schizophrenia Bulletin,* 30–74.

Garmezy, N., with Streitman, S. (1974). Children at risk: The search for antecedents of schizophrenia. I. Conceptual models and research methods. *Schizophrenia Bulletin, 8,* 14–90.

Geertz, C. (1973). *The interpretation of cultures.* New York: Basic Books.

Geinisman, Y., & Bondareff, W. (1976). Decrease in the number of synapses in the senescent brain: A quantitative electron microsopic analysis of the dentate gyrus molecular layer in the rate. *Mechanics of Aging and Development, 5,* 11–24.

Gergen, K. (1977). Stability, change, and chance in understanding human development. In N. Datan & H. Reese (Eds.), *Life–span developmental psychology: dialectical perspectives on experimental research* (pp. 136–158). New York: Academic Press.

Gergen, K. (1980). The emerging crisis in life–span development theory. In P. Baltes & O. G. Brim, Jr. (Eds.), *Life–span development and behavior* (Volume 3). New York: Academic Press.

Gibson, A. J., Moyes, I. C. A., & Kendrick, D. (1980). Cognitive assessment of the elderly long–stay patient. *British Journal of Psychiatry, 137,* 551–557.

Giel, R., Dijk, S., & van Weerden–Dijkstra, J. R. (1978). Mortality in the long–stay population of all Dutch mental hospitals. *Acta Psychiatrica Scandinavica, 57,* 21–28.

Ginnett, L. E., & Moran, L. J. (1964). Stability of vocabulary performance by schizophrenics. *Journal of Consulting Psychology, 28,* 178–179.

Gittleman–Klein, R., & Klein, D. (1969). Premorbid social adjustment and prognosis in schizophrenia. *Journal of Psychiatric Research, 7,* 35–53.

Gjerde, P. F. (1983). Attentional capacity dysfunction and arousal in schizophrenia. *Psychological Bulletin, 93,* 57–72.

Goffman, E. (1961). On the characteristics of total institutions. In D. R. Cressey (Ed.), *The prison.* New York: Holt, Reinhart and Winston.

Goffman, E. (1962). *Asylums.* Chicago: Aldine.

Goldberg, S. C., Schooler, N. R., Hogarty, G. E., & Roper, M. A. (1977). Prediction of relapse in schizophrenia outpatients treated by drug and sociotherapy. *Archives of General Psychiatry, 1977, 34,* 171–184.

Golden, C. J. (1976). Identification of brain disorders by the Stroop Color and Word Test. *Journal of Clinical Psychology, 32,* 654–658.

Golden, C. J., Hammeke, T. A., & Purisch, A. D. (1978). Diagnostic validity of a standardized neuropsychological battery derived from Luria's neuropsychological tests. *Journal of Consulting and Clinical Psychology, 46,* 1258–1265.

Golden, C. J., Hammeke, T. A., & Purisch, A. D. (1980). *The Luria-Nebraska neuropsychological battery manual.* Los Angeles: Western Psychological Services.

Golden, C. J., MacInnes, W. D., Ariel, R. N., Reudrich, S. L., Chu, C., Coffman, J. A., Graber, B., & Bloch, S. (1982). Cross–validation of the ability of the Luria–Nebraska Neuropsychological Battery to differentiate chronic schizophrenics with and without ventricular enlargement. *Journal of Consulting and Clinical Psychology, 50,* 87–95.

Golden, C., Moses, J. A., Zelazowski, R., Graber, B., Zatz, L. M., Horvarth, T. B., & Berger, P. A. (1980). Cerebral ventricular size and neuropsychological impairement in young chronic schizophrenics. *Archives of General Psychiatry, 37,* 619–623.

Goldfarb, A. (1962). Prevalence of psychiatric disorders in metropolitan old age and nursing homes. *Journal of the American Geriatrics Society, 10,* 77–84.

Goldfrank, L., & Bresnitz, E. (1974). Toxicological emergencies: Phenothiazines. *Hospital Physician, 6,* 42–53.

Goldstein, G. (1978). Cognitive and perceptual differences between schizophrenics and organics. *Schizophrenia Bulletin, 4,* 160–185.

Goldstein, G., & Halperin, K. M. (1977). Neuropsychological differences among subtypes of schizophrenia. *Journal of Abnormal Psychology, 86,* 34–40.

Goldstein, C., & Kyc, F. (1978). Performance of brain–damaged, schizophrenic, and normal subjects on a visual searching task. *Perceptual and Motor Skills, 46,* 731–734.

Goldstein, G., & Neuringer, C. (1966). Schizophrenic and organic signs and the Trail Making Test. *Perceptual and Motor Skills, 22,* 347–350.

Goldstein, K. (1944). Methodological approach to the study of schizophrenic thought disorder. In J. S. Kaisanin (Ed.), *Language and thought in schizophrenia.* New York: W. W. Norton.

Goldstein, R. H., & Salzman, L. F. (1967). Cognitive functioning in acute and remitted psychiatric patients. *Psychological Reports, 21,* 24–26.

Goldstein, K., & Scheerer, M. (1941). Abstract and concrete behavior: An experimental study with special tests. *Psychological Monographs, 53,* (No. 2).

Goodman, A. B., & Siegel, C. (1986). Elderly schizophrenic inpatients in the wake of deinstitutionalization. *American Journal of Psychiatry, 143*(2), 204–207.

Gorham, D. R. (1956). A proverbs test for clinical and experimental use. *Psychological Reports, 1,* 1–12.

Gottesman, I. I., & Shields, J. (1973). Genetic studies of schizophrenia as signposts to biochemistry. In L. L. Iversen & S. P. R. Rose (Eds.), *Biochemistry and mental illness* (pp. 165–174). London: Biochemical Society.

Gottesman, I. I., & Shields, J. (1976). A critical review of recent adoption, twin, and family studies of schizophrenia: Behavioral genetics perspectives. *Schizophrenia Bulletin, 2,* 360–401.

Gottesman, I. I., & Shields, J. (1982). *Schizophrenia, the epigenetic puzzle.* Cambridge, New York: Cambridge University Press.

Gottsdanker, R. (1982). Age and simple reaction time. *Journal of Gerontology, 37,* 342–348.

Granacher, R. P., Jr. (1981). Differential diagnosis of tardive dyskinesia: An overview. *American Journal of Psychiatry, 138,* 1288–1297.

Greenblatt, D. J., Allen, M. D., & Shader, R. I. (1977). Toxicity of high–dose fluazepam in the elderly. *Clinical Pharmacology and Therapeutics, 21,* 355–361.

Greenblatt, D. L., Stotsky, B. A., & DiMascio A. (1968). Phenothiazine-induced dyskinesia in nursing home patients. *Journal of the American Geriatric Society, 16,* 27–34.

Greenblatt, M., Levinson, D., & Williams, R. (1957). *The patient and the mental hospital.* New York: Free Press/Macmillan.

Groninger, L. D. (1979). Predicting recall: The "Feeling–that–I–will–know" phenonomenon. *American Journal of Psychology, 92*(1), 45–58.

Gross, G., & Huber, G. (1973). Zur Prognose der Schizophrenien. *Psychiatria Clinica, 6,* 1–16.

Gudelsky, G. A., Annunziato, L., & Moore, K. E. (1978). Localization of the site of the haloperidol induced prolactin mediated increase of dopamine turnover in the median eminence: Studies in rats with complete hypothalamic deafferentations. *Journal of Neurological Transmission, 42,* 181–192.

Gunderson, J. G., & Kolb, J. E. (1978). Discriminating features of borderline patients. *American Journal of Psychiatry, 135,* 792–796.

Gurland, B., Copeland, J., Kelleher, M., Kuriansky, J., Sharpe, L., & Dean, L. (1983). *The mind and mood of aging: The mental health problems of the community elderly in New York and London.* New York: Haworth Press.

Gurland, B., Kurlansky, J., Sharpe, L., Simon, R., Stiller, P., & Birkett, P. (1977–78). The comprehensive assessment referral evaluation (CARE) – rationale, development, and reliablility. *International Journal of Aging and Human Development, 8,* 9–42.

Gurland, B. J., Yorkston, N. J., Goldberg, K., Fleiss, J. L., Sloane, R. B., & Cristal, A. H. (1972). The structured and scaled interview to assess maladjustment (SSIAM): II. Factor analysis, reliability, and validity. *Archives of General Psychiatry, 27,* 264–267.

Gutmann, D. (1975). Parenthood: Key to the comparative psychology of the life cycle? In N. Datan & L. Ginsberg (Eds.), *Life–Span Developmental Psychology* (pp. 167–184). New York: Academic Press.

Gutmann, D. (1977). The cross–cultural perspective: Notes toward a comparative psychology of aging. In J. Birren & K. W. Schaie (Eds.), *Handbook of the Psychology of Aging* (pp. 302–326). New York: Van Nostrand Reinhold.

Gyldensted, C. (1977). Measurement of the normal ventricular system and hemispheric sulci of 100 adults with computed tomography. *Neuroradiology, 14,* 183–192.

Halperin, K. M. (1975). *Relation between neurological and neuropsychological deficits and process–reactive schizophrenia.* Unpublished master's thesis, University of Kansas.

Hamilton, Vernon. (1963). IQ changes in chronic schizophrenia. *British Journal of Psychiatry, 109,* 642–648.

Hamlin, R. M. (1969). The stability of intellectual function in chronic schizophrenia. *Journal of Nervous and Mental Disease, 149,* 497–503.

Hammer, M., MaKiesky–Barrow, S., & Gutwirth, L. (1978). Social networks and schizophrenia. *Schizophrenia Bulletin, 4*(4), 525–552.

Hanson, D., Gottesman, I., & Heston, L. (1976). Some possible indicators of adult schizophrenics inferred from children of schizophrenics. *British Journal of Psychiatry, 129,* 142–154.

Hanson, D., Gottesman, I., & Meehl, P. (1977). Genetic theories and validation of psychiatric diagnoses: Implications for the study of children of psychizophrenics. *Journal of Abnormal Psychology, 86,* 575–588.

Harding, C. M., & Brooks, G. W. (1980). Longitudinal assessment of a cohort of chronic schizophrenics discharged 20 years ago. *The Psychiatric Journal of the University of Ottawa, 5,* 274–278.

Harding, C. M., & Brooks, G. W. (1984). Life assessment of a cohort of chronic schizophrenics discharged 20 years ago. In Mednick, Harway, & Finello (Eds.), *Handbook of longitudinal research* (Vol. II) (pp. 375–393). New York: Praeger Press.

Harding, C. M., Brooks, G. W., Ashikaga, T., Strauss, J. S., & Breier, A. (in press *a*). The Vermont longitudinal study of persons with severe mental illiness: I. Methodology, study sample and overall current status. *American Journal of Psychiatry.*

Harding, C. M., Brooks, G. W., Ashikaga, T., Strauss, J. S., & Breier, A. (in press *b*). The Vermont longitudinal study: II. Long–term outcome for DSM–III schizophrenia. *American Journal of Psychiatry.*

Harding, C. M., & Strauss, J. S. (1985). The course of schizophrenia: An evolving concept. In M. Alpert (Ed.), *Controversies in schizophrenia: Changes and constancies* (pp. 339–353). New York: Guilford Press.

Hareven, T. (1980). The life–course of aging in historical perspective. In K. Back (Ed.), *Life–course: Integrative theories and examplary populations* (pp. 9–26). Boulder, CO: Westview Press.

Harrow, M., & Adler, D. (1974). *Are schizophrenics concrete?* Presented to the 46th annual meeting of the Midwestern Psychological Association, Chicago, IL.

Harrow, M., Adler, D., & Hanf, E. (1974). Abstract and concrete thinking in schizophrenia during the prechronic phases. *Archives of General Psychiatry, 31,* 27–33.

Harrow, M., Bromet, E., & Quinlan, D. (1974). Predictors of posthospital adjustment in schizophrenia: Thought disorders and schizophrenic diagnosis. *Journal of Nervous and Mental Disease, 158,* 25–36.

Harrow, M., Buckley–Marengo, J., Growe, G., & Grinker, R. R., Sr. (1979). Schizophrenic deterioration and concrete thinking. *Scientific Proceedings of the 132nd Annual Meeting of the American Psychiatric Association.* Washington, DC: American Psychiatric Association.

Harrow, M., Grinker, R. R., Sr., Silverstein, M. L., & Holzman, P. (1978). Is modern–day schizophrenic outcome still negative? *American Journal of Psychiatry, 135,* 1156–1162.

Harrow, M., Grossman, L., Silverstein, M. L., & Meltzer, H. Y. (1982). Thought pathology in manic and schizophrenic patients: At hospital admission and seven weeks later. *Archives of General Psychiatry, 39,* 665–671.

Harrow, M., & Quinlan, D. (1985). *Disordered Thinking and schizophrenic psychopathology.* New York: Gardner Press.

Harrow, M., Silverstein, M. L., & Marengo, J. (1983). Disordered thinking: Does it identify nuclear schizophrenia? *Archives of General Psychiatry.*

Haug, H., Barmwater, U., Eggers, R., Fischer, D., Kuhl, S., and Sass, N.–L. (1983). Anatomical change in aging brain: morphometric analysis of the human prosencephalon. *Brain Aging: Neuropathology, Neuropharmocology. (Aging, Vol. 21),* 1–12.

Havighurst, R., & Albrecht, R. (1953). *Older people.* New York: Longmans Green.

Hawk, A. B., Carpenter, W. T., & Strauss, J. S. (1975). Diagnostic criteria and five–year outcome in schizophrenia: A report from the international pilot study of schizophrenia. *Archives of General Psychiatry, 32,* 343–347.

Haywood, H. C., & Modelis, I. (1963). Effect of symptom change on intellectual function in schizophrenia. *Journal of Abnormal and Social Psychology, 67,* 76–78.

Heaton, R. K., Baade, L. E., & Johnson, K. L. (1978). Neuropsychological test results associated with psychiatric disorders in adults. *Psychological Bulletin, 85,* 141–162.

Heaton, R. K., & Crowley, T. J. (1981). Effects of psychiatric disorders and their somatic treatments on neuropsychological test results. In S. B. Filskov & T. J. Boll (Eds.), *Handbook of clinical neuropsychology.* New York: Wiley.

Heaton, R. K., Vogt, A. T., Hoehn, M. M., Lewis, J. A., Crowley, T. J., & Stallings, M. A. (1979). Neuropsychological impairment with schizophrenics vs. acute and chronic cerebral lesions. *Journal of Clinical Psychology, 35,* 46–53.

Heinrich, K., Wagener, I., & Bender, H. J. (1968). Spate extrapyramidal hyperkinesen bei neuroleptischer langzeittherapie. *Pharmakopsychiatr Neuropsychopharmakol 1,* 169–195.

Hemsley, D. R. (1977). What have cognitive deficits to do with schizophrenic symptoms? *British Journal of Psychiatry, 130,* 167–173.

Henderson, G., Tomlinson, B. E., & Gibson, P. H. (1980). Cell counts in human cerebral cortex in normal adults throughout life using an image analyzing computer. *Journal of the Neurological Sciences, 46,* 113–136.

Henisz, J. (1966). A follow–up study of schizophrenic patients. *Comprehensive Psychiatry, 7,* 524–528.

Herbert, M. E., & Jacobson, S. (1967). Late paraphrenia. *British Journal of Psychiatry, 113,* 461–469.

Herron, W. G. (1962*a*). The process–reactive classification of schizophrenia. *Psychological Bulletin, 59,* 329–343.

Herron, W. G. (1962*b*). Abstract ability in the process–reactive classification of schizohrenia. *Journal of General Psychology, 67,* 147–154.

Hersen, M., Levine, J., & Church, A. (1972). Parameters of the spiral after–effect in organics, schizophrenics, and normals. *The Journal of Genetic Psychology, 120,* 177–187.

Hertler, C. A., Chapman, L. J., & Chapman, J. P. (1978). A scoring manual for literalness in proverb interpretation. *Journal of Consulting and Clinical Psychology, 46,* 551–555.

Hertzog, C., Schaie, K. W., & Gribbon, K. (1978). Cardiovascular disease and changes in intellectual functioning from middle to old age. *Journal of Gerontology, 33,* 872–883.

Hess, G. D., Joseph, J. A., & Roth, G. S. (1981). Effect of age on sensitivity to pain and brain opiate receptors. *Neurobiology of Aging, 2,* 49–56.

Heston L. (1970, January). The genetics of schizophrenic and schizoid disease. *Science, 167,* 249–256.

Hicks, P., Strong, R., Schoolar, J. C., & Samorajski, T. (1980). Aging alters amphetamine–induced sterotyped gnawing and nostriatal elimination of amphetamine in mice. *Life Sciences, 27,* 715–722.

Himmelhoch, J., Harrow, M., Tucker, F. J., & Hersch, J. (1973). *Manual for assessment of selected aspects of thinking on the object sorting test.* ASIS/NAPS #02206, New York: Microfiche Publications.

Hinterhuber, H. (1973). Zur Katamnese der Schizophrenien. Eine klinisch–statistische Untersuchung lebenslanger Verläufe. *Fortschritte der Neurologie-Psychiatrie, 41,* 527–558.

Hogarty, G. E., & Goldberg, S. C. (1973). Drug and sociotherapy in the aftercare of schizophrenic patients: One year relapse rates. *Archives of General Psychiatry, 28,* 54–64.

Hogarty, G. E., Goldberg, S. C., Schooler, N. R. (1974*b*). Drug and sociotherapy in the aftercare of schizophrenic patients. III. Adjustment of nonrelapsed patients. *Archives of General Psychiatry, 31,* 609–618.

Hogarty, G. E., Goldberg, S. C., Schooler, N. R., & Ulrich, R. F. (1974*a*). Drug and sociotherapy in the aftercare of schizophrenic patients. II. Two year relapse rates. *Archives of General Psychiatry, 31,* 603–608.

Holland, T. R., Levi, M., & Watson, C. G. (1979). Multivariate structure of associations between verbal and nonverbal intelligence among brain–damaged, schizophrenic, neurotic, and alcoholic patients. *Journal of Abnormal Psychology, 88,* 354–360.

Holland, T. R., & Wadsworth, H. M. (1976). Assessment of conceptual deficits in brain–damaged and schizophrenic patients. *Perceptual and Motor Skills, 43,* 951–957.

Holland, T. R., & Wadsworth, H. M. (1979). Comparison and combination of recall and background inference procedures for the Bender-Gestalt Test with brain–damaged and schizophrenic patients. *Journal of Personality Assessment, 43,* 123–127.

Holland, T. R., Wadsworth, H. M., & Royer, F. L. (1975). The performance of brain–damaged and schizophrenic patients on the Minnesota Perceptual–Diagnostic Test under standard and BIP conditions of administration. *Journal of Clinical Psychology, 31,* 21–25.

Holland, T. R., & Watson, C. G. (1980). Multivariate analysis of WAIS–MMPI relationships among brain–damaged, schizophrenic, neurotic, and alcoholic patients. *Journal of Clinical Psychology, 36,* 352– 359.

Hollander, E. (1964). *Leaders, groups, and influence.* New York: Oxford University Press.

Holzman, P. S., Levy, D. L., & Proctor, L. R. (1976). Smooth pursuit eye movements, attention, and schizophrenia. *Archives of General Psychiatry, 33,* 1415–1420.

Horine, L. C., & Fulkerson, S. C. (1973). Utility of the Canter Background Interference Procedure for differentiating among the schizophrenias. *Journal of Personality Assessment, 37,* 48–52.

Hornykiewicz, O. (1982). Brain catecholamines in schizophrenia—A good case for noradrenaline. *Nature, 199,* 484–486.

Hoyer, W. J., & Plude, D. J. (1980). Attentional and perceptual processes in the study of cognitive aging. In L. W. Poon (Ed.), *Aging in the 1980's.* Washington, DC: American Psychological Association.

Hoyer, W. J., Rebok, G. W., & Sved, S. M. (1979). Effects of varying irrelevant information on adult age differences in problem solving. *Journal of Gerontology, 34,* 553–560.

Huber, G. (Ed.). (1973). *Verlauf und Ausgang schizophrener Erkrankungen.* Stuttgart: Schattauer.

Huber, G. (Ed.). (1976). *Therapie, Rehabilitation und Prävention schizophrener Erkrankungen.* Stuttgart: Schattauer.

Huber, G., Gross, G., & Schuttler, R. (1975). A long–term follow–up study of schizophrenia: Psychiatric course of illness and prognosis. *Acta Psychiatrica Scandinavica, 52,* 49–57.

Huber, G., Gross, G., & Schuttler, R. (1979). *Schizophrenie. Eine Verlaufsund sozial–psychiatrische Langzeitstudie.* Berlin–Heidelberg–New York: Springer.

Huber, G., Gross, G., Schuttler, R., & Linz, M. (1980). Longitudinal studies of schizophrenic patients. *Schizophrenia Bulletin, 6*(4), 592–605.

Hultsch, D. F. (1969). Age differences in the organization of free recall. *Developmental Psychology, 1,* 673–678.

Hultsch, D. F. (1971). Organization and memory in adulthood. *Human Development, 14,* 16–29.

Hunter, R., Earl, C. J., & Thornicroff, S. (1964). An apparently irreversible syndrome of abnormal movements following phenothiazine medication. *Proceedings of the Royal Society of Medicine, 57,* 758–762.

Imlah, N. W. (1976). Long–term follow–up of drugs of schizophrenia. *British Journal of Clinical Pharmacology, 3*(2), 411–415.

Innes, G., & Miller, W. M. (1970). Mortality among psychiatric patients. *Scottish Medical Journal, 15,* 143–148.

Itil, T. M., & Soldatus, C. (1980). Epilepthogenic side effects of psychotropic drugs: Practical recommendation. *Journal of American Medical Association, 244,* 1460–1463.

Itoh, H. & Yagi, G. (1979). Reversibility of tardive dyskinesia. *Folia Psychiatrica et Neurologica Japonica, 33,* 43–54.

Jackman, H. L., & Meltzer, H. Y. (1980). Factors affecting determination of platelet monoamine oxidase activity. *Schizophrenia Bulletin, 6,* 259–265.

Jacobs, S., & Myers, I. (1976). Recent life events and acute schizophrenic psychosis: A controlled study. *Journal of Nervous and Mental Disease, 162,* 75–87.

Jacobson, G. F. (1974). Programs and techniques of crisis intervention. In S. Arieti (Ed.), *American Handbook of Psychiatry, Vol 2,* (pp. 810–825). New York: Basic Books.

Jaques, E. (1965). Death and mid–life crisis. *International Journal of Psychoanalysis, 46,* 502–514.

Jaser, R. (1928). Ueber den Einfluss des Greisenalters auf die Gestaltung schizophrener Prozesse. *Allgemeine Zeitschrift Fur Psychiatrie, 89,* 1.

Jensen, A. R. (1965). Scoring the Stroop test. *Acta Psychologica, 24,* 398–408.

Jeste, D. V., DeLisi, L. E., Zalcman, S., Wise, C. D., Phelps, B. H., Rosenblatt, J. E., Potkin, S. G., Bridge, T. P. & Wyatt, R. J. (1981). A biochemical study of tardive dyskinesia in young male patients. *Psychiatry Research, 4,* 327–331.

Jeste, D. V., Kleinman, J. E., Potkin, S. G., Luchins, D. J., & Weinberger, D. R. (1982). Ex uno multi: Subtyping the schizophrenic syndrome. *Biological Psychiatry, 17,* 199–222.

Jeste, D. V., Potkin, S. A., Sinha, S., Feder, S. L., & Wyatt, R. J. (1979). Tardive dyskinesia: Reversible and persistent. *Archives of General Psychiatry, 36,* 585–590.

Jeste, D. V., & Wyatt, R. J. (1981). Dogma disputed: Is tardive dyskinesia due to postsynaptic dopamine receptor supersensitivity? *Journal of Clinical Psychiatry, 42,* 455–457.

Jeste, D. V., & Wyatt, R. J. (1981). Changing epidemiology of tardive dyskinesia. *American Journal of Psychiatry, 138,* 297–309.

Jeste, D. V., & Wyatt, R. J. (1982a). *Understanding and treating tardive dyskinesia.* New York: Guilford Press.

Jeste, D. V., & Wyatt, R. J. (1982b). Therapeutic strategies against tardive dyskinesia: Two decades of experience. *Archives of General Psychiatry, 39,* 103–116.

Johnstone, E. C., Crow, T. J. Frith, C. D., Stevens, M., Kreel, L., & Husband, J. (1978). The dementia of dementia praecox. *Acta Psychiatrica Scandinavica, 57,* 305–324.

Johnstone, E. C., Crow, T. J., Frith, C. D., Husband, J., & Kreel, L. (1979). Cerebral ventricular size and cognitive impairment in chronic schizophrenia. *The Lancet, II,* 924–926.

Johnstone, E. C., Cunningham Owens, D. G., Gold, A., Crow, T. J., & Macmillan, J. F. (1981). Institutionalization and the defects of schizophrenia. *British Journal of Psychiatry, 139,* 195–203.

Jones, M., & Hunter, R. (1969). Abnormal movements in patients with chronic psychiatric illness. In G.E. Crane & R. Gardner, Jr. (Eds.), *Psychotropic drugs and dysfunctions of the basal ganglia.* Washington, D.C.: U.S. Government Printing Office.

Jones, M. B., & Offord, D. R. (1975). Independent transmission of IQ and schizophrenia. *British Journal of Psychiatry, 126,* 185–190.

Jung, C. (1933). *Modern man in search of a soul.* New York: Harcourt, Brace and World.

Jus, A., Pineau, R., Lachance, R., Relchat, G., Jus, K., Pires, P., & Villeneuve, E. (1976). Epidemiology of tardive dyskinesia: Part II. *Diseases of the Nervous System, 37,* 257–261.

Kafka, J. S. (1964). Technical applications of a concept of multiple reality. *International Journal of Psycho–Analysis, 45,* 575–578.

Kafka, J. S. (1971). Ambiguity for individuation—A critique and reformulation of double–bind theory. *Archives of General Psychiatry, 26,* 232–239.

Kafka, J. S. (1977). On reality: An examination of object constancy, ambiguity, paradox, and time. In J. H. Smith (Ed.), *Thought, consciousness, and reality,* Vol. 2 of *Psychiatry and the Humanities.* New Haven, CT: Yale University Press.

Kafka, J. S. (1980). The dream in schizophrenia. In J. M. Natterson (Ed.), *The dream in clinical practice* (pp. 99–110). New York–London: Jason Aronson.

Kafka, J. S. (1986). The schizophrenic's objects: Implications for treatment strategies. In D. B. Feinsilver, Ed., *Toward a comprehensive model for schizophrenic disorders: Essays in memory of Ping–Nie Pao* (pp. 289–297). Hillsdale, NJ: Analytic Press.

Kahneman, D. (1973). *Attention and effort.* Englewood Cliffs, NJ: Prentice Hall.

Kane, J. M., Woerner, M., Lieberman, J., & Kinon, B. (1984). Tardive dyskinsia in neuropsychiatric movement disorders. In D. V. Jeste & R. J. Wyatt (Eds.), (pp. 97–118). Washington, D.C.: American Psychiatric Press.

Kaplan, B. (Ed.). (1964). *The inner world of mental illness.* New York: Harper & Row.

Katan, M. (1949). Schreber's delusion of the end of the world. In W. Niederland (Ed.), *The Schreber Case: Psychoanalytic profile of a paranoid personality.* New York: Quadrangle Press–The New York Times.

Kaufmann, C. A., Jeste, D. V., Linnoila, M., Shelton, R., Kafka, M., & Wyatt, R. J. (in press). Noradrenergic and Neuroradiological abnormalities in tardive dyskinesia. *Biological Psychiatry.*

Kausler, D. H., & Kleim, D. M. (1978). Age differences in processing relevant versus irrelevant stimuli in multiple–item recognition learning. *Journal of Gerontology, 33,* 87–93.

Kay, D. W. K. (1959). Observations on the natural history and genetics of old age psychoses. *Proc. R. Soc. Med., 52,* 791–794.

Kay, D. W. K. (1962). Outcome and cause of death in mental disorders of old age: A long–term follow–up of functional and organic psychoses. *Acta Psychiatrica Scandinavica, 38,* 249–276.

Kay, D. W. K. (1963). Late paraphrenia and its bearing on the aetiology of schizophrenia. *Acta Psychiatrica Scandinavica, 39,* 159–169.

Kay, D. W. K. (1972, October). Schizophrenia and schizophrenia–like states in the elderly. *British Journal of Hospital Medicine,* 369–376.

Kay, D. W. K. (1975). Schizophrenia and schizophrenia–like states in the elderly. In T. Silverstone & B. Barraclough (Eds.), *Contemporary psychiatry.* British Journal of Psychiatry Special Publication No. 9. Headley: Ashford, Kent.

Kay, D. W. K., Beamish, P., & Roth, M. (1964*a*). Old age mental disorders in Newcastle upon Tyme. Part I: A study of prevalance. *British Journal of Psychiatry, 110,* 146–158.

Kay, D. W. K., Beamish, P., & Roth, M. (1964*b*). Some medical and social characteristics of elderly people under state care, *Sociological Review Monograph* (No. 5).

Kay, D. W. K., & Bergman, K. (1980). Epidemiology of mental disorders among the aged in the community. In J. Birren & B. Sloane (Eds.), *Handbook of mental health and aging* (pp. 34–56). Englewood Cliffs, NJ: Prentice–Hall.

Kay, D. W. K., Cooper, A. F., Garside, R. F., & Roth, M. (1976). The differentiation of paranoid from affective psychoses by patients' premorbid characteristics. *British Journal of Psychiatry, 129,* 207–215.

Kay, D. W. K., & Roth, M. (1961). Environmental and hereditary factors in the schizophrenia of old age ("late paraphrenia") and their bearing on the general problem of causation in schizophrenia. *Journal of Mental Science, 107,* 649–686.

Kay, D., & Roth, M. (1963). Schizophrenias of old age. In R. Williams, C. Tibbits, & W. Donahue (Eds.), *Processes of aging: Social and psychological perspectives.* (pp. 402–488). New York: Atherton Press/Prentice–Hall.

Kay, S. R. (1979). Schizophrenic WAIS pattern by diagnostic subtypes. *Perceptual and Motor Skills, 48,* 1241–1242.

Keith, S. J., & Buchsbaum, S. (1978). Workshop on factors related to premorbid adjustment. *Schizophrenia Bulletin, 4,* 252–257.

Kendler, K. S. (1980). The nosologic validity of paranoia (simple delusional disorder): a review. *Archives of General Psychiatry, 37,* 699–706.

Kendler, K. S., & Davis, K. L. (1981). The genetics and biochemistry of paranoid schizophenia and other paranoid psychoses. *Schizophrenia Bulletin, 7,* 689–709.

Kendler, K. S., & Hayes, P. (1981). Paranoid psychosis (delusional disorder) and schizophrenia. *Archives of General Psychiatry, 38,* 547–551.

Kendler, K. S., & Tsuang, M. T. (1981). Nosology of paranoid schizophrenia and other paranoid psychoses. *Schizophrenia Bulletin, 7,* 594–610.

Kenshalo, D. R. (1977). Age changes in touch, vibration, temperature, kinesthesis, and pain sensitivity. In J. E. Birren & K. W. Schaie (Eds.), *Handbook of the psychology of aging.* New York: Van Nostrand Reinhold.

Kety, S. S., Rosenthal, D., Wender, P. H., & Schulsinger, F. (1976). Studies based on a total sample of adopted individuals and their relatives: why they were necessary, what they demonstrated and failed to demonstrate. *Schizophrenia Bulletin, 2,* 413–428.

Kety, S. S., Rosenthal, D., Wender, P. H., Schlusinger, F., & Jacobsen, B. (1975). Mental illness in the biological and adoptive families of adopted individuals who have become schizophrenic: A preliminary report based on psychiatric interviews. In R. R. Fiere, D. Rosenthal, & H. Brill (Eds.), *Genetic research in psychiatry* (pp. 147–166). Baltimore, MD: Johns Hopkins University Press.

Kidd, K. (1978). A genetic perspective on schizophrenia. In L. Wynne, R. Cromwell, & S. Matthysse (Eds.), *The nature of schizophrenia: New approaches to research and treatment.* (pp. 70–75). New York: Wiley.

King, H. E. (1967). Trail Making performance as related to psychotic state, age, intelligence, education and fine psychomotor ability. *Perceptual and Motor Skills, 25,* 649–658.

Kingsley, L., & Streuning, E. L. (1966). Changes in intellectual performance of acute and chronic schizophrenics. *Psychological Reports, 18,* 791–800.

Klages, W. (1961). *Die Spaetschizophrenie.* Stuttgart: Enke.

Klawans, H. L., Jr. (1970). A pharmacologic analysis of Huntington's chorea. *European Neurology, 4,* 148–163.

Klawans, H. L., Goetz, C. G., and Perlik, S. (1980). Presymptomatic and early detection in Huntington's disease. *Annals of Neurology, 8,* 343–347.

Klawans, H. L., Jr., Paulson, G. W., Ringel, S. P., & Barbeau, A. (1972). Use of L–DOPA in the detection of presymptomatic Huntington's chorea. *New England Journal of Medicine, 286,* 1332–1334.

Kleinman, J. E., Bridge, T. P., & Karoum, F. (1980). Biochemical abnormalities in postmortem brain. In C. Baxter & T. Melnechuch (Eds.), *Perspectives in schizophrenia research* (pp. 221–223). New York: Raven Press.

Kleinman, J. E., Weinberger, D. R., Rogol, A. D., Bigelow, L. B., Klein, S. T., Gillin, J. C., & Wyatt, R. J. (1982). Plasma prolactin concentrations and psychopathology in chronic schizophrenia. *Archives of General Psychiatry, 39,* 655–657.

Kline, D. W., & Baffa, G. (1976). Differences in the sequential integration of form as a function of age and interstimulus interval. *Experimental Aging Research, 2,* 333–343.

Kline, D. W., & Birren, J. E. (1975). Age differences in backward dichoptic masking. *Experimental Aging Research, 1,* 17–25.

Kline, D. W., & Orme–Rogers, C. (1978). Examination of stimulus persistence as the basis for superior visual identification performance among older adults. *Journal of Gerontology, 33,* 76–81.

Kline, D. W., & Szafran, J. (1975). Age differences in backward monoptic visual noise masking. *Journal of Gerontology, 30,* 307–311.

Klonoff, H., Fibiger, C. H., & Hutton, G. H. (1970). Neuropsychological patterns in chronic schizophrenia. *Journal of Nervous and Mental Disease, 150,* 291–300.

Kluever, H. (1933). *Behavior mechanisms in monkeys.* Chicago: University of Chicago Press.

Knehr, C. A. (1962). Psychological assessment of differential impairment in cerebral organic conditions and in schizophrenics. *Journal of Psychology, 54,* 165–189.

Knight, R. G., & Russell, P. N. (1978). Global capacity reduction and schizophrenia. *British Journal of Social and Clinical Psychology, 17,* 275–280.

Knight, R. A., Sherer, M., & Shapiro, J. (1977). Iconic imagery in overinclusive and nonoverinclusive schiziphrenics. *Journal of Abnormal Psychology, 86,* 242–255.

Knight, R. A., Sherer, M., Putchat, C., & Carter, G. (1978). A picture integration task for measuring iconic memory in schizophrenics. *Journal of Abnormal Psychology, 87,* 314–321.

Koh, S. D. (1978). Remembering of verbal materials by schizophrenic young adults. In S. Shwartz (Ed.), *Language and cognition in schizophrenia.* New York: John Wiley and Sons.

Koh, S. D., Kayton, L., & Berry, R. (1973). Mnemonic organization in young nonpsychotic schizophrenics. *Journal of Abnormal Psychology, 81,* 299–310.

Koh, S. D., Marusarz, T. Z., & Rosen, A. J. (1980). Remembering of sentences by schizophrenic young adults. *Journal of Abnormal Psychology, 89,* 291–294.

Koh, S. D., Szoc, R., & Patterson, R. A. (1977). Short–term memory scanning in schizophrenic young adults. *Journal of Abnormal Psychology, 86,* 451–460.

Kokes, R. F., Strauss, J. S., & Klorman, R. (1977). Premorbid adjustment in schizophrenia: Concepts, measures, and implications: II. Measuring premorbid adjustment: The instruments and their development. *Schizophrenia Bulletin, 3,* 186–213.

Kolle, K. (1931). *Die Primäre Verruetchtheit Psychopathologische, klinishce Untersuchimgen.* Leipzig: Thieme.

Korboot, P., & Yates, A. J. (1973). Speed of perceptual functioning in chronic nonparanoid schizophrenics: Partial replication and extension. *Journal of Abnormal Psychology, 81,* 296–298.

Kraepelin, E. (1902). Dementia praecox. In E. Kraepelin, *Clinical psychiatry: A textbook for students and physicians,* 6th ed. Trans. by A. R. Diefendorf, Leipzig: Thieme.

Kraepelin, E. (1903–1904). *7th Edition. Psychiatrie: Ein Lehrubuch für Studierendè und Arzte.* Leipzig: Verlag von Johann Ambrosius Barth.

Kraepelin, E. (1909–1913). *8th Edition. Psychiatrie: Ein Lehrubuch für Studierende und Arzte.* Leipzig: Verlag von Johann Ambrosius Barth.

Kraepelin, E. (1971). *Dementia Praecox.* New York: Krieger Publishing Company.

Kramer, M. (1978). Population changes and schizophrenia, 1970–1985. In L. Wynne, R. Cronwell, & S. Matthysse (Eds.), *The nature of schizophrenia: new approaches to research and treatment* (pp. 545–571). New York: Wiley.

Kretschmer, E. (1918). *Der sensitive Beziehungswahn.* Berlin: Springer.

Krynicki, V. E., & Nahas, A. D. (1979). Differing lateralized perceptual-motor patterns in schizophrenic and non–psychotic children. *Perceptual and Motor Skills, 49,* 603–610.

Kuhl, D. E., Phelps, M. E., Markham, C. H., Metter, E. J., Riege, W. H., & Winter, J. (1982). Cerebral metabolism and atrophy in Huntington's disease determined by ^{18}FDG and computed tomographic scan. *Annals of Neurology, 12*: 425–434.

Kumar, M. S. A., Chen, C. L., & Huang, H. H. (1980). Pituitary and hypothalamic concentration of met–enkephalin in young and old rats. *Neurobiology of Aging, 1,* 153–156.

L'Abte, L., Boelling, G. M., Hutton, R. D., & Mathews, D. L., Jr. (1962). The diagnostic usefulness of four potential tests of brain damage. *Journal of Consulting Psychology, 26,* 479.

La Rue, A., Dessonville, C., & Jarvik, L. F. (1980). Aging and mental disorders. In J. E. Birren & K. W. Schaie (Eds.), *Handbook of the psychology of aging* (pp. 664–702). New York: Van Nostrand Reinhold.

Labhardt, F. (1963). Die schizophreni ½ ahnlichen Emotionspsychosen. *Monograph. Gesamtgebiet Neurology Psychiatry.* Heft: *102,* Springer: Berlin.

Lachman, R., Lachman, J. L., & Butterfield, E. C. (1979). *Cognitive psychology and information processing: An introduction.* Hillsdale, NJ: Lawrence Erlbaum.

Laing, R. D. (1971). *The divided self: An existential study in sanity and madness.* Middlesex, England: Penguin Books.

Lamb, H. R., & Goertzel, V. (1977). The long–term patient in the era of community treatment. *Archives of General Psychiatry, 34,* 679–682.

Langfeldt, G. (1937). The prognosis in schizophrenia and the factors influencing the course of the disease. *Acta Psychiatrica Scandinavica, Suppl. 13.*

Laska, E., & Bank, R. (Eds.). (1975). *Safeguarding psychiatric privacy: Computer systems and their uses* (pp. 71–178). New York: Wiley.

Lawton, P. (1972). Schizophrenia forty–five years later. *The Journal of Genetic Psychology, 121,* 133–143.

Learoyd, B. M. (1972). Psychotropic drugs in the aging patient. *Medical Journal of Australia, 1,* 1131–1133.

Lee, T., & Seeman, P. (1980). Elevation of brain neuroleptic/dopamine receptors in schizophrenia. *American Journal of Psychiatry, 137,* 191–197.

Leff, J., Kuipers, L., Berkowitz, R., Eberlein–Fries, R., & Sturgeon, D. (1982). A controlled trial of social intervention in the families of schizophrenic patients. *British Journal of Psychiatry, 141,* 121– 134.

Lehman, R. A. W., Chelune, G. J., & Heaton, R. K. (1979). Level and variability of performance on neuropsychological tests. *Journal of Clinical Psychology, 35,* 358–363.

Lemert, E. (1951). *Social pathology.* New York: McGraw–Hill.

Levenson, A. O., Beard, O. W., & Murphy, M. L. (1980). Major tranquilizers and heart disease: To use or not to use. *Geriatrics, 39,* 55–61.

Levine, J., & Feirstein, A. (1972). Differences in test performance between brain–damaged, schizophrenic, and medical patients. *Journal of Consulting and Clinical Psychology, 39,* 508–511.

Lewine, R., Strauss, J. S., & Gift, T. E. (1981). Sex differences in age at first admission for schizophrenia. *American Journal of Psychiatry, 138,* 440–444.

Lewis, R. E., Nelson, R. W., & Eggrtsen, C. (1979). Neuropsychological test performance of paranoid schizophrenic and brain–damaged patients. *Journal of Clinical Psychology, 35,* 54–59.

Lilliston, L. (1973). Schizophrenic symptomatology as a function of probability of cerebral damage. *Journal of Abnormal Psychology, 82,* 377–381.

Lindelius, R. (1970). A study of schizophrenia. A clinical, prognostic and family investigation. *Acta Psychiatrica Scandinavica, Suppl. 216.*

Linden, M. E. (1955). Transference in gerontologic group psychotherapy: studies in gerontologic human relations. *International Journal of Group Psychotherapy, 5.*

Liptzin, B., & Babigian, H. (1972). Ten years experience with a cumulative psychiatric patient register. *Methods for Information in Medicine, 11,* 238–242.

Loranger, A. W. (1984). Sex differences in age at onset of schizophrenia. *Archives of General Psychiatry, 41:* 157–161.

Lovibond, S. H., & Holloway, I. (1968). Differential sorting behavior of schizophrenics and organics. *Journal of Clinical Psychology, 24,* 307–311.

Lubin, A., Gieseking, C. F., & Williams, H. L. (1962). Direct measurement of cognitive deficit in schizophrenia. *Journal of Consulting Psychology, 26,* 139–143.

Luborsky, L. (1962). Clinicians' judgments of mental health: A proposed scale. *Archives of General Psychiatry, 7,* 407–417.

Luria, A. R. (1973). *The working brain.* New York: Basic Books.

Madden, J. J., Lukan, J. A., Kaplan, L. A., & Manfredi, H. M. (1952). Nondementing psychoses in older persons. *Journal of American Medical Association, 150,* 1567–1570.

Magaro, P. A. (1980). *Cognition in schizophrenia and paranoia.* Hillsdale, NJ: Lawrence Erlbaum.

Magaro, P. A. (1981). The paranoid and the schizophrenic: The case for distinct cognitive style. *Schizophrenia Bulletin, 7,* 632–661.

Maggi, A., Schmidt, M. J., Ghetti, B., & Enna, S. J. (1979). Effect of aging on neurotransmitter receptor binding in rat and human brain. *Life Sciences, 24,* 367–374.

Maher, B. (1966). *Principles of psychopathology.* New York: McGraw-Hill.

Makman, M. H., Ahn, H. S., Thal, L. J., Sharpless, N. S., Drokin, B., Horwitz, S. G., & Rosenfeld, M. (1979). Aging and monoamine receptors in brain. *Federation Proceedings, 38,* 1922–1926.

Malamud, N. (1967). Psychiatric disorder with intracranial tumors of limbic system. *Archives of Neurology, 17,* 113–123.

Malec, J. (1978). Neuropsychological assessment of schizophrenia versus brain damage: A review. *Journal of Nervous and Mental Disease, 166,* 507–516.

Man, P. L., & Chen, C. H. (1973). Rapid tranquilization in acutely psychotic patients with intramuscular haloperidol and chlorpromazine. *Psychosomatics, 14,* 59–63.

Mann, D. M. A., Lincoln, L., & Yates, P. O. (1980). Changes in monoamine containing neurons of the human CNS in senile dementia. *British Journal of Psychiatry, 136,* 533–541.

Mann, D. M. A., & Yates, P. O. (1979). The effects of aging on the pigmented nerve cells of the human locus ceruleus and substantia nigra. *Acta Neuropathologica, 47,* 93–97.

Mann, D. M. A., & Yates, P. O. (1981). Dementia and cerebral noradrenergic innervation. *British Medical Journal, 282,* 465–474.

Mann, D. M. A., Yates, P. O., & Stamp, J. E. (1978). The relationship between lipofuscin pigment and aging in the human nervous system. *Journal of the Neurological Sciences, 37,* 83–93.

Manschreck, T. C., Maher, B. A., Rucklos, M. E., Vereen, D. R., Jr., & Ader, D. N. (1981). Deficient motor synchrony in schizophrenia. *Journal of Abnormal Psychology, 90,* 321–328.

Marengo, J., Harrow, M., Lanin–Kettering, I., & Wilson, A. (1985). A manual for assessing aspects of idiosyncratic thinking and speech on verbal tests. In M. Harrow & D. Quinlan (Eds.), *Disordered thinking and schizophrenic psychopathology.* New York: Gardner Press.

Marengo, J., Harrow, M., & Rogers C. (1980). *A manual for scoring abstract and concrete responses to the proverbs test.* American Society for Information Services, National Auxilliary Publication Service #03646, New York: Microfiche Publications.

Marinow, A. (1974). Klinisch–statistische und katamnestische Untersuchungen an chronisch Schizophrenen 1951-1960 und 1961-1970. *Archiv fur Psychiatrie und Nervenkrankheiten, 218,* 115.

Marinow, A. (1981). Ueber Verlauf, Ausgang und Prognose bei Schizophrenen. In Huber (Hrsq) Schizophrenie. Stand und Entwicklungstendenzen der Forschung. Stuttgart–New York: Schattauer, 135-149.

Marsden, C. D., Tarsy, D., & Baldessarini, R. J. (1975). Spontaneous and drug–induced movement disorders in psychotic patients. In D. F. Benson & D. F. Blumer (Eds.), *Psychiatric aspects of neurological disease.* New York: Grune and Stratton.

Martensson, E., & Roos, B. E. (1973). Serum levels of thioridazine in psychiatric patients and health volunteers. *European Journal of Clinical Pharmacology, 6,* 181–186.

Martin, J. P. (1968). Choreatic syndromes. In P. J. Vinken & G. W. Bruyn (Eds.), *Handbook of clinical neurology* (pp. 435–439). New York: Wiley.

Martin, P. J., Friedmeyer, M. H., Sterne, A. L., & Brittain, H. M. (1977). IQ deficit in schizophrenia: A test of competing theories. *Journal of Clinical Psychology, 33,* 667–672.

Marusarz, T. Z., & Koh, S. D. (1980). Contextual effects on the short-term memory retrieval of schizophrenic young adults. *Journal of Abnormal Psychology, 89,* 683–696.

Matthysse, S., & Kidd, K. (1976). Estimating the genetic contribution of schizophrenia. *American Journal of Psychiatry, 133,* 185–191.

Mayer, W. (1921). ber paraphrene psychosen Zentralblalt für diegesante. *Neurologie und Psychiatrie, 71,* 187–206.

Mayer–Gross, W., Slater, E., & Roth, M. (1954). *Clinical psychiatry,* London: Baillière, Tindall and Cassell Limited.

McDonough, J. M. (1960). Critical flicker frequency and the spiral after–effect with process and reactive schizophrenics. *Journal of Consulting Psychology, 24,* 150–155.

McGeer, P. L., & McGeer, E. G. (1978). Aging and neurotransmitter systems. In C. E. Finch, D. E. Potter, & A. D. Kenney (Eds.), *Parkinson's Disease: II. Aging and neuroendocrine relationships* (pp. 41–58). New York: Plenum Press.

McGeer, P. L., McGeer, E. G., & Suzuki, J. S. (1977). Aging and extra-pyramidal function. *Archives of Neurology, 34,* 33-35.

McGhie, A. (1966), Psychological studies of schizophrenia. *British Journal of Medical Psychology, 39,* 281-288.

Meese, W., Kluge, W., Grumme, T., & Hopfenmuller, W. (1980). CT evaluation of the CSF spaces in healthy persons. *Neuroradiology, 19,* 131-136.

Messing, R. B., Vasquez, B. J., Samaniego, B., Jensen, R. A., Martinez, J., & McGaugh, J. L. (1981). Alterations in dihydromorphine binding in cerebral hemispheres of aged male rats. *Journal of Neurochemistry, 36,* 784-790.

Meyer, L., & Goran, F. (1979). Schizophrenic reactions in the Serial Spiral After-Effect Test. *Scandinavian Journal of Psychology, 20,* 55-58.

Miller, S., Saccuzzo, D., & Braff, D. (1979). Information processing deficits in remitted schizophrenics. *Journal of Abnormal Psychology, 88,* 446-449.

Mirsky, A. F., DeLisi, L. E., Buchsbaum, M. S., Quinn, O. W., Schwerdt, P., Siever, L. J., Mann, L., Weingartner, H., Zec, R., Sostek, A., Alterman, I., Revere, V., Dawson, S. D., & Zahn, T. P. (1984). The Genain Quadruplets: Psychological studies. *Psychiatry Research, 13,* 77-93.

Mitchell, J.C. (1969). Concept and use of social networks. In J.C. Mitchell (Ed.), *Social networks in urban situations.* Manchester: Manchester University Press.

Mitsuda, H., & Fukuda, T. (1974). *Biological mechanisms of schizophrenia and schizophrenia-like psychoses.* Tokyo: Igaku Shoin Ltd.

Molchanova, E. K. (1975). Results of continuous study of population of schizophrenic patients greater than 60 years of age. *Zhurnal Nevropatologii I Psikhiatrii Imeni S. S. Korsakova, 73,* 898-905.

Monagle, R. D., & Brody, H. (1974). The effects of age upon the main nucleus of the inferior olive in the human. *Journal of Comparative Neurology, 155,* 61-66.

Moran, L. J., Gorham, D. R., & Holtzman, W. H. (1962). Volcabulary knowledge and usage of schizophrenic subjects: A six-year follow-up. *Journal of Abnormal and Social Psychology, 61,* 246-254.

Moreno, J. L. (Ed.). (1960). *The sociometry reader.* Glencoe, IL: Free Press.

Morgan, D. G., May, P.C. & Finch, C. E. (1987). Dopamine and serotonin systems in human and rodent brain: Effects of age and degenerative disease. *Journal of the American Geriatrics Society,* in press.

Morgan, D. G., Marcusson, J. O., Winblad, B., & Finch, C. E. (1984). Reciprocal changes in D-1 and D-2 dopamine binding sites in human caudate nucleus and putamen during normal aging. (3H) Fluphenazine as a dopamine receptor ligand. *Society of Neuroscience Abstracts* (Vol. 9).

Morrison, J., Clancy, J., Crowe, R., & Winokur, G. (1972). The Iowa 500: I. Diagnostic validity in mania, depression and schizophrenia. *Archives of General Psychiatry, 27,* 457-461.

Morrison, J., Winokur, G., Crowe, R., & Clancy, J. (1973). The Iowa 500:

The first follow-up. *Archives of General Psychiatry, 1973, 29,* 678–682.

Mosher, L. R., & Keith, S. J. (1980). Psychosocial treatment : Individual group, family and community support approaches. *Schizophrenia Bulletin, 6,* 10–41.

Mosteller, F., & Tukey, J. W. (1977). *Data analysis and regression.* Reading, MA: Addisson–Wesley.

Munnichs, J. (1966). *Old age and finitude: A contribution to psychogerontology.* New York: Karger.

Murphy, G. J. E., Wetzel, R. O. (1980). Suicide risk by birth cohort in the United States 1949–1974. *Archives of General Psychiatry, 37,* 519.

Müller, C. (1959). *Ueber das Senium der Schizophrenen.* Basel: Karger.

Müller, C. (1963). The influence of age on schizophrenia. In R. Williams, C. Tibbitts, & W. Donahue (Eds.), *Processes of aging: Social and psychological aspects* (Volume I). New York: Atherton Press.

Müller, C. (1971). Schizophrenia in advanced age. *British Journal of Psychiatry, 118,* 347–348.

Müller, C. (1981). Psychische Erkrankungen und ihr Verlauf sowie ihre Beeinflussung durch das Alter. Bern–Stuttgart–Wien: Huber.

Müller, C., & Ciompi, L. (1976). The relationship between anamnestic factors and the course of schizophrenia. *Comprehensive Psychiatry, 17,* 387–393.

Müller, C., & Le–Dinh, T. (1976). Aging of schizophrenic patients as seen through the Rorschach test. *Acta Psychiatrica Scandinavica, 53,* 161–167.

Nachmani, G., & Cohen, B. D. (1969). Recall and recognition free learning in schizophrenia. *Journal of Abnormal Psychology, 74,* 511–516.

Nagatsu, T., & Undenfriend, S. (1972). Photometric assay of dopamine-betahydroxylase activity in human blood. *Clinical Chemistry,* 980–983.

Nahas, A. D. (1976). The prediction of perceptual motor abnormalities in paranoid schizophrenia. *Research Communications in Psychology, Psychiatry and Behavior, 1,* 167–181.

Neale, J. M., McIntyre, C. W., Fox, R., & Cromwell, R. L. (1969). Span of apprehension in acute schizophrenics. *Journal of Abnormal Psychology, 74,* 593–596.

Neisser, U. (1967). *Cognitive psychology.* New York: Appleton–Century–Crofts.

Neufeld, R. W. J. (1977). Components of processing deficit among paranoid and nonparanoid schizophrenics. *Journal of Abnormal Psychology, 86,* 60–64.

Neufeld, R. W. J., & Broga, M. I. (1981). Evaluation of information sequential aspects of schizophrenic performance: II. Research strategies and methodological issues. *Journal of Nervous and Mental Disease, 169,* 569–579.

Neugarten, B. (1969). Continuities and discontinuities of psychological issues into adult life. *Human Development, 12,* 121–130.

Neugarten, B. (1973). Personality change in late life: A developmental perspective. In C. Eisdorfer & M. P. Lawton (Eds.), *The psychol-*

ogy of adult development and aging (pp. 311–335). Washington, DC: American Psychological Association.

Neugarten, B. (1979). Time, age, and the life–cycle. *American Journal of Psychiatry, 136,* 887–884.

Neugarten, B., & Hagestad, G. (1976). Aging and the life course. In R. Binstock & E. Shanas (Eds.), *Handbook of aging and the social sciences* (pp. 35–55). New York: Van Nostrand–Reinhold.

Neugarten, B., & Moore, J. (1968). The changing age–status system. In B. Neugarten (Ed.), *Middle–age and aging: A reader in social psychology* (pp. 5–20). Chicago: The University of Chicago Press.

Neugarten, B., Moore, J., & Lowe, J. (1965). Age norms, age constraints, and adult socialization. *The American Journal of Sociology, 70,* 710–717.

Neugarten, B., & Peterson, W. (1957). A study of the American age-grade system. *Proceedings of the Fourth Congress of the International Association of Gerontology, 3,* 497–502.

Neugebauer, R. (1980). Formulation of hypotheses about the true prevalence of functional and organic psychiatric disorders among the elderly in the United States. In: B. P. Dohrenwend, B. S. Dohrenwend, M. S. Gould, B. Link, R. Neugebauer, & R. Wunsch–Hitzig (Eds.), *Mental illness in the United States: Epidemiological estimates* (pp. 95–112). New York: Praeger.

New York State Department of Social Services (1980). *Survey of the needs and problems of single room occupancy hotel residents on the upper west side of Manhattan.* New York.

Niederland, W. (1974). *The Schreber Case: Psychoanalytic profile of a paranoid personality.* New York: Quadrangle Press–The New York Times.

Nies, A., Robinson, D. S., Davis, J. M., & Ravaris, L. (1973). Changes in monoamine oxidase with aging. In C. Eisdorfer & W. E. Fann (Eds.), *Psychopharmacology and aging* (pp. 41–54). New York: Plenum Press.

Nies, A., Robinson, D. S., Lamborn, K. R., & Lampert, R. P. (1973). Genetic control of platelet and plasma monoamine oxidase activity. *Archives of General Psychiatry, 28,* 834–837.

Noreik, K., Astrup, C., Dalgrad, O. S., & Holmboe, R. (1967). A prolonged follow–up of acute schizophrenic and schizophreniform psychoses. *Acta Psychiatricia Scandinavica, 43,* 432–443.

Nuechterlein, K. H. (1977). Reaction time and attention in schizophrenia: A critical evaluation of the data and theories. *Schizophrenia Bulletin, 3,* 373–428.

Nyback, H., Wiesel, F. A., Berggren, B. M., & Hindmarsh, T. (1982). Computed tomography of the brain in patients with acute psychosis and in healthy volunteers. *Acta Psychiatrica Scandinavica, 65,* 403–414.

Odegaard, O. (1953). New data on marriage and mental disease. The incidence of psychoses in the widowed and the divorced. *Journal of Mental Science, 99,* 778–785.

Offord, D. R. (1974). School performance of adult schizophrenics, their siblings and age mates. *British Journal of Psychiatry, 125,* 12–19.

Offord, D. R., & Cross, L. A. (1971). Adult schizophrenia with scho–

lastic failure or low IQ in childhood. *Archives of General Psychiatry, 24,* 431–436.

Oltmanns, T. F., & Neale, J. M. (1975). Abstract conceptulization in schizophrenia: A fundamental psychological deficit? *Perceptual and Motor Skills, 41,* 807–811.

Oltmanns, T. F., & Neale, J. M. (1978). Abstraction and schizophrenia: Problems in psychological deficit research. In B. A. Maher (Ed.), *Progress in experimental personality research* (Vol. 8). New York: Academic Press.

Orme, J. E., & Smith, M. R. (1964). Psychological assessments of brain damage and intellectual impairment in psychiatric patients. *British Journal of Social and Clinical Psychology, 3,* 161–167.

Owen, J. D. (1970). *The effects of chlorpromazine on performance of schizophrenic patients on two tests for brain damage and related measures.* Unpublished doctoral dissertation, Washington University.

Owens, D. G. C., Johnstone, E. C., & Frith, C. D. (1982). Spontaneous involuntary disorders of movement: Their prevalence, severity, and distribution in chronic schizophrenics with and without treatment with neuroleptics. *Archives of General Psychiatry, 39,* 452–461.

Panse, F. & Klages, W. (1964). Klinish–psychopathologische. Beobachtungen bei chronischem Missbrauch von Ephredrin und verwandten Substanzen. *Archiv fur Psychiatrie und Nervenkrankheiten, 206,* 69.

Pardue, A. M. (1975). Bender–Gestalt Test and background interference procedure in discernment of organic grain damage. *Perceptual and Motor Skills, 40,* 103–109.

Parsons, O. A., & Klein, H. P. (1970). Concept identification and practice in brain–damaged and process–reactive schizophrenic groups. *Journal of Consulting and Clinical Psychology, 35,* 317–323.

Pattison, E. M., deFrancisco, D., Wood, P., Frazier H., & Crowder, J. (1975). A psychokinship model for family therapy. *American Journal of Psychiatry, 132*(11), 1246–1251.

Pearlson, G. D., Veroff, A. E., & McHugh, P. R. (1981). The use of computed tomography in psychiatry: Recent applications to schizophrenia, manic–depressive illness and dementia syndromes. *Johns Hopkins Medical Journal, 149,* 194–202.

Penn, R. D., Belanger, M. G., & Yasnoff, W. A. (1978). Ventricular volume in man computed from CAT Scans. *Annals of Neurology, 3,* 216–223.

Perlmutter, M. (1978). What is memory aging the aging of? *Developmental Psychology, 14,* 330–346.

Perris, C. (1974). A study of cycloid psychoses. *Acta Psychiatrica Scandinavica Suppl. 253.*

Perry, E. K. (1980). The cholinergic system in old age and Alzheimer's disease. *Age and Ageing, 9,* 1–8.

Perry, E. K., Blessed, G., Tomlinson, B. E., Perry, R. H., Crow, T. J., Cross, A. J., Dockray, G. J., Dimaline, R., & Aggregui, A. (1981). Neurochemical activities in human temporal lobe related to aging and Alzheimer–type changes. *Neurobiology of Aging, 2,* 251–256.

Perun, P., & Bielby, D. (1980). Structure and dynamics of the individual life–course. In K. Back (Ed.), *Life course: Integrative theories and exemplary populations* (pp. 97–120). Boulder, CO: Westview Press.

Pfeiffer E. (1976). Psychotherapy with elderly patients. In L. Bellak &

T. B. Karasu (Eds.), *Geriatric psychiatry* (pp. 191–205). New York: Grune & Stratton.

Pfeiffer, E. (1977). Psychopathology and social pathology. In J. E. Birren & K. W. Schaie (Eds.), *Handbook of the psychology of aging* (p. 652). New York: Van Nostrand Reinhold.

Pfohl, B., & Winokur, G. (1983). The micropsychopathology of hebephrenic/catatonic schizophrenia. *Journal of Nervous and Mental Disorders, 171,* 296–300.

Pharr, D. R., & Connor, J. M. (1980). Memory scanning in a visual search task by schizophrenics and normals. *Journal of Clinical Psychology, 36,* 625–631.

Phillips, L. (1953). Case history data and prognosis in schizophrenia. *Journal of Nervous and Mental Disease, 117,* 515–525.

Phillips, W. M., Phillips, A. M., & Shearn, C. R. (1980). Objective assessment of schizophrenic thinking. *Journal of Clinical Psychology, 36,* 79–89.

Physicians' Desk Reference 35th ed. (1982). Oradell, N.J.: Medical Economics Co.

Pic'l, A. K., Magaro, P. A., & Wade, E. A. (1979). Hemispheric functioning in paranoid and nonparanoid schizophrenia. *Journal of Biological Psychiatry, 14,* 891–903.

Pickar, D., Vartanian, F., Bunney, W. E., Jr., Maier, H. P., Gastpar, M. T., Prakash, R., Sethi, B. B., Lideman, R., Belyaev, B. S., Tustusulkovskaja, V. A., Jungkunz, G., Nedopil, N., Verhoeven, W., & van Proag, H. (1982). Short term nalaxone administration in schizophrenic and manic patients. *Archives of General Psychiatry, 39,* 313–319.

Plum, F., & Posner, H. (1980). *Diagnosis of stupor and coma.* Philadelphia: F. A. Davis Publishers.

Pollack, M., Levenstein, S., & Klein, D. F. (1968). A three–year posthospital follow–up of adolescent and adult schizophrenics. *American Journal of Orthopsychiatry, 38,* 94–109.

Poon, L. W., Walsh–Sweeney, L., & Fozard, J. L. Memory skill training for the elderly: Salient issues on the use of imagery mnemonics. In L. W. Poon, J. L. Fozard, L. S. Cermak, D. Arenberg, & L. W. Thompson (Eds.), *New directions in memory and aging: Proceedings of the George Talland Memorial Conference.* Hillsdale, NJ: Lawrence Erlbaum.

Post, F. (1962). The impact of modern drug treatment on old age schizophrenia. *Gerentologia Clinica, 4,* 137–146.

Post, F. (1966). *Persistent persecutory states of the elderly.* Oxford: Pergamon Press.

Post, F. (1978). The functional psychoses. In A. D. Isaacs & F. Post (Eds.), *Studies in geriatric psychiatry.* New York: Wiley.

Post, F. (1980). Paranoid, schizophrenia–like, and schizophrenic states in the aged. In J. E. Birren & R. B. Sloan (Eds.), *Handbook of mental health and aging* (pp. 591–615). Englewood Cliffs, NJ: Prentice–Hall.

Pradhan, S. N. (1980). Central neurotransmitters and aging, *Life–sciences, 26,* 1643–1656.

Prien, R. F., Haber, P. S., & Caffey, E. M. (1975). The use of psychoactive drugs in elderly patients with psychiatric disorders: Survey conducted in twelve Veterans Administration hospitals. *Journal of the American Geriatrics Society, 23,* 104–112.

Puente, A. E., Heidelberg–Sanders, C., & Lund, N. (1982). Detection of brain–damage in schizophrenics as measured by the Whitaker Index of Schizophrenic Thinking and the Luria–Nebraska Neuropsychological Battery. *Perceptual and Motor Skills, 54,* 495–499.

Purisch, A. D., Golden, C. J., & Hammeke, T. A. (1978). Discrimination of schizophrenia and brain–injured patients by a standardized version of Luria's neuropsychological tests. *Journal of Consulting and Clinical Psychology, 46,* 1266–1273.

Rabbitt, P. M. A. (1965). An age–decrement in the ability to ignore irrelevant information. *Journal of Gerontology, 20,* 233–238.

Rabbitt, P. (1977). Changes in problem solving ability in old age. In J. E. Birren & K. W. Schaie (Eds.), *Handbook of the psychology of aging.* New York: Van Nostrand Reinhold.

Ranje, C., & Ungerstedt, U. (1977). High correlations between number of dopamine cells and motor performance. *Brain Research, 134,* 83–93.

Rapaport, D., Gill, M. M., & Schafer, R. (1968). *Diagnostic psychological testing.* R. R. Holt (Ed.). New York: International Universities Press.

Rappaport, S. R., & Webb, W. B. (1950). An attempt to study intellectual deterioration by premorbid and psychotic testing. *Journal of Consulting Psychology, 14,* 95–98.

Raskind, M., Alvarez, C., & Herlin, R. N. (1979). Fluphenazine enanthate in the outpatient treatment of late paraphrenia. *Journal of the American Geriatrics Society, 27,* 459–463.

Raskind, M. A., Alvarez, C., Pietrzyk, M., Westerland, K., and Herlin, S. (1976). Helping the elderly psychiatric patient in crisis. *Geriatrics, 31,* 51–56.

Reid, W. H., Moore, S. L., & Zimmer, M. (1982). Assessment of affect in schizophrenia: Reliability data. *Journal of Nervous and Mental Disease, 170*(5), 266–269.

Reidenberg, M. M., Levy, M., Warner, H., Coutinho, C. B., Schwartz, M. A., Yu, G., & Cheriplo, J. (1978). The relationship between diazepam dose, plasma level, age and central nervous system depression in adults. *Clinical Pharmacology and Therapeutics, 23,* 371–374.

Reifler, D. V., Larson, E., & Hanley, R. (1982). Coexistence of cognitive impairment and depression in geriatric outpatients. *American Journal of Psychiatry, 139,* 623–626.

Rennie, T. C. (1939). Follow–up study of 500 patients with schizophrenia admitted to the hospital from 1913 to 1921. *Archives of Neurology and Psychiatry, 42,* 877–891.

Retterstöl, N. (1966). *Paranoid and paranoiac psychoses.* Olso/Bergen/Tromso: Scandinavian University Books.

Retterstöl, N. (1970). *Prognosis in paranoid psychoses.* Oslo Munksgaard, Copenhagen: Universitetsforlaget.

Reveley, A. M., Reveley, M. A., Clifford, C. A., & Murray, R. M. (1982). Cerebral ventricular size in twins discordant for schizophrenia. *The Lancet I,* 540–541.

Rieder, R. O., Donnelly, E. F., Herott, J. R., & Waldman I. N. (1979). Sulcal prominence in young chronic schizophrenic patients: CT scan findings associated with impairment on neuropsychological tests. *Psychiatry Research, 1,* 1–8.

Riederer, P., & Wuketich, S. (1976). Time course of nigrostriatal degeneration in Parkinson's disease. *Journal of Neural Transmission, 38,* 277–301.

Riegel, K. (1979). *Foundations of dialectical psychology.* New York: Academic Press.

Riemer, M. D. (1950). A study of the mental status of schizophrenics hospitalized for over 25 years into their senium. *Psychiatry Quarterly, 24,* 309.

Riley, M. (1971). Social gerontology and the age stratification of society. *The Gerontologist, 11,* 79–87.

Riley, M. (1973). Aging and cohort succession: Interpretations and misinterpretations. *The Public Opinion Quarterly, 37,* 35–49.

Riley, M. (1976). Age strata in social systems. In R. Binstock & E. Shanas (Eds.), *Handbook of aging and the social sciences.* New York: Van Nostrand Reinhold.

Robinson, D. S. (1975). Changes in monoamine oxidase and monoamines with human development and aging. *Federation Proceedings, 34,* 103–107.

Robinson, D. S., Davis, J. M., Nies, A., Bunney, W. E., Davis, J. N., Colburn, R. N., Bourne, H. R., Shaw, D. M., & Coppen, A. J. (1972). Aging, monoamines and monoamine oxidase levels. *The Lancet I,* 290.

Robinson, D. S., Sourkes, R. L., Nies, A., Harris, L. S., Spector, S., Bartlett, D. L., & Kaye, I. S. (1977). Monoamine metabolism in human brain. *Archives of General Psychiatry, 34,* 89–92.

Rogers, J., & Bloom, F. E. (1985). Neurotransmitter metabolism and function in six aging central nervous systems. In C. E. Finch & E. L. Schneider (Eds.), *Handbook of Biology of Aging* (pp. 645–691). New York: Van Nostrand Reinhold.

Romel, T. E. (1970). The course of periodic schizophrenia according to the finding of long–term follow–up studies. *Zhurnal Nevropatologii I Psikhiatrii Imeni S. S. Korsakova, 70,* 430–435.

Rosen, B., Klein, D. F., & Gittleman–Klein, R. (1971). The prediction of re–hospitalization: The relationship between age of first psychiatric treatment contact, marital status and premorbid asocial adjustment. *Journal of Nervous and Mental Disease, 152,* 17–22.

Rosenblatt, J. E., Pert, C. B., Colison, J., van Kammen, D. R., Scott, R., & Bunney, W. E. (1979). Measurement of serum neuroleptic concentration by radioreceptor assay. *Communications in Psychopharmacology, 3,* 153–158.

Rosenthal, D. (1963). *The Genain Quadruplets.* New York: Basic Books.

Rosenthal, D. (1970). *Genetic theory and abnormal behavior.* New York: McGraw–Hill.

Rosow, I. (1976). Status and role change through the life span. In R. Binstock & E. Shanas (Eds.), *Handbook of aging and the social sciences* (pp. 457–482). New York: Van Nostrand–Reinhold.

Rosow, I. (1978). What is a cohort and why? *Human Development, 21,* 65–75.

Roth, J. (1963). *Timetables: Structuring the passage of time in hospital treatment and other careers.* Indianapolis: Bobbs–Merrill.

Roth, M. (1955). The natural history of mental disorders in old age. *Journal of Mental Science, 101*(4), 281–301.

Roth, M. (1980). The diagnosis of dementia in late and middle life. In J. A. Mortimer (Ed.), *The epidemiology of dementia.* Oxford University Press.

Roth, M., & Morrissey, J. D. (1952). Problems in the diagnosis and classification of mental disorder in old age. *Journal of Mental Science, 98,* 66–80.

Roth, M., Tomlinson, B. E., & Blessed, G. (1967). The relationship between quantitative estimates of dementia and of degenerative changes in the cerebral grey matter of elderly subjects. *Proceedings of the Royal Society of Medicine, 60,* 254–260.

Rousey, C. L. (1971). Psychological reactions to hearing loss. *Journal of Speech and Hearing Disorders, 36:3,* 382–389.

Russell, P. N., Bannatyne, P. A., & Smith, J. F. (1975). Associative strength as a mode of organization in recall and recognition: A comparison of schizophrenics and normals. *Journal of Abnormal Psychology, 84,* 122–128.

Russell, P. N., & Beekhuis, M. E. (1976) Organization in memory: A comparison of psychotics and normals. *Journal of Abnormal Psychology, 85,* 527–534.

Russell, P. N., Consedine, C. E., & Knight, R. G. (1980). Visual and memory search by process schizophrenics. *Journal of Abnormal Psychology, 89,* 109–114.

Russell, P. N., & Knight, R. G. (1977). Performance of process schizophrenics in tasks involving visual search. *Journal of Abnormal Psychology, 86,* 16–26.

Ryder, N. (1965). The cohort as a concept in the study of social change. *American Sociological Review, 30,* 843–861.

Saccuzzo, D. P. (1977). Bridges between schizophrenia and gerontology: Generalized or specific deficits? *Psychological Bulletin, 84,* 595–600.

Saccuzzo, D. P., Hirt, M., & Spencer, T. J. (1974). Backward masking as a measure of schizophrenia. *Journal of Abnormal Psychology, 83,* 512–522.

Saccuzzo, D. P., & Miller, S. (1977). Critical interstimulus interval in delusional schizophrenics and normals. *Journal of Abnormal Psychology, 86,* 261–266.

Salthouse, T. A., & Somberg, B. L. (1982). Isolating the age deficit in speeded performance. *Journal of Gerontology, 37,* 56–63.

Sanders, R., Smith, R. S., & Weinman, B. S. (1967). *Chronic psychoses and recovery.* San Francisco: Jossey-Bass.

Sappenfield, B. R., & Ripke, R. J. (1961). Validities of three visual tests for differentiating organics from schizophrenics and normals. *Journal of Clinical Psychology, 17,* 276–278.

Sartorius, N., Jablensky, A., & Shapiro, R. (1977). Two year follow–up of the patients included in the WHO International Pilot Study of Schizophrenia. *Psychological Medicine, 7,* 529–541.

Sartorius, N., Jablensky, A., & Shapiro, R. (1978). Cross–cultural differences in the short-term prognosis of schizophrenic psychoses. *Schizophrenia Bulletin, 4,* 102–113.

Satz, P. (1966). A block rotation task: The application of multivariate and decision theory analysis for the prediction of organic brain disorder. *Psychological Monographs, 80,* (21, Whole No. 629).

Schatzman, M. (1973). *Soul murder: Reseach in the family.* New York: The New American Library.

Scheff, T. J. (1960). *Being mentally ill.* Chicago: Aldine.

Scheibel, A. B. (1978). The hippocampus: Organizational patterns in health and senescence. *Mechanisms of Ageing and Development, 9,* 89–102.

Schmidt, R. H., Ingvar, M., Lindvall, O., Steneri, U., & Bjorkland, A. (1982). Functional activity of substantial nigra grafts reinnervating the striatum: Neurotransmitter metabolism and [14C] 2–deoxy–D–glucose autoradiography. *Journal of Neurochemistry, 38,* 737–748.

Schmolling, P., & Lapidus, L. B. (1977). Effect of enriched stimulus and instructional conditions on verbal abstracting ability in acute schizophrenics. *Psychological Reports, 41,* 1203–1210.

Schonecker, M. (1957). Ein eigentmliches syndrom in oralen bereich bei megaphenapplikation. *Nervenarzt, 28,* 35.

Schooler, N., Hogarty, G., & Weissman, M. (1978). *Social Adjustment Scale for Schizophrenia, (SASII).*

Schreber, D. (1955). *Memoirs of my nervous illness* (1903) Trans. by I. Macalpine & D. Hunter. London: William Dawson.

Schwartz, C. C., Müller, C., Spitzer, R. L., Goldstein, J., & Serrano, O. (1977). *Community care schedule.* New York State Psychiatric Institute.

Schwartzman, A. E., & Douglas, V. I. (1962). Intellectual loss in schizo–phrenia: Part I. *Canadian Journal of Psychology, 16,* 1–10.

Schwartzman, A. E., Douglas, V. I., & Muir, W. R. (1962). Intellectual loss in schizophrenia: Part II. *Canadian Journal of Psychology, 16,* 161–186.

Sechehaye, M. (1951). *Autobiography of a schizophrenic girl.* New York: Grune & Stratton.

Seidl, L. G., Thornton, G. F., Smith, J. W., Cluff, L. E. (1966). Studies on the epidemiology of adverse drug reactions. III. Reactions in patients on a general medical service. *Bulletin of the Johns Hopkins Hospital, 119,* 299.

Seltzer, M. (1976). Suggestions for the examination of time–disordered relationshpis. In J. Gubrium (Ed.), *Time, Roles and Self in Old Age* (pp. 111–125). Human Sciences Press.

Severson, J. A., & Finch, C. E. (1980). Reduced dopaminergic binding with aging in the rodent striatum. *Brain Research, 192,* 147–162.

Severson, J. A., Marcussen, J., Winblad, B., & Finch, C. E. (1982). Age–correlated loss of dopaminergic binding sites in human basal ganglia. *Journal of Neurochemistry, 39,* 1623–1631.

Shapiro, J. (1971). *Communities of the alone: working with single–room occupants in the city.* New York: Association Press.

Shapiro, R., & Shader, R. (1979). Selective review of results of previous follow–up studies of schizophrenia and other psychoses. In World Health Organization's *Schizophrenia: An international pilot study.* Chichester, England: J. Wiley & Sons, Inc.

Shih, J. C., & Young, H. (1978). The alteration of serotonin binding sites in aged human brain. *Life Sciences, 23,* 1441–1448.

Siede, H., & Muller, H. F. (1967). Choreiform movements as side effects of phenothiazine medication in geriatric patients. *Journal of the American Geriatric Society, 15,* 517–522.

Sigwald, J., Bouttier, D., Raymondeaud, C., & Piot, C. (1959). Quatre cas de dyskinesie facio–bucco–lingui–masticatrice a evolution prolongee secondaire a un traitment par les neuroleptiques. *Revue Neurologique, 100,* 751–755.

Silverman, I. (1963). Age and the tendency to withhold response. *Journal of Gerontology, 18,* 372–375.

Simon, S. H. (1967). Effect of tranquilizers on the Trail Making Test with chronic schizophrenics. *Journal of Consulting Psychology, 31,* 322–323.

Singer, E., Garfinkel, R., Cohen, S. M., & Srole, L. (1976). Mortality and mental health: Evidence from the Midtown Manhattan restudy. *Social Science and Medicine, 10,* 517–525.

Slater, E., Beard, A. W., & Glithero, E. (1963). The schizophrenic–like psychoses of epilepsy. *British Journal of Psychiatry, 109,* 95–150.

Smith, A. (1964). Mental deterioration in chronic schizophrenics. *Journal of Nervous and Mental Disease, 139,* 479–487.

Smith, A. D. (1980). Age differences in encoding, storage and retrieval. In. L. W. Poon, J. L. Fozard, L. S. Cermak, D. Arenberg, & L. W. Thompson (Eds.), *New directions in memory and aging: Proceedings of the George Talland Memorial Conference.* Hillsdale, NJ: Lawrence Erlbaum.

Smith, J. M., & Baldessarini, R. J. (1980). Changes in prevalence, severity and recovery in tardive dyskinesia with age. *Archives of General Psychiatry, 37,* 1368–1373.

Smith, J. M., Oswald, W. T., Kucharski, T. L., & Waterman, L. J. (1978). Tardive dyskinesia: age and sex differences in hospitalized schizophrenics. *Psychopharmacology, 58,* 207–211.

Smith, R. (1961). Cultural differences in the life cycle and the concept of time. In R. Kleemeier (Ed.), *Aging and leisure* (pp. 84–112). New York: Oxford University Press.

Smith, T. E., & Boyce, E. M. (1962). The relatonship of the Trail Making Test to psychiatric symptomatology. *Journal of Clinical Psychology, 18,* 450–454.

Snyder, S. H. (1981). Dopamine receptors, neuroleptics and schizophrenia. *American Journal of Psychiatry, 138,* 460–464.

Sokolovsky, J. & Cohen, C. (1981). Toward a resolution of methodological dilemmas in network mapping. *Schizophrenia Bulletin, 7,* 109–116.

Sorokin, P., & Merton, R. (1937). Social time: A methodological and functional analysis. *The American Journal of Sociology, 42,* 615–629.

Spaulding, W., Rosenzweig, L., Huntzinger, R., Cromwell, R. L., Briggs, D., & Hayes, T. (1980). Visual pattern integration in psychiatric patients. *Journal of Abnormal Psychology, 89,* 635–643.

Spence, J. T. (1963). Patterns of performance on WAIS similarities in schizophrenic, brain–damaged and normal subjects. *Psychological Reports, 13,* 431–436.

Spitzer, R. L., Endicott, J., & Robins, E. (1977). *Research diagnostic criteria (RDC) for a selected group of functional disorders* (3rd ed.). New York: Biometrics Research, New York Psychiatric Institute.

Spitzer, R. L., Gibbon, M., & Endicott, J. (1975). *The Global Assessment Scale (GAS)*. New York State Psychiatric Institute.

Spokes, G. S. (1979). An analysis of factors influencing measurements of dopamine, noradrenaline, glutamate decarboxylase and choline acetylase in human post–mortem brain tissue. *Brain, 102,* 333–346.

Spring, B., & Zubin, J. (1977). Vulnerability to schizophrenic episodes and their prevention in adults. In G. Albee & J. Joffe (Eds.), *Primary prevention of psychopathology. I: The issues (pp. 254–284).* Hanover, NH: The University Press of New England.

Stanton, A., & Schwartz, M. (1954). *The patient and the mental hospital.* New York: Free Press/Macmillan.

Steffy, R. A., & Galbraith, K. A. (1974). A comparison of segmental set and inhibitory explanations of crossover pattern in process schizophrenic reaction time. *Journal of Abnormal Psychology, 83,* 227–233.

Steger, R. W., Sonntag, W. E., Van Vugt, D. A., Forman, L. J., & Meites, J. (1980). Reduced ability of naloxone to stimulate LH and testosterone release in aging male rats: Possible relation to the increase in hypothalamic met–enkephalin. *Life Sciences, 27,* 747–753.

Stein, M. I. (1949). Personality factors involved in temporal development of Rorschach responses. *Rorschach Research Exchange and Journal of Projective Techniques, 3,* 355–414.

Stephens, J. H. (1970). Long–term course and prognosis in schizophrenia. *Seminars in Psychiatry, 2,* 464–485.

Stephens, J. H. (1978). Long–term prognosis and follow–up in schizophrenia. *Schizophrenia Bulletin, 4*(1), 25–47.

Stephens, J. H., & Astrup, C. (1963). Prognosis in "process" and "non-process" schizophrenia. *American Journal of Psychiatry, 119,* 945–953.

Stephens, J. H., Astrup, C., & Mangrum, J. C. (1966). Prognostic factors in recovered and deteriorated schizophrenics. *American Journal of Psychiatry, 122,* 1116–1121.

Sternberg, D. E., Van Kamen, D. P., Lerner, P., & Bunney, W. E. (1982). Schizophrenia: Dopamine B–hydroxylase activity and treatment response. *Science, 216,* 1423–1425.

Sternberg, E. (1979). Neuere klinische Forschungsrichtungen in der sowjetischen Psychiatrie. *Fortschritte der Neurologie–Psychiatrie, 47,* 1–23.

Sternberg, E. (1981). Verlaufsgesetzlichkeiten der Schizophrenie im Lichte von Langzeituntersuchungen bis zum Senium. In G. Huber (Ed.), *Schizophrenie. Stand und Entwicklungstendenzen der Forschung* (pp. 251–262). Stuttgart–New York: Schattauer.

Sternberg, S. (1966). High–speed scanning in human memory. *Science, 153,* 652–654.

Sternberg, S. (1975). Memory scanning: New findings and current controversies. *Quarterly Journal of Experimental Psychology, 27,* 1–32.

Steronko, R. J., & Woods, D. J. Impairment in early stages of visual information processing in nonpsychotic schizophrenic individuals. *Journal of Abnormal Psychology, 87,* 481–490.

Stevens, B. C. (1969). Marriage and fertility of women suffering from schizophrenia or affective disorders. *Maudsley Monograph* (No. 19). London: Oxford University Press.

Stotsky, B. A. (1977). Psychoses in the elderly. In C. Eisdorfer & W. E. Fann (Eds.), *Psychopharmacology and aging* (pp. 193–202).

Strain, G. S., & Kinzie, W. B. (1969). Reducing misdiagnosis of schizophrenic patients on a test for brain damage. *Journal of Clinical Psychology, 25,* 262.

Strain, G. S., & Kinzie, W. B. (1970). Improving prediction of brain damage with the Tactile Performance Test for a psychiatric population. *Perceptual and Motor Skills, 30,* 143–146.

Straube, E., Barth, U., & Konig, B. (1979). Do schizophrenics use linguistic rules in speech recall? *British Journal of Social and Clinical Psychology, 18,* 407–415.

Strauss, J. S., & Carpenter, W. T., Jr. (1972). Prediction of outcome in schizophrenia. I. Characteristics of outcome. *Archives of General Psychiatry, 27,* 739–746.

Strauss, J. S., & Carpenter, W. T., Jr. (1974). The prediction of outcome in schizophrenia. II. Relationships between predictor and outcome variables: A report from the WHO International Pilot Study of Schizophrenia. *Archives of General Psychiatry, 31,* 37–42.

Strauss, J. S., & Carpenter, W. T., Jr. (1977). Prediction of outcome in schizophrenia. III. Five–year outcome and its predictors. *Archives of General Psychiatry, 34,* 159–163.

Strauss, J. S., & Carpenter, W. T., Jr. (1979). The prognosis of schizophrenia. In L. Bellack (Ed.), *Disorders of the schizophrenic syndrome* (pp. 472–491). New York: Basic Books.

Strauss, J. S., & Carpenter, W. T., Jr. (1981). *Schizophrenia.* New York: Plenum Press.

Strauss, J. Carpenter, W., & Bartko, J. (1974). The diagnosis and understanding of schizophrenia. Part III. Speculations on the processes that underlie schizophrenia symptoms and signs. *Schizophrenia Bulletin, 11,* 61–75.

Strauss, J. S., Klorman, R., & Kokes, R. F. (1977). Premorbid adjustment in schizophrenia: Concepts, measures and implications. V. The implications of findings for understanding, research, and application. *Schizophrenia Bulletin, 3,* 240–244.

Strauss, J. S., Kokes, R. F., Carpenter, W. T., Jr., & Ritzler, B. A. (1978). The course of schizophrenia as a developmental process. In L. C. Wyne, R. L. Cromwell, & S. Matthysse (Eds.), *Nature of schizophrenia: New findings and future strategies.* New York: Wiley.

Strauss, J. S., Kokes, R. F., Klorman, R., & Sacksteder, J. L. (1977). Premorbid adjustment in schizophrenia: Concepts, measures and implications. I. The concept of premorbid adjustment. *Schizophrenia Bulletin, 3,* 182–185.

Strömgren E. (1974). Psychogenic psychoses. In S. R. Hirsch & M. Shephard (Eds.), *Themes and variations in European psychiatry.* Bristol: Wright.

Strömgren, E. (1945). 'Pathogenese der verschiedenen Formen von psychogenen Psychosen', in memorial volume to Ernst Kretschmer on his seventieth birthday, Mehrdimensionale Diagnostik und Therapie (pp. 67–70). Stuttgart: Thieme.

Stroop, J. R. (1935). Studies of interference in serial verbal reactions. *Journal of Experimental Psychology, 18,* 643–662.

Sugarman, A. A., William, B. H., & Adelstein, A. M. (1964). Haloperidol in the psychiatric disorders of old age. *American Journal of Psychiatry, 120,* 1190.

Sutter, J. M., & Chabert, G. (1967). Réflexions sur 80 schizophrénies remontant à plus de 10 ans. A la recherche de lignes de partage naturelles du groupe des schizophrènes. *Encéphale, 56,* 439–458.

Talman, W. T., Snyder, D., & Reis, D. J. (1980). Chronic lability of arterial pressure produced by destruction of A2 catecholamine neurons in brainstem. *Circulation Research, 46,* 842–853.

Tanna, V. L. (1974). Paranoid states: a selected review. *Comprehensive Psychiatry, 15,* 453–470.

Tanner, R. H., & Domino, E. F. (1977). Exaggerated response to (+) amphetamine in geriatric gerbils. *Gerontology, 23,* 165–173.

Taylor, M. A., Abrams, R., & Gaztanaga, P. (1975). Manic–depressive illness and schizophrenia: A partial validation of research diagnostic criteria utilizing neuropsychological testing. *Comprehensive Psychiatry, 16,* 91–96.

Taylor, M. A., Greenspan, B., & Abrams, R. (1979). Lateralized neuropsychological dysfunction in affective disorder and schizophrenia. *American Journal of Psychiatry, 136,* 1031–1034.

Taylor, M. A., Redfield, J., & Abrams, R. (1981). Neuropsychological dysfunction in schizophrenia and affective disease. *Biological Psychiatry, 16,* 467–477.

Terry, R. D., & Wisniewski, H. M. (1975). Structural and chemical changes of the aged human brain. In S. Gershan & A. Raskin (Eds.), *Aging, Vol. 2, Genesis and treatment of psychological disorders in the elderly* (pp. 127–141). New York: Raven Press.

Thiener, E. C., Hill, L. K., Latham, W. R., & McCarty, W. D. (1962). Validation study of the Kahn Test of Symbol Arrangement. *Journal of Clinical Psychology, 18,* 454–457.

Thornbury, J., & Mistretta, C. M. (1981). Tactile sensitivity as a function of age. *Journal of Gerontology, 36,* 34–39.

Till, R. E. (1978). Age–related differences in binocular backward masking with visual noise. *Journal of Gerontology, 33,* 702–710.

Tobin, J. M., Brousseau, E. R., & Lorenz, A. A. (1970). Clinical evaluation of haloperidol in geriatric patients. *Geriatrics, 25,* 119–122.

Traupmann, K. L. (1975). Effects of categoraztion and imagery on recognition and recall by process and reactive schizophrenics. *Journal of Abnormal Psychology, 84,* 307–314.

Traupmann, K. L. (1980). Encoding processes and memory for categorically related words by schizophrenic patients. *Journal of Abnormal Psychology, 89,* 704–716.

Tress, K. H., & Kugler, B. T. (1979). Interocular transfer of movement after–effects in schizophrenia. *British Journal of Psychology, 70,* 389–392.

Triggs, E. J., & Nation, R. L. (1975). Pharmacokinetics in the aged: A review. *Journal of Pharmacokinetics and Biopharmaceutics, 3,* 387–418.

Tsuang, M. M., Lu, L. M., Stotsky, B. A., & Cole, J. O. (1971). Halo-peridol versus thioridazine for hospitalized psychogeriatric patients: Double–blind study. *Journal of the American Geriatrics Society, 19,* 593–600.

Tsuang, M., & Winokur, G. (1974). Criteria for subtyping schizophrenia. Clinical differentiation of hebephrenic and paranoid schizophrenia. *Archives of General Psychiatry, 31,* 43–47.

Tsuang, M., & Winokur, G. (1975). The Iowa 500: Field work in a 35–year follow–up of depression, mania and schizophrenia. *Canadian Psychiatric Association Journal, 20,* 359–365.

Tsuang, M. T., Woolson, R. F., & Fleming, J. A. (1980). Premature deaths in schizophrenia and affective disorders. *Archives of General Psychiatry, 37,* 979–983.

Turbiner, M., & Derman, R. M. (1980). Assessment of brain damage in a geriatric population through use of a visual–searching task. *Perceptual and Motor Skills, 50,* 371–375.

Tutko, T. A., & Spence, J. T. (1962). The performance of process and reactive schizophrenics and brain injured subjects on a conceptual task. *Journal of Abnormal and Social Psychology, 65,* 387–394.

Tyrell, D. J., Struve, F. A., & Schwartz, M. L. (1965). A methodological consideration in the performance of process and reactive schizophrenics on a test for organic brain pathology. *Journal of Clinical Psychology, 21,* 254–256.

U. S. Department of HEW, (1978). *Statistical Reports on Older Americans: 3. Some Propsects for the Future Elderly Population.* DHEW Publication No. (OHDS) 78–20288.

Uhrbrand, I., & Faurbye, A, (1960). Reversible and irreversible dyskinesia after treatment with perphanazine, chlorpromazine, reserpine and electroconvulsive therapy. *Psychopharmacologia, 1,* 408–418.

United States Bureau of the Census. (1979). *Statistical abstract of the United States: 1979* (100th edition). Washington, D.C.: U.S. Government Printing Office.

Vaillant, G. E. (1962). The prediction of recovery in schizophrenia. *Journal of Nervous and Mental Disease, 135,* 534–543.

Vaillant, G. E. (1964). Prospective prediction of schizophrenic remission. *Archives of General Psychiatry, 11,* 509–518.

Vaillant, G. E. (1978). A 10–year follow–up of remitting schizophrenics. *Schizophrenia Bulletin, 4,* 78–85.

Vaillant, G. E. (1980). Adolf Meyer was right: Dynamic psychiatry needs the life chart. *NAPPH Journal, 11,* 4–14.

Van Dalen, D. B. (1973). *Understanding educational research.* New York: McGraw Hill.

Van Gennep, A. (1960). *The Rites of passage* (1908). Chicago: The University of Chicago Press.

Van Ree, J. M., & DeWied, D. (1981). Endorphins and schizophrenia. *Neuropharmacology, 20,* 1271–1277.

Vaughn, C. E., & Leff, J. P. (1976a). The measurement of expressed emotion in the families of psychiatric patients. *British Journal of Social Clinical Psychology, 15,* 157–165

Vaughn, C. E., & Leff, J. P. (1976b). The influence of family and social factors on the course of psychiatric illness. *British Journal of Psychiatry, 129,* 125–37.

Vijayashankar, N., & Brody, H. (1979). A quantitative study of the pigmented neurons in the nuclei locus coeruleus and subcoeruleus in man as related to aging. *Journal of Neuropathology and Experimental Neurology, 38,* 490–497.

Wahl, O. F., & Sieg, D. (1980). Time estimation among schizophrenics. *Perceptual and Motor Skills, 50,* 535–541.

Walker, E. (1981). Attentional and neuromotor functions of schizophrenics, schizoaffectives, and patients with other affective disorders. *Archives of General Psychiatry, 38,* 1355–1358.

Walsh, D. A. (1976). Age differences in central perceptual processing: A dichoptic backward masking invesitigation. *Journal of Gerontology, 31,* 178–185.

Walsh, D. A., & Thompson, L. W. (1978). Age differences in visual sensory memory. *Journal of Gerontology, 33,* 383–387.

Walsh, D. A., Till, R. E., & Williams, M. (1978). Age differences in peripheral visual processing: A monoptic backward masking investigation. *Journal of Experimental Psychology: Human Perception and Performance, 4,* 232–243.

Warner, H., Canfield, J., & Ban, T. A. (1969). An uncontrolled study with Thioxanthene. In Lehmann & Ban (Eds.), *The Thioxanthenes* (pp. 53–54). Basel and New York: F. Karger.

Watson, C. G. (1965). Intratest scatter in hospitalized brain–damaged and schizophrenic patients. *Journal of Consulting Psychology, 29,* 596.

Watson, C. G. (1965). WAIS error types in schizophrenics and organics. *Psychological Reports, 16,* 527–530.

Watson, C. G. (1965). WAIS profile patterns of hospitalized brain–damaged and schizophrenic patients. *Journal of Clinical Psychology, 21,* 294–296.

Watson, C. G. (1968). The separation of NP hospital organics from schizophrenics with three visual motor screening tests. *Journal of Clinical Psychology, 24,* 412–414.

Watson, C. G. (1971). Separation of brain–damaged from schizophrenic patients by Reitan–Halstead pattern analysis: An unsuccessful replication. *Psychological Reports, 29,* 1343–1346.

Watson, C. G. (1972). Cross–validation of a WAIS sign developed to separate brain–damaged from schizophrenic patients. *Journal of Clinical Psychology, 28,* 66–67.

Watson, C. G. (1973). A simple bivariate screening technique to separate NP hospital organics from other psychiatric groups. *Journal of Clinical Psychology, 29,* 448–450.

Watson, C. G., Thomas, R. W., Andersen, D., & Felling, J. (1968). Differentiation of organics from schizophrenics at two chronicity levels by use of the Reitan–Halstead organic test battery. *Journal of Consulting and Clinical Psychology, 32,* 679–684.

Watson, C. G., Thomas R. W., Felling, J., & Andersen, D. (1968). Differentiation of organics from schizophrenics with Reitan's sensory–perceptual disturbances test. *Perceptual and Motor Skills, 26,* 1191–1198.

Watson, C. G., Thomas, R. W., Felling, J., & Andersen, D. (1969). Differentiation of organics from schizophrenics with the Trail Making, Dynamometer, Critical Flicker Fusion, and Light–Intensity

Matching tests. *Journal of Clinical Psychology, 25,* 130–133.

Watson, C. G., & Uecker, A. E. (1966). An attempted cross–validation of the Minnesota Percepto–Diagnostic Test. *Journal of Consulting Psychology, 30,* 461.

Waugh, N. C., & Norman, D. A. (1965). Primary memory. *Psychological Review, 72,* 89–104.

Wechsler, D. (1955). *Wechsler adult intelligence scale manual.* New York: Psychological Corporation.

Wehler, R., & Hoffman, H. (1978). Intellectual functioning in lobotomized and non–lobotomized long term chronic schizophrenic patients. *Journal of Clinical Psychology, 34,* 449–451.

Weinberger, D. R., DeLisi, L. E., Perman, G., Targum, S., & Wyatt, R. J. (1982). CT scans in schizophreniform disorder and other acute psychiatric patients. *Archives of General Psychiatry, 39,* 778–783.

Weinberger, D. R., Torrey, E. F., Neophytides, A. N., & Wyatt, R. J. (1979a). Lateral cerebral ventricular enlargement in chronic schizophrenia. *Archives of General Psychiatry, 36,* 735–739.

Weinberger, D. R., Torrey, E. F., Neophytides, A. N., & Wyatt, R. J. (1979b). Structural abnormalities of the cerebral cortex in chronic schizophrenia. *Archives of General Psychiatry, 36,* 935–939.

Weinberger, D. R., Wagner, R. L., & Wyatt, R. J. (1983). Neuropathological studies of schizophrenia: A selective review. *Schizophrenia Bulletin, 9,* 191–212.

Weinberger, E., & Cermak, L. S. (1973). Short–term retention in acute and chronic paranoid schizophrenics. *Journal of Abnormal Psychology, 82,* 220–225.

Weingartner, H., Caine, E. D., Ebert, M. (1979). Imagery, encoding, & the retrieval of information from memory. *Journal of Abnormal Psychology, 88,* 52–58.

Weingartner, H., Cohen, R. M., Smallberg, S. Ebert, M., Gillin, J. C., & Sitaram, N. (1981). Memory failures in idiopathic dementia. *Journal of Abnormal Psychology, 90,* 187–196.

Weingartner, H., Ebert, M., Mikkelsen, E. J., Rapoport, J. L., Buchbaum, M. S., Bunney, W. E., Jr., & Caine, E. D. (1980). Cognitive processes in normal and hyperactive children and their response to amphetamine treatment. *Journal of Abnormal Psychology, 89*(1), 25–37.

Weinstein, S., & Johnson, L. (1964). The Bender–Gestalt Test in differential diagnosis of temporal lobectomy and schizophrenia. *Perceptual and Motor Skills, 18,* 813–820.

Weiss, B., Greenberg, L., & Cantor, E. (1979). Age–related alternations in the development of adrenegic denervation supersensitivity. *Federation Proceedings, 38,* 1915–1921.

Welford, A. T. (1977). Motor performance. In J. E. Birren & K. W. Schaie (Eds.), *Handbook of the psychology of aging.* New York: Van Nostrand Reinhold.

Wells, C. E. (1979). Diagnosis of dementis. *Psychosomatics, 20,* 517–522.

Welner, J., & Stromgren, E. (1958). Clinical and genetic studies on benign schizophreniform psychoses based on a follow–up. *Acta Psychiatrica Scandinavica, 33,* 377–399.

Wentworth–Rohr, I., & Macintosh, R. (1972). Psychodiagnosis with WAIS intrasubtest scatter of scores. *Journal of Clinical Psychology, 28,* 68.

Westerlundh, B., & Smith, G. (1983). Perceptgenesis and the psychodynamics of perception. *Psychoanalysis and Contemporary Thought, 6,* 597–640.

White, P., Hiley, C. R., Goodhardt, M. J., Carrasco, L. H., Keet, J. P., Williams, I. E. I., & Bowen, D. M. (1977). Neocortical cholinergic neurons in elderly people. *The Lancet I,* 668–671.

Wilford, J. (1971). The geriatric patient. In D. Rose (Ed.), *Audiological assessment* (pp. 281–315). Englewood Cliffs, NJ: Prentice–Hall.

Wimmer, A. (1916). Psykogene Sindesygdomoforder (Psychogenic varieties of mental diseases). In *St. Hans Hospital 1816–1916 Jubilee Publication,* (pp. 86–216). Copenhagen.

Wing, J. K. (1960). A pilot experiment on the rehabilitation of long-hospitalised male schizophrenic patients. *British Journal of prev. soc. med., 14,* 173–180.

Wing, J. K. (1961). A simple and reliable sub–classification of chronic schizophrenia. *Journal of Mental Science, 107,* 862.

Wing, J. K. (1975a). Impairments in schizophrenia: A rational basis for social treatment. In R. D. Wirt, G. Winokur, & M. Roff (Eds.), *Life history research in psychopathology* (Vol. IV). Minneapolis: University of Minnesota Press.

Wing, J. K. (Ed.). (1975b). *Schizophrenia from within.* London: National Schizophrenia Fellowship.

Wing, J. K. (1977). The management of schizophrenia in the community. In G. Usdin (Ed.), *Psychiatric medicine.* New York: Brunner, Mazel.

Wing, J. K. (1978a). Social influences on the course of schizophrenia. In L. C. Wynne, R. L. Cromwell & S. Matthysse (Eds.), *The nature of schizophrenia.* New York: Wiley.

Wing, J. K. (1978b). *Reasoning about madness.* London: Oxford University Press.

Wing, J. K., Bennett, D. H., & Denham, J. (1964). *The industrial rehabilitation of long–stay schizophrenic patients.* Medical Research Council Memo No. 42, London: H. M. S. O.

Wing, J. K., & Brown, G. W. (1970). *Institutionalism and schizophrenia: A comparative study of three mental hospitals 1960–1968.* London: Cambridge University Press.

Wing, J. K., Cooper, J. E., & Sartorius, N. (1974). *The description and classification of psychiatric symptoms: An instruction manual for the PSE and CATEGO system.* London: Cambridge University Press.

Wing, J. K., & Freudenberg, R. K. (1961). The response of severely ill chronic schizophrenic patients to social stimulation. *American Journal of Psychiatry, 118,* 311–322.

Wing, J. K., Leff, J. P., & Hirsch, S. (1973). Preventive treatment of schizophrenia: some theoretical and methodological issues. In J. Cole, A. Freedman, & A. Friedhoff (Eds.), *Psychopathology and psychopharmacology.* Baltimore: Johns Hopkins University Press.

Wing, L. (1981). Asperger's syndrome: a clinical account. *Psychological Medicine, 11,* 115–129.

Winokur, G. (1977). Delusional disorder (paranoia). *Comprehensive Psychiatry, 18,* 511–521.

Wise, C. D., Potkin, S. G., Bridge, T. P., Phelps, B. H., Cannon–Spoor,

H. E., & Wyatt, R. J. (1980). Sources of error in determination of platelet monoamine oxidase: A review of methods. *Schizophrenia Bulletin, 6,* 245–253.

World Health Organization (1973). *The international pilot study of schizophrenia.* Geneva: WHO.

World Health Organization (1979). *Schizophrenia: An international follow–up study.* New York: Wiley.

Wree, A., Braak, H., Schleicher, A., & Zilles, K. (1980). Biomathematical analysis of the neuronal loss in the aging human brain of both sexes, demonstrated in pigment preparations of the pars cerebellaris locus coerulei. *Analytical Embryology, 160,* 105–119.

Wright, D. M. (1975). Impairment in abstract conceptualization in schizophrenia. *Psychological Bulletin, 82,* 120–127.

Wright, R. E. (1981). Aging, divided attention, and processing capacity. *Journal of Gerontology, 36,* 605–614.

Wyatt, R. J., Potkin, S. G., Bridge, T. P., Phelps, B. H., & Wise, C. D. (1980). Monoamine oxidase in schizophrenia: An overview. *Schizophrenia Bulletin, 6,* 199–207.

Wyatt, R. J., & Torgow, J. S. (1976). A comparison of equivalent clinical potencies of neuroleptics used to treat schizophrenics and affective disorders. *Journal of Psychiatric Research, 13,* 91–98.

Yagi, J., Ogita, K., & Ohtsuka, N. (1976). Persistent dyskinesia after long–term treatment with neuroleptics in Japan. *Keio Journal of Medicine, 25,* 27–35.

Yamamura, H. I. (1981). Neurotransmitter receptor alterations in age–related disorders. In S. J. Enna, T. Samorajski, & B. Beer (Eds.), *Brain neurotransmitters and receptors in aging and age-related disorders* (pp. 143–147). New York: Raven Press.

Yates, A. J. (1966). Psychological deficit. In P. R. Farnsworth (Ed.), *Annual review of psychology.* Palo Alto, CA.: Annual Reviews.

Yates, A. J., & Korboot, P. (1970). Speed of perceptual functioning in chronic nonparanoid schizophrenics. *Journal of Abnormal Psychology, 76,* 453–461.

Yesavage, J. A., Holman, C. A., & Cohn, R. (1981). Correlation of thiothixene serum levels and age. *Psychopharmacology, 74,* 170–172.

Yolles, S., & Kramer, M. (1969). Vital statistics. In L. Bellak & L. Loeb (Eds.), *The schizophrenic syndrome* (pp. 66–113). New York: Grune & Stratton.

Zahn, T. P., Carpenter, W. T., & McGlashan, T. H. (1981). Autonomic activity in acute schizophrenia: I. Method and comparison with normal controls. *Archives of General Psychiatry, 38,* 251.

Zatz, L. M., Jernigan, T. L., & Ahumada, A. J. (1982). Changes on computed cranial tomography with aging: Intracranial fluid volume. *American Journal of Neuroradiology, 3,* 1–7.

Zigler, E., & Phillips, L. (1961). Social competence and outcome in psychiatric disorder. *Journal of Abnormal and Social Psychology, 63,* 264–271.

Zubin, J. (1977). Discussion of Section I. In J. Strauss, H. Babigian, & M. Roff (Eds.), *The origins and course of psychopathology.* New York: Plenum.

Zubin, J. (1978). Concluding remarks. In L. Wynne, R. Cromwell, & S.

Matthysse (Eds.), *The nature of schizophrenia: New approaches to research and treatment* (pp. 641–643). New York: John Wiley.

Zubin, J., & Spring, B. (1977). Vulnerability—A new view of schizophrenia. *Journal of Abnormal Psychology, 86,* 103–126.

Zubin, J., & Steinhauer, S. (1981). How to break the logjam in schizophrenia: A look beyond genetics. *Journal of Nervous and Mental Disease, 169,* 447–492.

Zukhovski, A. A. (1976). Clinical picture and dynamics of long–term late remissions in the outcome of schizophrenia. *Zhurnal Nevropatologii I Psikhiatrii Imenil S. S. Korsakova, 76,* 563–568.

Index